TRANSFORMING HAWAI'I

BALANCING COERCION AND
CONSENT IN EIGHTEENTH-CENTURY
KĀNAKA MAOLI STATECRAFT

I lele no ka lupe i ke pola
(It is the tail that makes the kite fly)

Mary Kawena Pukui, *'Ōlelo No'eau: Hawaiian Proverbs & Poetical Sayings* (1983)

TRANSFORMING HAWAI'I

BALANCING COERCION AND
CONSENT IN EIGHTEENTH-CENTURY
KĀNAKA MAOLI STATECRAFT

PAUL D'ARCY

PRESS

PACIFIC SERIES

Published by ANU Press
The Australian National University
Acton ACT 2601, Australia
Email: anupress@anu.edu.au

Available to download for free at press.anu.edu.au

A catalogue record for this book is available from the National Library of Australia

ISBN (print): 9781760461737
ISBN (online): 9781760461744

DOI: 10.22459/TH.06.2018

This title is published under a Creative Commons Attribution-NonCommercial-NoDerivatives 4.0 International (CC BY-NC-ND 4.0).

The full licence terms are available at creativecommons.org/licenses/by-nc-nd/4.0/legalcode

Cover design and layout by ANU Press. Cover photograph by Clement Faydi, flic.kr/p/Dp1PnX.

This edition © 2018 ANU Press

In memory of Kanalu G. Terry Young
Friend, Scholar and Mentor

Contents

List of Figures and Tables ix

Acknowledgements xi

Explanatory Note on the Use of Hawaiian Terms in this Book xix

Glossary of Hawaiian Terms xxi

List of Historical Personalities, Gods and Scholars xxvii

Introduction 1

1. Three Key Debates: Positioning Hawai'i in World History 5
2. Gathering Momentum: Power in Hawai'i to 1770 49
3. The Hawaiian Political Transformation from 1770 to 1796. 85
4. The Hawaiian Military Transformation from 1770 to 1796 109
5. The Pursuit of Power in Hawai'i from 1780 to 1796 147
6. Creating a Kingdom: Hawai'i from 1796 to 1819 181
7. The Hawaiian Achievement in Comparative Perspective. 221

Conclusion 249

Appendix 1: Hawaiian Military Activity 1778–97 255

Appendix 2: Firearms in Hawai'i, 1786–96 261

Appendix 3: A Note on Sources 263

Bibliography 271

Index 307

List of Figures and Tables

Figure 1: Ahupuaʻa divisions of Kohala District, Hawaiʻi 64

Figure 2: The Hawaiian archipelago 66

Figure 3: Hawaiʻi 68

Figure 4: Maui 72

Figure 5: Molokaʻi 75

Figure 6: Oʻahu 76

Figure 7: Kauaʻi 79

Table 1: Population estimates for Hawaiʻi 82

Figure 8: Possible population distribution, 1778 83

Table 2: Hawaiian chiefly rank system 91

Figure 9: The battle of Mokuʻōhai, 1782 155

Figure 10: The battle of ʻĪao, 1790 164

Figure 11: The battle of ʻAiea, 1794 174

Figure 12: The battle of Nuʻuanu, 1795 178

Table 1A.1: Military activity by month and locality, 1778–97 256

Table 1A.2: Areas Experiencing Hostile Armies, 1778–96 257

Table 2A.1: From 'Expenditures for the *Columbia*'s Outfit
   and Cargo', September 1790 261

Table 2A.2: Post-voyage inventory of Cptn Charles Bishop
   after a voyage to the north-west Pacific coast and Hawaiʻi,
   March 1796 (Canton) 262

ix

Acknowledgements

This book has been just over 30 years in the making. While indigenous Hawai'i holds a central place in much Pacific archaeological and anthropological discourse, this extraordinarily lengthy gestation was not due to the magnitude of the literature and sources to master. Indeed, my conclusions in this volume are essentially the same as my first full MA draft in the early 1990s, subsequently enriched by decades of exposure to wider circles of context. Rather, this length of production is more of a tribute to the incredible support I have received from a tight circle of friends, colleagues and family that carried me through some very rough times. This study began in the mid-1980s at the University of Hawai'i at Mānoa (UH Mānoa) as a comparative study of indigenous state formation in Hawai'i, Tonga and Tahiti. The sudden death of my younger brother, Nick; severe spinal damage from an association football injury; and becoming diabetic all in the space of two years ended my time at Hawai'i and saw me return to Aotearoa New Zealand. Many of my note cards, prepared in that pre-laptop era, were lost in transit from Hawai'i and so I had to revisit many of my sources and submit my study as an MA, focused solely on Hawai'i, at the University of Otago in 1992.

Work for Television New Zealand (TVNZ) followed, including being approached to join the Dunedin-based Natural History Unit in a joint project *The Seven Seas* with NHK of Japan. Funding fell through, but the project inspired me to explore my own maritime heritage out of Liverpool and the extraordinary affinity Pacific Islanders have with the sea, which I witnessed daily in Hawai'i. A PhD scholarship to The Australian National University in 1995 allowed me to escape years of casual work on the economic margins of Dunedin as a night watchman and gardener and produce a PhD on Pacific Islanders as maritime peoples. Securing a lectureship at Victoria University of Wellington (VUW) in 1997 provided welcome employment as the tertiary sector went through another of its increasingly frequent funding contractions. Full-time lecturing at

VUW and then James Cook University delayed my PhD submission and publication until 2006, just after I returned to ANU as a staff member. I published military aspects of my MA conclusions in article form in 2003, but only revisited my Hawai'i study seriously in 2007 with an intention of revising and publishing. The study has taken another 10 years to complete due to a combination of a flurry of new works on Kānaka Maoli (indigenous Hawaiians) during this time, significant teaching commitments, and increasingly community-orientated contemporary projects in the Pacific being given priority over my more historical work.

Ironically, over the last two years, I finished this project as I began it in the late 1980s, with my academic future uncertain, awaiting spinal surgery, but as always, supported, inspired and, ultimately, rescued by extraordinary friends and scholars to whom I am forever grateful and who inspire my optimism about our profession and humanity in general. Scholarship is always a collective endeavour and, in this case, especially so. A long list of helpers is therefore particularly in order for this project.

My undergraduate training at Otago University inclined me towards placing Pacific political and social evolution in global perspective, enriched by anthropological, sociological and archaeological theory. In taking an honours degree in Pacific and African history, I was fortunate to study under four exceptionally gifted scholars at Otago. The first was the brilliant South African historian, the late Professor John Omer-Cooper. John's 1966 *The Zulu Aftermath* remains a classic work on how to use oral history and read Western sources in new ways to reveal indigenous history running parallel to the Boer triumphalism that dominated South African history. John also introduced me to the revolution in the history of indigenous statecraft occurring in West and Central Africa in the 1970s and 1980s. The works of Djibril Niane on Mandingo history and traditional African history in general, Ivor Wilks on the Ashante, Saburi Oladeni Biobaku and P.C. Lloyd respectively on the Yoruba, and Jan Vansina and Thomas Reefe on Central African Savanna kingdoms have especially shaped my approaches to examining Hawaiian statecraft. More recent interactions with fellow Pacific specialists grounded in African studies, Dave Chappell and Pierre-Yves Le Meur, have reminded me of the intellectual dynamism and Pacific relevance of key studies on African societies.

The eccentric and intellectually gifted Professor Gordon Parsonson taught Pacific history from the inside looking out by combing the archives for glimpses of the indigenous Pacific past. His honours course used chapters of his draft indigenous history of the Pacific entitled *The Children of Maui* as weekly lectures. The draft book and the entire course were based largely on primary sources and depicted Pacific history as a series of internally driven revolutions well into the colonial era. Gordon's perfectionist streak means *The Children of Maui* remains unpublished, although he is now into his 90s. This is a tragedy as it remains the best work I have read on indigenous Pacific history. Social anthropologist the late Professor Peter Wilson and archaeologist Professor Atholl Anderson rounded out my education and left a passion for multidisciplinary approaches, and a deep and profound respect for 'big picture' anthropological theory based on astute fieldwork in the case of Peter, and meticulous excavations combined with theoretically lateral thinking in terms of where to look and what to look for in the deep Pacific past in the case of Atholl. Atholl's classic works on his Ngāi Tahu ancestors and John's on Bantu South Africa reinforced my belief in the need to walk over the sites that I write about with historical sources in my backpack. This was particularly revealing in assisting me to find the discrepancies in accounts of indigenous battles in Hawai'i that are discussed later in this book. While majoring in history honours, I also undertook two years of honours in geography, anthropology, and archaeology respectively. After graduation, I worked for two years on an Otago-based archaeological project.

The 1980s were times of bold theory in Pacific Studies, with major advances in studies of Hawai'i coming from archaeologists Patrick Kirch and Robert Hommon, and anthropologist Marshall Sahlins. While all three have continued to publish on Hawai'i, they have also largely continued to adhere to their fundamental theoretical stances formulated in the 1980s. Kirch has focused a great deal of attention in the last decade on incorporating Kānaka Maoli traditions recorded in the 19th century into his previous essentially archaeologically informed works on Hawai'i to support his interpretations of Kānaka Maoli political evolution. Their work continues to inspire and intellectually challenge my thinking.

While referring to traditions recorded by 19th-century Kānaka Maoli historians such as David Malo and Samuel Kamakau, few anthropologists and archaeologists have cited or even acknowledged the scholarship of the current generation of stunningly innovative Hawaiian/Kānaka Maoli scholars I met while at graduate school at UH Mānoa in the late 1980s: Lilikalā Kameʻeleihiwa, Jonathan Kay Kamakawiwoʻole Osorio, and the late Kanalu G. Terry Young, to whom this book is dedicated. This is especially surprising given the development of the UH Mānoa's

Kamakakūokalani Center for Hawaiian Studies to be arguably the best centre for indigenous scholarship in the Pacific today. The highlights of my coursework at UH Mānoa were the late Jerry Bentley's multidisciplinary course on world history, which emphasised the need to embrace the histories of non-Western peoples on their own terms, and David Hanlon's theoretically wide-ranging course on Micronesian history. Other students who inspired me and shaped my thinking included Lewis Mayo, who focused on Chinese and environmental history and who is still a close friend and also the most brilliant mind I have ever encountered; Bruce Campbell from Guam who introduced me to Micronesia and impressed upon me the need to give back to Pacific communities through items and knowledge they valued rather than academic learning alone; the late Teresia Teaiwa, who had already embraced multiple forms of indigenous self-expression as a means of developing indigenous voices informed, but not dictated, by more conventional academic scholarship; Dave Chappell, who had travelled the world, lived in Africa, and thinks deeply and writes profoundly about many key issues in Pacific and world history; Mike Pavkovic, whose thoughtful combination of classical studies and military history left a deep impression on me; and Dave French, whose profound knowledge of Amerindian cultures and fascination with Central Asian languages and history intoxicated me in our daily conversations. Dave shopped for me and visited me every day while I was bedridden for six months with a spinal injury, and did so while working full-time to put himself through graduate school. I could not have made it through those dark days without his help and support.

The completion of my MA on Hawai'i in the early 1990s at Otago was made possible by the friendship and support of the entire department, and my supervisor Judy Bennett in particular. Modest and forthright in equal measure, Judy was supportive and constructively critical of my drafts. She also heightened my awareness of the importance of environmental history in processes of political and social evolution. Exchanges with John McNeill during this time as he was writing an article-length overview of the first environmental history of the Pacific, and the TVNZ project combined to establish environmental perspectives as fundamental to my historical analysis.

Environmental perspectives were combined with non-Western historiography for my PhD at ANU with a dream panel and an exceptional cohort of PhD students. Donald Denoon as my panel chair reunited me with my African studies, which he combined with his deep understanding of Papua New Guinea and big-picture, broad-brush approach to Pacific history and settler colonialism. Niel Gunson, Deryck Scarr, Mark Elvin and Tony Reid were always willing to discuss problems and methodologies as panel supervisors. Niel opened my eyes as never before to the richness and untapped potential of traditional Pacific histories contained in archives and remembered within the community that are still unfortunately rarely seen in modern academic studies of the Pacific. His students Kambati Uriam and Kieran Schmidt reinforced this potential with their detailed studies of the pre-European traditional history of Kiribati and Samoa respectively. Deryck's deep knowledge of Fijian traditional ways served to further move me towards the traditional history – environmental history trajectory that influenced this book. Tony's big-picture histories of South-East Asia served as models of what we could also do in the Pacific and started me on a long investigation of linkages between the two regions that colonial rule and colonial languages had combined to divide the two regions within academic expertise. Mark's brilliant environmental perspectives on Chinese history and profound knowledge of cultures of the sea throughout history inspired me. I was also reunited with my friend Lewis Mayo, who Mark was supervising on a Chinese environmental history topic centred on western Gansu. Lewis's work and encouragement, along with that of our fellow PhD cohort member, Vicki Luker, have influenced my work profoundly. Lewis and Vicki remain among my closest friends today.

It was during my PhD that I saw Kanalu for the last time when we were panellists together at the Pacific History Association conference in Hilo in July 1996. His talk preceded mine and was spellbinding in its emotion and brilliant in voicing the frustration of having your history articulated by outsiders while your own perspectives and understandings are sidelined. I remember frantically taking notes on almost every sentence he spoke and then being unable to focus on my own talk with my mind full of the brilliant insights and alternative ways of conceiving Hawaiian society that he had just outlined. His book came out soon afterwards and was a profound influence on this book and my thinking about Pacific history in general. To my knowledge, it was never reviewed by any Pacific journal nor cited since by any non-Hawaiian academics, despite a raft of studies being published in the last decade. Hawaiian scholarship has flourished since then, however, and Hawai'i remains one of the strongest centres for indigenous studies in the Pacific with Lilikalā Kame'eleihiwa still an intellectual force 30 years after her groundbreaking PhD was completed at UH Mānoa, and published as a book in 1992, and Kanalu's and my contemporary, Jon Osorio, publishing his equally superb historical study of early 19th-century Hawai'i in 2002. Cutting short my PhD scholarship to take up a teaching position at VUW reunited me with Teresia Teaiwa as she developed a Pacific Studies Program there, but delayed the submission of my PhD and stifled my publications while I developed numerous courses in Pacific, European and world history. Similar teaching to research imbalances followed in a new position at James Cook University in Townsville.

It was not until I returned to ANU as a staff member in 2006 that I could focus on research more than teaching. Here I linked up with Niel Gunson again and continued to learn much about traditional history from him. Vicki Luker has been a warm, inspiring and supportive colleague in the Department of Pacific and Asian History and as executive editor of the *Journal of Pacific History*. Stewart Firth and Greg Fry have been especially encouraging and supportive in pushing me to publish this study, while my departmental supervisor and mentor, Tessa Morris-Suzuki, has been a tower of strength and integrity, and an intellectual inspiration over the last decade. In recent years I have also been fortunate to work and often co-author with inspiring scholars in the Pacific: Tamatoa Bambridge from Tahiti; Zag Puas and Mymy Kim from Chuuk; Roannie Ng Shui from Samoa; Morgan Tuimaleali'ifano from the University of the South Pacific at Laucala and also Samoa; Colin Philp of Leleuvia, Fiji; Chels Marshall from Australia; Tanira Kingi, Jacinta Ruru, Jenny Bryant-Tokalau and Lyn Carter from Aotearoa New Zealand; and Daya Dakasi Da-Wei Kuan and Vavauni Ljaljegean from Taiwan. Daya's and my edited book on indigenous responses to climate change and globalisation will feature a stunning piece from Jon Osorio expressing the vital importance of place and belonging to Kānaka Maoli. I am also lucky to be working with a very supportive and intellectually inspiring editorial team on the next Cambridge History of the Pacific: Jane Samson, Matt Matsuda, Anne Perez-Hattori and Ryan Jones.

This work has been improved immeasurably by detailed anonymous referees' reports, and especially through a very careful and perceptive copyedit by my wonderful editor Justine Molony. It has been a pleasure from start to finish working with ANU Press' acting manager Emily Hazlewood and graphic designer Teresa Prowse. Teresa designed the cover and checked the manuscript, while Emily has done an enormous amount of work to improve this book, and displayed immense patience with my endless delays. All of the figures in this book were created to my specifications by Kay Dancey, Jenny Sheehan and Karina Pelling of CartoGIS, the Cartography Unit of ANU College of Asia and the Pacific. Both ANU Press and CartoGIS produce world-class outputs on a slender budget that defies belief. It is fitting that this study will be affiliated with my new workplace within ANU, the Department of Pacific Affairs (DPA) in the Coral Bell School of the College of Asia and the Pacific. DPA is a happy and productive workplace directed by a generous and visionary Pacific scholar and leader, Nicole Haley. Nicole and the Dean of the College of Asia and the Pacific, Michael Wesley, have been fundamental in facilitating my transfer and providing me with the welcoming and stable workplace I have long sought to join. DPA works for the Pacific and not merely on the Pacific – a vital distinction. Lastly and most importantly, I owe so much of my academic success to the support and love of my family: my mum and dad, Anne and Brian, who have always supported my scholarship and taught me what really mattered in life. Mum and Dad were founding members of the New Zealand Values Party that later evolved into the New Zealand Green Party. Above all, my wonderful wife Xiaoqin and son Christopher inspire and support, fill every day with joy and make my life complete.

Explanatory Note on the Use of Hawaiian Terms in this Book

Where possible Hawaiian terms have been used for specifically Hawaiian institutions or objects.

Aliʻi is used to refer to Hawaiian chiefs in general. Aliʻi nui refers to senior chiefs as opposed to those with relatively little genealogical status. Mōʻī were the rulers of discrete polities known as moku. Makaʻāinana refers to all commoners, most of whom cultivated the land. But, within this group, there were commoners who served in chiefly retinues, and such people are distinguished by the term kanaka. The basic local land division was known as an ahupuaʻa. Akua refers to gods as opposed to ʻaumakua (spirits). In general, I have used the term gods for the broader sense of the supernatural world. When referring to particular deities, they are mentioned by name rather than as akua. Temples are referred to as heiau. Because of the large number of Hawaiian words that are used in the text, these have not been italicised or underlined so as not to disrupt the flow of the narrative.

Hawaiʻi is used for both the culture in general and Hawaiʻi Island. Where there may be ambiguity in sentences between the two usages, Hawaiʻi Island is used for the latter, and Hawaiʻi for the former.

Glossary of Hawaiian Terms

ʻaha aliʻi	council of chiefs
ahu	boundary marker
ahupuaʻa	basic local community land division, under the control of a lesser chief known as an aliʻi ai ahupuaʻa
ʻāina	land in general
ai noa	'free eating' – eating to deliberately break and challenge traditional food kapu practised by Kaʻahumanu and her followers in 1819
akua	a god, spirit or deity
aliʻi	chief
aliʻi ʻai ahupuaʻa	chief of the basic local community
aliʻi ʻai moku	district chief
aliʻi akua	god king, term reserved for chiefs of the highest rank, especially piʻo rank
aliʻi nui	great chief, paramount chief of a discrete, unified polity, also known as a mōʻī
ʻauhau	tax
ʻaumakua	ancestral spirits and deities
ʻawa	kava (*Piper methysticum*), the root of which was used to make a psychoactive beverage consumed by chiefs
hakuʻāina	a landlord, most typically a konohiki or aliʻi ʻai ahupuaʻa level lesser chief

hale nauā	the house in which genealogical specialists gathered to ascertain the pedigrees of chiefs for decisions on their eligibility to join paramount chief's households
hanai	adopted child
haole	foreigners
heiau	temple
hoʻokupu	tribute
hoʻomana	to worship, to empower through worship
hula	traditional dance in various forms
ihe	a short spear measuring from two to 2.5 metres, thrown or used to thrust
ilāmuku	officer of the paramount chief's household responsible for maintaining the kapu associated with that household
ʻili; ʻili lele	subdivision of an ahupuaʻa
ʻili kūpono	a segment of the ʻili land division directly controlled by the paramount chief rather than the ahupuaʻa chief, the tribute from which was reserved for the paramount chief
kaʻa-kaua	sub-commanders within each retinue
kāhili	fly whisks or standards; symbols of chiefly rank
kahului	crescent formation with horns pointing towards the enemy
kahuna	person with specialist knowledge of valued skills, usually associated with favour from the gods such as canoe makers, herbal medicine specialists and priests
kahuna kuni	sorcery priests
kahuna nui	high priest
kahuna pule	priest, religious specialist
kalaimoku	war councillor, senior military adviser to rulers

kalana	subdivision of a moku (district)
kalo	taro (*Colocasia esculenta*)
kanaka	commoners recruited by aliʻi for their martial prowess
Kānaka Maoli	indigenous Hawaiians
kanaka no lua kaua	aliʻi and makaʻāinana who lived with the chief and did not desert him in battle
kapa	tapa, cloth made form the bark of the wauke (paper mulberry plant, *Broussonetia papyrifera*)
kapu	permanent or temporary sacred status through connection to the gods
kapu moe	prostrating taboo requiring commoners and lower ranked chiefs to lie prostrate in the presence of a high-status sacred chief
kaukau aliʻi	collective name for lesser grades of chiefs
kāula	prophet
kāuwa	underclass enslaved by their enemies or descended from other kāuwa. Used for human sacrifices at luakini heiau (temples)
koʻa	a fishing shrine dedicated to the god Kūʻula
kōʻele	land division worked by commoners, all the produce of which was reserved for the benefit of the konohiki and aliʻi
konohiki	land manager for an ahupuaʻa land unit on behalf of the aliʻi ʻai ahupuaʻa (chief in charge of the ahupuaʻa)
kūʻauhau	genealogical specialist within the paramount chief's retinue responsible for memorising the genealogies and moʻolelo of the aliʻi
kuhina	governors
kukulu	straight battleline
kula	dryland cultivation areas especially associated with ʻuala (sweet potato) cultivation

kupuna	elder, ancestor
loʻi	irrigated pond-field for growing taro
loko iʻa (loko, loko kuapā)	fishpond on reef flat enclosed by a stone wall
luakini heiau	temple where human sacrifice was offered
luakini kaua	temple dedicated to the war god Kū
luakini poʻokanaka	temple where human sacrifice was offered
māhele	the land reform process from 1846 to 1855 which replaced traditional landholding procedures with Western-style individual tenure parcels held by the Hawaiian Crown, the government, and individuals
makaʻāinana	commoner majority below the chiefly classes
makahiki	four month, rainy season period of ritual, celebrations, and chiefly tax collection commencing when Pleiades became visible in November, and dedicated to Lono, the god of rain-fed agriculture
makawalu	battle formation of small flexible groups for broken terrain
mālama	care for, management of resources or people
malo	loincloth
mana	signs of the gods' favour manifest in good fortune to people eliciting respectful treatment of individuals
moemoe	night attacks
moe-pu	aliʻi's chosen companions in death
mōʻī	paramount chief, see also aliʻi nui
moku	polities
moʻo	a land unit subdivision of an ʻili land unit
moʻokūʻahuhau	genealogical heritage
moʻolelo	traditional historical account
naha	one of the highest chiefly ranks

GLOSSARY OF HAWAIIAN TERMS

nī'aupi'o (Pi'o)	close consanguineous marriage between high-status chiefs resulting in offspring of the most sacred rank, the ali'i akua or ali'i kapu
noa	temporarily or permanently free of kapu (sacred status) by separation from the divine
'okana (also known as poko)	a subdistrict incorporating several ahupua'a
pahoa	a hardwood dagger measuring up to 60 centimetres
pahupū	literally, cut in half, name given to special group of Maui warriors in the era of Kahekili who tattooed half of their body with black dye
pa'i'ai	storable form of taro produced by steaming, mashing and pressing taro corm into hard dry cakes
palaoa pae	ruler's right to whalebone washed up on shore
peleleu	new larger, sturdy canoe design commissioned by Kamehameha after loss of much of his fleet between O'ahu and Kaua'i in 1796
pikoi	used as a throwing club to bring down fleeing enemy
poi	cooked and mashed corm of taro with water added
poi-po	ambushes
poko (also known as 'okana)	a subdistrict incorporating several ahupua'a
polulu	a long hardwood pike of up to six metres
pua'a	pig
pukaua	commander in chief
pu'uhonua	place of refuge and safety in times of conflict
pu'uku nui	chief treasurer
toa	warrior
'uala	sweet potato (*Ipomoea batatas*)
wahine	a woman, female

waiwai	literally plentiful water, applied to wealth in goods or property
wohi	high chiefly rank exempt from the prostrating tapu

List of Historical Personalities, Gods and Scholars

Alapaʻi	ruler who unified most of Hawaiʻi Island in the early 1700s
Iʻī, John Papa	19th-century Hawaiian historian
Kaʻahumanu	favourite wife of Kamehameha I, and effective ruler during the reign of Kamehameha II and III
Kaʻeokulani	Kahekili of Mauiʻs half-brother who controlled Kauaʻi in the late 1700s in alliance with Kalanikūpule against Kamehameha
Kahahana	ruler of Oʻahu in the late 1700s who was overthrown by Maui ruler Kahekili
Kahekili	ruler of Maui in the late 1700s who conquered Oʻahu
Kalanikūpule	Maui chief who succeeded Kahekili as ruler of Maui and Oʻahu in the late 1700s until defeated by Kamehameha
Kalaniʻōpuʻu	ruler of Hawaiʻi in the late 1700s who succeeded Alapaʻinui
Kamakau, Kēlou	19th-century Kānaka Maoli historian
Kamakau, Samuel M.	19th-century Kānaka Maoli historian
Kameʻeleihiwa, Lilikalā	contemporary Kānaka Maoli historian
Kamehameha	nephew of ruler of Hawaiʻi, Kalaniʻōpuʻu, unified the Hawaiian chain in 1790s

Kamehameha-nui	son of Maui ruler Kekaulike and nephew of Kalaniʻōpuʻu, ruler of Hawaiʻi Island, who succeeded his father as ruler of Maui in the mid-1700s
Kanaloa	one of the four principal gods of the Kānaka Maoli pantheon
Kāne	one of the four principal gods of the Kānaka Maoli pantheon, the creator god and god of waters and irrigation, to whom kalo (taro) was sacred
Kaumualiʻi	the last ruler of Kauaʻi before it was taken over by Kamehameha
Keawemauhili	half-brother of Hawaiʻi ruler Kalaniʻōpuʻu and influential warrior and chief supporting Kamehameha
Keʻeaumoku	powerful chief from Kona, Hawaiʻi, who supported Kamehameha throughout his lifetime
Kekūhaupiʻo	famous warrior of Hawaiʻi Island who mentored and advised Kamehameha
Keōpūolani	sacred daughter of Hawaiʻi chief Kīwalaʻō who became royal wife of Kamehameha
Keōua Kuahuʻula	younger son of Hawaiʻi ruler Kalaniʻōpuʻu who controlled south-east Hawaiʻi Island as a rival to Kamehemeha until killed by Kamehameha in 1791
Kepelino	19th-century Kānaka Maoli historian
Kīwalaʻō	oldest son of Kalaniʻōpuʻu who briefly succeeded his father as ruler of Hawaiʻi before being killed by Keʻeaumoku at the battle of Mokuʻōhai in 1782. His daughter, Keōpūolani, became the sacred wife of Kamehameha
Kūaliʻi	ruler of Oʻahu in the late 1600s and early 1700s

LIST OF HISTORICAL PERSONALITIES, GODS AND SCHOLARS

Kūkāʻili-moku	war god Kū, the carver of lands
Liholiho	son of Kamehameha who succeeded his father as King Kamehameha II in 1819, but died in London in 1824
Malo, David	19th-century Kānaka Maoli historian
Osorio, Jonathon Kay Kamakawiwoʻole	contemporary Kānaka Maoli historian
Peleiʻōhōlani	ruler of Oʻahu and Kauaʻi in the late 1700s
Piʻilani	ruler of Maui in the mid-1500s
Pukui, Mary Kawena	20th-century Kānaka Maoli scholar
ʻUmi-a-Līloa	first unifier of Hawaiʻi Island in the late 1500s
Young, Kanalu G. Terry	modern Kānaka Maoli historian

Introduction

Hawaiians figure prominently in literature on the transition from fragmented chiefdoms to a unified state. The conquest and unification of the Hawaiian Islands by Kamehameha I between 1782 and 1812 came at a time of increasing European contact, prompting many to attribute his success to European weapons and ideas. Kamehameha succeeded Kalaniʻōpuʻu as mōʻī (paramount chief) of leeward Hawaiʻi when he defeated the other contender, Kīwalaʻō, in battle in 1782. He went on to conquer all the islands in the Hawaiian archipelago apart from Kauaʻi and Niʻihau between 1790 and 1795 (see Figure 2). By 1812, he had overcome the last challenge to his rule and Kaumualiʻi of Kauaʻi had also acknowledged his primacy. No one seriously threatened his rule from then until his death in 1819.

This study examines the role of coercion in the unification of the Hawaiian Islands in the era of Kamehameha I. Hawaiʻi was rapidly transformed from a series of divided chiefdoms into a unified kingdom at a time of increasing European contact. As such, it is a topic that involves consideration of a range of issues that are central to human history. The study of conflict and its role in wider power relations is crucial for any study of human society. The formation of centralised polities that transcended local kin-based loyalties was a significant watershed in social evolution, while the impact of European contact on non-Western societies is a major theme in world history. Three interrelated themes in Hawaiian political evolution are examined in this book: the balance between coercion and consent, between structural trends and individual leadership qualities and specific historical events, and between indigenous and European factors.

The unification of Hawaiʻi took place relatively late in its history and within a single generation. The period between 1778 and 1819 is rich in both European and Hawaiian documentary sources. This was a time of increasing European penetration in to the Pacific. Kamehameha's use of European advisers and Western military technology has been cited as a major factor behind the victories that paved the way for unification. This has naturally raised the question of the degree to which European contact influenced the process of political centralisation. Was it an essential ingredient, or did it merely speed up an already existing process? The latter part of this study deals with these issues and offers particular insights into the impact of European firearms on traditional warfare in Hawai'i and elsewhere. Those asserting firearms as a significant factor in Kamehameha's wars of unification largely ignore the nature of Hawaiian warfare and do not consider warfare alongside the other forms of political control that were central to this process in Hawai'i.

The study of warfare in the non-Western world has been neglected until relatively recently. Pacific history is no exception. The few studies of warfare in Pacific history have been heavily influenced by anthropology, and tend to emphasise the cultural context behind acts of violence, rather than the actual fighting. By neglecting the narrative of events, they tend to treat warfare as a static institution rather than an evolving process. But, perhaps, the most pressing need is for an attempt to follow the lead of recent European military historiography and combine the study of tactics and weaponry with consideration of psychological and logistical factors, and the place of warfare in wider social relations. This study constructs such an approach by combining the best aspects of European and non-European military historiography. The resulting synthesis is a radical reinterpretation of Hawaiian warfare that treats it as an evolving process heavily imbued with cultural meaning, and characterised by fluid circumstances, including crucial turning points when choices were made to take elements of Hawaiian society on paths of development that proved decisive for political unification, but which were neither inevitable or predictable.

The timing of Hawaiian unification has also created a disciplinary boundary in studies on this topic that rarely transcends the juncture marked by European contact and the addition of European written observations to the body of sources available for the study of this era. This study challenges the standard historiography in arguing for a diminished role for Western weapons and ideas in unification and a greater role for indigenous institutions. It also argues against the tendency to examine history in the non-Western world in terms of generalised structural history rather than historically specific dynamics in which a number of historical trajectories were possible depending on choices made by indigenous actors. In arguing for a more wide-ranging approach to power that encompasses political, diplomatic, social, religious and economic institutions as well as military topics, this study also spans disciplinary divides and knits Western and non-Western historiography. This approach is adopted here as a model for studies of political evolution and the role of warfare in non-European societies beyond Hawai'i. This more comprehensive framework diminishes the role of warfare and violence and elevates the role of consent and compromise in securing long-term political power.

This study examines works from a number of disciplines, and depicts the struggle for power in Hawai'i as a complicated and dynamic process involving long-term, slowly evolving continuities as well as short-term perturbations that could alter existing structures. It argues that long-term, indigenous processes had more influence on centralisation in Hawai'i than is generally recognised, and that logistical and political consolidation was more important in chiefly struggles for power than battle tactics and weapons. At the same time, however, it is argued that the process of Hawaiian history suggests that more attention needs to be paid to detailing historical events in non-Western historiography to explain why and when processes occur. Having the necessary conditions for military victory and centralisation in place only ensured that there was a potential for unification; specific triggers and opportunities were also needed.

Perhaps the greatest omission in the standard discourse on the political evolution of Hawaiian society is the almost total exclusion of modern indigenous Hawaiian scholarship on this topic in favour of largely North America-based anthropologists and archaeologists. The Hawai'inuiākea School of Hawaiian Knowledge at the University of Hawai'i at Mānoa is the world's leading centre for scholarship on Hawai'i. The conclusions reached by its historians present forms of political leadership and socio-economic organisation that were much more consensus-based, and in which environmental guardianship played a more prominent role in assessing leaders than is usually allowed for. This is markedly different from the standard interpretations that are critiqued in this book. While it might be argued that such interpretations merely reflect worldwide contemporary priorities and values, the fact that these values are consistently represented in Hawaiian traditions and scholarship across the ages, and also find common ground with a host of independently arrived at conclusions by other Pacific island scholars, requires that such perspectives are considered seriously by scholars of the Pacific. Above all, this study finds indigenous Hawaiian approaches a much better fit with the historical evidence related to Hawaiian history than more conventional scholarship.

1

Three Key Debates: Positioning Hawai'i in World History

Hawai'i figures prominently in the archaeological and anthropological literature on the transition from chiefdoms to unified states. This introductory chapter compares and contrasts academic analysis of indigenous Hawaiian society with that of wider disciplinary and geographical entities for three key debates concerning the evolution of human societies. Hawai'i is central to a number of these debates, yet marginal to others. The first theme debated is the process of political consolidation from chiefdoms based on kin loyalty derived from blood links to states based on power vested in institutional office holders and membership based on territorial residency. The second is the role of coercion and consent in political consolidation. Research on the history of Hawai'i is poorly served in this regard, despite the fact that most investigators acknowledge that unification occurred in the 1790s as a result of an extensive military campaign and the major role ascribed to warfare in state formation in most locations beyond the Pacific. The third theme is the role of European influences in ensuring the Hawaiian archipelago was unified for the first time in its history, given that this unification occurred soon after regular contact with European naval and trade vessels was established and widely acknowledged structural prerequisites for state formation were in place in Hawai'i for some time before unification occurred.

The literature on the unification of Hawai'i largely ignores comparative world history, sociology and political science in which coercion is generally allocated a central role in state formation, but which, in Pacific case studies, are largely absent. Combining frameworks from these diverse bodies of literature suggests exciting and fruitful approaches to the study of this topic in the Pacific. Indeed, the broader questions about the manifestation and consolidation of power that are explored in this chapter offer lessons for all disciplines and all regions, trapped as we are within partial and subjective prisms of observation. Three main methodological points are advocated here: the value of reading and applying approaches from other disciplines; the value of reading and applying approaches from other regions (especially combining Western and non-Western historiography); and, perhaps more problematically, the importance of local context, which requires caution in applying externally generated frameworks of analysis without modification.

While state formation in the West and elsewhere is generally acknowledged to have been forged in the crucible of violence to overcome strong senses of local identity and affiliation that characterise most of humanity, countervailing forces promoting diversity are generally acknowledged more in discussion of Western nation states as the seed that spawned later democratic institutions. In contrast, pre-colonial, non-Western, orientalist states are portrayed as ultimately held together by despotism, or hopelessly fragmented to the point of being beyond control other than by the application of often externally imposed coercion. Such mindsets justified colonial rule and postcolonial interventions across the globe by former colonial states in 'failed states'. These approaches ignore the fact that many political evolutions across the globe were based on balancing power bases for stability rather than unifying for efficiency in the delivery of outcomes. In the former, representation and relative consensus was the key objective while, in the latter, the goal was to deliver results and ensure limited dissent to block this delivery. While citing 'traditional' sources that were collected soon after European contact and before Western influence destroyed or compromised their veracity, few Western academics of state formation in the Pacific cite current indigenous academics. These indigenous Pacific academics portray a very different configuration of power in which rule is more consent-based and consultative by both necessity and social values, often in fluid and evolving circumstances.

1. THREE KEY DEBATES

The dilemma of political consolidation: Focusing power while accommodating diversity

The investigation of state formation in Hawai'i has mainly been conducted by anthropologists and archaeologists. They see economic modes of production as the key to understanding political power in Hawai'i during the pre-unification period. This emphasis is, in part, a reflection of their disciplinary assumptions on the processes driving the evolution of human societies, which are in turn partly derived from the relative absence of written observations for the times and peoples they study, and the relative abundance of archaeologically accessible remnants of economic production, such as field systems and buildings. There is also a voluminous literature on state formation written by sociologists, political scientists and historians, who tend more to emphasise political accommodation and/or military domination as key processes, which is again, in part, a reflection of sources available and disciplinary assumptions. In the late 1950s, historian Karl Wittfogel linked the development of sociopolitical complexity to the need for coordinated management of large-scale irrigated agricultural complexes, such as those found in Hawai'i. He argued that irrigated taro fields produced sufficient surplus to feed the warriors and administrative officers needed to support more complex forms of political organisation.[1] More recently, archaeologist Patrick Kirch noted that intensive dryland agriculture gave rise to inherently unstable and expansive chiefdoms. According to him, variable rainfall reduced food security and necessitated the conquest of other agricultural land.[2] However, the economic structures seen by British explorer Captain James Cook in the 1770s existed long before unification and do not, therefore, explain why unification occurred when and as it did.

Archaeologist Timothy Earle departs from this economic focus. He notes that the same military power that allowed expansion also introduced internal instability because the ruler could not always rely on the loyalty of warriors serving under subordinate chiefs. He emphasises the importance of ideological factors in securing sustained loyalty. Most state-builders in

---

1   Karl Wittfogel, *Oriental Despotism* (New Haven: Yale University Press, 1957), pp. 241–43.
2   P.V. Kirch, *The Wet and the Dry: Irrigation and Agricultural Intensification in Polynesia* (University of Chicago Press, 1994), p. 8. Kirch has maintained this contention in his most recent works – see *How Chiefs Became Kings: Divine Kingship and the Rise of Archaic States in Ancient Hawai'i* (Los Angeles & London: University of California Press, 2010) and *A Shark Going Inland Is My Chief: The Island Civilization of Ancient Hawai'i* (Berkeley: University of California Press, 2012).

Polynesia faced similar problems. There was always the danger of chiefs close to power making a bid for supremacy. At the same time chiefs in areas away from the centre of power might be tempted to assert their independence. This latter prospect was sometimes enhanced by problems of communication along narrow trails or across stormy seas. These problems were also common to chiefdoms outside of Polynesia.[3] Agriculture is important to Earle for the symbolic value of the temples and fields constructed under chiefly supervision as well as for subsistence. According to Earle, 'these constructions of social labour encapsulated the social relations of the chiefdom or, more precisely, the historical events that defined these relations'. Reminders of chiefly power were all around, as was the place of commoners in the subsistence economy: 'The symbolic order was thus grounded and subsumed within the everyday practice of ritual and subsistence labour in the monuments and fields of the chiefs.'[4] While acknowledging the role played by coercion, the anthropologists Marshall Sahlins and Valerio Valeri also emphasise the importance of belief in the ideology of sacred chieftainship for power, particularly in securing compliance from maka'āinana (commoners) well into the post-unification period.[5]

In his 2010 study of Hawaiian political and social evolution, *How Chiefs Became Kings*, Kirch argues convincingly that, by the arrival of Cook in the 1770s, Hawaiian polities had developed an array of the institutions to support the centralisation and concentration of power under high chiefs. According to Kirch, these archaic Hawaiian states were characterised by:

> the development of class stratification, land alienation from commoners and a territorial system of administrative control, a monopoly of force and endemic conquest warfare, and, most important, divine kingship legitimated by state cults with a formal priesthood.[6]

Two years later, Kirch published a more comprehensive history of Hawai'i in *A Shark Going Inland is My Chief* in which he continues his consistent assertion that the driving influence on political evolution was population growth built on agricultural intensification. Once agricultural intensification had reached its limit in the 16th century, around the time

---

3   I.C. Campbell, *A History of the Pacific Islands* (Christchurch: University of Canterbury Press, 1989), p. 47.
4   Timothy K. Earle, *How Chiefs Come to Power: The Political Economy in Prehistory* (Stanford University Press, 1997), p. 184.
5   Marshall Sahlins, 'Other Times, Other Customs: The Anthropology of History', *American Anthropologist*, vol. 85 (3), 1983, esp. 522–23, and 535 n. 12; and Valerio Valeri, *Kingship and Sacrifice: Ritual and Society in Ancient Hawaii*, Paula Wissing (trans.) (University of Chicago Press, 1985a).
6   Kirch (2010), p. 27.

of ʻUmi-a-Līloaʼs reign on Hawaiʻi island and Piʻilani on Maui, the further expansion of political power lay in the conquest of other lands. In so doing Hawaiian polities moved from being ruled by chiefs who were considered kinsmen by their commoner followers to states ruled by divine kings. Kirch is more certain in *A Shark Going Inland Is My Chief* than in *How Chiefs Became Kings* that Hawaiʻiʼs political centralisation occurred more because of multiple indigenous factors than European influences, but still cannot explain unification without recourse to the influence of Western weapons, again with almost no discussion of the evidence for this.[7] While making much more use of indigenous traditions than in his previous works, he still favours his previous explanations of underlying influences.[8] Archaeologists are increasingly coming to realise that oral traditions must be better utilised not just as a sign of respect for indigenous peoples but as key sources to enhance and clarify archaeological evidence.[9]

Archaeologist Robert Hommon also published his *The Ancient Hawaiian State* in 2013. Hommon pioneered the close reading of recorded traditions alongside archaeological material in the 1970s and 1980s. In his 2013 work, however, he retreats from his earlier close reading of historical processes for specific islands to emphasise that Hawaiian chiefdoms on the eve of European contact were state-like in their shared structures of political economic and social organisation.[10] The discussion in chapters seven and eight of the authority–power spectrum in Hawaiian polities in the lead-up to unification under Kamehameha I is of particular interest for this study. While making a strong case for the presence of the component parts of political rule that are generally associated with states, the lack of discussion on processes leading to this and how these structures were enacted in local and specific contexts means that Hommon cannot adequately explain why Hawaiʻi unified when it did according to these pre-existing indigenous elements. Hommon agrees with Kirch in seeing the key driving force as being the structural instability of dryland production to support expanding populations and ambitions of dryland rulers in the eastern islands.[11] However, the link between this

---

7   Kirch (2012), p. 225.
8   Kirch (2012), pp. 68, 79. This under-utilisation of traditions was also noted in a review of Kirch (2012) by Kerri A. Inglis ('Review of P.V. Kirch, *A Shark Going Inland Is My Chief: The Island Civilization of Ancient Hawaiʻi*', *Journal of Interdisciplinary History*, vol. 44 (2), Autumn 2013, 269).
9   Peter M. Whiteley, 'Archaeology and Oral Tradition: The Scientific Importance of Dialogue', *American Antiquity*, vol. 67 (3), Jul. 2002, 405–15.
10 Robert J. Hommon, *The Ancient Hawaiian State: Origins of a Political Society* (New York and Oxford: Oxford University Press, 2013), p. 2.
11 Hommon (2013), pp. 7–8, 117–35.

instability and the development and/or sophistication of specific elements of coercive capacity or other elements of state rule before or after specific events in the late 18th century is not clearly made.

This work departs from both Kirch and Hommon in arguing for greater documentation of the role of coercive mechanisms in this process and in arguing that sacred kingship was not as crucial as they and most other anthropologists and archaeologists claim. Rather, I argue here that the late 18th century witnessed the development of sophisticated methods of power sharing, resource allocation and mobilisation of resources, which consolidated the rule of certain chiefdoms at the expense of others that did not embrace these tactics in a process that can be seen as a political and military revolution. All this is recorded in Hawaiian traditions, but only modern Kānaka Maoli scholars Kanalu G. Terry Young and Jonathan Kay Kamakawiwoʻole Osorio, as discussed below, have noted this in detailed reference to the recorded history of their ancestors.[12]

Anthropology and archaeology have been the main disciplines concerned with the investigation of state formation in pre-industrial Pacific Island societies. The Western intellectual traditions from which they derive have been heavily influenced by the idea of linear evolutionary progress. Through time, societies become increasingly complex in their organisation, more politically unified, with an increasing capacity to utilise resources more efficiently. The generally accepted model of social evolution portrays a progression from relatively egalitarian societies to socially stratified, centralised states, by means of a transition phase characterised by the development of social differentiation.[13] Sophistication in this body of Pacific-orientated literature is generally synonymous with greater mobilisation and concentration of resources by those in power, rather than a means of power sharing and balancing power, as argued by Kānaka Maoli scholars and scholars beyond the Pacific.

---

12   Kānaka Maoli is the term used by indigenous Hawaiians to describe themselves and their culture. The best examples of the revolution in Kānaka Maoli scholarship are Kanalu G. Terry Young, *Rethinking the Native Hawaiian Past* (New York: Garland Publishing Inc., 1998); and Jonathan Kay Kamakawiwoʻole Osorio, *Dismembering Lāhui: A History of the Hawaiian Nation to 1887* (Honolulu: University of Hawaiʻi Press, 2002).
13   Michael Mann, *The Sources of Social Power*, vol. 1 (Cambridge University Press, 1986), p. 35; Alexander Alland Jr, *To Be Human: An Introduction to Anthropology* (New York: John Wiley & Sons, 1980), pp. 438 ff.; and Joseph A. Tainter, *The Collapse of Complex Societies* (Cambridge University Press, 1988), pp. 24 ff.

Within mainstream Western literature on state formation, egalitarian societies are characterised by a lack of permanent hierarchical distinctions between individuals. Status is based on individual achievement rather than institutionalised rankings. Leadership tends to be minimal, and to be based on the power of persuasion. Leaders are usually only obeyed temporarily to achieve specific goals. Social organisation is based around small, intimate kin groupings. Few cooperative enterprises can be sustained for any length of time between two or more of these groupings. Resources are distributed throughout the community by the exchange of goods and services and there is very little accumulation of resources in the hands of any one individual. The route to elevated social status is to acquire resources and distribute them to attract followers. Accumulated goods are also used to enhance prestige through the holding of public feasts and gift giving. Elevated status is only maintained by continued success in the accumulation and judicious distribution of goods. The only significant form of sanction is appeal to public opinion, which acts as a strong constraint on behaviour.[14]

Some communities become ranked societies. Individuals are ranked hierarchically and those in higher ranks have greater access to resources and privileges. Differences in rank may become institutionalised and even hereditary. But power is still essentially based on collective consent rather than coercive capability. Authority can only be used for collective purposes. Consent is freely given and may be freely withdrawn by participants. High rank holders have status, make decisions and use material resources on behalf of the whole group. They do not possess coercive power beyond their own kin base, however, and cannot divert group resources for private use without risking other kin groups withdrawing their support. Polities are more federations than organic wholes, with an ever-present potential for fission.[15]

Authority rests on sacred status that is sometimes claimed to emanate from a divine source that is not open to challenge. The sacred ruler secures obedience through claims of membership or influence over the supernatural

---

14 Mann (1986), p. 37; Tainter (1988), p. 24; Bruce Trigger, 'Generated Coercion and Inequality: The Basis of State Power in the Early Civilizations', in Henri J.M. Claessen, Pieter van de Velde & M. Estelle Smith (eds), *Development and Decline, The Evolution of Sociopolitical Organization* (South Hadley, Mass.: Bergin and Garvey, 1985), p. 50.
15 Mann (1986), pp. 37, 52; Christopher S. Peebles & Susan M. Kus, 'Some Archaeological Correlates of Ranked Societies', *American Antiquity*, vol. 42 (3), 1977, 421–22; B.G. Trigger, *Times and Traditions: Essays in Archaeological Interpretation* (Edinburgh University Press, 1978), pp. 197–99; Timothy Earle, 'The Evolution of Chiefdoms', *Current Anthropology*, vol. 30 (1), 1989, esp. 86; and Robert L. Carneiro, 'The Chiefdom: Precursor of the State', in Grant D. Jones & Robert R. Kautz (eds), *The Transition to Statehood in the New World* (Cambridge University Press, 1981), pp. 37–79.

world in societies where the supernatural are believed to have a major impact on man's fortunes. The problem with sacred authority is that, in claiming a power that transcends human power, the leader must retain sufficient distance from his subjects to develop an air of mystification, and yet not become so isolated as to risk losing popular appeal as head of a secular community. To intervene too blatantly in worldly affairs is to threaten the myth of divine control over the course of events.[16]

Rulers are able to use their sacred status to acquire goods and services in the name of ensuring supernatural support, but still need to redistribute goods and services to retain their secular support base. Accumulation of goods by leaders is also limited by the continued reliance on kinship as the basis of social and economic organisation. Family and kin groups tend to be primarily concerned with ensuring that their own needs are met rather than generating a large surplus for wider societal needs. Distinguished anthropologist of the Pacific Marshall Sahlins refers to this system as the Domestic Mode of Production. To Sahlins, households in this form of organisation are caught in a dilemma, 'temporising always between domestic welfare and broader obligations towards kinsmen in the hope of satisfying the latter without menacing the former'.[17] This curtailed the augmentation of production and polity and was the ultimate structural limitation on chiefdoms in Hawai'i and elsewhere.

Ranked societies span the full spectrum from near egalitarian to those with a marked concentration of power in the hands of a ruling body. In some ranked societies an absolute, uncontested highest rank emerges, with all other ranks' lineages being graded according to their relation to this focal point. Seniority is usually expressed in terms of genealogical proximity to the ultimate ancestors of the group, who are often associated with the gods. Leadership roles are usually reserved for those from higher ranks. Their authority derives from the belief that high genealogical rank endows them with exceptional powers or qualities through their connections with the gods. Periodic proof of the leader's abilities is required for the maintenance of authority. This type of authority is open to challenge from other competitors within the pool of genealogically qualified candidates, particularly when the incumbent is unsuccessful or fails to benefit his

---

16   Irving Goldman, *Ancient Polynesian Society* (University of Chicago Press, 1970), pp. xv–xxi; Sahlins (1983), p. 518; Alland (1980), p. 435; John Keegan, *The Mask of Command* (London: Penguin, 1987), p. 318; and Mann (1986), p. 158.
17   Marshall Sahlins, *Stone Age Economics* (Chicago: Aldine, 1972), pp. 41–100, 124–32, 148, esp. 125.

followers. Kinship is still the dominant form of social organisation, with open conflict tending to occur horizontally between groups, rather than vertically between classes within a group.[18]

Ranked societies are sometimes referred to as chiefdoms. Anthropologist Robert Carneiro defines a chiefdom as 'an autonomous political unit comprising a number of villages or communities under the permanent control of a paramount chief'.[19] To Carneiro, the major threshold in man's sociopolitical evolution was the move from egalitarian societies to stratified societies, as this represented the first transcendence of localised autonomy. From that point onwards, change was more quantitative than qualitative. Similarly, Earle believes the fundamental dynamics of chiefdoms are essentially the same as those of states. Many scholars disagree, pointing to the continuing tendency of ranked societies to fragment. They claim that the major threshold in human social evolution was the establishment of permanent centralised authority in the form of states.[20]

There is much debate on what characterises a state. Most definitions usually involve notions of centralised authority, territoriality and coercive capability. One of the most concise definitions is that of sociologist Michael Mann. To Mann:

> The state is a differentiated set of institutions and personnel embodying centrality, in the sense that political relations radiate outward to cover a territorially demarcated area, over which it claims a monopoly of binding and permanent rule-making, backed up by physical violence.[21]

The transition from advanced chiefdoms to states generally involves the conversion of temporary political authority and permanent religious centres into permanent political power, institutionalised and secularised in its access to coercive measures to quell internal dissent and prevent fission. A major part of the centralisation process is the breakdown of localised, kin-based loyalties, and their replacement with territorial affiliations. The domestic mode of production is supplemented or replaced with surplus-orientated forms of agricultural production and profit-orientated

---

18   Mann (1986), pp. 37, 527–30; Peebles & Kus (1977), pp. 421–22; Alland (1980), p. 450; and Stephanie Seto Levin, 'The Overthrow of the Kapu System in Hawaii', *Journal of the Polynesian Society*, vol. 77 (4), 1968, 403–05.
19   Carneiro (1981), pp. 37–45, esp. 45; Alland (1980), pp. 438–42; Peebles & Kus (1977), pp. 431–33; Sahlins (1983), pp. 521–22.
20   Earle (1997), p. 14; and Carneiro (1981), pp. 51–54, 70.
21   Mann (1986), p. 37.

commerce. The state's administrative structure supports itself by means of taxes and tributes levied on this surplus. Increasingly sharp vertical distinctions occur within the population as a consequence of declining kin-based obligations and affiliations.[22]

In a review of variations in power within West African kingdoms, historian P.C. Lloyd offers insights into the process of centralisation. The least concentrated forms of power consisted of rulers who were little more than arbitrators between the chiefs, in whom the real power lay. Autocratic rulers represented the most concentrated form of power. Although ultimately reliant on the goodwill of their chiefs, they were still able to manipulate them to achieve most of their aims. While all tended to be surrounded by a 'mystic aura', that 'surrounding the arbitrator is a substitute for control of physical force; that of the autocrat masks his secular power'.[23]

Effective political power required the possession of wealth and a personal following. Often the income from tribute, plunder and gifts was used to pay a personal staff. Initially salaried positions were rare in West African kingdoms. Senior office-bearers kept a proportion of the tribute collected and transmitted to higher authorities, while junior staff received free board and lodging. This limited the degree to which a ruler could increase his power at the expense of his chiefs for, to do so required gaining direct control over certain segments of the population, or establishing royal monopolies over certain types of trade. 'In a long established and politically stagnant kingdom, the allocation of these resources of wealth and people becomes institutionalised and difficult for a ruler, starting from a position of political weakness to alter.'[24]

To Lloyd, the key to the amount of power that can be concentrated in the hands of the ruler is the method of appointment to political office. He makes a crucial distinction between:

---

22 Mann (1986), p. 38; Tainter (1988), pp. 26–28; Henri J.M. Claessen & Peter Skalnik, 'The Early State: Models and Reality', in Henri J.M. Claessen & Peter Skalnik (eds), *The Early State* (The Hague: Mouton Publishers, 1978a), pp. 637–50; Grant D. Jones & Robert R. Kautz, 'Issues in the Study of New World State Formation', in Grant D. Jones & Robert R. Kautz (eds), *The Transition to Statehood in the New World* (Cambridge University Press, 1981), pp. 14–17.
23 P.C. Lloyd, 'The Political Development of West African Kingdoms', review article, *Journal of African History*, 9 (2), 1968, 324.
24 Lloyd (1968), pp. 326–27.

those chiefs who are elected to office by the members of a group – a descent group or segment of a royal lineage – and who primarily represent the interests of that group; and those chiefs who are appointed by the king and incumbent chiefs, whose loyalties lie primarily to the king.[25]

The degree to which appointed chiefs secured permanency of tenure, income independent of the ruler, and were organised into exclusive, discrete corporate entities would dictate the degree to which they could rival each other and the power of the king.

The series of stages in the transition from the early state into its mature form, proposed by European social scientists Henri Claessen and Peter Skalnik, outlines the common assumptions of this literature.[26] The first stage is the inchoate state. Here kinship, family and community ties still dominate political allegiances. The concept of a unified supra-community polity exists mainly in the minds of the ruling elite, while the bulk of the population still retains a parochial outlook. Economically, full-time specialists are rare, and taxation is poorly developed and usually on an ad hoc basis. Social differences are countered by close kin ties between rulers and ruled. The second stage is known as the typical state. Kinship ties are now counterbalanced by territorial affiliations. Competition and appointment to office exist beside the principle of hereditary offices. Economically, ties of redistribution and reciprocity still pervade relations between social strata. The transitional state is the final stage on the road to a mature state. Appointed officials whose loyalty is to the state rather than lineages or localities now dominate government administrative posts. The administration of laws and taxation is institutionalised. With the breakdown of horizontal ties, vertical divisions based on the uneven control of resources come to the fore. The significance of the private ownership of resources increases as communal ownership declines. This process also increases the potential for social differentiation.

---

25 Lloyd (1968), p. 324.
26 Claessen & Skalnik (1978a), pp. 559–60; Rolando Tamayo Y. Salmoran, 'The State as a Problem of Jurisprudence', in Henri J.M. Claessen & Peter Skalnik (eds), *The Study of the State* (The Hague: Mouton Publishers, 1981), pp. 405–06; Tainter (1988), pp. 27–28; Mann (1986), p. 68; Donald V. Kurtz, 'The Legitimation of Early Inchoate States', in Claessen & Skalnik (1981), pp. 178–83; Elizabeth M. Brumfiel, 'Aztec State Making: Ecology, Structure and the Origin of the State', *American Anthropologist*, vol. 85 (2), 1983, 276; R.M. MacIver, *The Web of Government* (rev. edn) (New York: The Free Press, 1965), pp. 36–37; Trigger (1985), pp. 46–52, 54, 57–60.

The mature state is usually distinguished from earlier forms primarily by the degree to which centralised power is institutionalised and legitimised. While the early state still tends to be based on appeal to sacred authority, the mature state claims legitimacy through the secular benefits it delivers to citizens. The ruler gradually comes to be portrayed as the embodiment of the authority of the state rather than as a source of sacred authority. The institutions of the state are depicted as impartial. With the institutionalisation of government, power endures beyond the lifetimes of individual office holders, although individual ability still plays an important role in the effectiveness of any office. The development of institutionalised administrative apparatus enhances state coercion by allowing the creation of professional standing armies supported by government taxes and dues.

Most scholars who discuss the transition from advanced chiefdoms to states emphasise the conversion of temporary political authority and permanent religious centres into permanent political power that is institutionalised and secularised in its access to coercive measures to quell internal dissent and prevent fission. They see the breakdown of localised, kin-based loyalties, and their replacement with territorial affiliations as essential to the centralisation process. The state's administrators support themselves by means of taxes and tribute levied on agricultural surplus.[27]

To anthropologist Elman Service, the rise of the state is more the result of an improved capacity for peacemaking than improved capacity for making war.[28] With the formalised resolution of conflicts, states are able to devote more of their energy to internal consolidation. Most enduring states recognise that unity and stability are achieved through the distribution of resources reflective of their internal balance of power. Emergent states usually succeed because they are not too intrusive, leaving much decision-making and regulatory power in the hands of family, local and occupational groupings. As long as central government does not interfere too much, it is in the interests of local leaders to support it. A challenge to one form of authority can threaten other sources of authority by bringing into question the idea of authority as eternal and unchanging.

---

27   Mann (1986), p. 38; Tainter (1988), pp. 26–28; Claessen & Skalnik (1978a), pp. 637–50; Jones & Kautz (1981), pp. 14–17.
28   Elman R. Service, *The Origins of the State and Civilization* (New York: W.W. Norton & Co., 1975), pp. 61, 100.

While there is broad agreement on the structural characteristics of the various phases of sociopolitical evolution, explaining how these patterns occur and evolve is a more contentious issue. Much explanation of social evolution in anthropology and sociology has tended to portray societies as integrated entities acting in a coherent manner similar to the behaviour of organic entities, such as the human body. This tradition was initially prominent in British anthropology's functionalist school and its principles were continued in general systems theory. This approach was heavily influenced by cybernetics, the study of regulating mechanisms in machines. Society is portrayed as a system of interrelated parts in which each element functions in such a way as to maintain the system as a whole. Like a thermostat, the system reacts to deviation from the norm. When thresholds are reached, the system brings itself back within the boundaries of the normal steady state, or homeostasis. Change is therefore usually the result of the intrusion of external factors, such as environmental change or contact with different societies. The degree of change is usually heavily influenced by societies' degree of success in incorporating new elements into existing structures.

General systems theory distinguishes between open and closed systems. Closed systems tend toward disintegration and entropy because of their inability to adapt to new circumstances, while open systems are dynamic and tend towards growth and internal differentiation. Increases in differentiation and internal integration occur because they confer a competitive advantage. Differentiation allows for increases in the quality of products through the increased skill factor that specialisation confers. Centralised, integrated structures increase efficiency by counteracting the duplication of resources and services, and providing overall coordination.[29]

Centralised control is important for the processing of information as well as the utilisation of energy. To coordinate internal components and react to external factors, a system must be able to gather, interpret and disseminate information to relevant sectors. The amount of information that can be processed by individuals, or groups, is finite. Information theory postulates that, as societies increase in size, the majority of individuals

---

29 Barbara Abbott Segraves, 'Central Elements in the Construction of a General Theory of the Evolution of Societal Complexity', in Colin Renfrew, Michael J. Rowlands & Barbara Abbott Segraves (eds), *Theory and Explanation in Archaeology: The Southampton Conference* (New York: Academic Press, 1982), pp. 288, 294–95; Peebles & Kus (1977), p. 428; Alland (1980), pp. 262, 323; and Frank Hole & Robert F. Heizer, *An Introduction to Prehistoric Archaeology* (2nd edn) (New York: Holt, Rinehart and Winston Inc., 1969), pp. 363, 373–81.

must surrender a direct role in the decision-making process to ensure that society can respond to challenges more efficiently. It becomes necessary for members to obey commands in crucial situations for the benefit of society as a whole. For example, martial law and non-consensus decision-making by the executive core of government commonly occur in times of war, as consensus-orientated decision-making could lead to fatal delays. The limits on information-processing capacity necessitate a hierarchical administrative structure. At each level, specific information is processed by specialists and passed on up the decision-making chain so that leaders are not overwhelmed by a mass of information. Political power usually involves influence on the content and targeting of the disseminated information, adding another potential avenue for rulers to consolidate or increase their influence.[30]

Internal divisions may be horizontal as well as vertical. Kinship, occupation, locality and other affiliations interact with class affiliations. Sociologist Michael Mann's definition of society as 'multiple overlapping and interconnecting networks of power'[31] can accommodate both horizontal and vertical divisions. It also suggests society is a series of spheres – economic, territorial, cultural and so on, that never coincide precisely. Mann notes that:

> Human beings do not create unitary societies but a diversity of intersecting networks of social interaction. The most important of these networks form relative stability around the four power sources in any given social space. But underneath, human beings are tunnelling ahead to achieve their goals, forming new networks, extending old ones, and emerging most clearly into our view with rival configurations of one or more of the principle power networks.[32]

There is considerable value in combining conflict-orientated and integration-orientated perspectives. Social action may be influenced by the combination of internal power relations and external pressures. Internal power will be based on the interplay of coercive capacity and the perceived benefits of loyalty to higher authority for individuals. External pressures will either allow leaders to consolidate their powers in the name

---

30 Segraves (1982), p. 297; Trigger (1985), pp. 48–49; Trigger (1978), pp. 194 ff., esp. 213–14; Tainter (1988), p. 91 ff.; Desmond Morris, *The Human Zoo* (London: World Books, 1971), chpt 1.
31 Mann (1986), p. 1.
32 Mann (1986), p. 16.

of preserving society's coherence, or allow existing contradictions to rise to the surface by diverting the power of existing leaders, or providing alternatives to their ideology and resource base.[33]

The development of states is sometimes explained as a result of internal responses to external pressures. At present, external pressures and elements in terms of European contact are the only theory that has been proposed to explain why Hawai'i became a state precisely when it did and not decades before, when all of the necessary internally generated conditions Kirch and others outline were already in place. According to this theory, societies change because they become hemmed in and their options are reduced or channelled. Similarly, a society is faced with a situation in which its breakup is impossible and unacceptable in the face of external pressure. The most common scenario is one of increasing population in circumstances of unchanging or declining agricultural capacity because of environmental degradation from overuse; natural disasters, such as drought; or territorial confinement because of antagonistic, powerful neighbours. Mann uses such a concept to explain why some societies developed as centralised states and others did not. According to Mann, they became 'caged' because of highly specific circumstances. The ancient river-valley civilisations of the Middle East, for example, became tied to increasingly large-scale, centrally coordinated, irrigation-based and sedentary river-valley farming with high population density only because their agricultural prosperity attracted less prosperous neighbours to press in on their borders and hem them in.[34]

External elements may also play a more active role by providing new sources of power. Trade goods, tribute from conquered territories or foreign mercenaries may upset the balance of power. As Lloyd suggests, one possible outcome is that:

---

33 Theda Skocpol, *States and Social Revolutions: A Comparative Analysis of France, Russia and China* (London: Cambridge University Press, 1979), pp. 18–24; Phil Kohl, 'Force, History and the Evolutionist Paradigm', in Mathew Spriggs (ed.), *Marxist Perspectives in Archaeology* (Cambridge University Press, 1984), pp. 129–30; and Mann (1986), p. 540.
34 Mann (1986), pp. 124–26. See also Robert L. Carneiro, 'A Theory of the Origin of the State', *Science*, vol. 169, 1970, 733–38; Henri J.M. Claessen & Peter Skalnik, 'The Early State: Theories and Hypotheses', in Claessen & Skalnik (1978b), pp. 3–30; Brumfiel (1983), pp. 262–63; and Earle (1989), pp. 84–86.

> The contest between the categories of office holders becomes more intense as established rules do not cover the allocation of the new resources. It is through the resolution of such contests, that one is most likely to follow the changes taking place in the political structure.[35]

Territorial expansion is often cited as a major factor behind centralisation. Discussing Oyo in Nigeria, historian Robin Law notes, 'The connection is two fold. First, the territorial expansion of the empire created administrative problems to which centralisation was a response. And second, the process of imperial expansion created the resources which made centralisation possible'.[36]

Expansion can also create and accentuate internal tensions. Because the new territories might incorporate culturally distinct or hostile peoples, a standing army might be needed to garrison new areas and protect barriers. Resources from these outer areas may provide the revenue for such a force. A number of African kingdoms witnessed the erosion of established chiefly power in the kingdom's heartland, as the ruler was able to create his own power base in the provinces by utilising provincial resources. Indeed, expansion was sometimes initially motivated by attempts to resolve or at least divert attention from internal tensions.[37] Most states have been characterised by an ongoing dialectic between central authorities seeking to consolidate power and senior officials attempting to convert their positions to a more independent and permanent basis. Both were confronted with demands for increased local autonomy.

As societies increase in size they confront a series of thresholds beyond which structural differentiation and functional specialisation must increase if internal coherence is to be maintained. Political expansion increases the resource base, but runs the risk of overextending the realm because more resources might be needed to maintain coherence than were gained through expansion.[38] Without structural changes, the society may collapse or fragment. Societies are particularly open to change during such times of systemic stress. The inability to resolve crises often results in rapid change. There is always a tendency to be more willing to

---

35   Lloyd (1968), p. 322. See also Earle (1989), p. 86.
36   Robin Law, *The Oyo Empire c. 1600 – c. 1836: A West African Imperialism in the Era of the Atlantic Slave Trade* (Oxford: Clarendon, 1977), p. 241.
37   Law (1977), pp. 241 ff.; and Lloyd (1968), pp. 328–29.
38   Campbell (1989), p. 47; and Mark Elvin, 'Three Thousand Years of Unstable Growth: China's Environment from Archaic Times to the Present', *East Asian History*, no. 6, 1993, esp. p. 18.

risk tragedy or the unknown rather than endure prolonged frustration. A society's development often consists of long periods of relative stability interspersed with periods of rapid change. All aspects of society are not necessarily transformed to the same degree during times of rapid change. Continuity and change exist side by side.[39]

Centralised states are only one possible form of organisation and are not necessarily the logical conclusion of any social process. Power is not one-dimensional. Mann distinguishes between intensive and extensive power. The former consists of concentrated power emanating from the centre that is often weak at the periphery. The latter consists of a more diffused form of power, usually involving a balance of power between localities and interest groups. Even intensive power usually involves a balance of power between various factions at the centre of power. It may be more appropriate to view state-building as the judicious balancing of power alongside attempts to concentrate that power, particularly in the early stages of state formation.[40] It is argued in this book that this theory best fits the observed pattern of events and structures of organisation on the ground during Kamehameha's period. The limits on chiefly coercive power required compromises to accommodate diffuse sources of power. This contention runs counter to the theories of Kirch and others outlined above that chiefly monopolies of power allowed them to concentrate and utilise more and more of their societies' resources. On the other hand, there is no reason why societies cannot revert to older or less centralised forms of organisation. Devolution, decline, involution and stagnation are also possibilities, the last three largely involuntary, but the first in keeping with how the majority of humans have organised themselves for millennia.[41]

An important distinction is made in modern political science discourse on Pacific Island states between the processes of state formation and nation-building. Writing on post-2000 conflict in Melanesia, conflict resolution expert Sinclair Dinnen notes that post 2000, international

---

39   Tainter (1988), pp. 194–96, 200; Mann (1986), p. 61; Jones & Kautz (1981), pp. 28–30; Kohl (1984), p. 130; Jonathan Friedman, 'Catastrophe and Continuity in Social Evolution', in Renfrew, Rowlands & Segraves (1982), pp. 179 ff.
40   Mann (1986), pp. 532–35. See also Colin Renfrew, 'Space, Time, and Man', in *Transactions of the Institute of British Geographers*, New Series, vol. 6, 1981, 257–78; R.C.C. Law, 'The Constitutional Troubles of Oyo in the Eighteenth Century', *Journal of African History*, vol. 12 (1), 1971, 25–44; and Law (1977).
41   Friedman (1982), pp. 177–78, 181–82.

interventions to restore peace and state services combine nation-building and state formation. By overly focusing on achieving 'good governance' in institutions for the state delivery of services, planners neglected the critical need for a joint focus on state and civil society relations. Effective nation-building requires 'developing a shared sense of political community that is capable of binding together the population of a given state'.[42] Dinnen and many other political scientists point out that, in much of the world, nationalism often preceded state formation.[43] While archaeology and anthropological discourse on state formation in the indigenous Pacific emphasises the breakdown of community loyalty and its replacement by loyalty to a territorial entity as a key process in the development of states, this study and that of Kānaka Maoli and other Pacific scholars emphasises that, to be enduring, polities rather need to broaden and enhance the strength of local bonds to embrace a wider state entity. This is a crucial distinction, the wider implications of which we discuss in the conclusion with reference to its implications for scholarship and contemporary state-building interventions.

In their 2008 book *Intervention and State-building in the Pacific*, political scientists Greg Fry and Tarcisius Kabutaulaka note that the legitimisation of the doctrine of 'cooperative intervention' was first needed to justify Australian-led intervention in response to civil strife within neighbouring Melanesian nations. They note the importance of 'establishing political acceptance of the project among those affected by it'.[44] The interventionist, state–institution centred approach critiqued by Fry and Kabutaulaka rests on two flawed and interrelated assumptions that run counter to the conclusions reached in this study of the nature of power and authority in Hawai'i. The first is the idea that centralised institutional efficiency is at the core of converting 'failed states' into functioning states. The centralised state model of Europe advocated by many international bodies seeking to resolve conflict only became efficient after prolonged periods

---

42   Sinclair Dinnen, 'The Twin Processes of Nation Building and State Building', *State, Society and Governance in Melanesia Briefing Note*, no. 1/2007 (State, Society and Governance in Melanesia Program, The Australian National University, 2007), pp. 1–2.
43   Dinnen (2007), p. 3. See also Charles Tilly, *Coercion, Capital, and European States AD 990–1992* (rev. edn) (Oxford: Blackwell, 1992); Charles Tilly, *Trust and Rule* (Cambridge University Press, 2005); and Benedict R. Anderson, *Imagined Communities: Reflections on the Origin and Spread of Nationalism* (rev. edn) (London: Verso, 1991).
44   Greg Fry & Tarcisius Tara Kabutaulaka, 'Political Legitimacy and State-building Intervention in the Pacific', in Greg Fry & Tarcisius Tara Kabutaulaka (eds), *Intervention and State-building in the Pacific: The Legitimacy of 'Cooperative Intervention'* (Manchester & New York: Manchester University Press, 2008), p. 3.

of nation-building in Europe – a period of social identity-building must precede state formation based on developing effective state institutions so as to engender loyalty from citizens working in these institutions and communities seeking to benefit from them in excess of what they can provide themselves for kin and community. The Hawaiian polity accommodated multiple power sources and local identities through both necessity and design.

This conceptualisation of accumulated power as being more diffuse and balanced well beyond centralisation than the preceding theories admit is also the belief of the current generation of indigenous Hawaiian scholars.[45] The work of the late Kanalu Young and Jonathan Osorio is particularly compelling and persuasive in this regard. Despite the acclaimed international reputation of the Hawaiʻinuiākea School of Hawaiian Knowledge at the University of Hawaiʻi at Mānoa and Ka Haka ʻUla O Keʻelikōlani, College of Hawaiian Language of the University of Hawaiʻi's Hilo campus as leading centres of indigenous scholarship, none of the Western scholars of Hawaiian indigenous society cite Young and Osorio, or even include them in their bibliographies. Osorio's work has been highly praised by a number of reviewers in leading history journals, making its omission from bibliographies of books on indigenous Hawaiian society even more astounding, while Young's stunningly insightful work has not even been reviewed by the *Journal of Pacific History*. Their mentor, Lilikalā Kameʻeleihiwa, is recognised only marginally, and her emphasis on the nurturing element of chiefly rule is not mentioned.[46] The same modern texts that praise the insights of mid-19th-century Hawaiian sources into their fast eroding culture, amidst European inroads and general indifference to Hawaiian beliefs, commit the same oversight in their own time against the cultural successors of scholars such as the Kānaka Maoli historians David Malo and Samuel Kamakau. It is the contention of this work that, in so doing, these scholars also misrepresent the nature of chiefly power and basis of social cohesion in Hawaiian society.

Young's 1998 *Rethinking the Native Hawaiian Past* challenged scholars to rethink standard approaches to the study of Hawaiian history outlined above by demonstrating a different history that is based on concepts derived from the Hawaiian language and oral traditions. Through

---

45   Indigenous Hawaiian and Kānaka Maoli are used interchangeably in this book.
46   Lilikalā Kameʻeleihiwa, *Native Land and Foreign Desires* (Honolulu: Bernice P. Bishop Museum Press, 1992).

detailed and nuanced studies of incidents and cultural institutions that have been largely overlooked in most academic studies of Hawai'i, Young revealed how lower ranked retainers acted as the glue that kept the polity together as intermediaries and messengers between the rulers and the ruled. Young noted that approaches to traditional Hawai'i have tended to focus on the ali'i nui (high chiefs) as leaders of a stratified society, and on the decisions they made in the context of the arrival of the haole (foreigners). This over-emphasis on the power and influence of high chiefs inadvertently marginalised other crucial institutions and internal interactions that provided stability and cohesion. Young's focus is on the vital role and evolving history of his ancestors, the kaukau ali'i. The kaukau ali'i performed a variety of supporting roles for the high chiefs, such as childcare, redistributive service for the welfare of the community, as well as forming a key element of fighting contingents. Young argues convincingly that these roles provided Hawaiian society with coherence and resilience in changing circumstances. These tasks structured the flow of daily life and their detailing does much to undermine the idea of high chiefs as despots ruling by fear. Kaukau ali'i also had empowerment strategies to advance their own interests. By shifting the focus of historical study from the high chiefs to the chiefly servers, a new perspective emerges in which the rulers are more in touch with those they rule and the flow of information and requests is more two-way than top-down.

Publication of Osorio's *Dismembering Lāhui* followed soon after Young's work. Osorio examines the effects of introducing Western-style law codes on indigenous Hawaiians between the first constitution in 1840 and the so-called Bayonet Constitution in 1887, which marked the constitutional transfer of political power to resident Westerners. While focused on the period after the unification process of Kamehameha I, Osorio's work is highly relevant because it demonstrates the long process that centralisation requires and extends Young's focus on the key role of lesser ali'i in maintaining social coherence in a time of transition, in this case as lesser known legislators. Osorio makes good use of legislative records and native petitions to government to ascertain the outlook of those outside the elite at a time when the new legislative body brought commoner and chief together.

Another important body of scholarship on Eastern Polynesian societies, which emerged parallel to these streams in the 1980s, has also received less recognition globally but adds support to the image of a less dictatorial and despotic form of governance proposed by Young and Osorio. In this era, over a century of Aotearoa/New Zealand Māori protest at land alienation and breaches of faith by the Crown finally led to the formation of the Waitangi Tribunal to investigate injustices against Māori and to assist the Crown's attempts to address grievances. A great deal of research on indigenous histories and ways of viewing land, sea and social relations, which was conducted to make the case for compensation and restitution before the tribunal, combined with a renaissance in Māori assertions of cultural identity to produce a profound cultural and academic revolution. Across Eastern Polynesia, indigenous scholars and community leaders are emphasising that political power was always more consensus-based than most academics claim, and that the effective exercise of this community-based, consensual power required a strong basis of environmental guardianship.[47] This vision is in direct contrast to the majority of academic theories outlined above. This contemporary Polynesian construction of statecraft cannot be dismissed as a romanticised version of the past because of the detailed evidence that Young and Osorio use to support their claims and because this vision also finds support in state theory and observations from history, political science and sociology, as outlined above. This body of observation characterises the role and reality of government as creating balance and seeking broad consensus among competing interest groups rather than concentrating or even monopolising power in the hands of the state. We argue here that this vision is also a better fit with events and underlying processes that are said to have been at play in the Hawaiian unification process.

Guns, hearts and minds: Balancing coercion and consent in the pursuit of power

No scholar who claims that Kamehameha's victories were due to European weapons discusses their use in battle. Weapons are simply assumed to have conferred a decisive advantage on and off the battlefield. This inflates the

---

47   Tamatoa Bambridge (ed.), *The Rahui: Legal pluralism in Polynesian traditional management of resources and territories* (Canberra: ANU Press, 2016); M. Mulholland & V. Tawhai (eds), *Weeping Waters: The Treaty of Waitangi and Constitutional Change* (Wellington: Huia, 2010); Jacinta Ruru, 'The Right to Water as the Right to Identity: Legal Struggles of Indigenous peoples of Aotearoa New Zealand', in F. Sultana & A. Loftus (eds), *The Right to Water: Politics, Governance and Social Struggles* (Abingdon, UK: Earthscan, 2012), pp. 110–22; and Okusitino Māhina, 'The Poetics of Tongan Traditional History, Tala-ē-fonua: An Ecology-Centred Concept of Culture and History', *Journal of Pacific History*, vol. 38 (1), 1993, 109–21.

importance of weapons in warfare, and coercion in political consolidation. In so doing, this body of scholarship ignores and runs counter to the analysis of 40 years of scholarship on the impact of Western weaponry by Pacific historians, which has consistently concluded that Western firearms and cannon were not decisive in warfare and political consolidation.[48] Earle, for example, claims that:

> Warfare was a strategy that determined real political relationships in the Hawaiian Islands. Succession was won on the battlefield, and rival island paramount chiefs continually confronted each other in battles of conquest. Until the introduction of western weapons, these conquests were effective only up to the natural boundaries of the major islands and their immediately neighboring islands. Complete unification of the major islands through conquest failed, and the Hawaiian state emerged only when an effective new military technology was introduced. Until then, though bound together through marriage and intrigue, the islands remained divided into separate chiefdoms focused on the islands of Hawai'i, Maui, O'ahu and Kaua'i.[49]

Warfare is not considered to be as important as the sacred status of chiefs in the accumulation of power and influence in Hawai'i. However, as well as the above-noted absence of analysis of the use of coercion in political power, those advocating the role of chiefs' sacred status as a key to commanding obedience rarely examine the degree to which coercion, or the latent threat of coercion, secured the loyalty of the population within the sacred chiefs' territories. Earle, in noting that the same military power that allowed expansion also introduced internal instability, even suggests coercive power might have threatened chiefly power rather than reinforced it, as the ruler could not always rely on the loyalty of warriors serving under subordinate chiefs.[50]

Very little has been written about Hawaiian warfare during this time of transition or any other time. Indeed, few have even considered the extent to which leaders were able to use violence to command obedience in indigenous Hawaiian society from 1778 to 1819. Some articles have appeared on the role of firearms and beachcombers in Kamehameha's

---

48   Dorothy Shineberg, 'Guns and Men in Melanesia', *Journal of Pacific History*, vol. 6, 1971, 61–82; K.R. Howe, 'Firearms and Indigenous Warfare: A Case Study', *Journal of Pacific History*, vol. 9, 1974, 21–38; and Paul D'Arcy, 'Māori and Muskets from a Pan-Polynesian Perspective', *New Zealand Journal of History*, vol. 34 (1), April 2000, 117–32.
49   Earle (1997), p. 140.
50   Earle (1997), pp. 105–10.

victories. Most authors assume that firearms secured victory without investigating the nature of the fighting that took place in the 1790s. Ethnographers such as Peter Buck provide inventories of Hawaiian weaponry, while archaeologist and ethnographer Kenneth Emory's chapter on warfare in *Ancient Hawaiian Civilization* relies heavily on two 19th-century writers: Malo and the missionary William Ellis. Both of these sources describe warfare as a series of general principles. As a result, Emory's work does not distinguish between pre- and post-unification practices, nor does it portray warfare as a process that was modified according to circumstances. Historian Gavan Daws contrasts tactical procedures and rituals with the grim reality of battle in Kamehameha's time, but spends less than a page on this subject.[51] Earle's study emphasises the importance of coercion, but more as a destabilising force than as a factor assisting unification. Two non-academic studies touch upon this topic: Neil Dukas's *Military History of Sovereign Hawaii* and Richard Tregaskis's *The Warrior King*. Dukas's 2004 work is a brief, popular history dealing largely with the period after the one considered here, has few footnotes and a tendency towards an uncritical reading of sources. Dukas follows the format of the ethnographic sources consulted and presents Hawaiian warfare for much of the period prior to 1819 as a static set of rules and practices rather than an evolving process. Tregaskis's book is a work of historical fiction.[52] The largest study of warfare in Hawai'i is James Fitzsimmons's 1969 Masters' thesis from the University of Hawai'i at Mānoa, 'Warfare in Old Hawaii'. The study is particularly insightful on the post-unification era.[53]

This neglect of warfare and other forms of coercion as influences on political evolution is somewhat at odds with social science and historical practice elsewhere in the world. Distinguished anthropologist Robert Carneiro has consistently argued and documented how war existed before states and how war was a major, if not the major, influence on the development of first chiefdoms and then states and how, in turn, war was transformed by

---

51 Peter Buck, 'Warfare and Weapons', in *Arts and Crafts of Hawaii* (Honolulu: Bernice P. Bishop Museum, 1964), pp. 417–64; J. Feher, *Hawaii: A Pictorial History* (Honolulu: Bernice P. Bishop Museum, 1969), pp. 117–19; Kenneth P. Emory, 'Warfare', in E.S.C. Handy et al., *Ancient Hawaiian Civilization – A Series of Lectures Delivered at the Kamehameha Schools* (rev. edn), (Tokyo: Charles E. Tuttle Company, 1965); and Gavan Daws, *Shoal of Time: A History of the Hawaiian Islands* (Honolulu: University of Hawai'i Press, 1968a), p. 31.
52 Neil Dukas, *Military History of Sovereign Hawaii* (Honolulu: Mutual Publishing, 2004); and Richard Tregaskis, *The Warrior King: Hawaii's Kamehameha the Great* (London: Macmillan, 1973).
53 James Patrick Fitzsimmons, 'Warfare in Old Hawaii: The Transformation of a Poleomological System', MA Thesis, University of Hawai'i, 1969.

states.[54] Carneiro echoes anthropologists and archaeologists of Hawai'i in assigning a key role to political control of agricultural surpluses to supply and fund the organs of state, but places key emphasis on armies as well, not only as beneficiaries of agricultural output, but also as contributors by conquering more agricultural land to increase the output available to rulers. In this, he also finds common ground with Charles Tilly, the renowned scholar of Western and comparative state formation.[55] Tilly notes the variability of state formation processes and configurations, so that caution is needed in applying models from one context to another as is attempted in this book. The revised approach to state-building attempted here is, however, a better fit between observed outcomes and asserted processes. In essence, however, the three components are common and crucial to all processes of political development: coercion, or the ability to harm or disrupt persons, possessions or social relations; resources, or the material means to enforce political will; and commitment, or relations between social entities that promote their taking account of each other. In other configurations of power discussed below, this last category is usually associated with the term consent.[56]

In the last three decades, military history, political theory and European-orientated state-formation literature have recognised the need for a more wide-ranging vision of the role of violence in power relations. No leader can rule by coercive means alone. Power is now usually portrayed as multifaceted: involving military, economic, organisational and ideological dimensions. This literature has been synthesised into a paradigm-shifting theoretical framework for the study of coercion as a political tool that has, however, largely bypassed Pacific Studies. While Pacific specialists tend to analyse warfare as a cultural act whose form and function varies between cultures, contemporary Western military historians emphasise the importance of logistical, organisational and psychological factors.[57] Both groups' approaches call for a re-evaluation of the significance of European weaponry and mercenaries in the Hawaiian wars of unification.

---

54   Robert L. Carneiro, 'War and Peace: Alternating Realities in Human History', in S.P. Reyna & R.E. Downs (eds), *Studying War: Anthropological Perspectives* (Langhorne, Penn.: Gordon and Breach, 1994), p. 14.
55   Decades of Tilly's thinking are admirably and concisely summarised in his 'States, State Transformation, and War', in Jerry H. Bentley (ed.), *The Oxford Handbook of World History* (Oxford, University Press, 2011), esp. pp. 178–85. His ideas on the role and limits on coercion in state power are most thoroughly covered in his *Trust and Rule* (2005), and *Coercion, Capital, and European States AD 990–1992* (1992).
56   Tilly (2011), p. 180.
57   D'Arcy (2000).

On the one hand, warfare was a stage for the enhancement of personal status while, on the other, it carried more sanguine aims that were achieved through long-term attrition rather than by dramatic victories in the course of a day.

Until the 1970s, military history conventionally focused on fighting methods and weaponry. Battles were decisive turning points in human history. Warfare was analysed in terms of generalship, tactics and strategy. The latter two were discussed in terms of abstract principles of warfare that, if applied correctly, enhanced the chances of victory. Great generals controlled their men like so many chess pieces to outmanoeuvre their opponents and then deliver the decisive blow. The object of manoeuvring was to concentrate your strength at a decisive point where the enemy was weaker. Battles were described in discrete phases, rather than as a flow of confusing and overlapping incidents. Firepower and the shock of the charge were the principal ways of delivering the decisive blow. Advances in the striking power of hand-to-hand weapons or to the range, volume and accuracy of missile weapons provided a decisive advantage. This belief fuelled many arms races throughout history.[58]

Recent studies have challenged many of these conventions. Studies on military technology show that its performance in combat is usually well below that achieved in peacetime tests and training exercises. Calculations of peacetime military strength are usually quantitative, as size is more tangible than operational capability. The shrapnel shell favoured by many armies in World War I was found to be far less effective than believed when a shell accidentally exploded among a group of scientists after the war and all escaped unscathed.[59]

Strategic and tactical plans rarely go as smoothly as portrayed in conventional military texts and battle maps. War seldom goes according to plan. Rather, war is a risky enterprise with an unpredictable outcome. Nations can prepare for war, but they can never practice for the real thing. Men tend to blunder through the experience rather than control events. Order is usually created in memoirs, official records and history books produced only after the fact. Operating principles espoused in military

---

58 John Keegan, *The Face of Battle* (London: Penguin, 1976), pp. 25 ff.; and Michael Howard et al., 'What is Military History?', in Juliet Gardiner (ed.), *What is History Today?* (London: Macmillan, 1988), pp. 4–17.
59 James F. Dunnigan, *How to Make War: A Comprehensive Guide to Modern Warfare* (New York: William Morrow & Co., 1982), pp. 216, 231, 243–44.

texts distort this reality by relying on simplified accounts of extreme cases – the great triumphs and the great disasters of military history, such the campaigns of Julius Caesar or Napoleon's demise at Waterloo. The reality is often much less spectacular. For most of history, warfare has not been dramatically decisive, but a rather cautious, piecemeal and indecisive business with little overall grand strategy. The urge to play safe and think of defence has been just as prominent as the desire for dramatic victories and bold campaigns. Perceptions, however, often remain unchanged by experience. James Dunnigan believes history shows armies remember no more of the past than their oldest members. Peacetime armies are transformed into fighting organisations through a bloody process of trial and error, only to forget these lessons in the next lengthy period of peace.[60]

There has been, since 1970, a renaissance in studies on psychological factors in warfare. In his 1976 book *The Face of Battle*, John Keegan points out that the physical disintegration of an army in battle must be preceded by its moral disintegration. As such, the study of battle must be necessarily social and psychological. For Keegan, the study of battle is the study of group solidarity and its correlate, the disintegration of human groups. He focuses on the behaviour of men: 'men striving to reconcile their instinct for self-preservation, their sense of honour and the achievement of some aim over which other men are ready to kill them'.[61]

The uninitiated often view the onset of war with enthusiasm. Defeat, wounding or dying are seen as remote prospects. But, as battle approaches, enthusiasm tends to turn to apprehension. Armies use pre-battle ceremonies involving religious rites or military reviews as necessary symbolic thresholds at which men pause to mentally prepare themselves for the coming shock. Without these ceremonies, armies often fight with much less resolve, as is sometimes the case in unanticipated encounters. Once in battle, many find the stress of combat preferable to the anxious wait just prior to combat. The extreme danger and stress of battle increases energy and hones physical functions. Every act has a new feeling of significance not experienced in the daily activities of everyday life. The simple desire to survive is a powerful stimulant. Dunnigan notes that heroes are often simply men who become cornered and see no other option than to fight their way to safety. The first sight of a dead body in

---

60 Dunnigan (1982), pp. 216, 233; and Keegan (1987), pp. 6–7.
61 Keegan (1976), pp. 302–03.

battle is usually a great shock. Until then, death is a remote experience for young men. Experiencing the sight of death reminds combatants that they are potential victims as well as potential victors.[62]

A group of combatants can be likened to a crowd. Crowds have personalities that affect the actions of those within them. Crowds are easily panicked. Indeed, it is a difficult task just to keep men on the battlefield let alone inspire them to acts of bravery.[63] Physical coercion plays its part. Dereliction of duty usually carries severe penalties in most armies. Less obvious influences play a significant role. The 'warrior myth' is commonly used to distract attention from the brutal reality of a violent and often anonymous, meaningless death. The 'warrior myth' tells of battles won, heroic deeds of individual valour that confer lasting immortality and fame on their instigators. The generally poor treatment of veterans by modern societies has done little to overturn the myth. While, however, there are young men eager to prove their manhood, and veterans seeking to enhance their status and justify their sacrifices, the 'warrior myth' will continue to endure.[64]

Modern practice emphasises the importance of drill and discipline in the armed forces. In the physically and emotionally taxing environment of battle, drill and discipline are something to fall back on as automatic responses drummed into the consciousness by constant repetition. A group of drilled men tend to have a collective psychology that differs from and overrides individual identities and fears. But the most commonly cited influence behind keeping men in battle is small unit cohesiveness. Small groups that fight and live together tend to establish a strong sense of comradeship and loyalty. Group cohesion may be increased by symbols of membership, such as uniforms or regimental flags. The fear of being seen to shirk one's duty in front of comrades acts as a strong counter to the concern for personal survival. The fear of losing one's reputation as a man among close associates is often held more dearly than life itself.[65]

---

62 Keegan (1976), pp. 259–65, 281, 333–34; Dunnigan (1982), pp. 210, 236; Paul Fussel, *The Great War and Modern Memory* (Oxford University Press, 1975), p. 327; Ronald J. Glossop, *Confronting War: An Examination of Humanity's Most Pressing Problem* (North Carolina: McFarland, 1983), pp. 79–80.
63 Keegan (1976), pp. 174–75; and Gwynne Dyer, *War* (New York: Crown Publishers, 1985), p. 142.
64 Dyer (1985), pp. 13–15.
65 Dyer (1985), pp. 12–13; Dunnigan (1982), p. 211; Keegan (1976), pp. 51, 176; and John Keegan & Richard Holmes, *Soldiers. A History of Men in Battle* (New York: Viking, 1985), pp. 18, 42, 261.

While morale is a decisive factor, élan alone will not carry the day against equally motivated opponents with superior weapons. This lesson was learnt by Scottish Highlanders at Culloden and by countless indigenous societies in the late 19th century against European forces armed with modern, rapid-firing weapons. Similarly, morale and weaponry are of limited value if an army cannot be maintained and supplied in the field. The process of producing and supplying enough to feed and arm troops is a major undertaking. Ultimately, the art of winning battles is really no more than the art of the logistically possible. Throughout history logistical problems have been major constraints on warfare. If wars progress beyond the initial encounters, they generally settle down into struggles of attrition. Battles are relatively infrequent in war.

While archaeologists of Hawai'i have emphasised the importance of agricultural production for providing a surplus on which chiefs could draw for political consolidation, none have realised how crucial logistical supplies were to military victory in chiefly societies. Humans have been dispersed in agricultural communities for much of history. Urban centres and assembled armies represent unusual concentrations of humanity that pose logistical problems. This century's advances in food storage and transportation have helped considerably but, for most of history, warring armies have had to live off the land, or severely restrict their movements to localities with stored caches of supplies and adequate amounts of drinking water. Many armies were little more than temporarily assembled levies who were expected to feed themselves. This was especially true in economies that generated limited agricultural surpluses beyond subsistence needs. Such societies could not spare the manpower or food for prolonged campaigns, so that fighting had to be brief and organised around agricultural seasons.[66]

Some armies disintegrated, without ever coming into contact with their enemies, because of inadequate supplies and poor preventive measures to avoid the outbreak of disease. Until relatively recently, disease often accounted for more deaths and incapacitation than battle casualties in warfare. Public health practices are usually difficult to implement in the field and, for much of human history, such practices were at best primitive. The medical treatment of wounds has usually been inadequate.

---

66   Tilly (2011), pp. 184–85; Keegan & Holmes (1985), pp. 146–50, 225; and Robert S. Smith, *Warfare and Diplomacy in Pre-Colonial West Africa* (Norwich, Great Britain: Methuen, 1976), pp. 42–43.

In Europe, for example, there was very little provision for getting the wounded to hospitals and treating them until well into the 19th century. Treatment was a traumatic experience of amputations and removal of projectiles without anaesthetics. Sanitation was usually appalling. It was not until after 1850, when disinfectants began to be used consistently, that deaths from complications and infections of battle wounds regularly fell below deaths in battle. It was not until World War II that the chances of surviving a wound increased significantly with the use of antibiotics and blood transfusions.[67]

Other aspects of human activity, however, affect military capacity besides food production. Warfare is a manifestation of the societies that raise armies to pursue it, and the economies, technologies and worldviews that those societies sustain. Fighters must be motivated enough to risk their lives, while the rest of society must make sacrifices to ensure that the war effort is kept supplied. The waging of war will be heavily influenced by the organisation of society, and particularly its solidarity in supporting its leaders. Warfare needs to be examined in a wider context. No such breadth of vision has been attempted for Hawaiian society, despite the wealth of relevant information available.

***

Warfare is only one form of coercion, and coercion is only one means of exercising political control. Organised violence occurs within societies as well as between them. Violence need not be direct and physical. Sociologist Johan Galtung has coined the phrase 'structural violence' to describe inequalities and social restrictions on members of a society. To Galtung, the mere absence of war is only a negative peace. True positive peace involves both the absence of hostilities and injustices.[68] This distinction is important for any discussion of warfare. Control is about more than just coercive ability. Coercion alone will never secure lasting compliance. Indeed, as political theorist Hannah Arendt has argued, the resort to violence is a sign of a loss of true power, which ultimately rests on a society's willingness to be governed.[69] From this perspective, Hawaiian traditions on the virtues of chiefly benevolence towards followers can be viewed as

---

67 Dunnigan (1982), pp. 323–27; Keegan & Holmes (1985), pp. 145–49.
68 Johan Galtung, 'Twenty-five Years of Peace Research: Ten Challenges and Some Responses', *Journal of Peace Research*, vol. 22 (2), 1985, 145–46.
69 Hannah Arendt, *On Violence* (Orlando, Florida: Harvest Press, 1970), p. 56.

much as reflection of a fundamental reality of power as self-serving myth-making. It was a reality of power that Kamehameha embraced and his rivals ignored, to their ultimate demise.

Concepts of power vary. Power is generally portrayed as the ability to ensure one's desires are carried out even in the face of opposition, or as resting on the consent of a community. The latter is often referred to as legitimised power, or authority. The key distinction is between consent and coercion. Power can be seen to rest ultimately on coercive capacity, with the exercise of authority also resting on the threat of sanctions as the price of disobedience. Alternatively, authority can be seen as not only an aspect of power, but as the basis of power. According to this scenario, resort to physical violence is a sign of the erosion of power. The supreme exercise of power is to avert conflict and grievances by influencing, shaping and determining the perceptions of others. Although it is generally conceded that a balance between sanctions and benefits is needed to secure enduring compliance, most writers tend to emphasise the ultimate primacy of one of these two aspects of power.[70] In reality, however, power involves a judicious balance between coercion and consent. Retaining power involves knowing just how far coercion can be exercised without risking a counterproductive backlash. An early concession may alleviate the need for excessive violence later on in the face of mounting opposition. To French anthropologist Maurice Godelier, violence and consent are inseparable. The violence of the dominant is only useful if it secures the consent of the dominated. Obedience becomes preferable to sanctions.[71]

Anthropologist Peter Wilson noted that the exercise of power does not necessarily require physical actions:

> Power as production of an intended effect, when given the meaning 'to make an impression', can be extended to the successful fulfillment of deception, to the successful creation of an illusion, and, most important of all, to the conviction that one sort of effect (the impression) may be taken to be a reliable confirmation of another sort of effect. In short, by producing something that makes a great impression it is possible to confirm the possibility of the capacity to produce other, more material

---

[70] Stephen Lukes, 'Power and Authority', in R. Nisbett & T. Baltimore (eds), *A History of Sociological Analysis* (New York: Basic Books, 1978), pp. 633, 637; Keegan (1987), p. 315; Johan Galtung, *The European Community: A Superpower in the Making* (London: George Allen and Unwin, 1973), p. 35; and Arendt (1970), pp. 43 ff.

[71] Maurice Godelier, 'Infrastructures, Societies, and History', *Current Anthropology*, vol. 19 (4), 1978, 767; Keegan (1987), p. 315; and Galtung (1973), p. 35.

effects without actually having to do so ... In this way, for example, a candidate, by making an impression, establishes a claim to power without ever demonstrating the power to lead.[72]

There are good reasons for those in power to exercise restraint. Actual capacity can only be determined when it is unleashed. Such an occurrence is wrought with unknowns. Victory, or catastrophe may result. Powerful backlashes may be generated. Restraint from using power may enhance one's power because perceptions of potential power are often much greater than the reality. As noted above, it can be argued that resort to physical coercion is a sign of the loss of power as its potential consequences have failed to deter possible opponents.

Adherence to prescribed behaviour occurs for a variety of reasons. One may conform out of fear of sanctions for not doing so. Conformity may arise through belief that the behaviour demanded is either justified, necessary, or will serve one's own interests. Consent may also be founded on the belief that alternative courses will not return the same benefits. Conformity may simply occur through force of habit, with those concerned never encountering alternative conceptions that challenge prevailing norms. The behaviour of any individual may involve the interaction of all or some of these forms of consent – fear, acquiescence, attachment, indifference and habit.[73]

Four spheres of human activity are generally cited as avenues for the pursuit of power. These are: economic activity, the use of coercion, organisational institutions for governing society, and the definition of norms and values.[74] Economic activity involves human activities and social relations for the production and distribution of goods and services. The elements of production are human labour, natural materials, and technological means for converting materials into useful resources. Economic power involves securing subsistence needs through the social organisation of the extraction, transformation, distribution and consumption of objects of nature. Most Marxists emphasise the importance of controlling modes of production, especially human labour. Others, such as Karl Polanyi,

---

[72] Peter J. Wilson, *The Domestication of the Human Species* (particularly chpt 5, 'The Surrealities of Power', pp. 117–50) (New Haven: Yale University Press, 1988), p. 118.
[73] Lukes (1978), pp. 643 ff.; and Joseph V. Femia, *Gramsci's Political Thought Hegemony, Consciousness, and the Revolutionary Process* (Oxford: Clarendon Press, 1981), pp. 37–40, 45.
[74] Mann (1986), pp. 20–49.

stress the importance of controlling the distribution of resources through trade and exchange networks. Earle sees the ultimate value of economic control as the ability to buy compliance through rewards or deprivations.[75]

Coercive power derives from control of the tools of coercion: weapons and obedient manpower. Coercive capacity is a relative measure. What matters is the gap between potential opponents' strength. The military and economic spheres are related not merely through payments to secure obedience and the logistical requirements of an army but also in terms of social organisation. Hunter–gatherer societies use weapons of the hunt against human rivals. The use of cavalry in feudal Europe required the decentralisation of power, as cavalry were expensive to maintain and the main form of wealth was land rather than a concentrated source, such as commerce. Earle notes that, in such decentralised systems, military strength is problematic as warriors, who are the basis of chiefly power, are also potential usurpers.[76]

While Marxist theory tends to dismiss government institutions as merely tools of a ruling class united by economic interests, some sociologists make a strong case for viewing government as a distinct power base. Class interests do not necessarily correlate with those of government administrative bodies. Once the functions of government are institutionalised, the foundations for new power networks are established. Loyalty to the state, or even bodies within government's administrative apparatus, replaces other loyalties based on economic interests or blood relations.[77] Governments in modern states tend to monopolise coercive force. The norms of society are codified into laws administered through a judiciary, and backed up by the threat of the use of governmental coercive apparatus for noncompliance. At the same time government is dependent on taxes and levies to support its administrative apparatus. Government is usually portrayed as a mutually beneficial contract between citizens and the state in which the citizen surrenders certain aspects of personal freedom in return for enhanced security.[78]

A number of commentators claim the crucial means of control is in determining the norms and values of society. R.C. MacIver asserts:

---

75   Earle (1997), p. 6; Mann (1986), p. 24; Segraves (1982), p. 297.
76   Earle (1997), p. 8, Mann (1986), pp. 25–26, 48–49; and Michael Howard, *War in European History* (Oxford University Press, 1976), pp. 1–3.
77   Mann (1986), pp. 10–11; Skocpol (1979), pp. 25–30.
78   Alland (1980), pp. 447–51.

> Every society is held together by a myth-system, a complex of dominating thought-forms that determines and sustains all its activities. All social relations, the very texture of human society are myth-born and myth-sustained.[79]

If one concept of reality is dominant, all modes of thought and behaviour will be infused with its spirit. It is this situation that Italian political theorist Antonio Gramsci refers to as hegemony. If desirable concepts are associated with existing institutions, and external influences restricted, then it will be difficult for alternative images of society to emerge. Groups, while discontented with their lot, are nevertheless unable to locate the source of their discontent because of restricted insight into the alternatives.[80]

Although norms and values can be manipulated to legitimise or hide the realities of power, there are limits. Ideologies are unlikely to attain a hold over people if they merely serve to justify inequality and domination. They must be at least plausible to be generally adhered to without the threat of sanction to back them up. Ideologies are able to legitimise power when they are able to capture and articulate peoples' experiences and desires.[81] Attitudes and beliefs are influenced by their application in practice. The basis of authority can change through time. The resilience of any normative structure in the wake of change will depend on its flexibility and ability to mould perceptions of new elements into existing worldviews through control of information dissemination.

It is important to distinguish between the four avenues of power and the enactment of power. The four modes of power are merely the realms within which the play for power is enacted. Networks of individuals attempting to utilise the four avenues to further their own interests create power. The success or failure of any network depends on its organisation of its resources to achieve its goals. Utilisation rather than possession is the key element. As MacIver points out,

---

79 MacIver (1965), p. 4.
80 Femia (1981), pp. 24, 43–44, 120.
81 Mann (1986), p. 23; MacIver (1965), pp. 56–58; and John Kenneth Galbraith, *The Anatomy of Power* (London: Corgi, 1985), pp. 39–40, 43.

> To say that in the struggle of groups the most powerful wins is to say nothing, for the power of a group is no simple function of the force it disposes; it depends no less on its solidarity, its organizing ability, its leadership, the resources and its resourcefulness, its tenacity of purpose, and other things.[82]

The four modes of power offer alternative or combinable organisational means of social control. Domination is as much a matter of relative organisational coherence as it is a trade-off between coercion and consent.

The interaction between the modes of power and their enactment in combination is perhaps most clearly articulated by Canadian economist and diplomat J.K. Galbraith in his *The Anatomy of Power*, which traces the evolution of power in the European world. He distinguishes underlying sources of power from avenues of power. Galbraith lists the sources of power as personality, organisation and property. These equate to the four spheres just discussed in that, in Galbraith's scheme, economic activity and use of coercion are combined as property. By personality, Galbraith means traits such as physique, confidence, persuasiveness and intellect that allow individuals to rise above their fellow men and secure compliance. Such qualities are usually associated with leadership. Any organisation involves the coming together of those of similar interests, values or perception. The pursuit of power requires the submission of a sufficiently large body of adherents to the purpose of the organisation; internal coherence is a key factor. Property refers to material objects whose desirability makes them useful commodities for purchasing compliance. To a lesser extent, property may enforce compliance if it is in the form of coercive instruments wielded by a coherent group.[83]

The key to power lies in the effective combination of the sources of power. To Galbraith, organisation is the ultimate source of power. Personality and property have effect only with the support of organisation. Personality alone may allow an individual access to power, but the individual needs the support of an organisation to maintain that power. Whether personality secures property or a following of adherents, no individual can maintain this hold without support. Galbraith points out that many leaders rule not so much because of their ability to ensure compliance but because they head an organisation whose coherence

---

82 MacIver (1965), p. 12; and Mann (1986), pp. 6–7, 518, 523.
83 Galbraith (1985), pp. 23–25.

of belief is already in place. On the other hand, strong leaders can ensure an organisation maintains its direction and coherence. Property only becomes an avenue for power when organisations control and utilise property for their own ends.[84]

Galbraith distinguishes the three ways that the sources of power may be utilised as: condign power, compensatory power and conditional power. Condign power secures compliance through the imposition of unpleasant and painful alternatives for noncompliance with the group's wishes. Compensatory power ensures adherence to the group's objectives by rewarding compliant individuals. In each case, individuals are aware that they are submitting. In contrast, conditioned power works to ensure that submission is not recognised. By influencing beliefs, the course of action desired is made to seem natural and appropriate.[85] The power of an organisation depends on its association with other sources of power, and its control over all modes of power. An organisation is strong when it has access to all modes of power, and weak when access is missing. Galbraith detects the gradual emergence of organisation to replace property and personality as the dominant source of power.[86]

Western influence versus indigenous continuity in Hawai'i's unification

The inability of any of the theories in the previous section to adequately explain why the conquest and unification of the Hawaiian Islands by Kamehameha I occurred specifically between 1782 and 1812, during a time of increasing European contact, has prompted the attribution of his success to European weapons and ideas. Scholars are divided on the degree to which European influences facilitated political unification. Anthropologist Irving Goldman believes Europeans merely precipitated a process of unification that would have occurred without their presence.[87] Historian Gavan Daws is more circumspect when he states that:

---

84 Galbraith (1985), pp. 55–56, 65.
85 Galbraith (1985), pp. 4–6.
86 Galbraith (1985), pp. 89 ff., esp. 131–32.
87 Goldman (1970), p. 200.

Whether, undisturbed by contact with the West, Hawaiian society would ever have crossed the line from tribalism to some sort of unified primitive state, is problematical. Certainly the chances for new experiments in power politics provided by the appearance of white men with advanced military technology transformed Hawaiian traditional society in the space of one or two generations.[88]

Most academics conclude that European contact had a significant influence on unification. They generally echo Daws in assigning particular importance to European weapons to explain how Kamehameha was able to unify the archipelago.[89]

So far, scholars have been unable to explain the unification of the Hawaiian Islands from the late 1780s onwards solely by pre-existing factors in Hawaiian society on the eve of sustained European contact. Hawai'i is a prominent focus of one of the strengths of Pacific Studies – the dynamics of culture contact and interactions between Europeans and Pacific Islanders. Pacific Studies has led the way in examining the cultural logic behind the exchange of items and ideas between Europeans and Islanders. Island beaches are portrayed as transformative spaces and processes where objects, ideas and individuals move between cultures, mediated by power relations and acculturation.[90]

The decade of the 1980s, which saw the reorientation of Pacific anthropology towards greater focus on the interaction between cultural structures and historical processes, was a time when historians were coming out of two decades of adjusting their focus from history as primarily a sequence of events to one more focused on the social, economic and ideological structures underlying actions. Works like E.P. Thomson's *The Making of the English Working Class* highlighted the history of this usually neglected group in historical narratives.[91] The working of underlying structures into the narrative of events is no easy task. What has tended to emerge from attempts to marry structure and event was what anthropologist Nicholas

---

88 O.A. Bushnell (ed.), *The Illustrated Atlas of Hawaii*, text by Gavan Daws (10th edn) (Honolulu: Island Heritage, 1987), p. 14.
89 For example, H.E. Maude, 'Beachcombers and Castaways', in H.E. Maude, *Of Islands and Men: Studies in Pacific History* (Melbourne: Oxford University Press, 1968), pp. 156–57; and M. Kelly (ed.), *Hawaii in 1819: A Narrative Account by Louis Claude de Saules de Freycinet* (Honolulu: Bernice P. Bishop Museum Press, 1978), p. 103 n. 24.
90 A good example of this approach is Greg Dening's *Islands and Beaches: Discourse on a Silent Land, Marquesas 1774–1880* (Honolulu: University of Hawai'i Press, 1980), pp. 3, 157–61, esp. 159.
91 E.P. Thompson, *The Making of the English Working Class* (London: V. Gollancz, 1980).

Thomas calls 'systemic history' – analysis that is more structure than process.[92] The idea persists that culture changes round the edges as a result of cultural interaction and changed circumstances, but the core remains intact, changing very gradually if at all. Interestingly, Pacific historian J.W. Davidson reached similar conclusions a decade before, despite coming from an intellectual tradition that emphasises historical processes over cultural beliefs.[93]

According to this systemic history school of thought, Pacific Islander political and social philosophy centred on the idea of melding local and exotic elements. Daws, for example, notes that power in Hawai'i was 'always violent, always usurping, came from the outside, and belonged to strangers. But authority was always legitimate, always came from within, belonged to those born with it, belonged to natives'.[94] Sahlins notes similarities between Polynesian ideas of political sovereignty and those noted in the ancient Indo-European civilisations by the classical scholar Georges Dumézil. Polynesian rulers are conceived of as hostile strangers who are gradually absorbed and domesticated by indigenous locals, this process being symbolised by their induction into the local pantheon of gods. All strangers are conceived in this way and expected to act as their predecessors did. To Sahlins, history re-enacts the myth. In more general terms, Polynesian philosophy conceives society of being made up of a combination of opposed, yet complementary qualities. He emphasises that these dichotomies are fluid and contextual. At the moment of intrusion, for example, the immigrant is male, aggressive and from the sea, while the locals are female, receptive, fertile and of the land. Hawaiians referred to their chiefs as sharks that walked on land – wild elements that needed controlling. History taught that strangers came to overthrow rulers. They then married the highest born local women to gain legitimacy, as they rarely had sufficient numbers to sustain their position

---

92 Nicholas Thomas, *Out of Time: History and Evolution in Anthropological Discourse* (2nd edn) (Ann Arbor: The University of Michigan, 1996), p. 96.
93 J.W. Davidson, 'Lauaki Namalau'ulu Mamoe: A Traditionalist in Samoan Politics', in J.W. Davidson & Deryck Scarr (eds), *Pacific Island Portraits* (Canberra: Australian National University Press, 1970), p. 267.
94 Gavan Daws, 'The Death of Captain Cook', *Pacific Islands Monthly*, April 1984, 15–17, and May 1984, 51–53, 16.

without local cooperation.[95] More recently, Sahlins refined his structure of the conjuncture concept to give more influence to individuals and localities relative to general structures and word systems.[96]

Europeans may also have seemed usurping strangers arriving to challenge local rulers, as had been the pattern since the dawn of time.[97] Most scholars suggest that encounters with Europeans were radically different to previous encounters.[98] Prior to their arrival, most outsiders had broadly similar appearance and ways of behaving, regardless of whether they were drift voyagers or visiting kin. Even hostile invaders usually came from a world known to the communities they attacked. Other Islanders might not speak the same language, but they generally acted in ways that made sense to those encountering them.

Not all scholars subscribe to this perspective. Historian Ian Campbell points out that Pacific history has vacillated between explanations of culture contact that emphasise differences in cultural understanding, and those that opt for explanations based on desires to advance one's interests in terms of power, material possessions and physical comforts. Campbell takes issue with the idea that most conflicts occurred in contact situations because Islanders did not share the European belief about private property. Europeans often took offence when Islanders took goods without asking permission. Literary scholar the late Bill Pearson's idea that Islanders believed they had the right as hosts to take visitors' goods is based on one reference to the reception of Kau Moala in Futuna. It is not clear that this was the practice elsewhere. Campbell demonstrates that there was a clear distinction between open attempts to take goods off Western vessels, and attempts to conceal them. He demonstrates that Polynesians had the concept of property rights and punished theft severely.[99]

---

95 Marshall Sahlins, 'The Discovery of the True Savage', in Donna Marwick (ed.), *Dangerous Liaisons: Essays in Honour of Greg Dening* (History Department, University of Melbourne, 1994), pp. 63–65, 69.
96 Marshall Sahlins, 'Structural Work: How Microhistories Become Macrohistories and Vice Versa', *Anthropological Theory*, vol. 5 (1), 2005, 5–30.
97 Greg Dening, *Performances* (Melbourne University Press, 1996), pp. 64–65; Daws (1984), p. 16; and Marshall Sahlins, *Historical Metaphors and Mythical Realities: Structure in the Early History of the Sandwich Islands Kingdom* (Ann Arbor: University of Michigan Press, 1981), pp. 129 ff.
98 For example, see Mālama Meleisea & Penelope Schoeffel, 'Discovering Outsiders', in Donald Denoon (ed.), *The Cambridge History of the Pacific Islanders* (Cambridge University Press, 1997), pp. 120–21.
99 I.C. Campbell, 'European–Polynesian Encounters: A Critique of the Pearson Thesis', *Journal of Pacific History*, vol. 29 (2), 1994, 223–25, 229.

Campbell suggests that these situations reveal not a clash of two cultures, but the moderation of cultural practices to suit what both sides realised was an unusual situation. The result was a culture of contact, where unusual patterns of behaviour occurred in response to the presence of the unfamiliar and uncertain. Polynesians would initially apply rituals and practices normally used to greet strangers, but they might also practice unusual behaviour, such as giving their women for material gain and to placate the foreigners. Similarly, Europeans sometimes overlooked theft in the name of maintaining peace.[100] Campbell also suggests that references to Europeans as *papalangi, papaa, etua* was not a mark of respect associating them with the gods, but a temporary label denoting anything unfamiliar and yet to be understood.[101] The equivalent contemporary term would be UFO. Gunson notes that *papaa* was simply the word for foreigner in Eastern Polynesia, while some early European sources translated *papalangi* as the word for the land of strangers, and others defined it as cloth from the sky (European manufactures).[102]

Europeans had an uneven impact in the pre-colonial Pacific. The size of their presence varied enormously. Māori were the only group in the Pacific Islands to become a minority in their own land before 1870. Elsewhere, Western settlement was limited to a few thousand people concentrated around one or two port towns, or a handful of beachcombers. In many locations, contacts were limited to visits from naval and trading vessels manned by crews of five to a few hundred men.[103] Few were able to impose their will without naval support. Even then, naval expeditions soon had to move on. Most local economies were able to meet the demand for provisions from visiting vessels, providing they did not outstay their welcome.[104] Most localities hosted larger groups than these in the course of their normal social relations. The desire for Western goods did, however, cause some communities to alter production. This was perhaps

---

100 Campbell (1994), pp. 230–31.
101 I.C. Campbell, 'Polynesian Perceptions of Europeans in the Eighteenth and Nineteenth Centuries', *Pacific Studies*, vol. 5 (2), 1982, 65–69, esp. 67–69.
102 Niel Gunson, 'The Coming of Foreigners', in Noel Rutherford (ed.), *Friendly Islands: A History of Tonga* (Melbourne: Oxford University Press, 1977), pp. 93, 259–60 n. 34.
103 On ships' complements see W. Kaye Lamb (ed.), *The Voyages of George Vancouver 1791–1795*, vol. 3 (London: The Hakluyt Society, 1984), p. 819. Crew numbers on British naval vessels ranged from 70 to 115 men.
104 See, for example, Ross H. Cordy, 'The Effects of European Contact on Hawaiian Agricultural Systems – 1778–1819', *Ethnohistory*, vol. 19 (4), 1972, 400–03.

most notable around ports like Honolulu, where food was grown to cater to the Western palates of crews from whaling fleets and trading vessels, and Māori growing flax to trade for muskets.[105]

Introduced diseases were the element of Western contact that Island communities were least able to counteract. The fatal impact thesis is most often associated with the trauma caused by introduced diseases. Fatal impact was brought into question in the 1960s and 1970s as many estimates of death rates were lowered, and significant variation in the demographic history of individual islands and communities was recognised.[106] The idea of Western contact as fatal has experienced a resurgence in the last two decades with the advent of environmental histories that include disease among the exotic invaders.[107] These decades have also seen the rise of a body of literature that seeks to re-examine the impact of European colonialism from the perspective of indigenous people. These works often include significant upward revisions of populations at contact. Such revisions require far greater death rates to reach the population figures recorded later in the 19th century. This perspective has been most forcefully articulated in the work of David Stannard, professor of American Studies at the University of Hawai'i, on the demographic collapse of the Hawaiian population.[108]

Medical historian Donald Denoon presents a comprehensive overview on the heated debate over the causes and extent of Pacific Islander depopulation as a result of Western diseases. This issue rose to prominence in 1989 when Stannard published a book arguing that the indigenous Hawaiian population at European contact was at least double former estimates, so that post-contact depopulation until the first accurate census was truly catastrophic. While debate raged within the world of Pacific scholarship about Stannard's method for calculating contact populations

---

105 See, on Hawai'i, Cordy (1972), pp. 402, 407, 411–12; and Samuel M. Kamakau, *Ruling Chiefs of Hawaii* (Honolulu: Kamehameha Schools Press, 1961), p. 190. On Aotearoa, see James Belich, *Making Peoples: A History of the New Zealanders from Polynesian Settlement to the End of the Nineteenth Century* (Auckland: Penguin, 1996), p. 152.
106 See, in particular, Norma McArthur, *Island Populations of the Pacific* (Canberra: Australian National University Press, 1967). My overview of the historiography of disease in the Pacific Islands is based on Victoria Luker, 'Mothers of the Taukei: Fijian Women and "the Decrease of Race"', PhD Thesis, The Australian National University, 1997, pp. 5–13.
107 Most notably, Alfred W. Crosby, *Ecological Imperialism: The Biological Expansion of Europe, 900–1900* (Cambridge University Press, 1986).
108 See, particularly, David Stannard, *Before the Horror: The Population of Hawai'i on the Eve of Western Contact* (Honolulu: Social Science Research Institute, University of Hawai'i, 1989).

and whether depopulation primarily resulted from epidemics or disease-induced infertility,[109] epidemiologist Stephen Kunitz developed a more wide-ranging analysis which opened up the debate. Kunitz argued that the key factors affecting the rate of depopulation were not so much biological as social, economic and political. While epidemics could cause high death rates among populations with no exposure and immunity to them, the key was post-epidemic recovery which required social stability. Kunitz demonstrated that the areas with the most severe depopulation on record were areas where European colonisation and dispossession disrupted indigenous societies. As Denoon notes, 'Depopulation was for Stannard a cause, for Kunitz an effect, of dispossession'.[110] Denoon also makes the important point that specific localised circumstances, such as local diet and the presence of malaria, led to variation in depopulation.

Conclusion: Towards a framework for examining political consolidation

The wealth of material available on the unification period allows Hawaiian warfare to be examined along the lines advocated above. Ideally, the study of warfare should consider logistical and motivational factors as well as tactics and technology. Warfare is only one aspect of coercion, and coercion is only one aspect of power. Power is exercised by means of sanctions, rewards or the conditioning of social attitudes. Four aspects of human activity exist as possible avenues for power: the production and distribution of goods and services, the administration of society, coercive mechanisms, and the definition of norms and values. For power to be enduring it must also secure a degree of consent from a significant proportion of the population.

Theories on the centralisation process emphasise the institutionalisation and secularisation of the basis of power, and the importance of the breakdown of localised, usually kin-based, loyalties. During this process,

---

109 See, for example, Andrew F. Bushnell, '"The Horror" Reconsidered: An Evaluation of the Historical Evidence for Population Decline in Hawai'i, 1778–1803', *Pacific Studies*, 16 (3), 1993, 115–61.
110 Stephen J. Kunitz, *Disease and Social Diversity: The European Impact on the Health of Non-Europeans* (Oxford University Press, 1994); and Donald Denoon, 'Pacific Island Depopulation: Natural or Un-natural History?', in Linda Bryder & Derek A. Dow (eds), *New Countries and Old Medicine* (Auckland: Pyramid Press, 1994), p. 325.

tools of coercion become increasingly concentrated in the hands of the central governing body. Centralised, coercive power is still limited, so that there is a need to establish a workable balance of power between powerful groups within the polity. Centralisation is by no means inevitable. This study proposes that Kamehameha's successful centralisation of the islands was as much a victory of the arts of peacemaking as the arts of war. It is argued that those who insist that European firearms gave him the decisive military advantage needed to secure unification overestimate the capabilities of firearms and the degree to which victory in battle translates into lasting power in human history.

To fully accommodate these multiple considerations, this study seeks to combine long-term ecological perspectives alongside cultural attitudes and institutions, and the process of day-to-day living and making decisions over choices that can fundamentally change the trajectory societies and individuals take. Kirch and Sahlins' post-contact study of Anahulu on Oʻahu represents the high point of the structural history (as defined by Thomas) of Hawaiʻi, in its blend of emphasis on the influence of long-term environmental influences and cultural institutions on Hawaiian responses to the era of increasing exposure to European influences.[111] Sahlins is more comfortable in knitting structural history with specific events and actors than Kirch, but still favours structures incorporating new elements than transforming them.[112] In *How Chiefs Became Kings*, Kirch is almost defensive when he states that he has not pointed to a time when chiefdoms can be said to be archaic states in Hawaiʻi, as this was a process rather than an event.[113] He goes on to assert that social scientists, such as archaeologists, are superior to historians and other humanities scholars because they seek underlying reasons for actions, while 'To historians or humanists content with a strictly narrative mode of analysis, this may be the end of the road'.[114] Ironically, the historian he cites most in the book, Fernand Braudel, was a leading advocate of the long durée as the ultimate causation behind events, and he changed the face of history decades ahead of the social scientists who Kirch cites as his influences.

---

111 P.V. Kirch & Marshall Sahlins, *Anahulu: The Anthropology of History in the Kingdom of Hawaii*, vol. 1: *Historical Ethnography* (The University of Chicago Press, 1992).
112 Sahlins (1981).
113 Kirch (2010), p. 178.
114 Kirch (2010), p. 176.

The analytical framework designed by Braudel can accommodate the range of influences needed for the broad approach to warfare, coercion and political centralisation outlined above. Braudel examined historical processes by means of a three-tier temporal scheme. His three temporal levels were geographical time, social time and individual time. Geographical time consists of permanent, or slowly changing, elements of the natural environment. These consist of certain features of the natural environment such as mountain ranges and climate. Social time incorporates aspects of human activities that endure beyond any single individual's lifetime. Social institutions, economic and demographic trends all fall into this category. Finally there is the timescale of individual lifetimes and specific events. Influences from all three groupings interact continuously. A combination of the physical environment, society's technological capacity, social and political organisation, and beliefs determine the parameters of historical action. Within these longer term structures, a number of futures are possible. Any single event will be the result of inherited structural restraints and specific actions.[115]

This work argues against the conventional historiography that indigenous influences were at least as important as introduced European elements. It also adopts a specifically historical approach in arguing that specific events and individuals were as important as structural features in shaping the Hawaiian Kingdom. A number of futures are possible within any combination of longer term structural parameters. Structures determine what can happen, but events determine what actually happens. History is rich with examples of critical junctures, the 'what ifs' of history. How would Europe have developed if the young Napoleon Bonaparte had not been turned down for a place on the ill-fated La Perouse expedition to the South Pacific?[116] For this reason, detailed narratives are produced alongside more general discussions of the nature of Hawaiian society. Because of the controversy over the degree of European influence on Hawaiian state-building, specific, datable references have been used as much as possible. Local cultural, economic and political variation within the Hawaiian archipelago is also examined. In this way, the specifics of time and place are not subsumed under more widely applicable structural features described in the next three chapters.

---

115 Fernand Braudel, *On History*, Sarah Mathews (trans.) (University of Chicago Press, 1980), pp. 4, 26; and Ian Hodder, 'The Contribution of the Long Term', in Ian Hodder (ed.), *Archaeology as Long-term History* (Cambridge University Press, 1987), pp. 1–8.
116 Daws (1968a), p. 28.

The organisation of this work reflects the interaction between structure and process that is at the heart of the historical process. The next chapter examines the environmental and agricultural foundations and structures of power that emerged in various localities across Hawai'i from first settlement to the late 1700s. Chapters 3 and 4 examine the transformation of political and military structures of power between 1778 and 1796. Chapter 5 details the course of events in conflicts between chiefs from 1778 to 1796, when broadly similar structures of power were used differently, resulting in varying fortunes for chiefly rivals. Chapter 6 carries on this detailed interaction between broad structures and specific events and decisions to examine how military victory was converted into enduring control of all inhabited islands of the Hawaiian archipelago under one ruler for the first time in Kānaka Maoli history. An attempt is made to attribute change to Hawaiian or European actions and ideas respectively in Chapter 7. The search for Hawaiian precedents prior to the unification process in the four decades centred on Kamehameha's last major military victory in 1795 is an important part of this study. Only once indigenous precedents have been identified can attempts be made to evaluate the degree to which European agency influenced the formation of the Hawaiian Kingdom. We conclude by placing the Hawaiian achievement in wider Pacific and global contexts.

2
Gathering Momentum: Power in Hawai'i to 1770

The structure of Hawaiian polities worked against the concentration of power in the hands of one ruler. Yet, in the late-18th century, it took Kamehameha – a young ali'i from Hawai'i – less than 20 years to unify the archipelago, with the exception of Kaua'i and Ni'ihau, under his rule. The timing of this achievement has led a number of scholars to attribute his success to European ideas and European military hardware. Such a viewpoint ignores the significant changes that had taken place in Hawai'i during the 200 years preceding the birth of Kamehameha. By the late 18th century Hawaiian mō'ī were pushing the limits of sacred power as they strove to enhance their control over subjects and rivals. The history of Hawai'i between 1778 and 1796 represents a continuation of historical patterns of political struggle that were only partly modified by European influences before unification.

Hawaiian society has, thus far, been studied in a fragmented, discipline-specific way that has produced divergent and partially correct interpretations. When these perspectives are viewed in combination with greater emphasis placed on indigenous traditions, it becomes apparent that Hawai'i was becoming more politically sophisticated in the centuries leading up to unification, and that mounting competitive pressures between polities resulted in political and military transformations that were already well under way by the time of the arrival of Captain James Cook in the late 1770s. The drama of culture contact, the death of Cook at the hands of Hawaiians in 1779, and the wealth of European eyewitness accounts have meant that these profound internal transformations have largely been ignored by scholars in favour of the drama of culture contact and adjustment. Archaeological remains and a variety of indigenous traditions provide evidence of the development of sophisticated logistical capacity and arts of government well before Cook's sails pierced Hawai'i's horizons. These institutions and practices had sufficient momentum and logic of their own to explain Kamehameha's successful unification of the archipelago. The unification of the Hawaiian Islands owes more to this indigenous political legacy and a specific set of local circumstances than to the new influences brought by strangers from across the sea.

Sacred genealogies and patterns on the land: Indigenous and archaeological models of political evolution to 1770

Archaeological evidence suggests that humans first settled in the Hawaiian Islands at least 1,000 years ago, and probably came from the Marquesas Islands. Artefacts and words from linguistic reconstructions of the Proto-Polynesian language suggest that these early colonists were skilled mariners, who cultivated tropical root crops and harvested marine resources. It seems likely that they introduced domestic pigs, dogs, and chickens to the chain. They were probably organised into kin groups led by chiefs. The presence of the term toa (warrior) in early language reconstructions implies that, even at this early date, warfare was a fact of life.[1]

Patrick Kirch defines the initial colonisation period in Hawai'i as 1000–1200 AD. During this era, small groups established permanent coastal settlements in windward sites with fertile soil and access to permanent streams and marine resources. Bone remains from early sites show evidence of fishing, shellfish collection, bird hunting and animal husbandry. There are also indications of agriculture, including the introduction of

---

1 Kirch (2012), pp. 120–26; Kirch (2010), pp. 17–24; P.V. Kirch, *Feathered Gods and Fishhooks: An Introduction to Hawaiian Archaeology and Prehistory* (Honolulu: University of Hawai'i Press, 1985), pp. 67–88; and Yosihiko H. Sinoto, 'The Marquesas', pp. 110–34; H.D. Tuggle, 'Hawaii', pp. 167–99 and Ross Clark, 'Language', pp. 266–68, in Jesse D. Jennings (ed.), *The Prehistory of Polynesia* (Canberra: Australian National University Press, 1979).

coconut trees. Kirch considers this period as one of consolidation rather than population expansion. Rank differentiation between chiefs and commoners was probably not great, while bonds of kinship continued to be the main social cement.[2]

The Early Expansion Period of Kirch's scheme encompasses the next two centuries from 1200–1400 AD. By the close of this period, small settlements were dispersed throughout ecologically favourable areas of all major islands. These early sites became the core areas of what would later become territorially defined political units; and were often separated by mountain ranges and relatively unproductive lands. The elaboration and specialisation of fishing gear in this period suggest a successful adaptation to local marine resources. Increased dog and pig remains suggest the expansion of agriculture, as these animals were fed on agricultural produce at European contact. Excavations suggest that, during this period, agricultural fields began to expand from valley floors onto surrounding slopes. Kirch speculates that, while the total population of the archipelago was expanding, it was still relatively limited.

The Late Expansion Period was followed by a period of expansion and upheaval between 1400 and 1650 AD. Most archaeologists of Hawai'i agree that the archipelago experienced a major population increase in this era. Kirch's speculation that the population grew to several hundred thousand is based on evidence of major agricultural intensification and the expansion of settlement into leeward areas and agriculturally marginal, arid zones. Kirch believes this population take-off gave rise to a number of major technological, social and political changes. The concentration of settlement in favoured localities now gave way to dispersed settlement across a variety of ecological zones. This expansion of settlement coincided with the extension and intensification of all aspects of agricultural production. The first clear evidence of agricultural irrigation occurs in this period in well-watered valleys, while vast upland field systems were developed where soils and rain permitted, most notably on the leeward

---

2   The standard accepted archaeological developmental sequence for Hawai'i is best outlined by Kirch. Timelines developed by other contemporary archaeologists of Hawai'i, such as Robert Hommon, Timothy Earle, and Ross Cordy are only cited in the following footnotes as they significantly diverge from this standard sequence. The following summary is outlined in Kirch (2010), pp. 126–28.

slopes of Kona and Kohala on Hawai'i Island. Fishponds were also developed in this period. Embryonic states begin to emerge towards the end of this period and population growth peaked and then stabilised.[3]

Major changes in social and political organisation occurred, with the structures witnessed by Cook's expedition in the 1770s evolving in this period. Artefacts used as symbols of chiefly rank at contact became common, which suggests the consolidation of rank differentiation at this time. Settlement expansion is seen as a key factor in the breakdown of kin-group organisation and its replacement with territorial affiliations and class-based social organisation. Robert Hommon suggests that, as all the best agricultural land came into use, it became necessary to define territorial boundaries more precisely. Ahupua'a land units may have begun to develop at this time. Kin-group solidarity may have begun to erode due to dispersed settlement, while the general economic self-sufficiency of most ahupua'a and their increasing populations may have reduced the need for exchanges of food and marriage partners between localities.[4]

Hawaiian traditions confirm that changes to landholding occurred in this era. A council of chiefs on O'ahu elected Ma'ilikukahi as mō'ī, in part, to act as a mediator. According to Abraham Fornander, a Swede who settled in Hawai'i in 1842, 'He caused the island to be thoroughly surveyed, and the boundaries between different divisions and lands to be definitely and permanently marked out, thus obviating future disputes between neighbouring chiefs and landholders'.[5] Maui was also divided into districts, sub-districts and smaller divisions by the kahuna Kalaikaohi'a in the reign of the Maui mō'ī Kaka'alaneo. A chiefly supervisor was assigned to each land division. Within a few generations, a similar process was carried out on Hawai'i by mō'ī 'Umi-a-Līloa.[6]

---

3   On population growth and plateauing, see P.V. Kirch, '"Like Shoals of Fish": Archaeology and Population in Pre-contact Hawai'i', in P.V. Kirch & J.L. Rallu (eds), *The Growth and Collapse of Pacific Island Societies: Archaeological and Demographic Perspectives* (Honolulu: University of Hawai'i Press, 2007), pp. 52–69. On transformative features during this era see also Robert J. Hommon, 'Social Evolution in Ancient Hawaii', in P.V. Kirch (ed.), *Island Societies: Archaeological Approaches to Evolution and Transformation* (Cambridge University Press, 1987), pp. 60–67; Hommon (2013), pp. 227 ff.
4   Hommon (2013), pp. 228–35; Hommon (1987), p. 65; R.J. Hommon, 'The Formation of Primitive States in Pre-contact Hawaii', PhD Thesis, University of Arizona, 1976, pp. 230–31.
5   Abraham Fornander, *Ancient History of the Hawaiian People to the Times of Kamehameha 1*, vol. 2: *An Account of Polynesian Race*, (Rutland, Vermont: Charles E. Tuttle Company, 1969), p. 89. See Kirch (2012), pp. 131 ff. on Ma'ilikukahi.
6   M.W. Beckwith, *Hawaiian Mythology* (Honolulu: University of Hawai'i Press, 1970), p. 383; and Kamakau (1961), pp. 17–20.

Kirch associates these changes to landholding and land administration, which were first initiated on Oʻahu by Maʻilikukahi, with a profound change in social organisation that increased chiefly power over commoners. In this period, land units moved from being controlled by genealogical lineages to a situation where commoners, who were known as makaʻāinana, formed a distinct class that was separated from their former lineage chiefs, and worked the land under the direction and control of the chiefly class. Makaʻāinana rights to land resided in the chief who ruled their land at the time, and became divorced from multi-generational genealogical ties to the land that were remembered in family moʻolelo (histories). Soon makaʻāinana were forbidden from claiming and reciting genealogies greater than two generations. The power of paramount chiefs became increasingly associated with divine status, which justified the demands for more tribute that increasingly came to be used to support paramount chief's households, warriors and administrative officers.[7] Kirch posits that this pattern of social relations became universal throughout the islands, although the unstable nature of dryland agriculture pressured mōʻī in leeward Hawaiʻi and Maui, who were more reliant on this form of agriculture, to demand more from their subjects and to be more orientated to wars of aggression to seize agricultural land.[8] Kirch, however, sees the period from Maʻilikukahi's reforms until the era of unification of the archipelago under Kamehameha as one of the elaboration of existing sociopolitical structures rather than as a period of significant structural reform. To Kirch, the underlying influences on this elaboration of paramount chiefly power were status rivalry and usurpation between chiefs, elite marriage and endogamy to raise one's chiefly status, intensification of agricultural production to increase the paramount's resource base to support his military and administrative forces, elaboration of chiefly ritual and human sacrifice to enhance divine status, and the application of force, war and territorial conquest to increase the paramount chief's mana and resource base.[9]

The longstanding, evolving and relatively uniform sociopolitical structure of government behind unification suggested by Kirch and others is most comprehensively outlined by Hommon. Society was divided into two socio-economic classes – a producer class of makaʻāinana, whose social links and work were highly localised in orientation, and the aliʻi, who

---

7   Kirch (2010), pp. 34, 47–50, 66–67, 89–91.
8   Kirch (2010), pp. 53–54, 90–91, chpts 4 & 5; Kirch (2012), pp. 222–25.
9   Kirch (2010), p. 121.

maintained kinship links throughout the archipelago and controlled all positions of influence in government and religion, as well as determining makaʻāinana access to land, for which the latter paid a rent to them. Government of moku consisted of either one paramount or two co-rulers, who delegated power to multiple levels of administrators drawn from the chiefly class right down to highly localised levels. These delegated administrators supervised agricultural production, tax collection, military command and the supervision of public works, such as temple construction and irrigation works. Armies of up to 15,000 men were mobilised by individual mōʻī by the 1790s, with the fighting core also drawn from chiefly ranks and supplemented by an indeterminate number of makaʻāinana conscripts or recruits.[10]

Not all archaeologists and anthropologists adhere to this analysis. Marshall Sahlins's classical analysis of the problems for domestic modes of production that were caused by increased demands for tribute has already been noted. Archaeologist Michael Kolb asserted that this era on Maui witnessed a move from increased demands for produce as tribute by paramount chiefs to demands instead for corvée labour for use in temple construction, in keeping with the increasing emphasis on the divinity of ruling chiefs. Kolb concluded that this increased the bonds between ruler and ruled as their demands on their followers switched from taking an increasing share of makaʻāinana production as ritual tribute to greater makaʻāinana participation in communal building projects that were shared by the ruler and the ruled.[11] Critiquing Kolb, Valerio Valeri noted that this may have in fact had the opposite effect, as such large-scale communal building projects affected the amount of time that was available to be devoted to agricultural production, which was the central focus of makaʻāinana life. Valeri went on to note that:

> [Moreover,] a system of ritual consumption allowed the ruler to attract and keep a large number of clients and subordinate chiefs who could be used to stabilise his rule by use of force directed against the ruled but especially against rivals ... The sacrificial polity was all the more successful the more it could finance its ritual consumption with plunder and conquest rather than mere 'taxation'. The Hawaiian political system was not able to transcend its predatory stage completely – at least not until the late 18th century.[12]

---

10   Hommon (2013), pp. 3–4, 25–38.
11   Michael J. Kolb, et al., 'Monumentality and the Rise of Religious Authority in Precontact Hawaiʻi [and Comments and Reply]', *Current Anthropology*, vol. 35 (5), Dec. 1994, 527–28, 530–31.
12   Valerio Valeri, comment on Kolb, in Kolb (1994), p. 542.

In response, Kolb noted that '[P]olitical rule is always a delicate balance between consensus and coercion, and it is clear that the emphasis in Hawai'i shifted from the former to the latter'.[13]

Despite the widespread support among archaeologists for this hypothesis, there are a number of problems with its assumptions. Firstly, if all moku contained the same structures of power and governance, why did one succeed where all others failed? Leeward Maui and Hawai'i are asserted to have had the most effective states because of their ability to conduct expansionary wars of conquest within and between islands, yet neither was able to consolidate conquests until the 1790s. Why? I suggest that the process of consolidation mattered more than the process of conquest, as shown by the contrasting fortunes of Kamehameha and Kahekili in the last decades of the 18th century. Furthermore, the major structural changes in military and political organisation that occurred in the late 18th century can explain why unification occurred in the 1790s and not before. Hawaiian traditions also demonstrate the ongoing strength of local countervailing power structures that limited the power of mōʻī over their subjects, as illustrated by Kanalu Young. Finally, the limits on coercive power to ensure compliance meant that paramount chiefs, by necessity, had to restrict their demands and produce benefits to ensure loyalty. The alliance of interests between ali'i and maka'āinana posited by Lilikalā Kameʻeleihiwa and Jon Osorio is a better fit with the realities of power and the course of events than the predominant archaeological models.

As discussed in Chapters 3 and 4, the ongoing strength of local power bases beyond those controlled by ali'i nui in Kamehameha's era raises questions about the degree to which class had replaced blood as the prime affiliation for the majority of the population. It is worth noting Hommon's observation that the ali'i probably only made up 1–2 per cent of the entire population.[14] History demonstrates that no amount of martial ability or sacred legitimacy can keep such a small elite in power if it alienates the rest of the population. Even though it is now acknowledged by archaeologists that the ali'i classes substantially increased as a proportion of the population in the late pre-unification era, this was still not on a scale where they could alone supply the military and administrative needs of paramount chiefs who had alienated their maka'āinana subjects. At this early stage, the mōʻī's control over landholding probably required even more of a consensus than it did in Kamehameha's early years. The mōʻī

---

13 Kolb (1994), p. 543.
14 Hommon (2013), p. 17.

Maʻilikukahi played the role of mediator, while Maui's reforms were initiated by a kahuna, with the mōʻī Kakaʻalaneo's influence unclear. Just prior to ʻUmi-a-Līloa's unification of Hawaiʻi, the dominant aliʻi on the island, Hakau, had offended two elderly men called Nunu and Kakohe. They 'became angered and gave the land to ʻUmi'.[15] The positions of Nunu and Kakohe are not stated, but their actions were a clear indication of the need for sensitive diplomacy by power brokers. At this stage, local kin groups probably still exercised political influence, albeit on a diminishing scale. Were Nunu and Kakohe lineage heads or aliʻi with armed retinues?

While land reforms may have set in train processes that increased chiefly power relative to commoners, it was warfare that consolidated this power. Competition for arable land precipitated inter-group warfare. Hawaiian traditions mention antagonism between chiefs in leeward and windward areas of Hawaiʻi in this era. While the windward areas were based on long-established, stable economies, those to the leeward expanded rapidly, but were unstable because of partial reliance on unpredictable yields from marginal, drought-prone and possibly overused lands. The greater effort required to break in and maintain drier lands served to enhance chiefly power in leeward areas by providing a need for coordinated supervision above the lineage level. Marginal and fluctuating surpluses may have pressured rulers to enhance their logistical base through conquest rather than risk commoner dissent by drawing too heavily on production not normally earmarked for the support of chiefly retinue. There was a noticeable increase in the prominence of leeward chiefs relative to those from windward areas of Hawaiʻi from the time that ʻUmi-a-Līloa moved his main residence from Waipiʻo in Hāmākua to Hōnaunau in Kona. This move was preceded by a struggle between ʻUmi and his genealogically senior half-brother Hakau at Waipiʻo. Umi was initially forced to take refuge in the dry tablelands of Hāmākua, where he gathered disgruntled elements of the local population around him until he was strong enough to topple Hakau.[16]

---

15 Dorothy Kahananui (ed.), *Ka Mooolelo Hawaii* (Honolulu: University of Hawaiʻi, Committee for the Preservation and Study of Hawaiian Language, Art and Culture, 1984), p. 223; and Kamakau (1961), p. 12.
16 David Malo, *Hawaiian Antiquities*, Nathaniel B. Emerson (trans.) (Honolulu: Bernice P. Bishop Museum, 1951), p. 258; Kamakau (1961), p. 62; E.S.C. Handy & E.G. Handy, *Native Planters of Old Hawaii: Their Life, Lore, and Environments* (Honolulu: Bernice P. Bishop Museum, 1972), pp. 533–35; Hommon (1976), pp. 285–86; P.V. Kirch, *The Evolution of the Polynesian Chiefdoms* (Cambridge University Press, 1984), p. 236; Kirch (1985), pp. 306–07; Hommon (1976), p. 67; and Kirch (1994), pp. 261–62.

To Kirch, this era was a crucial watershed in Hawaiian political evolution. Strong population growth based on irrigated taro and aquaculture that had favoured chiefs from the older western islands of Kaua'i and O'ahu reached its limits, and people moved into drier lands as wet taro lands could no longer accommodate the population. The dominant rulers in this era, 'Umi-a-Līloa of Hawai'i and Kiha-a-Pi'ilani of Maui, were both usurping younger siblings who moved away from the long-established irrigated taro lands to new dryland sweet potato-based lands in response to this pressure. This dryland agriculture favoured the eastern islands of Maui and Hawai'i. Around this time larger and more complex temple sites began to flourish, and large royal centres in locations identified as the heartlands and residences of particular rulers occur in the archaeological record. These dryland systems were vulnerable to drought, making them potentially unstable as more and more people would come to rely on their produce unless more land could be incorporated in the realm to allow agricultural expansion. At the same time, these dryland chiefs used ritual and temples to garner more of the harvest to feed their military and administrative contingents and increasingly needed new lands to distribute as incentives to followers.[17]

In his detailed history of O'ahu, however, Ross Cordy suggests that the pinnacle of O'ahu chiefs' power occurred during the 1600s and 1700s up until their conquest by chiefs from Maui in the 1780s. It is also interesting to record that the chiefs of O'ahu were considered to be more inclined towards cooperation than competition, unlike their leeward neighbours. This argues against the efficacy of centralised power and in favour of the more localised, counterbalancing power, as argued by modern Hawaiian scholars. As events transpired, Kahekili, the Maui conqueror of O'ahu, failed to win the loyalty of the long independent O'ahu lesser ali'i and this fatally weakened his bid for leadership over the entire chain.[18] Further debate on Kirch's proposed timeline is raised by Hommon's dating of irrigated taro agricultural systems reaching their capacity to support an expanding population to the period 1680–1790. This is much later than Kirch, and the fact that it occurred on the eve of unification is not really explored by Hommon.[19]

---

17   Kirch (2012), pp. 92–103.
18   Ross Cordy, 'The Rise and Fall of the O'ahu Kingdom: A Brief History of O'ahu History', in Janet Davidson, Geoffrey Irwin, Foss Leach, Andrew Pawley & Dorothy Brown (eds), *Oceanic Culture History: Essays in Honour of Roger Green*, New Zealand Journal of Archaeology Special Publication, Dunedin, 1996, esp. pp. 600–03; and Ross Cordy, *The Rise and Fall of the O'ahu Kingdom* (Honolulu: Mutual Publishing, 2002).
19   Hommon (2013), p.7.

Kirch's final evolutionary phase dates from 1650 to 1778 AD. In the 1980s, Kirch dated the end of this era to 1795 – ahead of Cook's arrival in 1778 – because Kirch believed the old political order of competing chiefdoms was not structurally altered until 1795, and it was only in the 1790s that visits by trade vessels began to seriously influence Hawaiian culture. As noted in Chapter 1, however, Kirch has recently altered this stance as he believes Hawaiian polities were archaic states by the time Cook arrived, but fails to discuss how these structures enabled Kamehameha to unify the islands, while his rivals, with similar structures of governance and power, could not. In *How Chiefs Became Kings*, Kirch outlines the distinct political histories of each major island, but does not emphasise structural differences in their respective organisation of power beyond the potential ecological instability of those based primarily on dryland agricultural systems, which promoted a need to expand and seize more agricultural land. Kirch proposed that the era after 1650 witnessed the 'elaboration of the existing social order and of further intensification of the means of production along lines firmly established'.[20] Hawaiian traditions suggest that this period was characterised by intense inter-chiefly rivalry and warfare. This is supported by archaeological evidence, which reveals an increase in the size, and possibly number, of luakini heiau during this period. Luakini heiau first appear in the latter part of the Expansion Period, and may signal the rise of the chiefly adherence to the war god Kū. References to Kū are found in traditions relating to 'Umi-a-Līloa. Hommon's analysis of Hawaiian traditions suggests that, in the centuries leading up to contact, accession to political office and the establishment and maintenance of political boundaries were increasingly based on the application of force rather than the exercise of genealogical prerogatives.[21]

Traditions reveal a cyclical pattern of conquests, attempts to integrate conquered lands, followed by the contraction or even disintegration of polities. Wars extended between islands, with Moloka'i serving both as a battleground and a prize for the chiefs of O'ahu and Maui, while east Maui was periodically occupied or raided by forces from Hawai'i. Territorial conquests were rarely retained beyond the lifetime of the conquering paramount, or his immediate successor. Weak or ageing mō'ī always faced the prospect of being usurped by ambitious subordinates, particularly junior collateral kin. Successful challenges are usually explained in the traditions

---

20   Kirch (1985), pp. 305–06.
21   Hommon (1976), pp. 55, 278–80; Kirch (1985), p. 305; Kirch (2010), pp. 103–16.

as the result of increasingly oppressive or demanding incumbents alienating their subjects and making them amenable to challenges by rival chiefs who were perceived to be more benevolent and just.[22]

The administrative and coercive capacity of Hawaiian mōʻī in the 1770s was insufficient for the imposition of effective centralised rule. Political and military structures, however, were far from stagnant. Generations of Hawaiian aliʻi and their advisers devoted much time and energy into enhancing chiefly power. It is important to take this long heritage of political struggle into account when analysing the unification of the islands in the decades following Cook's discovery of Kauaʻi in 1778.

The importance of geography: Variation between localities

Local differences in resources and geographical barriers to communication played a significant role in shaping the struggle for power between chiefs. The natural environment not only influenced agricultural production and population concentrations, but also the ease of communication between localities. These were important considerations for the essentially decentralised polities of 18th-century Hawaiʻi. They also influenced warfare, as most armies depended on local resources for sustenance. Ecological diversity and barriers to communication also created variation in cultural practices and political coherence between polities (moku) presided over by high chiefs (aliʻi nui) within the broad pattern just described.

The Hawaiian archipelago has a wide variety of environments. The landscape is essentially the result of volcanic activity modified by wind and rain. The islands are the emergent tips of a chain of volcanoes that rest on the Pacific Plate. The oldest islands are to the north-west, while the youngest volcanoes are in the south-east. Many, such as Kilauea on Hawaiʻi, are still active. The older the islands, the more they have been eroded by weathering agents such as rainfall and wave action. Kauaʻi and Oʻahu are heavily dissected by erosion, resulting in well-developed valley floors and coastal plains, while the younger volcanic slopes of Haleakalā on Maui, and Mauna Kea and Mauna Loa on Hawaiʻi have been only slightly eroded. Changes in sea level during the Pleistocene resulted in

---

22 Kirch (2010), pp. 103–16; Kirch (1985), p. 307; Hommon (1976), pp. 160–62.

high sea cliffs in some places while, at places like Honolulu and 'Ewa on O'ahu, drops in sea level exposed coral reefs which formed the base for large leeward plains.[23]

The islands' north-west–south-east alignment means that their mountains block the prevailing north-easterly trade winds to produce a distinct dry leeward, wet windward dichotomy. When the moisture-laden trade winds encounter the steep volcanic ranges they are forced upward, leading to rapid condensation and rainfall. Rainfall is highest on the windward slopes, and then decreases rapidly towards the leeward coasts. On O'ahu, for example, rainfall in the windward coast near Kāne'ohe averages around 1,875 millimetres annually, rises to over 6,250 millimetres at the crest of the Ko'olau Mountains, and drops to less than 500 millimetres on the leeward coast near 'Ewa. Rainfall is seasonally variable. The months from October to April are generally wetter, while the period from May to August is considerably drier. The wetter months are also a time of stormy seas that curtail inter-island travel. The major exception to this pattern is the Kona district of Hawai'i, where the peak rainfall months are June to August. This is because of moist southerly winds, known as Kona winds, which are common during this time.[24]

Ancient Hawaiian society was unable to cultivate much of the archipelago's landmass. Rainfall and local geology combine to determine the degree of erosion, vegetation patterns and food crops. The greater part of Hawai'i's land area consists of lithosols, either recent lava flows or older, weathered saprolites. All are of limited use for agriculture. The lithosols of the older, more eroded upland slopes have more depth, but the most productive soils for Hawaiian cultivation technology were the alluvial and colluvial soils of windward and leeward valley bottoms. Varying soil fertility and orographic rainfall produced a pattern of dry forest on lower slopes giving way to wet, dense forest on upper slopes, and alpine scrub on the highest peaks. Coastal plains were covered with a variety of grasses, shrubs, swamp and stands of screw pine.[25]

The isolation of the chain resulted in a relatively restricted range of terrestrial fauna and flora prior to Polynesian settlement. The endemic fauna, beyond seabirds and native geese, was of limited use for food.

---

23   Kirch (1985), pp. 24–25; and Department of Geography, University of Hawai'i at Mānoa, *Atlas of Hawaii* (2nd edn) (Honolulu: University of Hawai'i Press, 1983), pp. 36–37.
24   Kirch (1985), p. 25; Handy & Handy (1972), pp. 16–17.
25   Kirch (1985), pp. 28–31; Kirch (2012), p. 154; Handy & Handy (1972), p. 7.

There were no suitable beasts of burden. While the marine resources of the archipelago were less abundant than in other parts of Polynesia, the sea was still a rich reservoir of food. Reef and lagoon complexes were limited, and many areas lacked sheltered inshore fisheries and safe coastal waters to travel in. Large stretches of rugged coastline made access to marine resources difficult, and travel potentially dangerous.[26]

The physical environment also posed other hazards. Unusually heavy rains in the mountains resulted in flash floods in the valleys, while tsunami in the north Pacific periodically threatened low-lying coastal areas. Volcanic activity is another ongoing hazard, particularly on Hawai'i. This volcanic regime also provided Hawaiians with a number of potentially useful stone resources for tools and building. Perhaps the most consistent and significant natural hazard to man has been the ever-present threat of drought, particularly in leeward areas.[27] While rich marine environments reduced reliance on agriculture in some localities, local soil and water regimes were the critical determinants of a community's viability.

Most settlements in the late 18th century were situated within 10 kilometres of the coast. They were dispersed along much of the coastline to varying degrees of intensity. Although early explorers refer to several 'villages' of up to 70 or 80 structures each, most residences were more dispersed. In places, they formed an almost continuous ribbon development of individual dwellings set along the coastline or scattered among fields and groves of fruit trees.[28] French explorer Jean François de La Perouse noted such a pattern of dwellings on a fertile section of the coastline of south-east Maui, describing:

> dwellings which are so numerous, that a space of three or four leagues may be taken for a single village, but all the houses are upon the sea shore, and the mountains seem to occupy so much of the island, that the habitable part of it appears to be scarcely half a league broad.[29]

---

26   Kirch (1985), pp. 30–32; and Robert J. Hommon, *Use and Control of Hawaiian Inter-Island Channels: Polynesian Hawaii: A.D. 1400–1794* (Honolulu: Office of the Governor of Hawaii, 1975), pp. 113–48.
27   Kirch (1985), p. 33; and James Jackson Jarves, *History of the Hawaiian Islands* (4th edn) (Honolulu: Henry M. Whitney, 1872), pp. 214–70.
28   Cordy (1972), p. 406; Kirch (1985), p. 179; Tuggle (1979), p. 182; Samwell, in J.C. Beaglehole (ed.), *The Journals of Captain James Cook on his Voyages of Discovery*, vol. 3: *The Voyage of the Resolution and Discovery* (Cambridge: The Hakluyt Society, 1967) 3:2; Clerke, in Beaglehole (1967) 3:1, pp. 592–93, 1175–76; and King, in Beaglehole (1967), 3:1, p. 283.
29   L.A. Milet-Mureau (ed.) *A Voyage Round the World, Performed in the Years 1785, 1786, 1787 and 1788 by J.E.G. de La Perouse*, vol. 2 (London: J. Johnson Printer, 1798), pp. 37–38.

The basic local social and economic unit was an ahupua'a. These generally consisted of long narrow strips of land extending inland from the coast for a distance of several miles. They incorporated a variety of environments from inshore fisheries to forested uplands, providing residents with access to a wide range of resources. The seaward boundary of ahupua'a was defined as the depth the tallest man could wade out to at low water. Beyond that, the six monthly fishing kapu applied.[30] This pattern varied to accommodate topographical features, such as steep-walled windward valleys, or to compensate for local scarcity by increasing land area. Districts as a whole tended to centre on resource-rich localities. The ideal was a fertile, well-watered locality with accessible and abundant offshore fishing. District boundaries were often in less well-endowed areas.[31]

Taro grown in irrigated, well-watered valleys and 'uala (sweet potato) grown on dry slopes represent the extremes of Hawaiian agricultural practice. A variety of subsistence regimes existed within these parameters. Local production generally involved multiple cropping, with irrigated and non-irrigated fields often sitting adjacent to each other. Dry-field cultivation ranged from swidden to permanent fields with capacity enhanced by mulching. Broadly speaking, two major environmental zones supported the majority of the Hawaiian population. Each had a distinctive crop regime, one based on irrigated fields and the other on dry-field cropping.[32] Permanent streams and fertile alluvial soil allowed the year-round cultivation of wet taro in the steep-walled valleys of the windward coasts. Swamps, streambeds and artificially irrigated fields provided suitable areas for cultivation. Sugar cane, banana and 'ulu (breadfruit) were often grown on the banks separating flooded taro fields, and in non-irrigated areas. Larger leeward valleys with reasonable, but less reliable, rainfall in their upper reaches could also support irrigated fields, but tended to have a higher proportion of their land planted in dryland crops.[33]

---

30 Archibald Campbell, *A Voyage Round the World from 1806 to 1812* (Honolulu: University of Hawai'i Press, 1967 (1822)), pp. 142–43.
31 Tuggle (1979), p. 181.
32 Cordy (1972), p. 396; Kirch (1984), p. 168; Kirch (1985), p. 31; Tuggle (1979), p. 173.
33 T. K. Earle, 'Prehistoric Irrigation on the Hawaiian Islands', *Archaeology and Physical Anthropology in Oceania*, vol. 15 (1), 1980, 1–28; George Vancouver, *A Voyage of Discovery to the North Pacific Ocean and Round the World*, vol. 3 (London: John Stockdale, 1801), pp. 360–65; and Archibald Menzies, *Hawaii Nei 128 Years Ago* (Honolulu: T. H. Press, 1920), pp. 23–24.

The other significant environmental zone was slopes or lowlands that lacked permanent streams, but had sufficient rainfall or humidity to allow cultivation of dry taro and ʻuala. Both crops were planted in non-irrigated fields, often surrounded by low stonewalls to block runoff and covered in mulch to retain moisture. Sugar cane, paper mulberry, banana and breadfruit were often planted in groves or on stone walls separating fields. In some areas, such as the wet, humid lowlands of Puna on Hawaiʻi, breadfruit was a major crop. Beyond these two zones, limited water generally restricted crops grown to ʻuala and occasionally yams, with occasional clusters of sugar cane and bananas when local regimes allowed. Mounds of earth and stone were used to enhance the growing environment. These techniques were also used in drier areas within the two main regimes.[34]

Variation in cultivation influenced social and political organisation as well as economic organisation. Intensive dry-field cultivation requires a much higher labour input than irrigated taro cultivation. While wet taro systems require limited attention beyond initial field and irrigation ditch construction, dry-field systems need continual mulching and weeding after the fields have been cleared of stones and rocks and the ground broken for planting. The prominence of intensive dry-field systems in leeward areas of Maui and Hawaiʻi resulted in the drafting of women into the agricultural workforce. Discussing regional variation within the Hawaiian Islands, Kirch draws attention to a passage in Kamakau, which states that:

> All the work outside the house was performed by the men, such as tilling the ground … This was the common rule on Kauai, Oahu, and Molokai, but on Maui and Hawaii the women worked outside as hard as the men, often cooking, tilling the ground, and performing the duties in the house as well. At the time when Kamehameha took over the rule from Hawaii to Oahu it was not uncommon to see the women of Hawaii packing foods on their backs, cooking it in the imu, and cultivating the land … On Maui the men showed their wives where their [garden] patches were and while they went to do other work the women brought the food and firewood from the upland … This is why the chiefs of Hawaii imposed taxes on men and women alike and got the name of being oppressive to the people, while the chiefs on Oahu and Kauai demanded taxes of the men alone.[35]

---

34 Menzies (1920), p. 75 (dry-field systems); King, in Beaglehole (1967), 3:1, p. 521 (mulching); and Cordy (1972), pp. 395–96; and Handy & Handy (1972), p. 152 (breadfruit).
35 Kamakau (1961), pp. 238–39; and P.V. Kirch, 'Regional Variation and Local Style: A Neglected Dimension in Hawaiian Prehistory', *Pacific Studies* (Laie), vol. 13 (2), 1990a, 48–49.

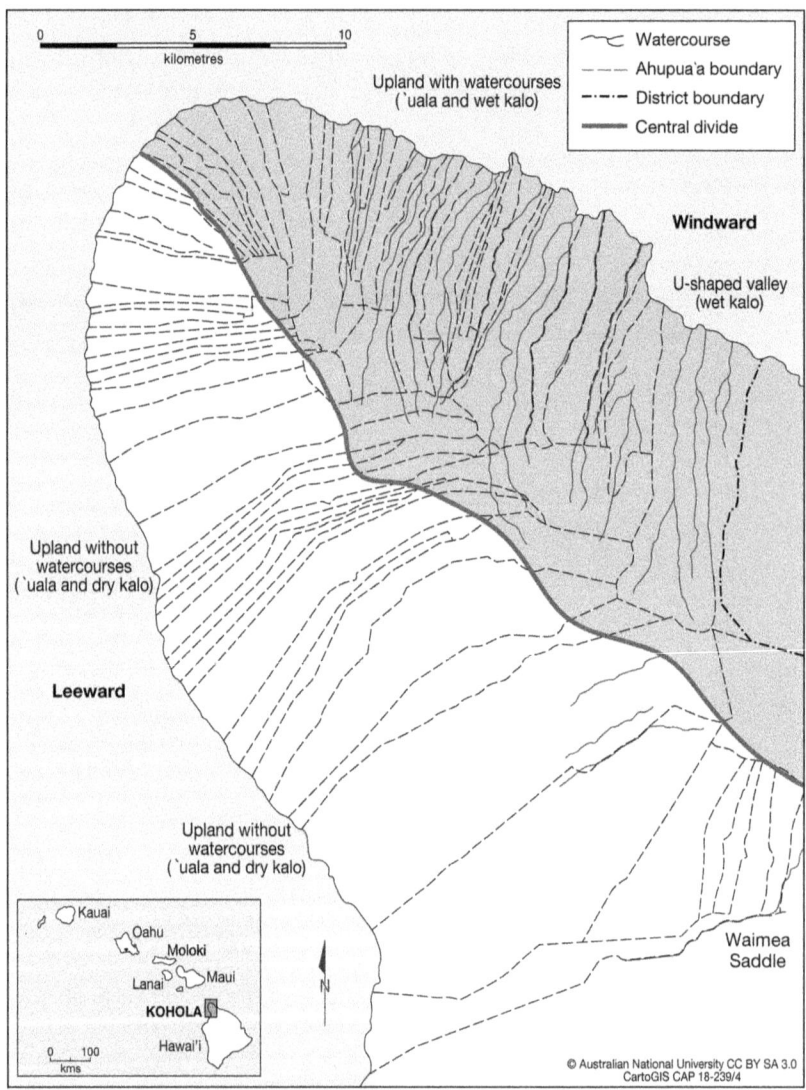

Figure 1: Ahupua'a divisions of Kohala District, Hawai'i
Source: CartoGIS, The Australian National University.

Kirch notes that the increased demand on female labour in these areas may have negatively influenced female fecundity. This in turn may have influenced the human resources available for agriculture and warfare. Archaeological investigations suggest there was a significant intensification of dry-field cultivation in leeward areas of Maui and Hawai'i in the two centuries before the age of Kamehameha. While these systems were capable of prolific yields they were also dependent on rainfall. Increasing yields through intensifying production in existing areas or expanding into areas of less reliable rainfall ran the risk of relying on an unpredictable rainfall regime. It was a shaky basis upon which to expand the population or increase the level of chiefly expropriations. Dry-field systems were potentially more politically unstable than wet taro systems because of the additional labour demands placed on maka'āinana by ali'i, and the pressure to conquer more lands to increase agricultural output.[36]

The natural environment also influenced sociopolitical organisation by affecting communications. Wide and often dangerous channels separated some of the main islands. These channels tended to divide the inhabited islands into four distinct areas whose external ties were somewhat weaker than their internal links. These areas were Kaua'i and Ni'ihau; O'ahu; Moloka'i, Lāna'i, Maui and Kaho'olawe; and Hawai'i. The 117-kilometre-wide channel between Kaua'i and O'ahu was particularly hazardous. Although the right trade winds allowed the 46-kilometre 'Alenuihoha channel between Maui and Hawai'i to be crossed in either direction in a couple of hours, they could also produce very rough seas. On the other hand, the close grouping of Maui, Moloka'i, Lāna'i and Kaho'olawe provided a partly enclosed, and relatively sheltered body of water that facilitated canoe travel.[37]

Political groupings were influenced by island alignments. Powerful moku tended to centre on one of the four major islands: Kaua'i, O'ahu, Maui and Hawai'i. Kaua'i dominated Ni'ihau, and Maui dominated Lāna'i and Kaho'olawe. Moloka'i sometimes served as a battlefield between the forces of O'ahu and Maui. Neither could establish permanent control over Moloka'i, which remained largely independent until the latter part of the 18th century. By then, east Maui was also a regular site for confrontations between the forces of Maui and Hawai'i mō'ī.[38]

Religious practices and other cultural differences may also have been influenced by the relative separation of the inhabited islands into four clusters. Fishhooks and food pounders from the material culture of Kaua'i, for example, are distinct from those of other islands in the chain. Chiefly dynasties tended to be associated with god forms distinct from those of

---

36   Kirch (1985), p. 303.
37   Kirch (1985), pp. 22–23; Hommon (1975), pp. 161–70; Tuggle (1979), pp. 171–72.
38   Hommon (1976), p. 55.

their rivals. A large number of gods (akua) were worshipped for a variety of purposes. Occupational groupings, localities, families, gender and class divisions all had their own gods, although most seem to have been subsumed under four major gods: Kū, Lono, Kāne and Kanaloa. While the rulers of Oʻahu and Hawaiʻi both worshipped aggressive forms of Kū as their war god, that of the former was Ku-honeʻenuʻu, while the latter's was Kūʻkāʻili-moku. The hierarchy of Kū, Lono, Kāne and Kanaloa may only have become the pattern for the whole group after Kamehameha's unification of the islands. Temple types on Kauaʻi suggest that Luakini poʻokanaka were usually dedicated to Kāne and to a lesser extent Kanaloa, rather than to Kū, as was the case on Hawaiʻi. Some luakini poʻokanaka on Maui were even dedicated to Kāne. Pele, the goddess associated with volcanoes, was particularly worshipped on volcanically active Hawaiʻi. Cultural differences were probably more profound among makaʻāinana than among the more mobile chiefly elite.[39]

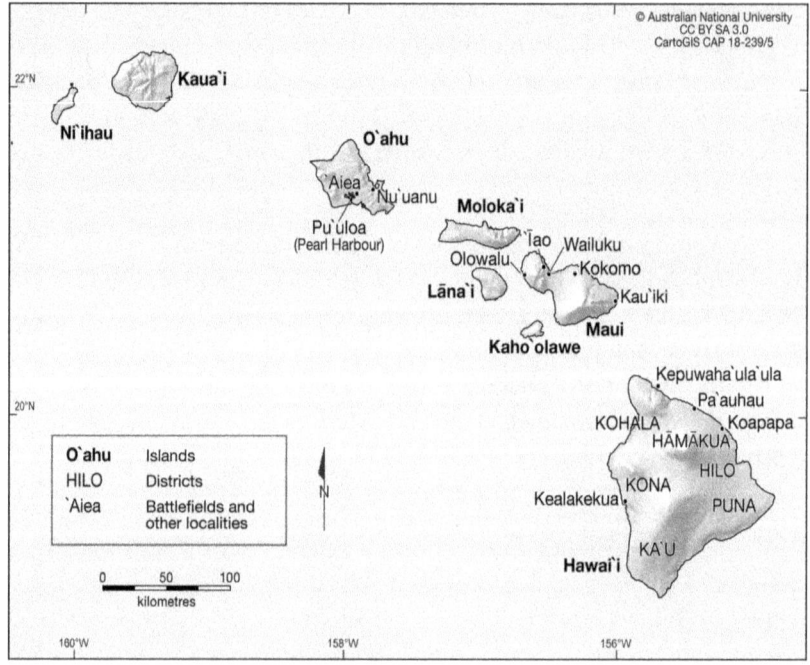

Figure 2: The Hawaiian archipelago
Source: CartoGIS, The Australian National University.

---

39 Kirch (1994), p. 263; Valeri (1985a), pp. 184–85; Kirch (1985), pp. 99–100; and Handy & Handy (1972), pp. 79–83.

Local resource bases, political traditions and spatial relationships

The decentralised nature of Hawaiian polities and their administrative capabilities restricted their geographical extent. The smaller islands leeward of Hawai'i were geographically more coherent and each tended to form a single moku, apart from during brief succession disputes. In contrast, Hawai'i fluctuated between unity under a single mōʻī and division between rival rulers, with large tracts of forested uplands and lava fields providing a buffer between the core areas of their respective domains. All moku were made up of a number of discrete localities. The resources of each locality, and the relationships between localities played a crucial role in shaping the unification process.

Hawai'i (see Figure 3) has a landmass greater than that of the other seven inhabited islands combined. It is made up of five overlapping volcanoes, the most prominent being Mauna Loa and Mauna Kea. As the least eroded island in the group, it has sizeable valleys restricted to the windward side of the Kohala Mountains. There is a sharp windward–leeward dichotomy, with no permanent flowing streams on the western side from South Point to Upolu Point. Forested uplands in the interior exacerbated political as well as climatic differences between windward and leeward areas. Canoe travel was often used, although no reefs protected the coastline.[40]

The saddle between Mauna Kea and Mauna Loa still has traces of ancient trails reflecting its role as a crossroads for windward–leeward communication. These narrow trails were poor avenues for the passage of armies and were ideal settings for ambushes. It was not good country for manoeuvring, as the Welsh naval surgeon on Cook's third voyage David Samwell noted on a trip inland from Kealakekua Bay. He described how, 'the Underwood Which grows here render[s] the Woods Impassable everywhere out of the common Paths, many of which we met intersecting each other in various directions'.[41] The interior's main assets for Hawaiians were the extensive basalt adze quarries on Mauna Kea, and the fertile Waimea Saddle between Hāmākua and Kohala. The saddle is 790–900 metres above sea level, and also formed the only relatively open corridor between the windward and leeward coasts.

---

40   Kirch (1984), pp. 182–86; and Kirch (1985), pp. 154, 179.
41   Samwell, in Beaglehole (1967), 3:2, p. 1166.

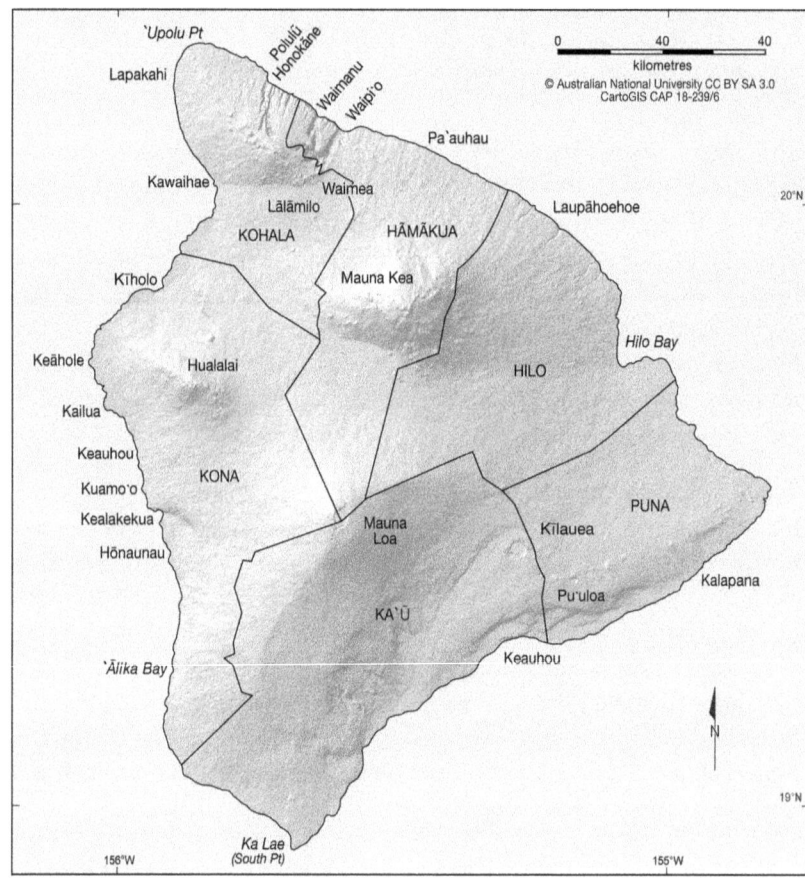

Figure 3: Hawai'i
Source: CartoGIS, The Australian National University.

Fierce rivalry existed between windward and leeward ali'i nui and their followers. In Kamehameha's time, the main centre of power on the windward coast was the district of Hilo, home to the important ali'i nui families of I and Keawe.[42] Hilo hosted a large population, mostly concentrated in the vicinity of Hilo Bay. Here, a number of permanent waterways, nightly showers and moist, warm, north-east trade winds provided a climate that allowed the year-round planting of dry-field crops as well as irrigated field systems. Northern Hilo's population was based in a number of scattered settlements around gulches with permanent streams that were terraced to grow wet taro. The land from Hilo Bay

---

42 W.D. Westervelt, 'Kamehameha's Method of Government', *31st Annual Report of the Hawaiian Historical Society for the Year 1921* (Honolulu 1922), p. 28.

south to the border with Puna was barren and lava strewn, with few permanent waterways. This part of Hilo contained only scattered pockets of agriculture and few residents.[43]

Puna has no permanent streams, but is blessed with substantial areas of light and fertile volcanic soils and ample rainfall, particularly in its wet, humid coastal lowlands. This allowed year-round planting of dry-field taro and ʻuala. Puna was also the main breadfruit-growing area in the chain. Breadfruit trees provided a significant source of carbohydrates and, in good years, could provide food for eight months of the year. Puna was one of the most fertile and populous areas in indigenous Hawaiʻi.[44] Cook's expedition found settlement spread along most of the coastline. Samwell commented that from the sea Puna had:

> the most fertile & pleasant appearance of any place we have seen at these isles, being almost entirely covered with groves of Coconut and other fruit trees, among which on small green plots stand their Houses near the seaside.[45]

Puna allied itself politically with Hilo or Kaʻū in Kamehameha's time, and never formed the core area of support for any aliʻi nui seeking to rule Hawaiʻi.

The inhabitants of Puna's neighbouring district of Kaʻū mainly lived inland among their cultivations. Some of these were up to 12 kilometres from the coast. Settlement of the barren lava coast was generally limited to fishing camps used to exploit Kaʻū's rich offshore fishing – the waters off South Point were the richest fishing grounds exploited by Hawaiians. The inland fields produced dry taro and ʻuala, and depended on rainfall, especially winter rains brought by the onset of Kona storms. Member of the Vancouver naval expedition to Hawaiʻi Archibald Menzies found the interior belt of settlement fertile and heavily populated. Kaʻū traditions, however, refer to severe droughts that occasionally forced locals to seek temporary refuge in Puna or Kona when reservoirs or dried fish, preserved ʻuala, and famine foods were exhausted. Despite this, Kaʻū remained

---

43   Cordy (1972), p. 396; Handy & Handy (1972), pp. 104, 152, 538–39; King, in Beaglehole (1967), 3:1, p. 605; Cook, in Beaglehole (1967), 3:1, p. 484; and Joseph Ingraham, in Mark D. Kaplanoff, *Joseph Ingraham's Journal of the Brigantine Hope on a Voyage to the Northwest Coast of North America 1790–1792* (Barre, Mass.: Imprint Society, 1971), pp. 65–66.
44   Cordy (1972), p. 396; Handy & Handy (1972), pp. 104, 152, 539–41.
45   Samwell, in Beaglehole (1967), 3:1, p. 1156.

politically independent well into Kamehameha's time. The rulers of Ka'ū generally allied with those of Puna and Hilo against the leeward chiefs in Kamehameha's era.[46]

The district of Hāmākua extended along the windward coast from Hilo. Most of the eastern Hāmākua coast was lined with cliffs and streaked with spectacular waterfalls as streams from the interior abruptly ended their procession to the sea. These streams formed deep gulches that broke up the relatively wet, forested upland plateau behind the coast. This upland area supported dispersed dwellings scattered among mulched fields of dry-field taro and 'uala.[47] The two great valleys of Waipi'o and Waimanu at the western end of Hāmākua contained extensive wet taro cultivation and supported substantial populations.[48] Hawaiian traditions record Waipi'o as the ancient seat of the first unifier of Hawai'i. By the late-18th century, Waipi'o was no longer a centre of power. Western Hāmākua and the Waimea Saddle now formed a zone of rivalry astride the most accessible land route between windward and leeward spheres of influence.

The populous north Kona coastline from Kailua to Keouhou was the major centre of political power on the leeward coast in the late 18th century. Early European explorers reported a number of 'villages' and archaeological remains show the area contained a number of substantial heiau. Relatively high rainfall allowed the cultivation of breadfruit near the coast. Extensive dry-field systems, measuring nearly 5 kilometres in width and extending for 29 kilometres parallel to the coast, were constructed further inland to take advantage of the increased rainfall at higher altitude. This area of the Kona coast also contains rich offshore fishing grounds.[49] Further south, Kealakekua Bay supported a sizeable population, despite its arid appearance, because moisture from fog and late afternoon showers allowed the cultivation of 'uala and dry taro on the slopes behind the bay.[50]

---

46   Handy & Handy (1972), pp. 273, 276, 543–621; Cordy (1972), p. 396; Menzies (1920), pp. 185–86; and Cook, in Beaglehole (1967), 3:1, pp. 485–86.
47   Handy & Handy (1972), pp. 532, 537–38; Cook, in Beaglehole (1967), 3:1, pp. 476, 478; King, in Beaglehole (1967), 3:1, p. 605; Menzies (1920), p. 51.
48   Handy & Handy (1972), pp. 273, 535–36; Samwell, in Beaglehole (1967), 3:2, pp. 1152–53.
49   Clerke, in Beaglehole (1967), 3:1, pp. 591–92; King, in Beaglehole (1967), 3:1, pp. 607–08; Menzies (1920), p. 75; and Vancouver (1801), bk 5, pp. 100–02; Handy & Handy (1972), p. 273; Kirch (1984), p. 182; Kirch (1985), p. 164; and Hommon (1976), p. 57.
50   Clerke, in Beaglehole (1967), 3:1, p. 592; Cordy (1972), p. 396; Handy & Handy (1972), p. 522; Kirch (1985), pp. 3, 164; and David Stannard, 'Disease and Infertility: A New Look at the Demographic Collapse of Native Populations in the Wake of Western Contact', *Journal of American Studies*, 24 (3), 1990, 3.

South again, beyond Kealakekua Bay, was the major religious complex of Hōnaunau, which housed bones of mōʻī descended from the original unifier of the islands, ʻUmi-a-Līloa. Hōnaunau also supported a sizeable population, again by taking advantage of the more suitable climate of the rain-fed inland slopes.[51] The rest of southern Kona supported only a few coastal settlements of fishermen and appeared to Samwell to be ʻa rugged, barren place almost entirely covered with lavaʼ. [52] These fishing communities were able to supplement their catch with dry-field crops planted eight to 11 kilometres inland.

Kohala was closely allied to Kona by the time Kamehameha rose to political prominence. Beyond the arid and lava-strewn shores of Kawaihae Bay, the Kohala Mountains provided a good environment for intensive cultivation. The upper part of the leeward slopes received enough rainfall to support a considerable dry-field system there. ʻUala and dry taro was grown along a 24-kilometre strip that was nearly 5 kilometres wide in places. This complex supported a considerable population based in coastal settlements.[53] High rainfall carved five deep valleys into the windward Kohala coast north of Waipiʻo and Waimanu in Hāmākua. Wet taro was grown in their alluvial flats, although their permanent streams were prone to flooding. Rugged bluffs and steep slopes restricted land communication between the valleys.[54] The other major population concentration in Kohala was the previously mentioned Waimea saddle. Its rich soils and local rainfall were supplemented with irrigation channels tapping streams from the Kohala Mountains to water extensive fields of dry taro and ʻuala.[55]

Maui is the second largest island in the chain (see Figure 4), and consists of two shield volcanoes connected by an isthmus formed from the merging of their lava flows. The western volcano is much older than its eastern neighbour, Haleakalā. As a result, the West Maui Mountains are more eroded, with deep valleys radiating out from their central spine on both leeward and windward sides. The geologically younger slopes of Haleakalā are less deeply incised. Haleakalā is now dormant, but was still active as

---

51   Kirch (1985), p. 162; and Kirch (1984), p. 256.
52   Samwell, in Beaglehole (1967), 3:2, p. 1157; Kirch (1985), p. 160; and Handy & Handy (1972), p. 523.
53   King, in Beaglehole (1967), 3:1, p. 608; Vancouver (1801), bk 5, pp. 104–06; Cordy (1972), pp. 396; Kirch (1984), pp. 182–86; Kirch (1985), pp. 167, 169, 175–77; and Hommon (1976), p. 57.
54   H.D. Tuggle & M.J. Tuggle-Tomanari, ʻPrehistoric Agriculture in Kohala, Hawaiiʼ, *Journal of Field Archaeology*, vol. 7 (3), 1980, 303–05; and Kirch (1985), p. 178.
55   Vancouver (1801) bk 5, p. 106; Kirch (1984), p. 186; and Kirch (1985), p. 177.

late as 1790. Steep, narrow and difficult to negotiate inland trails crossed the central spine of the West Maui Mountains and Haleakalā. Most travel was conducted along the coast, either by canoe or along the Alaloa (Great Road). This was a well-maintained trail that circled the coastline of Maui. Its construction dated to the reign of Kiha-a-Pi'ilani, the mō'ī who unified Maui in the 16th century. The isthmus also provided an easy route between the windward and leeward coasts of west Maui. There was little or no reef development, and the coastline was particularly rugged in the north-east.[56]

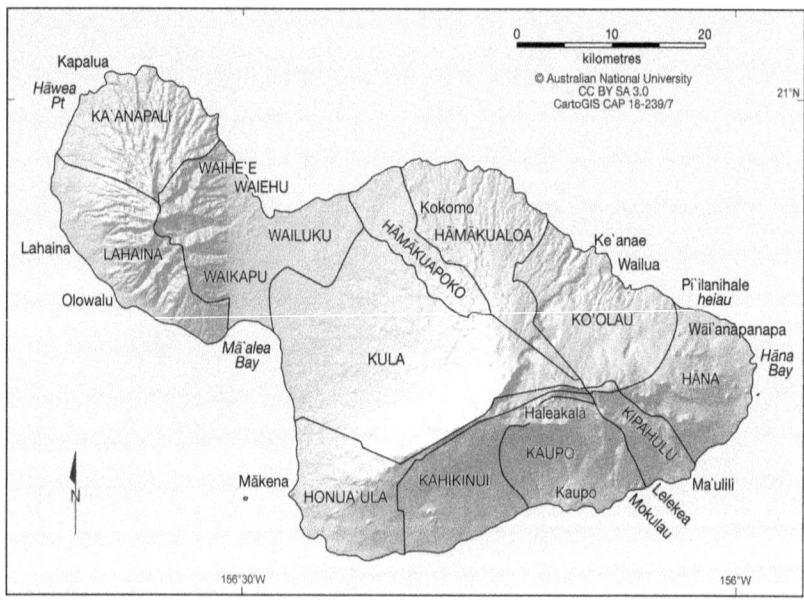

Figure 4: Maui
Source: CartoGIS, The Australian National University.

Maui remained unified through to Kamehameha's time, thanks in part to the relative ease of movement around the island. The seat of power for the ruling dynasty of Maui was the Wailuku area on west Maui's windward coast. Here four permanent streams issued forth from the mountains to form broad fertile alluvial fans on the coastal plain that supported extensive irrigated taro fields. The small size of local districts suggests this fertile area supported a dense population. The area was known as Nā Wai 'Ehā (the four streams), and its four districts centred on the streams they

---

56   Kirch (1985), pp. 134–35; Handy & Handy (1972), pp. 470, 489–90.

were named after: Waiheʻe, Waiehu, Wailuku and Waikapu. There were more permanent streams further up the windward coast of west Maui in Kaʻanapali. These also seem to have supported irrigated taro complexes.[57]

The leeward coast of west Maui was also heavily populated. The coastal lowlands contained scattered patches of irrigated taro surrounded by dry taro and ʻuala with groves of coconut and breadfruit trees. The importance of water was demonstrated by the arid nature of this coast away from irrigated areas. Even in times of drought, however, water to sustain crops on the coastal lowlands could be drawn from the upper reaches of large leeward valleys like the Olowalu that extended deep into the mountains. There were also coastal springs in places. Lahaina's rich offshore fisheries and irrigated fields made it a particularly favoured leeward locality that was often used as a residence by Maui mōʻī.[58]

Further east along the leeward coast, water was not so readily available. The district of Kula on the south-west slopes of Haleakalā was arid and sparsely populated. Its inhabitants relied on ʻuala and fishing for their sustenance. The remaining leeward districts of Honuaʻula, Kahikinui, Kaupo and Kipahulu contained more substantial populations because of the higher rainfall received by their inland slopes. Dry-field systems dominated by ʻuala occupied the slopes between 400 and 700 metres altitude in all four districts. While fishing was good off Kula and Honuaʻula, it was generally poor along the rest of this coastline. Most settlements were located up the slopes among the cultivation zone rather than on the coast.[59]

Rainfall increases towards the eastern end of this south-eastern coast towards the start of the windward coast in the district of Hana. The eastern coast of Hana had relatively wet uplands, which allowed the development of extensive fields of mulched dry taro and ʻuala, and almost continuous coastal settlement among fruit trees. The windward coast of Hana and its neighbour Koʻolau contained permanent streams and supported a dense population practicing irrigated agriculture. The irrigated taro

---

57   Handy & Handy (1972), pp. 272, 496–98; and Kirch (1985), p. 135.
58   King, in Beaglehole (1967), 3:1, p. 583; Clerke, in Beaglehole (1967), 3:1, p. 570; Vancouver (1801), bk 3, p. 326; Menzies (1920), pp. 103–04; and Handy & Handy (1972), pp. 272, 492–94.
59   Vancouver (1801), bk 3, pp. 291, 327; La Perouse, in Milet-Mureau (1798), pp. 40–41, 53–55; Handy & Handy (1972), pp. 276, 507–11; and Kirch (1985), pp. 135–38.

fields of Keʻanae and Wailua-nui in Koʻolau were particularly productive. The political significance of this area is suggested by the massive heiau of Piʻilanihale in Hana, perhaps the largest heiau in the islands.[60]

Hawaiian traditions concerning Maui do not indicate that east Maui aliʻi ever challenged the rule of mōʻī based in west Maui. The Maui mōʻī Kahekili's ignorance of local springs while besieging Kaʻuiki Head in Hana in 1783, and the apparent cooperation between local residents and aliʻi from Hawaiʻi in the 1770s and 1780s, suggest east Maui may not have been as fully integrated into the moku of Maui as is generally accepted. Hana and Koʻolau were separated from west Maui by the districts of Hāmākualoa and Hāmākuapoko. Both districts were situated on gently sloping lands that were too low to catch the moist north-easterly trade winds until they were well inland. Rainfall was limited near the coast and only small gulches crossed their slopes. The coastal bays generally provided good fishing and ʻuala was grown further up the slopes with breadfruit and banana trees planted in gulches. The large number of narrow ahupuaʻa in these districts suggests a relatively high population.[61]

The rulers of Maui dominated their leeward neighbours on Lānaʻi and Kahoʻolawe. These two islands were located in a rain shadow area leeward of Maui's high mountains and their aridity was not helped by their relatively low elevation. Kahoʻolawe is the smallest and most arid of the main islands. It has steep cliffs around most of its coastline and only intermittent rainfall, and seems to have been abandoned by the late 18th century.[62] Lānaʻi had some valley development on its windward side, but had no permanent streams and received only seasonal rainfall. Most fell on the island's central plateau. Despite this, most settlement by Kamehameha's time seems to have been along the coast. Lieutenant James King, of Cook's voyage, noted that, in places, 'the Island look'd very Pleasant, and the borders seemed full of Villages'.[63] With generally poor offshore fishing and limited reef development, the population relied on ʻuala, yams and dry taro.

---

60 Cook, in Beaglehole (1967), 3:1, p. 474; Samwell, in Beaglehole (1967), 3:2, p. 1151; Vancouver (1801), bk 3, p. 289; Handy & Handy (1972), pp. 272, 498, 502; Cordy (1972), p. 396; and Kirch (1985), pp. 135, 144.
61 Handy & Handy (1972), p. 498.
62 King, in Beaglehole (1967), 3:1, pp. 583, 609, 3:2, p. 1218; Vancouver (1801), bk 3, pp. 301–02 (Mar. 1793); and Kirch (1985), pp. 144–47.
63 King, in Beaglehole (1967), 3:1, p. 610; Clerke, in Beaglehole (1967), 3:1, p. 570; Samwell, in Beaglehole (1967), 3:2, p. 1220; Handy & Handy (1972), p. 276; and Kirch (1985), pp. 132–34.

Molokaʻi is an elongated island formed from two volcanoes linked by a central saddle (see Figure 5). Its east–west alignment meant that the windward face of the East Molokaʻi Mountains caught most of the moist trade winds, leaving the rest of the island largely deprived of rainfall. Whereas the permanent streams of the windward district of Koʻolau carved deep, steep-sided valleys that broke up the high sea cliffs of this coast, leeward eastern Molokaʻi possessed only intermittent streams in shallow gulches. Low-lying western Molokaʻi was even drier. While the ocean crashed directly against the rugged windward coast of Koʻolau, the leeward shore of Molokaʻi was blessed with reefs that enclosed broad shallows in which extensive fishponds were developed, particularly in eastern Molokaʻi.[64]

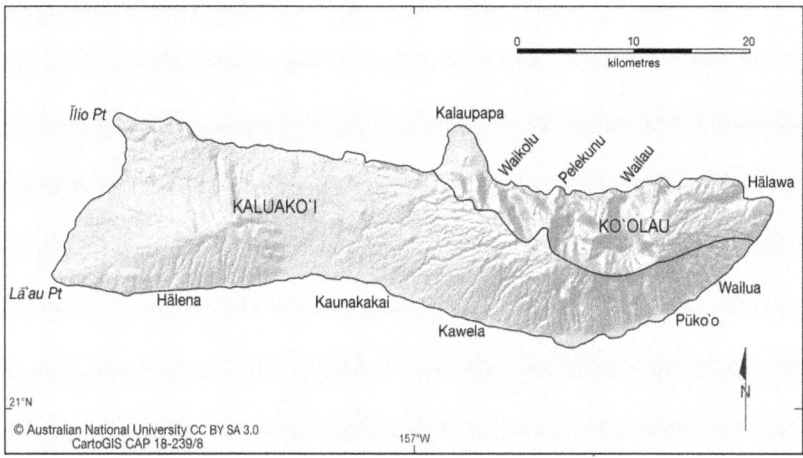

Figure 5: Molokaʻi
Source: CartoGIS, The Australian National University.

The population of the windward district of Koʻolau was concentrated in four great valleys and grew irrigated taro, while the population of leeward Kona was dispersed along the central and eastern sections of the south coast and relied on upland dry-field systems and inshore fisheries for sustenance. The only permanent stream on this coast was at Kawela, where irrigated taro was grown.[65] The western third of Molokaʻi was used only for fishing camps and the quarrying of basalt for adze production. Few people lived here and the

---

64   Kirch (1985), p. 130.
65   Clerke, in Beaglehole (1967), 3:1, p. 571; King, in Beaglehole (1967), 3:1, pp. 609–10; Handy & Handy (1972), pp. 511–20; and Kirch (1985), pp. 131, 134 (Koʻolau); and Samwell, in Beaglehole (1967), 3:2, p. 1220; Vancouver (1801), bk 3, p. 334; Handy & Handy (1972), p. 515; Kirch (1985), pp. 130–31 (Kona).

whole area made up only one ahupuaʻa.⁶⁶ Molokaʻi was not a major power in the wars between mōʻī, but its abundant fishponds and lush windward valleys attracted the attention of mōʻī from Oʻahu and Maui. The fierce rivalry between Koʻolau and Kona aliʻi often lead to war, and facilitated the intervention of its more powerful neighbours on Oʻahu and Maui.

The eastern coast of Oʻahu is visible from western Molokaʻi on clear days. Oʻahu was shaped by lava flows from its two volcanoes, resulting in two parallel mountain ranges separated by a plateau (see Figure 6). There was a considerable leeward zone beyond the windward Koʻolau Mountains. This zone included the unusual feature of large coastal plains in the districts of ʻEwa and Kona. In contrast, the windward coast was relatively narrow and consisted largely of deep valleys often ending in cliffs at the watershed, whose permanent streams created alluvial fans at the coast. Unlike most of the other inhabited islands, Oʻahu had well-developed reefs around large sections of its windward and leeward coasts.⁶⁷

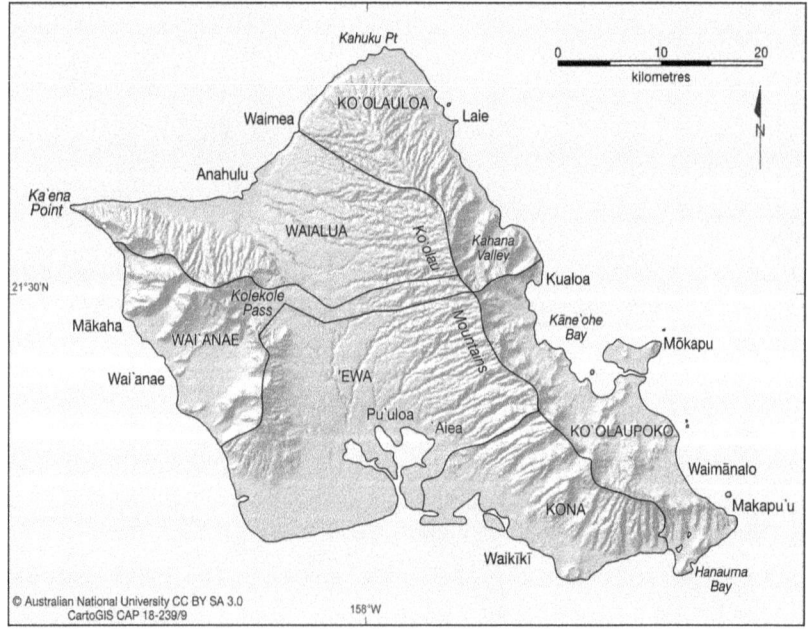

Figure 6: Oʻahu
Source: CartoGIS, The Australian National University.

---

66   Vancouver (1801), bk 3, p. 334; Handy & Handy (1972), p. 514; Kirch (1985), p. 134 (western Molokaʻi).
67   Kirch (1985), p. 107.

Scottish sailor Archibald Campbell, who became part of Kamehameha's retinue, considered Oʻahu to be the most fertile island in the archipelago in 1810.[68] The windward district of Koʻolaupoko was the most bountiful and populous district on Oʻahu. Centred on Kailua and Kāneʻohe, its heavy rainfall, permanent streams and rich soils in its valley bottoms and flood plains produced one of the most productive wet taro areas in the islands. In addition, its offshore reefs allowed the development of extensive fishponds and provided a sheltered inshore fishery.[69] The great valleys of Koʻolauloa between Laie and its boundary with Koʻolaupoko also produced a rich harvest of wet taro. Although the coastal plain here is not as extensive as at Koʻolaupoko, its reefs and sheltered bays provide good fishing. The Koʻolau Mountains decreases in height beyond Laie, resulting in a decrease in rainfall. Here the land is less weathered and prone to drought. King still found the area to be full of 'villages' in the 1770s.[70]

Across the Koʻolau Mountains from Koʻolaupoko lay Kona, the most fertile district of leeward Oʻahu. Despite its leeward climate, Kona's broad coastal plain sustained wet taro fed by permanent streams from the large valleys behind it that reach deep into the Koʻolau Mountains. Fishponds lined Kona's reef-fringed coast, although offshore fishing was relatively poor. Kona supported a large population by the 1770s.[71] The other leeward districts of Oʻahu were noticeably more arid than Kona, and probably less densely populated. The scarcity of water on the ʻEwa plain meant that most of the population of the district of ʻEwa lived around the shores of Puʻuloa (Pearl Harbour). Here they were able to tap the rich concentration of fish and shellfish in the harbour. Dry-field agriculture predominated, although some irrigated taro grew on the narrow plain between the harbour and the foothills of the Koʻolau Mountains along streams that flowed into the harbour.[72] The Waiʻanae coast fell within the rain shadow area of the Waiʻanae Mountains. Enough rain fell to sustain extensive cultivation of dry-field crops, particularly ʻuala. Some irrigation was possible in the upper reaches of larger valleys near the watershed of the

---

68   Campbell (1967), p. 109.
69   Clerke, in Beaglehole (1967), 3:1, p. 571; Handy & Handy (1972), pp. 271–72, 452–60; Kirch (1985), pp. 107–13; and Stannard (1989), p. 57.
70   King, in Beaglehole (1967), 3:1, p. 610; and Handy & Handy (1972), pp. 271–75.
71   Vancouver (1801), bk 3, pp. 360–65; Menzies (1920), pp. 23–24; Handy & Handy (1972), pp. 235, 270, 278–84; and Kirch (1985), pp. 107, 116–17.
72   Gilbert J. McAllister, *Archaeology of Oʻahu*, Bernice P. Bishop Museum Bulletin 104 (Honolulu: 1933), p. 29; Handy & Handy (1972), pp. 469–70; Kirch (1985), p. 107; and Stannard (1989), p. 24.

Wai'anae Mountains. The Wai'anae coast provided good offshore fishing but, Wai'anae was remote from the centres of power, and its ali'i do not seem to have been influential players in O'ahu politics.[73]

The interior of 'Ewa and Wai'anae, between the two mountain ranges, was sparsely populated. It was traversed by trails linking Puuloa to the Waialua coast, and the Wai'anae coast through Kolekole Pass.[74] The population of the Waialua district lived mainly on the coastal plain of O'ahu's north-west coast. This plain was highly cultivated, despite low rainfall at the coast, thanks to streams that had their sources deep in the Ko'olau Mountains. Captain Charles Clerke, an officer on the Cook expedition, described the land around Waimea Bay as 'a fine expanse of Low Land bounteously cloath'd with Verdure, on which were situated many large Villages and extensive plantations'.[75] The district did not have good offshore fishing and its coastal waters were largely unprotected by reefs.

The mō'ī of O'ahu drew the core of their support in this period from Kona and Ko'olaupoko. Linked by the Nu'uanu Pass and the eastern coastal plain, their combined resources provided perhaps the most concentrated resource base in the archipelago. Waikiki, Nu'uanu and Kailua are mentioned as royal residences or patrilineal estates of 18th-century mō'ī. The unification of O'ahu seems to have been a relatively late event and 18th-century traditions refer to armed resistance to O'ahu mō'ī from ali'i in 'Ewa and Wai'anae, and, to a lesser extent, Waialua and Ko'olauloa.[76]

O'ahu's Waialua coast faces Kaua'i, the oldest of the inhabited islands (see Figure 7). Kaua'i's mountainous core was heavily eroded over centuries to form broad valleys that deposited large alluvial fans at the coast. The heavy rainfall in the interior centred on Mount Wai'ale'ale, and gave rise to a number of significant waterways.[77] Hawaiian traditions suggest the Kahakumakalina family provided most Kaua'i mō'ī up until the late 18th century. From an early period, their principal residence was at Wailua in the district of Puna. This was one of the most sacred sites in

---

73 Vancouver (1801), bk 3, pp. 365–66; Handy & Handy (1972), pp. 271, 275–76; R.C. Green, *Makaha Valley – Prior to 1880 A.D.*, Pacific Anthropological Records no. 31 (Honolulu: Bernice P. Bishop Museum, 1980), esp. p. 75; and Kirch (1985), pp. 107–08.
74 John Papa I'i, *Fragments of Hawaiian History* (Honolulu: Bernice P. Bishop Museum, 1959), pp. 89 ff.; and Kirch (1985), p. 108.
75 Clerke, in Beaglehole (1967), 3:1, pp. 572–73; King, in Beaglehole (1967), 3:1, pp. 584, 610; Handy & Handy (1972), pp. 271, 275, 467; Kirch (1985), p. 108; and Kirch & Sahlins (1992).
76 Fornander (1969), pp. 270–82, 289–91, 297; and Handy & Handy (1972), pp. 278, 480.
77 Handy & Handy (1972), pp. 269–70; and Kirch (1985), pp. 99–100.

the archipelago, and there were a large number of heiau in its vicinity. Wailua was situated on the lower reaches of the Wailua River, the largest waterway in the islands. The river enabled the large-scale cultivation of wet taro. Breadfruit was another prominent food source in this area. Just north of Wailua was another extensive area of irrigated taro cultivation at Kapaʻa. The third major population centre of Puna was at Hulēʻia in the south where good offshore fishing supplemented fishponds, wet taro and ʻuala. The combined resources of Puna and its political dominance on Kauaʻi suggest it had a considerable population.[78]

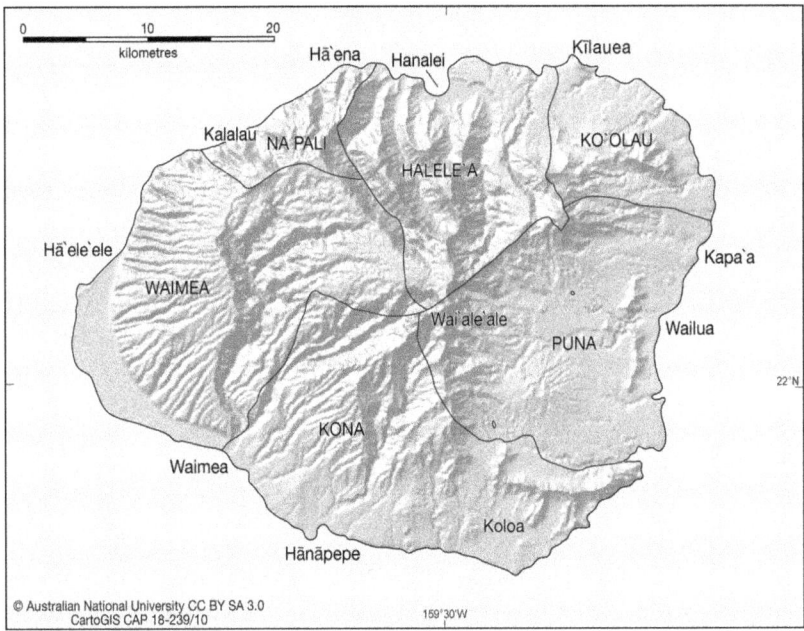

Figure 7: Kauaʻi
Source: CartoGIS, The Australian National University.

To the north and west of Puna were the three windward districts of Koʻolau, Haleleʻa and Nā Pali. Broad fertile valleys with permanent streams supported large-scale irrigated taro complexes in Koʻolau and Haleleʻa. Cultivation was particularly concentrated in the Hanalei Bay area of Haleleʻa, where a number of valleys converged to produce a substantial coastal plain of fertile alluvial soil. The valleys and the plain were

---

78 Fornander (1969), pp. 291, 293; Handy & Handy (1972), pp. 152–53, 269, 423, 425; and Kirch (1985), pp. 99–100.

extensively irrigated, and fishponds dotted the coastal plain. In contrast, Nā Pali consisted of deep, but narrow, valleys separated by razorback ridges and coastal cliffs. Most valleys seem to have been cultivated to some degree and, today, many still show signs of ancient irrigation systems. The Nā Pali coast was a rich deep-sea fishing area. While the combined population of these three windward districts was probably large, this does not seem to have translated into political influence. Puna remained dominant, and what opposition there was usually emanated from the large leeward district of Kona.[79]

The large leeward district of Kona contained the whole south-western part of the island. Although it was significantly drier than the other half of Kaua'i, it extended into the rain-drenched central plateau and included two large, permanently flowing watercourses. These flowed down the Waimea and Hanapepe valleys and allowed the cultivation of irrigated taro alongside dry-field crops up to 12 kilometres inland. The southern coast, east of Waimea, supported dry-field cultivation, particularly of 'uala. Breadfruit thrived along most of the coast between Waimea and Wailua. This coast seems to have supported many people, judging from Cook's observation that it had many villages. The Koloa area may have formed the third significant centre of population in Kona after Waimea and Hanapepe.[80] The island of Ni'ihau lay off the Kona coast and had a relationship with Kaua'i that was similar to Lāna'i's with Maui. Kaua'i dominated Ni'ihau politically. Low-lying and drought-prone, Ni'ihau was home to a population who depended on yam cultivation and temporarily abandoned their island during severe droughts and sought refuge on Kaua'i.[81] Waimea was a rich resource base for the I'ihiwalani family, the junior branch of the royal line, to pursue their rivalry with their senior relatives in Wailua.[82]

---

79 Handy & Handy (1972), pp. 421 (Ko'olau), 269, 417 (Halelea), and 269, 414 (Nā Pali); Timothy K. Earle *Economic and Social Organization of a Complex Chiefdom — Halelea District, Kauai, Hawaii*, University of Michigan – Anthropological Paper no. 63 (Ann Arbor: 1978), p. 9; and Kirch (1985), p. 99.
80 Cook, in Beaglehole (1967), 3:1, pp. 264, 269–72, 427; Clerke, in Beaglehole (1967), 3:1, p. 575; Samwell, in Beaglehole (1967), 3:2, p. 1082; Handy & Handy (1972), pp. 152–53, 269–70, 275, 393, 429, 477; Cordy (1972), p. 396; and Kirch (1985), p. 99.
81 Cook, in Beaglehole (1967), 3:1, pp. 275–79; Vancouver (1801) bk 3, p. 386; Handy & Handy (1972), pp. 432–34; and Kirch (1985), p. 166.
82 Fornander (1969), p. 293.

The translation of observations on settlement patterns into actual population figures is a difficult task. No accurate census of the Hawaiian population was taken until well into the 19th century, and few areas were visited for any length of time by Cook's expedition. Regional settlement surveys by archaeologists help fill the gaps in places. Land records from the mid-19th century also help illustrate settlement patterns, although change during the intervening decades must be allowed for. Until recently, most estimates of the Hawaiian population in 1778 were based upon King's observations. King initially estimated the population to be 500,000, but later revised this down to 400,000. His figures were based on house counts at Kealakekua Bay and Waimea on Kaua'i. These were then extrapolated to cover the length of coastline that King estimated to be inhabited. He estimated that around a quarter of the coastline was inhabited, with little or no settlement of the interior. Most modern scholars have estimated the Hawaiian population in 1778 at between 200,000 and 300,000. The lack of firm evidence, however, means that these estimates are largely speculation.[83]

In 1989, David Stannard proposed a radical revision of the Hawaiian population in 1778 to at least 800,000. He attacked the rather shaky basis of most previous estimates, and suggested King's figure was a considerable underestimate. More than a quarter of the coastline was occupied, including marginal areas, as were inland zones. He suggests that Kealakekua Bay and Waimea did not represent the most densely populated areas in the islands, as both were in leeward zones where rainfall patterns restricted cultivation. He asserted that windward areas with more consistent rainfall probably supported greater population densities than most leeward areas.

Stannard supported his upward revision of the Hawaiian population by providing evidence to show that this was possible according to the islands' potential agricultural production and accepted models of population growth. Stannard argues that such growth rates were not significantly curtailed by traditional warfare, infanticide, abortion, sacrificial killings or pre-European disease and general health. He notes that rapid and significant population decline among populations not previously exposed to European diseases usually followed first contacts with Europeans. Stannard points out that to take account of the impact of introduced

---

83 Stannard (1989), pp. 2–14; Terry L. Hunt, 'Book Review of David Stannard, *Before the Horror*', *Pacific Studies* (Laie), vol. 13 (3), 1990, 256; and P.V. Kirch, (1990b), p. 394.

disease, Hawai'i State statistician Robert Schmitt's contact population should be much higher, as it is nearly the same as missionary William Ellis's estimate of the population four decades later (see Table 1).[84]

Stannard's study prompted much debate. Most responses have been positive, but a number of valid criticisms have been raised. His negative assessment of the carrying capacity of Kealakekua Bay and Waimea relative to windward areas underestimates the productivity of these areas, and exaggerates the difference between leeward and windward production. His claim that windward chiefs usually prevailed in battle over leeward chiefs is not supported by Hawaiian traditions in general, and certainly not by the one reference he cites to back up his claim. Stannard tends to rely on average carrying capacity rather than the more significant denominator, the carrying capacity of areas during drought and other hard times. None of these points, however, invalidate Stannard's criticism of previous population estimates. They suggest that Stannard's estimate needs modification rather than radical alteration.[85]

Table 1: Population estimates for Hawai'i

Island	1779 (King)	1779 (Schmitt)	1779 (Stannard)	1823 (Ellis)
Hawai'i	150,000	90,000	340,000	85,000
Maui	65,400	52,000	260,331	65,082
Kaho'olawe	?	?	?	?
Lāna'i	?	3,500	11,879	2,970
Moloka'i	?	9,000	44,549	11,137
O'ahu	76,200	42,000	220,927	55,231
Kaua'i	64,000	25,000	81,502	20,375
Ni'ihau	?	750	7,774	1,944
Total	355,600	222,250	966,962	241,739

Sources: Schmitt (1971), p. 242; Stannard (1989), p. 54; Kirch (2010), p. 138.

Estimating the indigenous population of Hawai'i in the era of Kamehameha I with any degree of accuracy is impossible. What is more important for this study is the relative distribution of the population. This study generally supports Stannard's argument for an upward revision of Hawaiian

---

84   Stannard (1989), pp. 29, 37–45 (agricultural production), 32–37 (population growth models), 45–50, 60.
85   Kirch (2010), pp. 31–33, 128–31; P.V. Kirch, 'Review of David Stannard, *Before the Horror*', *The Contemporary Pacific*, vol. 2, Fall 1990b, 395; and Hunt (1990), p. 260.

population estimates. Deaths resulting from warfare and sacrifice seem to have been relatively low, but estimates of the typical ratio of combatants to total population argue for a population in excess of Schmitt's figure. The review of settlement patterns supports Stannard's speculation about the extent of Hawaiian settlement, and of the agricultural potential of the archipelago. However, the fragility of overextending agricultural capacity in areas of unreliable rainfall was also noted. The diversity of settlement concentrations revealed by the above locality survey argues against generalising from particular localities (see Figure 8). Windward localities, such as Hilo Bay, Nā Wai 'Ehā and Ko'olaupoko, were probably more productive than Kealakekua Bay and Waimea, as Stannard claims, but other windward localities, such as eastern Hāmākua on Hawai'i and Hāmākuapoko on Maui, were probably not as well populated. Furthermore, North Kona and leeward Kohala were probably more densely populated than either Kealakekua Bay or Waimea. While Schmitt and Stannard agree on the population ratios between islands, this is largely due to their use of Ellis's 1823 estimates for each island. By this time, disease and increased mobility may have distorted traditional population patterns. Our review of local resources suggests population estimates for O'ahu and Kaua'i may err on the low side.

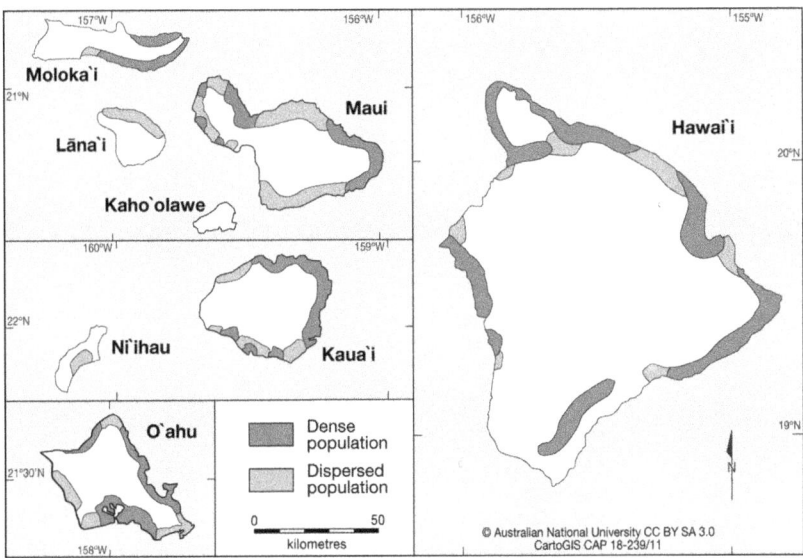

Figure 8: Possible population distribution, 1778

Source: CartoGIS, The Australian National University.

The distribution of resources just described conferred distinct advantages on the occupants of certain favoured localities. But the diffuse nature of power within moku restricted the degree to which such geographical advantages could be converted into lasting political benefits. The expectation of reciprocity underlying maka'āinana obedience to sacred leaders, and the limited coercive power of those leaders relative to subordinate ali'i, combined to restrain the concentration of power by mō'ī. The relative power of the leaders of different localities varied over time. The pursuit of status and power by individual mō'ī, and the pressures caused by expanding populations in a variety of local environments, altered the relationship between localities over time. Environmental constraints on economic activity and social and political barriers to the expansion of power by mō'ī were often challenged. Occasionally they were pushed back. Unification was possible, but by no means certain.

3

The Hawaiian Political Transformation from 1770 to 1796

No one alive in 1778 would have predicted that the Hawaiian Islands would be unified in their lifetime, or that Kamehameha would be the chief to bring it about. To understand how the potential for unification noted by scholars became a reality requires a detailed examination of political and military structural transformations that picked up momentum after 1770. Robert Hommon discusses global writings on warfare and state formation in *The Ancient Hawaiian State*, including the work of Charles Tilly and Robert Carneiro, and makes a strong connection between the two. Hommon concludes that warfare was a causative link but not a crucial factor in Hawaiian state formation because war was pursued by states and non-states alike. Rather, to Hommon, the key influence on Hawaiian state formation was the political innovation of 'both holding centralised political power and delegating it'.[1] This and the following chapter contest Hommon's dichotomy by arguing that changes to the nature of political and military power in the late 18th century were interrelated. Escalating chiefly rivalries spurred military reforms and forced chiefs to delegate authority to accommodate a structure of warfare that mobilised and relied upon a greater proportion of the polities' residents and resources. Hawaiian society became more militarised as chiefs threw off the vestiges

---

1   Hommon (2013), pp. 238–40.

of sacred power that had come to constrain them, and altered their warfare to make it more efficient, even though this resulted in an erosion of chiefly status on the battlefield.

The structure of consent: Religious beliefs and social relationships

Hawaiian polities on the eve of Kamehameha's wars of unification are best characterised as politically advanced chiefdoms according to the standard framework outlined in Chapter 1. The authority of the chiefs rested heavily upon their sacred status. Secular power was relatively loose and decentralised, with limited development of centralised coercive and administrative structures. Yet, by the late 18th century, Hawaiian society was moving towards instituting features that are more usually associated with early states. Localised kinship affiliations were weak and the courts of ruling chiefs contained the seeds of centralised administrative structures. But, perhaps the most noticeable feature of this period was the tension between the increasing resort to coercive power and continued reliance on sacred legitimacy. By 1770, Hawaiian chiefs were reaching the limits of sacred power.

Religious ritual played a prominent role in the organisation of Hawaiian life in this period. Gods and spirits of dead ancestors influenced the affairs of mortals. Natural phenomena were interpreted as supernatural omens, and all actions took into consideration the utterances of spirit mediums and oracles. The gods were appealed to for protection from hostile forces and ceremonies involving prayers and offerings were enacted seeking assistance in various undertakings.

The four major gods: Kū, Lono, Kāne and Kanaloa, were general categories rather than specific gods. Each god category encompassed a wide variety of particular forms. For example, Kū, in his violent form, was the war god of the Hawaiian chiefs yet, through this association with war, Kū was also connected with prosperity and fertility as the dividends of victory. There was no fixed hierarchy within the Hawaiian pantheon. Because of often multiple associations, the relative importance of gods depended upon the context in which they were worshipped. Changing hierarchies and associations within the pantheon occurred as the perceived needs of supplicants varied in time and place.[2]

While the Hawaiians did not distinguish between supernatural and human agency as modern European society does, they did draw a sharp distinction between kapu (sacred) and noa (non-sacred) elements. Kapu status, which carried restrictions to isolate its possessor from other elements, signalled a close association with the supernatural world, whose powers were so great that they needed to be approached with caution. Valerio Valeri maintains that improper contact between kapu and noa elements also threatened the efficacy of kapu elements in Hawai'i. Revised interpretations in the 1980s, however, suggest that noa referred to the subject in question being free of the restrictions that kapu status conferred. This interpretation is consistent with revisions of kapu and noa elsewhere in Polynesia. It is now believed that, apart from certain highly sacred individuals who were always kapu, most men and certain women moved between states of kapu and noa depending on circumstances.[3]

Daily activities were regulated by a relatively fixed and regular system of prohibitions. These were also known as kapu. Kapu intruded into all aspects of life, reinforcing social divisions by restricting contact between genders, separating sacred and profane classes, and dictating the conduct of daily activities such as eating, work and leisure. Kapu also served to organise the year's activities. The year was divided into the ceremonial periods of Kau and Ho'oilo, which roughly corresponded to the dry and rainy seasons respectively. During Kau, four kapu periods were observed each month, each of two to three days' duration. The attendance of chiefs and priests at temples was required during these periods, and commoners' activities

---

2   On Hawaiian religion in general, see Valeri (1985a), pp. 4, 13, 31, 58–66. On divination, see Thomas G. Thrum (ed.), *Fornander Collection of Hawaiian Antiquities and Folklore*, vol. 6 (Honolulu: Bernice P. Bishop Museum, 1919–20), pp. 70–86. On the Hawaiian pantheon, see Malo (1951), pp. 83–85; Mary W. Beckwith, (ed.), *Kepelino's Traditions of Hawaii* (Honolulu: Bernice P. Bishop Museum, 1937), p. 10; Kamakau (1961), pp. 200–03; Handy & Handy (1972), p. 14; Rev. John F. Pogue, *The Mooolelo of Ancient Hawaii*, Charles W. Kenn (trans.) (Honolulu: Topgallant, 1978 (1858)), pp. 45–48; Valerio Valeri, 'The Transformation of a Transformation: A Structural Essay on an Aspect of Hawaiian History (1809–1819)', *Social Analysis*, vol. 10, May 1982, 4; and Valeri (1985a), pp. 9, 187.
3   See Valeri (1985a), pp. 84–86, 111; and Caroline Ralston, 'Sanctity and Power: Gender in Polynesian History – Introduction', *Journal of Pacific History*, vol. 22 (3), 1987, 115.

were restricted.⁴ In Hoʻoilo, a harvest festival known as the makahiki dominated the ceremonial calendar. During the makahiki in Hoʻoilo, events observed during Kau were suspended, as were temple building and warfare while Lono, as the god of fertility, achieved temporary ascendancy over the war god form of Kū.

The makahiki season roughly coincided with the period of October to January on the European calendar and centred upon the collection of first fruits' offerings to Lono in thanks for a successful crop. In its final phase, images of the god were carried around each island. According to Kēlou Kamakau, the passage of the god image around the island lasted 23 days. A strict kapu on warfare and offshore fishing applied during this time. The giving of tribute to Lono by each local community, public feasts and entertainment – such as dancing and boxing contests – marked the images' journey. The makahiki ended with the rite of Kaliʻi, in which the followers of Kū reasserted the dominance of their god, and the images of Lono were set adrift in a canoe. At the end of the makahiki, the paramount chief would dedicate a temple to Lono in preparation for a year of peace, or to Kū in preparation for war. The dedication of such a temple involved a major commitment in terms of labour and offerings, as well as a long and complex ceremony.⁵

The kapu divided Hawaiian society in to two distinct groups: the chiefs (aliʻi), and the commoners (makaʻāinana). Although both were believed to have descended from the god Papa and his consort Wakea, only the aliʻi were deemed to be sacred. This was because the aliʻi were considered to have descended directly from the gods while the makaʻāinana were only connected to the gods through junior branches of lineages. Status was more a function of genealogical seniority than of age or gender. A person from a genealogically senior branch outranked older generations of junior branches. Chiefs were ranked according to the purity of their descent from the gods. Each rank was associated with a personal kapu that was conferred at birth. The higher the rank, the stricter the kapu.

---

4   On kapu in general, see Sahlins (1981), p. 52; and Levin (1968), p. 413. On the annual ritual cycle, see Malo (1951), pp. 31–33, 240; Beckwith (1937), pp. 80–84; Pogue (1978), pp. 40–45; and Valeri (1985a), pp. 194–98. On social kapu, see Caroline Ralston, 'Hawaii 1778–1854: Some Aspects of Makaʻāinana Response to Rapid Cultural Change', *Journal of Pacific History*, vol.19 (1), 1984, 23–24. On monthly kapu, see Iʻī (1959), pp. 33–46.

5   Malo (1951), pp. 142–52; Thrum, vol. 6 (1919–20), p. 40; Handy & Handy (1972), pp. 329–68; Valeri (1985a), pp. 200–33; Sahlins (1981), pp. 18–30; Marshall Sahlins, *Islands of History* (Ann Arbor, University of Michigan Press, 1985), pp. 115–22; and Marshall Sahlins, 'Captain Cook at Hawaii', *Journal of the Polynesian Society*, vol. 98 (4), 1989, 387–93.

3. THE HAWAIIAN POLITICAL TRANSFORMATION FROM 1770 TO 1796

As sacredness was hereditary, marriage was an important determinant of rank. Because of the association of high rank with closeness to the gods, much importance was attached to the rank of candidates for the part of paramount chief (mōʻī). Mōʻī and their nuclear families sought to conceive unions that would produce offspring of the highest possible rank. The ranks that could result from various unions and their associated kapu are outlined in Table 2.[6]

The ruling chief, and his offspring from unions with high-ranking female chiefs formed a small, incestuous group that made up the senior branch of the chiefly stratum. They were known as the aliʻi nui. All other aliʻi were viewed as collateral junior branches of the chiefly stratum and, therefore, less suitable candidates to be paramount, although they were by no means wholly excluded from contention. The dividing line between junior aliʻi and makaʻāinana was defined by the individual's relationship to the incumbent mōʻī. Chiefly status was determined at the accession of a new ruler during the hale nauā ceremony, where a link with the ruler's ancestral line was sought. In general, an aliʻi's importance varied inversely with the number of generations required to prove the link. According to David Malo, the questioning only extended to the 10th ascending generation.[7] Failure to prove such a link condemned lesser aliʻi to the ranks of the makaʻāinana. There does not seem to have been any upward mobility in rank from the status of makaʻāinana. By the late 18th century the rift between aliʻi and makaʻāinana was profound. Just as incestuous marriages kept the senior branch of the chiefly elite small and selective, the hale nauā ceremony kept the ranks of the aliʻi restricted. Makaʻāinana did not maintain lengthy family genealogies, and made up the vast majority of the population.

The relationship between the mōʻī and his makaʻāinana subjects was one of mutual obligations and duties. The makaʻāinana provided labour and taxes in kind to support their ruler in return for his mediation with the most powerful gods to secure bountiful harvests, and protection from potential threats. The aliʻi nui were able to do this because of their close connection with the gods. Indeed the highest ranking aliʻi seem to have been considered

---

6   Levin (1968), p. 408; Malo (1951), p. 52; Pogue (1978), p. 60; Lilikalā Kameʻeleihiwa, 'Land and the Promise of Capitalism: A Dilemma for the Hawaiian Chiefs of the 1848 Māhele', PhD Thesis, University of Hawaiʻi at Mānoa, 1986, p. 24; and Sahlins (1985), pp. 20–21. See also Levin (1968), pp. 408–11; Malo (1951), pp. 54–57, 80; and Beckwith (1937), pp. 195–96.
7   Malo (1951), p. 192; Hommon (1976), pp. 27–48; Hommon (1987), p. 57; and Kirch (1984), p. 57.

to possess certain attributes that were characteristic of gods. Depictions of ali'i and gods closely echoed each other in terms of their ranks, associated kapu, and insignia. Whether ali'i nui were considered to be living gods is uncertain, however, it is clear that deceased ali'i of the senior branch were considered to be 'aumakua (ancestral spirits) of their successors. In 1819, for example, 'A house was built for Kamehameha's bones for the purpose of deifying him so that he could become an 'aumakua – a family god'.[8] 'Aumakua were believed to influence the affairs of humans.

The significance attached to religious ritual meant that priests (kahuna) occupied an important role in Hawaiian society as appellants to, and interpreters of the gods. There were a number of regular orders of kahuna as well as less conventional kahuna that were usually associated with prophecy or sorcery. Unexpected deaths were often put down to sorcery, and an important member of any mō'ī's personal pantheon was his sorcery deity to assist him against his enemies and their sorcerers. War gods and sorcery gods were used to destroy rivals. The importance attached to these gods by ruling chiefs is suggested by their epithet: *mau akua 'imi aupuai* (gods who sought kingdoms).[9] High priests (kahuna nui) were closely linked to high chiefs. Knowledge of the most important ritual and learning was restricted to these two groups. A detailed account of the Hoomanamana priestly order, which was recorded in the mid-19th century, suggests that these orders were organised into specialised divisions, such as prophecy and medicine, each of which was associated with a specific god.[10] One had to excel at all of the specialties within one's particular priesthood before being considered worthy of becoming a high priest. Most high-ranking kahuna seem to have been drawn from the ali'i class. Senior kahuna advised mō'ī upon ritual and spiritual matters, and were much valued as a significant part of any ruler's legitimacy rested upon his ritual efficacy. Some kahuna nui, like Kalanihula of the Hawai'i, served as advisers to successive generations of mō'ī, and were invaluable advisers on secular aspects of rule as well as ritual. Others had

---

8   Kahananui (1984), p. 211. On mō'ī as intermediary between gods and humans, see Valeri (1985a), pp. 86–87; Levin (1968), pp. 407–08; and Kame'eleihiwa (1986), pp. 34, 43. On mō'ī as 'aumakua, see Valeri (1985a), pp. 145–53; Sahlins (1981), p. 25; Marshall Sahlins, *How 'Natives' Think: About Captain Cook, For Example* (University of Chicago Press, 1995), p. 25; Malo (1951), pp. 104–06; and Beckwith (1937), p. 13. On the afterlife, see Thrum, vol. 5 (1918–19), p. 572; and Pogue (1978), pp. 56–58.
9   On priests in general, see Malo (1951), pp. 112–14; Sheldon Dibble, *A History of the Sandwich Islands* (Honolulu: Thos. G. Thrum, 1909), p. 83; King, in Beaglehole (1967), 3:1, p. 629; Valeri (1985a), p. 138; Levin (1968), pp. 410–11; and Sahlins (1995), pp. 121–22. On sorcery, see Malo (1951), pp. 96–97; I'ī (1959), p. 8; Vancouver (1801) bk 3, p. 375; and Valeri (1982), p. 25.
10 Thrum, vol. 6 (1919–20), pp. 68–70, 74.

an even more direct connection to the secular power of the high chiefs. Koa, the old priest encountered by James Cook in 1779, had once been a famous warrior.[11]

Table 2: Hawaiian chiefly rank system

Rank	Rank of child	Membership criteria	Associated kapu
Highest	Nī'aupi'o	Parents both of highest rank	Kapu moe
	Pi'o	Offspring of full-sibling marriage of nī'aupi'o rank	Kapu moe
	Naha	Offspring of half-sibling marriage of nī'aupi'o rank	Kapu noho
	Wohi	Offspring of nī'aupi'o, pi'o, or naha father with close female relative	Kapu wohi
	Papa	Offspring of nī'aupi'o, pi'o, or naha mother with a lower ranking chief	
	Lōkea	Offspring of high-ranked father with mother of a relative through younger siblings	
	Lā'au ali'i	Parents are children of high chiefs through secondary matings	
	Kaukau ali'i	Flexible term signifying an inferior or dependent status; descendants of high chiefs through collateral branches	
Lowest	Ali'i noanoa	Literally 'without kapu' – offspring of a high chief and a commoner woman – not recognised as ali'i unless special provision made	

Source: Kirch (2010), p. 36.

The mō'ī remained the supreme mediator between men and the gods. Only the mō'ī and, perhaps, the most senior kahuna could communicate with the most powerful gods of the Hawaiian pantheon. Only ali'i of the senior branch could conduct human sacrifice, the supreme appeal to the gods.[12] This special relationship with the gods was not, however, accepted unquestioningly. Failure to prove the existence of this relationship through the successful completion of temple ritual, and tangible signs of the god's favour like success in war and prosperity in peace, threatened the security of the mō'ī's rule.

---

11   On priests, see Beckwith (1937), pp. 60–62, 140, 192; Malo (1951), p. 149; Hommon (1975), p. 149; and Levin (1968), p. 416. On kahuna as advisers, see Kamakau (1961), p. 173. On Koa, see Sahlins (1995), p. 49, citing James Cook & James King, *A Voyage to the Pacific Ocean … on His Majesty's Ships Resolution and Discovery*, vol. 3 (Dublin: Chamberlaine et al., 1784), pp. 3, 69.
12   Valeri (1985a), pp. 140–42; and Malo (1951), p. 53.

This relationship between the mōʻī and gods was conceived of in terms of mana. Mana was divine energy that could be conferred or withdrawn by the supernatural world. Objects and persons were merely mediums and reservoirs for mana. Mana also derived from the accumulated achievements of ancestors, so that aliʻi attempted to locate and desecrate the secreted remains of their enemies' ancestors. Some emblems of chiefly status were made from the bones of slain rival aliʻi. The ruling chief obtained mana from his sacred status, but this could diminish without concrete achievements. Defeat in warfare and natural disasters within a mōʻī's lands were seen as indications of the god's withdrawal of mana. As such, the leadership was open to challenge by ambitious rivals. The relative mana of rival aliʻi was put to the test in wars between rival ruling chiefs, succession disputes and rebellions. The mōʻī was not always the highest ranking aliʻi. Kamehameha was of the wohi rank and secured the rule of the leeward districts of Hawaiʻi by defeating the higher ranking nīʻaupiʻo aliʻi, Kīwalaʻō.[13]

The sacred and secular aspects of aliʻi power complemented each other, as aliʻi believed favour by the gods would attract many followers, and these followers would provide him with a secular power base with which to achieve what his reputation suggested he was capable of. In other ways, the sacred and secular aspects of a ruler's power were not so compatible. As Valeri notes, 'The [King] thus must maintain his transcendence, to be separated from all men, but at the same time he must enter into a contract with them to demonstrate his power … created by society through a myriad of rules of separation, the king's divinity incurs a debt in relation to society that it must pay sooner or later'.[14]

From sacred to secular power? Balancing coercion and consent

The kapu of the aliʻi was a double-edged sword. This was particularly true of the more demanding kapu of aliʻi of the senior branch. They needed to intervene in worldly affairs to assert their mana, yet did so surrounded and protected by kapu that restrained their actions. Some high-ranking

---

13   Valeri (1985a), pp. 99–100; see also Levin (1968), pp. 403, 410, 414–15; Malo (1951), p. 211; and Jocelyn Linnekin, 'Who Made the Feather Cloaks? A Problem in Hawaiian Gender Relations', *Journal of the Polynesian Society*, vol. 97 (3), 1988, 276, 277.
14   Valeri (1985a), p. 149.

ali'i had to travel at night so that their kapu that required maka'āinana to prostrate themselves in their presence did not disrupt daily activities, and so that the risk of polluting their status by coming into contact with impure persons and objects was lessened.[15]

By the late 18th century, kapu restrictions were being circumvented for political efficacy. A number of high-ranking ali'i interacted with maka'āinana. There are a number of references in Hawaiian traditions to mō'ī personally supervising the improvement of agricultural fields, even down to individual taro patches. Presumably, this involved some contact with the local cultivators, unless instructions were directed through the lesser ali'i who supervised particular localities for the ruler. Kamehameha certainly laboured in his own fields and was said to have been well liked by his maka'āinana subjects. Kalanikūpule, a young ali'i nui from the Maui ruling house, was also much loved by maka'āinana. Kamakau states that he would fraternise with even the humblest of his subjects.[16]

Ali'i nui also participated in battles. Some were killed in combat, and not necessarily by ali'i of similar rank. It is unclear if any rules of combat governed conduct towards ali'i nui in battle. Two incidents from the life of the nī'aupi'o ali'i Kīwala'ō, however, suggest a pattern. According to traditions, when Kīwala'ō intervened in a battle on Maui, he effectively ended the battle as the combatants were obliged to throw down their weapons and prostrate themselves in his presence. Yet, in a later battle at Moku'ōhai on Hawai'i, Kīwala'ō's supporters were routed when his slaying by the lesser ali'i Kalaimoku broke their morale.[17]

At Moku'ōhai, Kamehameha challenged Kīwala'ō for the right to succeed Kalani'ōpu'u as mō'ī of Hawai'i. The stakes were high, and a substantial demonstration of prowess and resolve may have been required to win over wavering supporters. It may also be significant that both Kīwala'ō and Kalaimoku were high-ranking ali'i. In contrast, the fight on Maui was between the forces of two well-established rulers – Kahekili of Maui and Kalani'ōpu'u of Hawai'i. Kamakau's description of Kīwala'ō's intervention here suggests that symbols of his high status were prominently displayed to signal his intentions. While ali'i wore distinctive yellow and red protective cloaks in battle, on this occasion

---

15   Valeri (1985a), p. 149; Malo (1951), pp. 54, 56–57; and I'ī (1959), pp. 51–52, 120.
16   Kamakau (1961), pp. 203 (Kamehameha), and 142–43 (Kalanikūpule).
17   On the battle on Maui, see I'ī (1959), p. 52; and Kamakau (1961), p. 88. On Moku'ōhai, see Kamakau (1961), pp. 120–22.

Kīwalaʻō was dressed in the garments of a chief and attended by Kameʻe-ia-moku bearing the spittoon and Ka-manawa carrying the Kāhili. As Kīwalaʻō advanced, splendidly arrayed, endowed with the kapu of a god and covered with the colors of the rainbow, down fell the fighting men of both sides prostrate to the ground because of his divine rank as a nīʻaupiʻo and the severe tabu that demanded prostration to avoid facing the sacred back of a chief. The soldiers of Maui wished to ignore the tabu, regretting the cessation of the fighting, but Kīwalaʻō continued on to Wailuku.[18]

Kīwalaʻō's success in ending the fighting, despite the Maui warriors' desire to press home their advantage, may also have been due to kinship links between prominent aliʻi within the rival camps. Kīwalaʻō was not only the son of Kalaniʻōpuʻu, but was also related to Kahekili. His two attendants, Kameʻeiamoku and Kamanawa, were Kahekili's half-brothers.

Another strategy used to overcome the restraining influence of kapu on the actions of mōʻī was the delegation of ritual obligations to close relatives. Kamehameha made his younger brother, Kealiʻimoikai, the sometime personal guardian of the ruler's (Kamehameha) kapu, thus freeing himself to more actively pursue secular and potentially defiling affairs of state. When Kamehameha had to cut short his ceremonial duties during the makahiki season in 1794 to accompany George Vancouver to Kealakekua Bay, he designated his half-brother to stand in for him, after first consulting with his kahuna.[19]

In some instances, kapu were modified to accommodate chiefly interactions with Europeans. But, in all cases, due consideration was given to ritual requirements. According to Vancouver, Kamehameha's reluctant modification of the 1794–95 makahiki came about because of Vancouver's threat to take his trade elsewhere. In the previous year, Vancouver's provisioning at Kealakekua Bay had been delayed while Kamehameha was in the process of being ritually purified as the makahiki drew to a close. Even in 1794, however, religious considerations were not overlooked, despite Vancouver's threat; makahiki ceremonies were merely delayed one lunar month to accommodate him.[20] Vancouver also relates how, in January 1794, the 10-day kapu of 'Hahcoo' (Haiku) that pertained to fishing was shortened by Kamehameha in the district that Vancouver

---

18 Kamakau (1961), p. 88.
19 Vancouver (1801), bk 5, p. 18.
20 Vancouver (1801), bk 5, p. 18 ; Valeri (1985a), pp. 229–30; and Sahlins (1989), p. 389.

was visiting to allow him to be supplied with fish. Vancouver was under the impression that this was allowable in Hawaiian custom if the 'king' so desired.[21]

By the late 18th century, observation of the makahiki may have been considered by rival mōʻī as merely a convenient breathing space between campaigns. The makahiki was a time when winter weather disrupted movement and much attention focused upon the planting of crops to take advantage of winter rains. The fact that a religious procession went throughout the mōʻī's domains and demanded offerings for Lono is seen by some as an indication that the makahiki served as a means of reasserting his power, with the offerings serving as de facto tribute.[22] Table A1, Appendix 1, shows that armies remained mobilised in the field during a number of makahiki seasons. Marshall Sahlins suggests that the makahiki kapu on warfare only applied when the image of Lono made its brief island circuit of around three weeks duration.[23] Whether this represented a compromise on earlier practice is unclear. Anthropologist Gananath Obeyesekere claims that fighting took place on Maui during the 1778–79 makahiki circuit, although he does not make the important distinction between fighting and mobilisation made here.[24]

It is apparent that there were tensions between aliʻi and kahuna during the 1770s. During Cook's visits to Kealakekua Bay, certain kahuna of Lono were friendly to the Europeans, even after the outbreak of hostilities between the English and supporters of the local mōʻī, Kalaniʻōpuʻu. Although Obeyesekere asserts that the priests identified with Lono were acting on Kalaniʻōpuʻu's orders, Cook's officers believed he was angry with them for giving Cook permission to use a temple site (heiau) without his consent. Captain Charles Clerke and others in Cook's expedition noted that the priests of Lono disliked the mōʻī's local representative, Koa. Gavan Daws has hypothesised that the apparent deification of Cook as Lono may have been an attempt by the kahuna of Lono to reassert themselves against the now politically dominant cult of Kū by associating their god with the power of the Europeans.[25]

---

21 Vancouver (1801), bk 5, pp. 30–31.
22 Peebles & Kus (1977), pp. 425–26.
23 Sahlins (1989), pp. 397–98, citing Kēlou Kamakau in Thrum, vol. 6 (1919–20), p. 40; Sahlins (1995), p. 26.
24 Gananath Obeyesekere, *The Apotheosis of Captain Cook: European Mythmaking in the Pacific* (Princeton University Press, 1992), p. 81; and Sahlins's reply (1995), pp. 36–37.
25 King, in Beaglehole (1967), 3:1, pp. 550–53, 559–60; Clerke, in Beaglehole (1967), 3:1, pp. 543–45. See also Sahlins (1985), pp. 124–25; Sahlins (1989), p. 400; Daws (1968a), p. 23; and Obeyesekere (1992), pp. 42, 92–94.

Sahlins argues that the followers of Kū and Lono conceived differing relationships with Cook. Kalaniʻōpuʻu gave his feather cloak and helmet to Cook as well as a royal flywhisk – all symbols of royal kapu status. In contrast, the high priest Kaʻo dressed Cook in a mantle of red tapa cloth. The same was done to images of gods in heiau. To Sahlins, this suggests that the mōʻī represented Cook in his own social image as a divine warrior, while the kahuna nui represented Cook as a manifestation of a god. Kalaniʻōpuʻu's exchange of names with Cook, and the latter's gifts to the mōʻī, as well as the Lono priests' surrender of iron adzes given to them by the British are all seen by Sahlins as being consistent with the ritual transfer of sovereignty from Lono back to Kū that ended every makahiki. Cook's out-of-season return a few days after his departure was therefore seen as a challenge to the sovereignty of Kalaniʻōpuʻu and Kū. It was the Kaliʻi ceremony in reverse. Kalaniʻōpuʻu's retainers naturally resisted Cook's attempts to take their mōʻī to sea, just as Lono's adherents ritually resisted the mōʻī's wading ashore to usurp Lono during the Kaliʻi ceremony.[26]

Other instances of kahuna seemingly coming into conflict with aliʻi occurred in this period. In the 1780s, such a conflict resulted in the ruler of Oʻahu, Kahahana, killing his kahuna nui, Kaopulupulu, after the latter's prolonged opposition to Kahahana's policy of appeasement towards his uncle, Kahekili of Maui.[27] While the kahuna nui of some priesthoods associated with the worship of Kū and Lono almost became hereditary, and had land granted to them by mōʻī,[28] the priesthoods do not appear to have developed independent power bases. What influence they exercised in the secular realm derived from the fortunes of their particular aliʻi, and the continued, although perhaps diminishing, importance of ritual to chiefly rule.

Although mōʻī do not seem to have tolerated open opposition from kahuna at this stage, they were still not willing or able to totally break with them. A major part of the ruler's authority still appears to have rested upon his sacred status, particularly with regard to the makaʻāinana majority. Hawaiian traditions abound with examples of rulers who were overthrown when they became unpopular for neglecting their ritual duties. Support

---

26   Sahlins (1985), pp. 123, 128–29; Sahlins (1995), pp. 60, 81, 132–34; refutes Obeyesekere (1992), pp. 58, 137–40, 187.
27   Fornander (1969), p. 278; Kamakau (1961), pp. 133–35.
28   Beckwith (1937), pp. 60–62, 140, 192; Malo (1951), pp. 149, 190; Hommon (1975), p. 149; and Levin (1968), pp. 416–17.

for Kahahana, for example, is said to have weakened significantly after his murder of Kaopulupulu.[29] The fact that some rulers sought the advice of renowned kahuna from outside of their realms suggests that their concerns went beyond purely secular affairs of state. Kamehameha, for example, sought the advice of the famous Kauaʻi soothsayer Kapoukahi, then resident on Oʻahu.[30] Some orders were, however, privileged over others. Sahlins notes that Kamehameha continued his predecessor Kalaniʻōpuʻu's practice of favouring the priests of Kū over those of Lono, with the latter having little influence in affairs of state.[31]

The modification of kapu and the subsidiary role of kahuna in Hawaiian politics do not necessarily reflect irreligious attitudes among the chiefly elite. Rather the beliefs of the aliʻi were influenced by the demand and need for tangible benefits in the competitive arena of chiefly politics. Although the gods were believed to be the source of power, their power rested upon men's worship, and particularly upon the sacrifices made to them. Worship was usually referred to as hoʻomana, translated by Valeri as 'to cause one to have mana, to empower'.[32] Gods and mōʻī needed adherents, and could lose support for not producing benefits. When the son of the aliʻi Kalaimoku died from a wound received during a sparring exercise with spears, anger at their god for allowing this to happen was expressed. Vancouver noted that a kapu due to begin on 23 January 1794 was suspended 'to manifest that they were offended with their deity for the death of this young chief'.[33] The kapu was again observed soon after, but only from sunset to the following sunrise instead of the usual two nights and one whole day, again to signal the community's resentment at their god. Kalaimoku ignored all kapu following the death of his son until 29 January.

Makaʻāinana seem to have generally adhered to the kapu of the gods and that of the aliʻi. The fact that secular sanctions against kapu-breakers existed, and were occasionally used, suggests that this adherence was not entirely due to belief in the underlying assumptions of the kapu system. To assess the degree to which the threat of chiefly punitive actions dictated

---

29 Fornander (1969), pp. 278–79. On Kahahana, see Kamakau (1961), pp. 134–35. On rebellions against mōʻī who neglected ritual duties, see Malo (1951), p. 252.
30 Fornander (1969), pp. 239–40.
31 Sahlins (1995), pp. 133–34.
32 Valeri (1985a), p. 98.
33 Vancouver (1801), bk 5, pp. 22, 27 (Jan. 1794).

makaʻāinana obedience, it is necessary to examine evidence on the religious beliefs of makaʻāinana, the conditions under which makaʻāinana lived, and whether they had the ability to change their circumstances.

Makaʻāinana were mainly concerned throughout the year with rituals surrounding subsistence and family affairs. They worshipped ancestral deities and spirits, usually in household shrines or small local shrines. Daily life was mostly influenced by kapu pertaining to gender and age distinctions among kinsmen. The persistence of this type of worship well into the 19th century is testament to the strength of belief at this level. Makaʻāinana also participated in larger agricultural rituals under the auspices of local aliʻi and kahuna of Lono.[34] Lono was a popular god among the makaʻāinana and not only was he worshipped in heiau, he was also the main deity worshipped in domestic shrines. In this respect Lono was 'the mediator between polity and society'.[35] Presumably the kahuna of Lono were the cultural intermediaries between chiefly and commoner cultures, the crucial conveyers of the ideology that justified the Hawaiian social order.[36]

Malo and the 19th-century Hawaiian cultural historian Kepelino state that kahuna were much respected by the common people.[37] The same could not be said, however, for the images of the gods. Ship's surgeon on Cook's expedition David Samwell noted that:

> Tho' they look upon these Idols as their Gods they pay no great reverence to them, for when any of us laughed at them and treated with Contempt even those we supposed the most sacred among them, the Indians instead of being offended, would join with us in ridiculing them and seemed to think as lightly of them as we did; and there was none of them that they would not sell even for trifles.[38]

Obviously such behaviour may reflect a disbelief in the power of idols rather than the gods they represented, and may also be the result of the ambiguities of intercultural interaction.

---

34   On makaʻāinana religious practices, see Malo (1951), pp. 82, 142; Levin (1968), p. 413; Sahlins (1981), p. 52; Hommon (1986), p. 58; and Kirch (1985), p. 7. On persistence of traditional beliefs after 1819, see K.R. Howe, *Where the Waves Fall: A New South Sea Islands History From First Settlement to Colonial Rule* (Sydney: Allen and Unwin, 1984), p. 168.
35   Sahlins (1989), p. 413.
36   Michelle Vovelle, *Ideologies and Mentalities*, Eamon O'Flaherty (trans.) (Cambridge: Polity Press, 1990), pp. 118–25.
37   Malo (1951), pp. 188–90, 197; and Beckwith (1937), p. 132.
38   Samwell, in Beaglehole (1967), 3:2, pp. 1185.

3. THE HAWAIIAN POLITICAL TRANSFORMATION FROM 1770 TO 1796

During Cook's visits, maka'āinana seem to have been genuinely overawed by ali'i nui and obedient of kapu. But in the absence of ali'i nui they were often less willing to adhere to kapu, even in the presence of lesser ali'i acting on behalf of the mō'ī. Incidents abound of maka'āinana meekly acquiescing to high-handed and often violent treatment at the hands of ali'i nui. In January 1778, for example, Cook's expedition saw a double canoe carrying the high-ranking Kaua'i ali'i Kāneoneo simply run over a number of smaller canoes occupied by maka'āinana without the slightest attempt to avoid them. The maka'āinana could not paddle out of the way because Kāneoneo's status demanded that they prostrate themselves face down in his presence.[39] Cook and his officers noted that Kalani'ōpu'u's kapu on trade was only broken when the old mō'ī was absent on campaign with his warriors. In one instance, an ali'i launched a canoe to prevent commoners breaking the kapu and coming out to trade, but he was driven off by a 'musquet fir'd over his head to make him disist'.[40] The maka'āinana continued to trade, apparently undaunted by the prospect of the ali'i's wrath when they returned to shore.

Lesser ali'i, in maintaining order at Kealakekua Bay during the absence of Kalani'ōpu'u, sometimes had to resort to physical force to expel maka'āinana from Cook's vessels. In the absence of the controlling influence of ali'i, crowds of maka'āinana could become quite troublesome. Maka'āinana women were particularly prominent in the infringement of kapu regulating contacts with foreign vessels. They often engaged in the forbidden act of eating kapu food in the company of members of the all-male crew. Such behaviour may explain why Malo claimed that the majority of women were irreligious.[41]

Outside situations involving contacts with Europeans, maka'āinana seem to have rarely offered open resistance to ali'i demands for labour, food tribute and military service. Malo provides the names of eight 'kings' killed by uprisings against their rule. Three were mō'ī, and the others were subordinate ali'i administering lands within their rulers' domains. All the

---

39   Cook, in Beaglehole (1967), 3:1, p. 281.
40   King, in Beaglehole (1967), 3:1, p. 511 (25 Jan. 1779); Samwell, in Beaglehole (1967), 3:2, pp. 1166–67; and Sahlins (1981), p. 49.
41   Malo (1951), p. 82. On maka'āinana in general, see King, in Beaglehole (1967), 3:1, p. 504; Clerke, in Beaglehole (1967), 3:1, p. 596; Samwell, in Beaglehole (1967), 3:1, p. 116; and Nathaniel Portlock, *A Voyage Round the World: But More Particularly to the North-West Coast of America, Performed in 1785, 1786, 1787 and 1788*, Bibliotheca Australiana no. 43 (New York: Da Capo Press, 1968), pp. 62–63. On maka'āinana women in particular, see Sahlins (1981), pp. 46 ff.; and Samwell, in Beaglehole (1967), 3:2, p. 1161.

revolts were said to have been motivated by the abuse of power rather than by a desire to overthrow the concept of divinely ordained aliʻi rule. These so-called 'commoner revolts' were actually led by chiefly rivals of the aliʻi concerned. Individual chiefs changed, but not the rule of chiefs.[42]

The issue of revolts raises the question of whether the relationship between the aliʻi and makaʻāinana gave the latter reason to seek change. Makaʻāinana spent most of their lives within highly localised units known as ahupuaʻa. These were land divisions with defined boundaries. The name ahupuaʻa derives from the fact that their boundaries were marked by altars (ahu) dedicated to Lono as rain god through offerings of hog's heads (puaʻa).[43] All of the inhabited islands in the chain were divided into ahupuaʻa. Most ahupuaʻa were only a few miles wide at the coast and extended some distance inland. In general they were relatively economically self-sufficient. Ahupuaʻa were divided into smaller sections that were held and worked by extended households of makaʻāinana. It appears that most households were able to be self-supporting from the lands they worked and, while there were some exchange networks between relations in food staples, these were probably conducted within the ahupuaʻa or, at most, with neighbouring ahupuaʻa. Makaʻāinana social organisation was based largely on affinal links rather than lineal descent relationships, which could rarely be traced beyond grandparents. There appears to have been no surviving traces of corporate kinship units by contact.[44]

Each ahupuaʻa was part of an autonomous polity known as a moku. Moku were ruled over by mōʻī. The ruling mōʻī appointed lesser aliʻi to control ahupuaʻa within his domains (aliʻi ʻai ahupuaʻa). These aliʻi in turn might appoint one or more overseers (konohiki) to organise work parties, collect tribute, mobilise makaʻāinana levies in time of war, and generally ensure that the mōʻī's interests were maintained. The relationship between the terms aliʻi ʻai ahupuaʻa and konohiki is blurred in places. Aliʻi ʻai ahupuaʻa were the highest level konohiki of an ahupuaʻa. Most konohiki were lesser aliʻi associated with the lineages of incumbent paramount chiefs or of

---

42 Malo (1951), p. 195; and Hommon (1975), pp. 160–63.
43 Handy & Handy (1972), pp. 18–19.
44 On ahupuaʻa, see Kirch (1985), p. 2; Hommon (1975), pp. 15–17; Hommon (1976), pp. 55–57; and Handy & Handy (1972), pp. 48–49. On makaʻāinana social organisation, see Hommon (1975), pp. 75 ff.; Jocelyn Linnekin, 'Statistical Analysis of the Great Māhele: Some Preliminary Findings', *Journal of Pacific History*, vol. 22 (1), 1987, 22–23; Ralston (1984), pp. 21–40; Sahlins (1985), pp. 22–25; and Kirch & Sahlins (1992), pp. 196–203.

senior aliʻi of their particular district within the moku.⁴⁵ Land records from the 1840s also reveal that there was a further category of supervisor below konohiki known as konohiki hope.⁴⁶

Makaʻāinana had the right to use and occupy land indefinitely as long as they were deemed to have met the tributary and labour demands of the aliʻi. Beneath the mōʻī, land was not 'owned' in the European sense, but rather rights of use were conferred, usually with the implied subordination of the recipient. The main requirement for maintaining land rights was the giving of hoʻokupu, in the form of produce from the land, especially its first fruits. These presentations were made to the land occupier's immediate overlord all the way up the chain to the mōʻī and beyond to the gods. Makaʻāinana could not own the land. Despite the periodic imposition of new konohiki at the accession of new mōʻī, makaʻāinana occupancy seems to have been relatively secure. Nineteenth-century land commission records suggest that the eldest son inherited most makaʻāinana land. It was not in the interests of aliʻi to disrupt cultivation by breaking this pattern, and makaʻāinana apparently had the right to abandon their land and move into the territory of another overlord if they were unfairly treated by their konohiki or aliʻi. This right is suggested by the Hawaiian phrase 'imi haku' (seeking a lord). It is important to note that the only recorded instances of attempts to change overlords in this period came from subordinate aliʻi and their retinues, rather than from communities of makaʻāinana. A notable example was Kaʻiana. Originally a vassal aliʻi of Kahekili of Maui, he fought against Kahekili on Oʻahu, fled to Kauaʻi after Kahekili's victory and, then, after a voyage to China aboard a European vessel, settled on Hawaiʻi under Kamehameha. In 1795 Kaʻiana turned against Kamehameha and joined Kalanikūpule, the son of Kahekili.⁴⁷

Kula lands and kōʻele lands were the only ahupuaʻa cultivation not organised into family plots. Kula lands were upland tracts and forests that were unsuited to intensive cultivation and which operated as common lands. Individual households were allowed to gather forest products and

---

45 On land divisions, see Kirch (1985), p. 2. On konohiki, see Jocelyn Linnekin, 'The Hui Lands of Keanae: Hawaiian Land Tenure and the Great Māhele', *Journal of the Polynesian Society*, vol. 92 (2), 1983, 185 n. 3; Kameʻeleihiwa (1986), p. 40; and Levin (1968), p. 410.
46 Kirch & Sahlins (1992), pp. 32–33.
47 On land-use rights, see Valeri (1985a), p. 155; Linnekin (1983), pp. 169–72; Linnekin (1987), p. 21; Handy & Handy (1972), pp. 41, 46–47; Cordy (1972), pp. 396–97; and Malo (1951), p. 16. On the right to change lords, see Valerio Valeri, 'The Conqueror Becomes King: A Political Analysis of the Legend of ʻUmi', in Antony Hooper & Judith Huntsman (eds), *The Transformation of Polynesian Culture*, Polynesian Society Memoir no. 45 (Auckland: 1985b), pp. 86–87; and Sahlins (1981), p. 36.

to plant scattered crops to supplement their own crops. Kō'ele lands were small tracts within each ahupua'a that were worked by maka'āinana as a whole, and whose entire harvest was solely for the use of ali'i. A study of land records pertaining to Halawa Valley on Moloka'i suggests that approximately one third of the valley's fields were under the control of konohiki and ali'i. Maka'āinana worked on the kō'ele fields one day in five.[48]

Early European visitors were struck by the poor physique of most maka'āinana when compared to the ali'i, who generally appeared robust and well built. James King's comment that the commoners were 'very tawny, thin and small, mean looking people'[49] is typical. He attributed this appearance to diet, and a lifestyle involving much hard labour. King also noted that he saw more deformed people in Hawai'i than in all the other lands that he had visited put together. Although evidence is limited, it seems more likely that the physique of the maka'āinana was the result of the composition of their diet rather than excessive appropriation of produce by the ali'i. As well as producing sustenance for maka'āinana households, Hawaiian agricultural systems were required to sustain ritual obligations and maintain chiefly retinues in both peace and in their efforts against their rivals. Such efforts might involve the periodic destruction or depletion of certain localities by marauding armed forces. The Halawa Valley figures suggest, however, that chiefly appropriations of food and labour were not excessive. Rather the widespread nature of the symptoms suggests a predominantly carbohydrate-orientated diet deficient in body building protein sources. The main staples of the Hawaiian diet were taro, 'uala (sweet potato) and, to a lesser extent, fish. Taro and 'uala are useful carbohydrate staples, but need supplementing with foods rich in proteins, fats, minerals and vitamins, such as fish and coconut, to be truly nutritional. The ali'i diet was supplemented with animal meat and the produce of specially constructed fishponds. These were largely reserved solely for ali'i consumption or, in the case of pigs, for ritual offerings.[50]

---

48   Kirch (1984), pp. 175–76.
49   King, in Beaglehole (1967), 3:1, pp. 611, 629.
50   Kirch (1985); Cordy (1972), pp. 395–96; Handy & Handy (1972), p. 75; Malo (1951), pp. 42–43, 78; Samwell, in Beaglehole (1967), 3:1, p. 184; and George Dixon, *A Voyage Round the World: But More Particularly to the North-West Coast of America, Performed in 1785, 1786, 1787 and 1788*, Bibliotheca Australiana no. 37 (New York: Da Capo Press, 1968), p. 275; Handy & Handy (1972), pp. 75–101; Emile Massal & Jacques Barrau, *Food Plants of the South Sea Islands*, South Pacific Commission Technical Paper no. 42 (Noumea: 1956), pp. 7–9; J.W. Purseglove, *Tropical Crops*, vol. 1: *Monocotyledons 1* (London: Longmans, 1972a), p. 64.

The political and religious affairs of the mōʻī and kahuna nui rarely intruded into the day-to-day life of makaʻāinana. The mōʻī's relative remoteness from the affairs of makaʻāinana, and the kapu that surrounded his person probably served to enhance the sacred aspect of his office by providing an aura of mystery. Religious ceremonies involving the mōʻī and kahuna nui, such as those during the makahiki and ceremonies dedicated to Kū as war god were usually conducted in large temples. The largest temples were the luakini heiau, also known as heiau poʻokanaka, where human sacrifices might be offered to Kū as god of war. Some agricultural rituals for Lono may also have taken place in these temples. These temples, which could only be constructed and dedicated on the command of a mōʻī,[51] made impressive stages upon which to enact the drama of Hawaiian ceremonies. Prior to the present technological age, monumental architecture of this nature was probably the greatest enduring manifestation of power. As Peter Wilson notes:

> The ancient monument brought the gods to earth and assembled together in one place the scattered powers of nature ... As the fusion of permanence and perfection such architecture was power, not a symbol of it.[52]

Ceremonies in these large temples involved complex rituals that demanded precise actions and chants from the kahuna, and long periods of silence from all others, and occasionally human sacrifice. To the makaʻāinana assembled to bear silent witness to the proceedings, it must have been an intimidating experience.

The threat of physical violence also played a role in the maintenance of social norms. When King asked a female makaʻāinana why the people obeyed the kapu surrounding the expedition's onshore observatory, she replied that they feared that the 'Etooa' (Akua) and 'Teree-oboo' (Kalaniʻōpuʻu, the local mōʻī) would kill them if they broke the kapu.[53] The removal of eyes, strangulation, and the shattering of heads and limbs with clubs were among the punishments meted out to kapu transgressors. Those not killed immediately were condemned to the status of kāuwa. Kāuwa were either kapu transgressors or defeated enemies from whose ranks human sacrifices were drawn. Ceremonies relating to the illness

---

51 On heiau, see Malo (1951), p. 160; Kirch (1985), pp. 257–60; Cook, in Beaglehole (1967), 3:1, p. 269; and Samwell, in Beaglehole (1968), 3:2, pp. 1177–78. On important heiau in Hawaiʻi, see Pogue (1978), p. 40. On ceremonies in heiau, see Sahlins (1981), p. 52.
52 Wilson (1988), p. 148.
53 King, in Beaglehole (1967), 3:1, p. 508.

of an ali'i nui, the consecration of temples and victory in war all might involve human sacrifice. Vanquished enemy rulers and other high-ranking enemy were sought for victory ceremonies. Otherwise, kāuwa in general sufficed. David Stannard notes that pigs and other animals were often substituted as sacrifices for humans.[54]

Retribution for breaking kapu was exacted upon the transgressor's family as a whole. All became kāuwa, as did their descendants. Kāuwa were avoided by maka'āinana, yet had a special relationship with ali'i, whose sacred status their transgressions threatened. The ali'i considered them as their gods and ancestral spirits and allowed them free access to their houses, a privilege denied to maka'āinana. This apparently contradictory relationship may be explained by the fact that the sacrificial deaths of kāuwa helped to restore order to the universe and appease the gods.[55]

Punishment of kapu violations was not applied consistently to both ali'i and maka'āinana, nor was physical sanction always clearly in pursuit of breaches of kapu. Offences that would result in the death of maka'āinana might only elicit a rebuke if the offender was an ali'i. When a handsome young ali'i was discovered to be the secret lover of Kamehameha's favourite wife, Ka'ahumanu, he was spared from execution because of his rank. Instead he was punished by the loss of all of his property. In January 1794, Vancouver learnt that a prominent ali'i's son had been mortally wounded in a spear contest with a man 'of mean rank'.[56] The unfortunate maka'āinana was seized the next day and had his eyes pulled out. He was left in this state for two days before being executed by strangulation with a rope.

During the dedication of a luakini heiau, Malo mentions a ceremony known as ka-papa-ulua. In this ceremony a kahuna, accompanied by several others, went to fish for ulua (crevalle) to dedicate at the heiau. If they failed to catch any ulua, Malo relates how they then returned to land and went from one house to another, shouting out to the people within and telling them some lie or other and asking them to come

---

54 Howe (1984), p. 166; and Stannard (1989), p. 61. On sacrifices, see Valeri (1985a), chpt 4. On kāuwa, see Valeri (1985a), p. 164; Malo (1951), pp. 68–70; and Beckwith (1937), p. 144.
55 Valeri (1985a), pp. 93, 374, n. 81; and Malo (1951), p. 68.
56 Vancouver (1801), bk 5, p. 20 (Jan. 1794). On adultery, see Hommon (1976), p. 167. On differences in punishment between chiefs and commoners, see Levin (1968), p. 414, citing I'ī (1959), p. 23; and Kamakau (1961), p. 17.

outside. If anyone did come out, they killed him and, thrusting a hook in his mouth, carried him to the heiau. If there were many people in the house, they resisted and thus escaped.[57]

The unfortunate victim was then offered as a sacrifice at the heiau. Although vague, the reference to dwellings with many people escaping sacrifice may indicate that the victims were loners or outcasts. Certainly this reference appears on the surface to suggest a more random violence than other references that are usually justified in terms of kapu violations.

The degree to which the threat of violent death secured social order is uncertain. Ceremonies involving human sacrifice did not appear to have been particularly numerous, nor were executions outside of ceremonies. In any case the ability of maka'āinana to disrupt the status quo was limited by their social and economic organisation. Any sense of class-consciousness was curtailed by the strong, localised affiliations that the economic self-sufficiency of most ahupua'a and limited social interaction between ahupua'a communities engendered. After commenting on the apparent frequency of battles between rival chiefs, King observed that 'the different Villages even had dislikes to each other which might lead one to suppose their contest[s] were too frequent'.[58] Much of this animosity may have been stifled by the control that ali'i exercised over life in general, or channelled into controlled activities such as the boxing and dancing competitions that were held during the makahiki. The periodic mock battles between communities that were used for military training may have fulfilled a similar role.[59] Given the prominence in Hawaiian traditions of revenge as a driving motive behind many antagonisms, and the belief in sorcery as a cause of misfortune and even death, it is probable that suspicion and mutual distrust often characterised relations between locations.

Ahupua'a communities were not, however, totally discrete. Drought-affected communities received supplies from elsewhere, or were temporarily evacuated to other ahupua'a or even to other districts. During drought, the inhabitants of Ni'ihau took temporary refuge in nearby southern Kaua'i, people from Ka'ū on Hawai'i moved as far away as the neighbouring districts of Puna or Kona; while communities in

---

57 Malo (1951), pp. 172–73.
58 King, in Beaglehole (1967), 3:1, p. 614.
59 Vancouver (1801), bk 3, pp. 252–58.

arid Kula on Maui were supplied with produce from Waikapu on the windward coast of west Maui.[60] Cook's visits to Kealakekua Bay seem to have attracted maka'āinana to the bay from surrounding areas. Sahlins notes that maka'āinana followed Cook's circuit of the island of Hawai'i in 1778–79 for at least part of the way, just as the annual procession of the Lono image gathered followers en route.[61] In the 1790s, Archibald Menzies noted that Vancouver's presence at Kealakekua resulted in maka'āinana arriving from 'several leagues' north and south of the bay.[62] Sources are silent on the impact that these journeys and military service outside home areas had on maka'āinana, who otherwise lived most of their lives within a single ahupua'a.

Distinctions within chiefly status softened the distinction between ali'i and maka'āinana, and served to modify any consciousness of exploitation as a class that maka'āinana may have harboured. The lowest ranking ali'i lived in daily contact with the maka'āinana of their locality. Through the hale nauā ceremony, these ali'i could become maka'āinana. Local ali'i 'ai ahupua'a and konohiki acted primarily as organisers of land-use rights, supervisors of supra-household activities and sources of security and justice rather than as agents of oppression. While maka'āinana could not become members of the ali'i, they could advance their position within their fixed status by rendering valuable service to their overlord, particularly in warfare. Maka'āinana might be rewarded by being made part of an ali'i's personal retinue, or by the granting of land for their use by grateful mō'ī. Hawaiians also distinguished maka'āinana who stood out from others because of their prosperity and skill in cultivation.[63] Such successful farmers must also have served to blur social boundaries.

The involvement of kaukau ali'i in supervision down to the local level meant that leadership skills beyond the control of family affairs were rare among maka'āinana. By the late 18th century, maka'āinana seem to have been dependent on ali'i leadership. When Kamehameha was away with his army in O'ahu in 1796 and a rebellion occurred back on Hawai'i, the rebellious ali'i encountered little resistance. The captain of a visiting European vessel found the population of one of Kamehameha's districts paralysed into inactivity when faced by their traditional enemies from the

---

60 Handy & Handy (1972), pp. 274, 510–11.
61 Sahlins (1989), p. 413; and King, in Beaglehole (1967), 3:1, pp. 561, 618.
62 Menzies (1920), p. 67.
63 Malo (1951), p. 56; Thrum, vol. 6 (1919–20), p. 178; and Levin (1968), p. 437.

other side of the island. They seemed incapable of mobilisation against the approaching danger, 'having no chief in whom they confided to lead them on'.[64] Kamehameha was left with no choice but to return from Oʻahu and crush the rebellion himself.

This incident suggests makaʻāinana played a limited role in warfare. For most makaʻāinana, warfare involved periods of heightened tensions, punctuated by brief periods of danger as opposing forces moved through or into their ahupuaʻa. The composition of fighting forces, however, still required the engagement and support of significant elements of the population beyond the upper echelons of the chiefly ranks. Heightening competition between chiefs in the late 18th century prompted the broadening of recruitment into core chiefly fighting contingents. This served to expand chiefs' military capacity against each other, but also increased the importance of ensuring the loyalty of chiefly subjects from the ranks of both kaukau aliʻi and makaʻāinana. It is unclear from moʻolelo the extent to which makaʻāinana with martial ability might be elevated to kaukau aliʻi status in this era, although the expansion of the aliʻi class in this late pre-unification era due to population expansion has already been hypothesised by a number of archaeologists. Enhanced coercive capacity against rivals came at the price of a diminished coercive gap between the ruler and those they already ruled over who, increasingly, formed the mainstay of armed contingents.

---

64 William Robert Broughton, *A Voyage of Discovery to the North Pacific Ocean Performed in His Majesty's Sloop Providence, and Her Tender, in the Years 1795, 1796, 1797, 1798* (New York: De Capo Press, 1967 (1804)), p. 69.

4

The Hawaiian Military Transformation from 1770 to 1796

In *How Chiefs Became Kings*, Patrick Kirch argues that the Hawaiian polities witnessed by James Cook were archaic states characterised by:

> the development of class stratification, land alienation from commoners and a territorial system of administrative control, a monopoly of force and endemic conquest warfare, and, most important, divine kingship legitimated by state cults with a formal priesthood.[1]

The previous chapter questioned the degree to which chiefly authority relied on the consent of the majority based on the belief in the sacred status of chiefs as opposed to secular coercion to enforce compliance. This chapter questions the nature of the monopoly of coercion that Kirch and most commentators ascribed to chiefs. It is argued that military competition forced changes in the composition and tactics of chiefly armies that threatened to undermine the basis of chiefly authority. Mass formations operating in drilled unison came to increasingly figure alongside individual warriors and chiefs' martial prowess as decisive factors in battle. Gaining military advantage against chiefly rivals came at the price of increasing reliance on lesser ranked members of ones' own communities. This altered military relationship in turn influenced political and social relations in ways that favoured rule based more on the consent and cooperation of the ruled than the threat of coercion against them for noncompliance. As armies became larger and stayed in the field

---

1   Kirch (2010), p. 27.

longer, the logistics of adequate and predictable agricultural production and supply became increasingly important and the outcome of battles came to be less decisive.

The structure of coercion

Most 19th-century ethnographers state that Hawaiian armies were constituted from general mobilisations of the mō'ī's subjects. As in most Polynesian societies, all adult males were potentially eligible for military service.[2] In reality, it appears that the brunt of any fighting fell upon a relatively small cadre that was occasionally supplemented by levied forces. In a battle drill witnessed by George Vancouver in 1793, two distinct types of combatant were apparent. Maka'āinana opened the exercise with disorganised skirmishing. When they had finished, well-drilled columns of men brandishing long spears came forward to spar. This confirms David Malo's distinction between half-trained, lightly armed troops, and other, more competent troops. Malo also noted that the latter included a distinct body of men known as papa kaua, who were armed with long spears and who probably guarded their 'king' in battle.[3] Samuel Kamakau's description of the armies of Ka'eokulani of Kaua'i and Kahekili of Maui in 1791 provides a further insight into the composition of Hawaiian armies during this era. According to Kamakau, Ka'eokulani's force consisted of 'chiefs, warriors, and paddlers', while Kahekili set out from Maui 'with his chiefs, both high and low, his warriors, the children of the chiefs, and among them Ka-niu-'ula, Ke-po'o-uahu' the pahupū', and other soldiers newly picked from O'ahu'.[4]

Hawaiian sources in general make it clear that every ali'i of any standing gathered around him a retinue, including many who constantly trained in the use of weaponry.[5] These chiefly retinues formed the nearest equivalent that the Hawaiians had to standing armies. Relatives were an important part of any retinue. Ali'i nui entered into sexual unions outside of political marriages designed to produce high-ranking offspring. The offspring of these secondary unions, and even offspring from secondary unions

---

2   William Ellis, *Polynesian Researches* (Tokyo: Charles E. Tuttle Company, 1969 (1859)), p. 149.
3   Vancouver (1801), bk 3, pp. 252–58; and Malo (1951), pp. 197, 294.
4   Kamakau (1961), p. 159.
5   For example, see Malo (1951), pp. 59, 191, 194, 196; I'ī (1959), p. 66; and Beckwith (1937), p. 124.

of the incumbent's parents, were often known as the 'backbone of the chief', in reference to their importance to their lord's fortunes. For those lacking lineage affiliations to influential chiefs, the prospect of becoming connected to an aliʻi's retinue was an attractive proposition. The women's relatives, therefore, welcomed the amorous advances of aliʻi towards makaʻāinana women.[6]

While the power and authority of the mōʻī was considerable, it was based on the loyalty of coercive forces drawn from lower ranked followers. These consisted of the kaukau aliʻi, on which Kanalu Young's groundbreaking study focused, who were lesser aliʻi associated with the ruling aliʻi and the offspring of such liaisons with women not until then connected to the chief's line. The term kaukau aliʻi was used by Kamakau as a collective term for the lowest five of the 11 chiefly ranks. The six highest chiefly grades filled roles as members of the chief's advisers and council, and acted as leaders of battleline sections during complicated moves, such as flank attacks, that required coordinated actions between units. The core of the fighting contingents, however, were made up of kaukau aliʻi.[7]

Young notes that the legendary reformer 'Umi-a-Līloa, who is regarded as a crucial figure in the evolution of chiefly power in Hawaiʻi, came from the ranks of the kaukau aliʻi. 'Umi was an aliʻi noanoa, the offspring of a union between someone from the three highest aliʻi nui ranks and a country person of no rank.[8] Through skills and proven ability he was able to rise to prominence as probably the most influential ruler of his generation. Young also notes that he was, however, exceptional in his ability.[9] In addition, kaukau aliʻi had connections with each other beyond their loyalty and empowerment as members of chiefly retinues. Young notes:

---

6   Malo (1951), p. 81; Levin (1968), p. 410; Valeri (1985a), p. 159; and Sahlins (1985), pp. 24, 130.
7   Young (1998), p. 34; and Samuel M. Kamakau, *Ka Poʻe Kahiko: The People of Old* (Honolulu: Bernice P. Bishop Museum, 1964), pp. 4–6, 73–74, 80. See also Valeri (1985a), pp. 86–93, where he compares and contrasts relations between chiefs and their retinues with European feudal relations and orientalist conceptions of Hawaiian power.
8   Young (1998), p. 43.
9   Young (1998), p. 90.

> Significant for the kaukau aliʻi story is that as lineages from west Hawaiʻi and east Maui continued to maintain their own lower level connections ... The chiefly servers [i.e., kaukau aliʻi] from the Moana kāne line followed the lead of their ranking superiors by engaging in noho [to stay, sleep, remain with] that were inter-island in scope.

Young goes on to note the potential implications of such relations beyond the chiefly retinue as:

> [If] too many of a particular lesser lineage were to noho with siblings or engage in the act of hoʻi [a sexual union of cousins], a challenge to Aliʻi. Nui supremacy might be suspected. A challenge to Aliʻi. Nui paramountcy could result if enough familial support for a strategic action was mustered.[10]

In his case study of the Moana lineage of kaukau aliʻi, Young notes how Moana women linked their group into powerful warrior lineages across moku boundaries – linking dryland agriculture-based Kona in eastern Hawaiʻi to Maui and to the powerful and numerous I clan of Hilo in windward Hawaiʻi, which commanded a powerful warrior force.[11] While archaeologists emphasise the logistical base for the evolution of Hawaiian political power, contemporary and past scholars of Hawaiian history emphasise the importance of blood ties and sociopolitical ties.

ʻUmi's road to power involved usurpation of an unpopular ruler by someone of lower rank by demonstrating leadership ability. This popular support was legitimised through engaging in noho with women of aliʻi nui rank and demonstrating the mana of Kū through achievements in battle or, more correctly, 'well organised, consensus-based, protocol-mandated acts of violence'.[12] A great deal of ability was required to make this transition. Inferior blood links and the inability to mobilise battle support from many quarters kept the vast majority of kaukau aliʻi out of contention for such usurping of power.[13] By the same token, however, the same need to mobilise and command the support from many quarters meant that aliʻi nui could not afford to alienate their followers with

---

10   Young (1998), pp. 48–49, 52–53.
11   Young (1998), pp. 56, 59, 64; and Edith Kawelohea McKinzie, *Hawaiian Genealogies: Extracts from Hawaiian Language Newspapers*, Ismael W. Stagner (ed.), no. 2, vol. 1, The Institute for Polynesian Studies (Lāʻie: 1983), p. 44.
12   Young (1998), p. 49.
13   Young (1998), p. 50.

oppressive or unpopular actions. Aliʻi nui had the right to put kaukau aliʻi to death for poor service, but this seems to have been rarely exercised in a relationship that was mutually beneficial.[14]

Retinues were bolstered from further afield. According to Malo, mock battles like the one witnessed by Vancouver were used, in part, 'to show the chiefs beforehand who among the people were warriors, so that they might be trained and brought up as soldiers'.[15] The use of the term 'people' is ambiguous in terms of distinguishing between aliʻi and makaʻāinana, although elsewhere Malo refers to 'commoners' who lived with the chief and did not desert him in battle. Such men were called kanaka-no-lua-kaua (men for the pit of battle). This epithet was also applied to aliʻi who demonstrated similar loyalty. Malo claims that warriors who distinguished themselves in battle were sometimes rewarded with feather cloaks.[16] Such cloaks were usually a symbol of chiefly status. Even if there was social mobility, the conveying of specific titles and regalia still suggests that social distinctions between aliʻi and makaʻāinana within retinues were retained.

Hawaiian terminology distinguishes between commoners who cultivated the land (makaʻāinana) and landless commoners (kanaka) who became clients or servants of an aliʻi. Nineteenth-century sources suggest that many of these were 'adventurers' who moved between different polities in search of service in the retinue of a lord under whom their personal fortunes would be enhanced.[17] It should be noted, however, that there was a marked increase in mobility after the unification of most of the archipelago in 1796. Such mobility may not have existed prior to this. On the other hand, it may explain the apparently contradictory image of generally passive and settled makaʻāinana moving on if their overlord alienated them. It was perhaps the support of kanaka, and not makaʻāinana, that rulers needed to retain. Makaʻāinana were ill suited to traditional Hawaiian warfare, if James King's poor opinion of their physique is correct. They would have lacked the necessary muscle to cope with the rigours of combat at close quarters. Hawaiian chiefs often asked David Samwell who were the 'tata toa' (kaua-koa) or fighting men among Cook's expedition, assuming that 'none are such but those who are tall and stout, the same as they are among them'.[18]

---

14 Young (1998), pp. 98–99.
15 Malo (1951), p. 66.
16 Malo (1951), pp. 61, 77.
17 Valeri (1985a), pp. 156, 159.
18 Samwell, in Beaglehole (1967) 3:2, p. 1193.

The most skilful warriors were the higher ranked aliʻi. Kamehameha, for example, was famous for his prowess in parrying and dodging spears. Important young chiefs received rigorous training in the arts of war.[19] The greatest contemporary warrior-chief on Hawaiʻi, Kekūhaupiʻo, trained Kamehameha. Kekūhaupiʻo belonged to the powerful Moana people of Kaʻawaloa in Kealakekua Bay, who also supplied the war leaders for mōʻī of the leeward coast. Abraham Fornander mentions that Kualoa in windward Oʻahu was noted as a place where young aliʻi received training in the arts of war and peace.[20] Aliʻi figure prominently in traditional accounts of battles, with the death of an important aliʻi often deciding the conflict. Vancouver found that many of his former chiefly acquaintances had died in the time between his first visit to the islands as a member of Cook's expedition and his return just over a decade later. He was told that most had died as a result of warfare.[21]

Aliʻi had much to motivate them to risk their lives in the pit of battle. Their mana and secular power were at stake. Sacred status alone could not attract adherents. The fortunes of the members of chiefly retinues were obviously linked to those of their lords. Decisive victory might mean a share in the division of the lands of the vanquished. Noticeable acts in battle might enhance an individual's status within the retinue – all would be aware of how past warriors had won immortality through their acts of courage and skill, and this knowledge served to inspire each new generation of young warriors. For makaʻāinana, the benefits of victory were less direct. Some might fight well enough to secure a place in the retinue. For most, the end of hostilities would have meant a return to their fields regardless of the outcome, providing they could avoid being killed in the interim. Other, more general influences probably shaped the attitudes of all combatants to varying degrees: social conventions concerning manliness, kin-group and retinue loyalties, the fear of losing face in front of one's associates, priestly claims of supernatural support, and the consequences of defeat.

The proportion of the total population involved in warfare is difficult to ascertain. The information that is available, however, tends to support the idea that armies mainly consisted of chiefly retinues. All references to the size of armed forces pertain to Hawaiʻi and may not be representative

---

19   Pierre Francois Peron, *A Frenchman in Hawaii, 1796*, Virginia Day (trans.) (Honolulu: White Knight Press, 1975), p. 6.
20   Kamakau (1961), p. 126 ; Fornander (1969), p. 278 ; Sahlins (1995), p. 48.
21   Vancouver (1801), bk 2, pp. 405–06.

of other islands in the chain. Sometime in the 18th century, prior to the arrival of Cook, Alapaʻinui, the ruler of Hawaiʻi, attacked Maui. Kamakau records that his army numbered 8,440 men. The Russian explorer Urey Lisiansky was told that Kamehameha's invasion force on Maui in 1790 numbered 8,000 men and travelled in 2,000 canoes. Lisiansky's source was John Young, who served Kamehameha from 1790 onwards. Young also informed traders Captain Charles Bishop and John Boit Jr that Kamehameha raised an army of 10,000 men on Hawaiʻi, and a fleet of 1,200 canoes for the conquest of the rest of the chain in 1795. Young told Lieutenant William Broughton of Vancouver's expedition that the army numbered 16,000 men, however, although the figure of 10,000 men is more consistent with the size of other Hawaiian armies.[22]

Fleet sizes were another indication of military strength. In 1791 the trader Joseph Ingraham recorded seeing a force of 700 canoes in which he estimated that there were 20,000 fighting men.[23] While an estimate taken from hundreds of canoes is of dubious value, the figure of 700 canoes is feasible given fleet sizes mentioned elsewhere. In January 1779, Cook's expedition witnessed the return of the Hawaiʻi ruler Kalaniʻōpuʻu from a campaign on Maui at the head of 150 canoes. While this fleet size is well below those of Alapaʻi and Kamehameha, it is important to note that Kalaniʻōpuʻu had left a garrison in east Maui. Furthermore, just prior to Kalaniʻōpuʻu's return, Samwell counted 150 large sailing canoes among an estimated 1,000 canoes in Kealakekua Bay.[24] Given such sailing canoes were used to transport troops, it would thus appear that Kalaniʻōpuʻu had by no means fully mobilised his resources.

Figures for specific areas of Hawaiʻi are in keeping with the previously suggested total of 8,000 to 10,000 men for the island as a whole. The island consisted of six districts. Fornander suggests that each of Kamehameha's four major chiefly supporters could muster at least 1,000 spears in battle. Their lands centred on two populous districts, Kona and Kohala. The Kona aliʻi, Kameʻeiamoku, was accompanied by 1,000 men

---

22 Kamakau (1961), p. 74; Urey Lisiansky *A Voyage Round the World in the Years 1803, 4, 5 and 6* (New York: De Capo Press, 1968 (1814)), p. 129; Michael Roe (ed.), *The Journal and Letters of Captain Charles Bishop on the North-West Coast of America in the Pacific and in New South Wales 1794–1799* (London: Cambridge University Press for the Hakluyt Society, 1967), p. 141; and John Boit Jr., *The Journal of a Voyage Round the Globe 1795 and 1796*, University of Hawaiʻi microfilm 2890 no. 1, n.d.
23 Ingraham, in Kaplanoff (ed.) (1971), p. 86; and Hommon (1975), pp. 151–57.
24 Hommon (1976), p. 303, citing Rickman. See also, King, in Beaglehole (1967) 3:1, p. 511; and Samwell, in Beaglehole (1967) 3:2, p. 1158.

when he visited Vancouver at Hawai'i in 1794.[25] Accounts of casualties resulting from the explosion of Kilauea volcano suggest that the army of Kamehameha's rival, Keōua, numbered perhaps 1,200 men at the time. One of Keōua's three columns was wiped out. William Ellis put the losses at 80 'warriors', the missionary James Jarves calculated 400 'human beings', Fornander counted '2,000 men', and missionary Sheldon Dibble refers to 400 'fighting men'.[26] At the time, Keōua controlled the Ka'ū and Puna districts. In addition to this force he had almost certainly left others to guard Ka'ū, and to control recently conquered Hilo. He was also nearing the end of a series of prolonged campaigns fought to defend his domains from the increasingly powerful Kamehameha.

As we have seen, the total size of the Hawaiian population at European contact has generated considerable debate. Robert Schmitt's and David Stannard's figures for the island of Hawai'i are 90,000 and 340,000 respectively. As neither figure is conclusive, it is appropriate to work with both. A fighting strength of 10,000 men would represent 11 per cent of Schmitt's estimate and 2.9 per cent of Stannard's figure.[27] Most studies of pre-industrial societies face similar problems concerning accurate measurements, but historian Michael Wood echoes the general consensus when, speaking of Bronze Age Greece, he asserts that '[T]he idea that anything near 10 per cent of a pre-industrial society could be mobilised for war is probably far-fetched'.[28] In such societies, an army of a few hundred well-armed men was a significant force, and expeditions of a few thousand men were considerable achievements both logistically and politically. If this is a correct assessment, then either Schmitt's figure errs on the low side, or late 18th-century Hawaiian society was more militarised than most other pre-industrial societies. References to the replacement of casualties suggest that full fighting strengths were rarely mobilised. In the 1770s, Kalani'ōpu'u is said to have lost 800 of his best fighters in one day's fighting on Maui. Yet, he soon after again attacked Maui at the head of a

---

25 Fornander (1969), pp. 315, 338.
26 John F. G. Stokes, 'Dune Sepulture, Battle Mortality and Kamehameha's Alleged Defeat on Kauai', *45th Annual Report of the Hawaiian Historical Society for the Year 1936* (Honolulu: 1937), pp. 36–39; and Fornander (1969), p. 324.
27 R. C. Schmitt, 'New Estimates of the Pre-censal Population of Hawaii', *Journal of the Polynesian Society*, vol.80 (2), 1971, 237–43. See also Table 1, Chapter 2.
28 Michael Wood, *In Search of the Trojan War* (London: Facts on File Publications, 1985), p. 158.

strong army. After the battle of Koapapa in the early 1790s, Kamehameha delayed his pursuit of the retiring army of Keōua to replace his losses. A few months later, Kamehameha invaded Keōua's territory.[29]

Although women accompanied Hawaiian armies, and some female ali'i fought in battle, most combatants appear to have been men.[30] If it is assumed that approximately half of the population was female, then a 10,000-man army represents 22 per cent of Schmitt's male population and 5.8 per cent of Stannard's. Obviously, as a percentage of healthy adult males, this figure would be even higher. In the case of Schmitt's figure, fighting forces would almost certainly have required the inclusion of maka'āinana, ali'i and kanaka. The evidence, therefore, suggests that the Hawaiian population was larger than Schmitt's estimate.

Maka'āinana levies certainly did march with chiefly retinues on some occasions. The degree to which maka'āinana were mobilised varied according to the nature of the undertaking, or the seriousness of the threat posed. Kamakau relates that, when an O'ahu army invaded Moloka'i in the mid-part of the 18th century, it was not until the fifth day of fighting that every able-bodied man within range of the battlefield came out of his house to fight.[31] Maka'āinana levies were almost certainly more useful defending their own localities than bolstering forces invading other polities or other islands for logistical reasons. Practice varied. Vancouver was told that just the principal chiefs of O'ahu and their warriors had gone to Moloka'i to prepare to fight Kamehameha in the early 1790s. Yet, in 1779, King was informed that most of the men in the Waimea area of O'ahu had accompanied the O'ahu ruler, Pelei'ōhōlani, to Moloka'i to fight against the forces of Maui.[32]

Success in war enhanced the ruler's control over his maka'āinana subjects in a number of ways. By protecting the heartland of his lands from aggressors, the mō'ī shielded its inhabitants and crops from the ravages of war. By carrying war to his enemy, the mō'ī could limit his demands upon his population through living off the lands of his enemy and, perhaps, even increasing his resources by incorporating enemy land into his own

---

29 Kamakau (1961), pp. 85–88, 152; Fornander (1969), p. 324; and Thrum, vol. 5 (1918–19), p. 472.
30 Ellis (1969), pp. 103–04, 124–25; and Fornander (1969), p. 324.
31 Kamakau (1961), p. 70.
32 Vancouver (1801), bk 2, p. 36; and King, in Beaglehole (1967) 3:1, p. 585.

realm. By also limiting the use of maka'āinana manpower in fighting forces, ali'i helped maintain a coercive gap between their small, but well-trained and relatively cohesive retinues, and the general population.

Most mō'ī seem to have realised the value of courting the loyalty of their subjects. The overuse of coercion might not lead to maka'āinana rebellions, but it did threaten to undermine the rule of the paramount by inducing sympathy for rival mō'ī or rebellious subordinate ali'i. The rebellion of the Puna ali'i Īmakakoloa in the early 1780s against his paramount, Kalani'ōpu'u, is said to have served as a rallying point for subjects disgruntled at excessive demands for provisions from Kalani'ōpu'u's court. The rebellion did not spread beyond Puna but, after his defeat, Īmakakoloa was assisted by his people to evade capture for one year. Īmakakoloa was eventually betrayed and captured when Kalani'ōpu'u began to ravage Puna to induce the local population to surrender him. Īmakakoloa was sacrificed to Kū, but Puna remained a source of sullen dissent to overlords from beyond its borders for years to come.[33]

Maka'āinana support was sometimes given to invaders who treated them well. When Kamehameha's brother, Kalanimalokuloku-i-Kapo'okalani, invaded east Maui in the mid-1780s, he won the goodwill of local maka'āinana by respecting their property. As a result, when Kahekili of Maui defeated him soon after, local inhabitants helped hide him from his pursuers until he could escape to Hawai'i. This raises questions about the relationship between Kahekili and his east Maui subjects. A few years earlier his army had exhausted local food resources in a prolonged siege of the stronghold of Ka'uiki Head at the eastern end of Maui following a period of Hawaiian control.[34]

Hawaiian ali'i must have been aware of their potential vulnerability as a small ruling elite. While no maka'āinana levy could resist drilled columns of chiefly retinues in hand-to-hand combat, the maka'āinana fighting elite witnessed by Vancouver in battle exercise used missile weapons. Such weapons could be great levellers. Many centuries before, Spartan hoplites – using similar tactics to those recorded by Vancouver – had been decimated by swarms of lightly armed Athenian skirmishers on the island of Spacteria. The skirmishers had refused to close with the Spartans and fight on their terms. Instead they had pelted them with a barrage

---

33 Fornander (1969), pp. 201–02.
34 Fornander (1969), pp. 216–17, 229; and Kamakau (1961), p. 143.

of missiles. The Spartans suffered heavy losses in the open and retreated to a fort at one end of the island. Here they eventually surrendered once they realised that their position was hopeless.[35]

When the aliʻi Kukeawe abused his position as Kahekili's regent on Maui during the latter's invasion of Oʻahu in the 1780s, he was confronted by local contingents and soundly defeated. The nature of the fighting is not mentioned, but it may be significant, given the course of events at Spacteria, that, after the initial encounter, Kukeawe retreated and fortified a position for refuge. When Kahekili's son, Kalanikūpule, returned from Oʻahu in response to this disruption, order was soon restored peacefully. Kalanikūpule was popular with the people of Maui. He agreed with the just nature of their grievance against Kukeawe and took no punitive action, thereby enhancing the rule of the Maui ruling family.[36]

Aliʻi and makaʻāinana generally stopped short of open confrontation. The limits of sacred power was ambiguously defined by fears and perceptions rather than sharply defined by confrontation. The pervading ideology elevated aliʻi above makaʻāinana by associating them with the gods and linking their sacred status to the wellbeing of the population as a whole. The latent threat of punitive measures was probably also a consideration in deterring makaʻāinana from openly questioning this worldview too vigorously. As long as their lives were reasonably comfortable according to the norms they were accustomed to, and better alternatives were either not envisaged, or not seen as realistic possibilities, makaʻāinana seem to have accepted their lot. For their part, the aliʻi generally exercised restraint in their dealings with commoners

Coercion played a prominent role in relations between aliʻi. The requirement of proving favour with the gods meant that the relative secular power of aliʻi was exposed through physical confrontation. According to Hawaiian genealogical rules, the most suitable successor to any ruler was the eldest son of his highest ranking wife. In reality, the complex social relations between aliʻi nui usually ensured a pool of several candidates with valid and comparable claims to the leadership. The incumbent did not always designate a successor and, if he did, the nominee was not necessarily his eldest son by his highest ranking wife.

---

35   Thucydides, *History of the Peloponnesian War*, Rex Warner (trans.) (rev. edn) (Middlesex: Penguin, 1972), bk 4, pp. 26–41.
36   Fornander (1969), p. 227; Kamakau (1961), p. 142.

The designation of an heir by the incumbent did not necessarily ensure a smooth transition of government. The legitimacy of any candidate depended upon proving their ritual and secular efficacy.[37]

A war of succession was always possible as rival candidates asserted their claims. Power became legitimacy. Kalaniʻōpuʻu perhaps acknowledged this in his designation of two heirs to succeed him. His son Kīwalaʻō was bequeathed the kingdom, while his nephew Kamehameha inherited the old ruler's war god Kūkāʻili-moku.[38] Indeed, the designation of an heir may have served only as a signal of the incumbent's wishes to his own retinue after his death to boast the secular power base of his favoured candidate for the ensuing succession struggle. Candidates had to secure a substantial power base to succeed. Supporters might begin to choose between potential candidates well before the death of the incumbent. The temptation to cover all options had to be balanced against the possibility of faring poorly in the eventual victor's division of rewards among his followers. The most longstanding and loyal supporters tended to receive the best lands to administer, while the vanquished faced the possibility of land loss, exile, relegation to makaʻāinana status, or death.

In the absence of a designated heir, the followers of the incumbent ruler faced a difficult choice. Their position depended on continued exhibitions of loyalty to their lord, yet they also had to give consideration to their future as the ruler aged. Structural tension, therefore, existed between the incumbent and his supporters, and potential successors and their supporters. The danger of usurpation by potential successors was probably a major reason why some sons of mōʻī were raised outside of their father's domains in the court of rival rulers. Because of widespread polygyny among aliʻi nui, the various sons of a mōʻī tended to have different mothers. Valerio Valeri notes that this often meant that each drew his support base from his matrilineal kin. Patrilineal kin would have conflicting loyalties and might end up as supporters of rival candidates.[39]

Traditions pertaining to the 18th century suggest that the various factions usually soon polarised into two opposing camps, each supporting a rival candidate for mōʻī. The stability of these unions was not necessarily

---

37 Levin (1968), pp. 403–18; Valeri (1985a), pp. 90–91; Marshall Sahlins & Dorothy Barrere, 'William Richards on Hawaiian Culture and Political Conditions of the Hawaiian Islands in 1841', *Hawaiian Journal of History*, vol. 7, 1973, 18–19.
38 Valeri (1985a), p. 91; and Levin (1968).
39 Valeri (1985a), pp. 90–91.

guaranteed beyond their immediate purpose, the defeat of the rival camp. Although warfare tended to be mostly directed against other polities as the new paramount consolidated his rule, the possibility of internal dissent was ever present, as the following prayer to Kū suggests:

-E molia aku [curse]
-I na kipi u waho ao
luko hoʻi [The rebels without and within]
-I ke ka ʻiliʻaina [who wish to seize the land][40]

While the conquest of one polity by another might result in significant changes in personnel, new mōʻī were rarely in a position to immediately impose their will. Hawaiian warfare rarely resulted in the decimation of the losing army. Existing power relations tended to be modified rather than overturned. To endure, the allocation of tenure rights and administrative positions required a subtle balance between attempts to put trusted followers in favoured positions and localities, and the need to recognise pre-existing power relations among aliʻi.

There was usually a body of powerful aliʻi who presided over territory made up of number of ahupuaʻa within each moku. These divisions were known as ʻokana or poko.[41] Important aliʻi who survived to reach old age were usually skilled warriors heading substantial retinues. Such men could not be ignored. Powerful aliʻi families, such as the Mahi and I families of Hawaiʻi, had estates that had been in their control for decades, if not centuries. Social scientist Stephanie Levin suggests that, prior to 1796, supporters of successful candidates were given lands contiguous to their traditional family lands, which, in effect, consolidated their holdings. Fornander distinguishes between hereditary estates and '[A]ll other lands' which 'were subject to change in the grand council of division' that marked the accession of a new ruler. Fornander goes on to state that such lands were not redistributed if 'their previous owners were of the court party or too powerful to be needlessly interfered with'.[42] In reality, there were probably few major changes in tenure, with the hale nauā ceremony and land redistribution serving mainly to regroup the chiefly elite closer to the new ruler by excluding more distant relatives.

---

40 Iʻī (1959), p. 37.
41 Malo (1951), p. 192; Handy & Handy (1972), pp. 46–48; and Hommon (1975), p. 18.
42 Fornander (1969), p. 300; and Levin (1968), pp. 418, 420.

The personal retinue of contending candidates in succession disputes generally only formed a small part of their forces. This was particularly true of younger candidates. Any coalitions required the support of older, more established aliʻi. For example, when most Kona and Kohala aliʻi threw their support behind Kamehameha to be the successor to Kalaniʻōpuʻu, he only controlled his family estate at Halawa in Kohala and some land granted to him in Kona and Hāmākua by Kalaniʻōpuʻu. The Kona/Kohala faction emerged out of fear that their rivals in Hilo and Puna would exercise more influence than they would over the other contender, Kīwalaʻō. Hawaiian traditions suggest that both Kamehameha and Kīwalaʻō were willing to compromise but that some of the older, more powerful aliʻi backing them pushed them into war. Conflict became inevitable when Kīwalaʻō's powerful and high-ranking uncle, Keawemauhili, influenced Kīwalaʻō's land distribution to ensure that he prospered, while the Kona/Kohala aliʻi, and even Kīwalaʻō's brother, Keōua, were disadvantaged.[43]

Around the same time, the unpopular ruler of Oʻahu, Kumahana, was overthrown and a 'council of chiefs' 'elected' Kahahana as his successor. This move bypassed Kumahana's children and eroded any entrenched power his family may have built up. Kahahana was the son of the prominent ʻEwa aliʻi Elani. He may have been chosen because of the fact that he had been brought up outside of Oʻahu at the court of the Maui ruler Kahekili and, therefore, did not have a personal power base on Oʻahu, as Kumahana had. As an outsider, he may have provided a suitable compromise to rival Oʻahu aliʻi within the assembled council.[44]

Once a successor had been decided, the realm was divided up into administrative units. Usually these seem to have conformed to the district boundaries, which were largely fixed and stable by the late 18th century. The court of the mōʻī crowned the previously described hierarchical administrative structure. The court contained a considerable number of councillors, specialists and other retainers, including a body of warriors. The court favoured certain localities over others, such as Waikiki and Kailua on Oʻahu, Wailua on Kauaʻi and Wailuku on Maui. These areas tended to be the fertile heartland of the moku, although the court did move around the ruler's land to ensure that the task of feeding its numbers did not always

---

43   Fornander (1969), pp. 300–03, 306–07.
44   Kamakau (1961), pp. 2128–29.

4. THE HAWAIIAN MILITARY TRANSFORMATION FROM 1770 TO 1796

fall upon any one locality.[45] These tours also allowed the mōʻī to assess the state of his lands and reaffirm his relationship with the subordinate aliʻi on whom he depended for district and local administration. As the mōʻī could not be in all places at once, messengers were used to convey orders and to act as the ruler's eyes and ears. They travelled by canoes and along a network of trails. As well as being trustworthy, messengers needed to have speed and stamina for conveying messages overland. When travelling by sea, they were provided with the best canoes and paddlers available. Some, perhaps even most, were of aliʻi rank.[46]

Even at the peak of any mōʻī's career, power remained essentially decentralised. No professional bureaucracy loyal to the ruling mōʻī had emerged to supplant subordinate aliʻi and their retinues' experts as administrative agents. Sources suggest that the mōʻī's retinue numbered anywhere from a few hundred to a few thousand men.[47] Malo mentions that subordinate chiefs also gathered warriors. At least four of Kamehameha's chiefly supporters could muster over 1,000 men in battle.[48] Their contingents were possibly agglomerations of the retinues of less powerful aliʻi, given that the battle witnessed by Vancouver engaged sides of only 150 men. Certainly King believed that the frequency of Hawaiian warfare gave 'weight and consequence to many lesser chiefs'.[49]

After a decade as ruler of the leeward areas of Hawaiʻi, and impressive victories against his rivals Kahekili and Kaʻeokulani, Kamehameha still acted with caution when dealing with his important subordinate aliʻi. Vancouver noted tensions among Kamehameha's main chiefly supporters on a number of occasions. In 1794 Vancouver was led to believe that Kamehameha had returned all but one of the knives recently stolen from him because it had been given to a 'person of much consequence, over whom Tamaahah did not wish to enforce his authority'. A few years earlier,

---

45   On mōʻī retinue, see Malo (1951), pp. 59–64, 187–95; Beckwith (1932), pp. 124–34; and Kirch (1984), pp. 258–59. On Kalaniʻōpuʻu's administration, see Kamakau (1961), p. 79. On a tour by Kalaniʻōpuʻu, see Fornander (1969), pp. 200–01.
46   On messengers, see Hommon (1975), pp. 103–08; and Kirch (1985), p. 266. On modes of travel, see Handy & Handy (1972), pp. 489–91; and Hommon (1975), pp. 161–70.
47   Kamakau (1961), pp. 7, 134, 156. See also Fornander (1969), p. 315; Dixon (1968), p. 78; Sahlins & Barrere (1973), p. 21; and Hommon (1975), p. 116.
48   Malo (1951), p. 194; and Fornander (1969), pp. 315, 338.
49   King, in Beaglehole (1967) 3:1, p. 614.

in 1790, Kamehameha had felt the need to take a considerable force with him to claim a European vessel and its sole survivor from his ali'i vassal a Kame'eiamoku after the latter had attacked and overwhelmed it.[50]

The mō'ī had to be both politician and warrior, maintaining his support base among his chiefly backers while successfully leading his followers against the forces of rival rulers to maintain his mana. Open dissent within the realm had to be dealt with before the flames of rebellion could take hold. Yet the excessive assertion of central authority raised the risk of alienating the population. The consolidation of power was also sought through marriage alliances between various collateral kin of the ruling house and other powerful families. Kamehameha married into the family of his slain rival, Kīwala'ō, to effect a reconciliation, and also to increase the status of his family by linking it with such a high-ranking family.[51]

Marriage unions could bestow significant influence on high-ranking female ali'i. High-ranking women might have many partners in their lifetimes. The formidable high-ranking Kaua'i ali'i Kamakahelei played a crucial role in deciding the leadership of Kaua'i in the 1770s and 1780s through her choice of, and influence over, marriage partners. Other chiefly women exercised significant influence in Hawaiian polities in this period. Kamehameha's favourite wife, Ka'ahumanu, had much influence with her Maui kinsmen and also attended Kamehameha's councils.[52] Some ali'i women even fought beside their spouses in battle. One such woman was Kalola, the wife of Kahahana, who joined her spouse's ill-fated stand against Kahekili's invading army at Nu'uanu on O'ahu in 1783.[53] Chiefly women, just like their male equivalents, controlled status symbols such as cloaks.[54] Given this evidence of female ali'i nui exerting significant political influence and fighting in battle, the possibility that such women controlled armed retinues of their own cannot be dismissed.

While some rulers, such as the Maui ruling line, entrusted important administrative posts to immediate family members, others gave these posts to affinal relations to keep power away from close, consanguineous relatives.

---

50   Fornander (1969), p. 230. See also Vancouver (1801), bk 3, p. 215 for 1790; and Vancouver (1801), bk 5, p. 26 for 1794.
51   Valeri (1985a), pp. 165–66, 168.
52   Sahlins (1985), p. 22. On Kamakahelei, see Valeri (1985a), p. 166. On Ka'ahumanu, see Sahlins (1981), p. 61; and Kame'eleihiwa (1987), pp. 107–08. On brother–sister bonds, see Ralston (1987), p. 117.
53   Fornander (1969), p. 224; and Ellis (1969), pp. 124–25.
54   Linnekin (1988), pp. 269–70.

This seems to have been particularly true of Hawai'i, where traditions abound about the usurpation of the leadership by junior collateral kin. On Maui, in contrast, the same line had ruled for generations and seems to have been relatively untroubled by serious internal strife in the period under consideration. The only dissent noted occurred around 1783, when some Maui ali'i fought against Kahekili during a rebellion on O'ahu.[55]

The formation of full-time military units loyal to the ruler has usually been crucial to the formation of centralised states in most parts of the world. There are strong indications that, by the 1770s, units of military specialists existed alongside chiefly retinues. Traditions pertaining to this decade refer to Kahekili's army consisting of 'chiefs, fighting men and left-handed warriors whose sling shots missed not a hair of the head or a blade of grass', as well as the po'ouahi (smoke head) and niu'ula (red coconut) 'divisions'. This force defeated and expelled Kalani'ōpu'u's army from Maui, prompting the Hawai'i ruler to spend a year reorganising his forces. He is said to have organised six brigades, with ali'i forming a bodyguard called keawe, and 'nobles' constituting two other units known as the alapa and pi'ipi'i respectively. The alapa were armed with spears and are said to have numbered around 800 men.[56]

By 1783, Kahekili's forces also included men known as pahupū (cut in two) because of their distinctive tattooing which covered one side of their body. Kahekili was also tattooed in this way.[57] Vancouver saw many of Kahekili's subjects with this pattern of tattoo and was told that it had been adopted recently with the purpose of intimidating enemy soldiers in battle.[58] The fact that Kahekili's nephew, Kīwala'ō, had his back tattooed like his uncles while visiting his mother, Kalola, on Maui dates this practice to at least as far back as 1781.[59] There appears to be no other record of this type of tattooing outside of Kahekili's realm. Kamakau distinguishes pahupū from chiefs and warriors when describing Kahekili's army in 1791. The ali'i Koi, Kuala-kia and Manu-o-kaniwi, are listed as 'leaders' of pahupū on O'ahu, which suggests that the tattoos signified membership of an organised body rather than functioning merely as an

---

55   Sahlins (1981), pp. 61–62; Levine (1968), p. 417; and Fornander (1969).
56   Kamakau (1961), p. 85; Thomas G. Thrum 'Hana of Historic Tradition and Romance', in Thomas G. Thrum (ed.) *The Hawaiian Almanac For 1919* (Honolulu: Thos. G. Thrum, 1919), p. 66; and Fornander (1969), p. 151.
57   Kamakau (1961), p. 135. Greg Dening, *History's Anthropology: The Death of William Gooch*, (Lanham, Maryland: University Press of America, 1988), pp. xvii, 10, 93.
58   Vancouver (1801) bk 3, Ch 8, p. 347.
59   I'ī (1959), p. 9.

instrument of terror in battle. In a reference concerning 1783, Kamakau lists the pahupū alongside the Poʻo-uwahi and Ka-niu-ʻula and labels them collectively as 'warrior companies'[60] led by chiefs.

It is unclear whether these units were kept together in times of peace or whether they were merely specialists from the various retinues assembled together in times of war for military advantage. Both Kahekili and Kalaniʻōpuʻu were powerful, established rulers by the 1770s and may have been able to create such power bases independent of their aliʻi vassals. The threat of invasion by the other may have helped justify such a move. Kalaniʻōpuʻu's reforms seem, however, to have been more a reorganisation of his chiefly fighting force rather than the creation of a new power base. The fact that Maui had been unified under a stable dynasty for centuries may have allowed Kahekili to make more substantial moves towards increasing his military capacity relative to his vassals. For all rulers, the continued importance to chiefly status of martial prowess remained a barrier to the expansion of their power base through the large-scale incorporation of makaʻāinana into their military forces.

The ability of any ruler to maintain a sizeable military force of his own was also restricted by the structure of the Hawaiian political economy. The existing military power of his more important vassals, and an economy geared to the needs of an essentially dispersed population, worked against such a concentration of power. Mōʻī had direct control over only a limited amount of land. Kamehameha's most noted landholding, for example, was Kuahewa in the upper Kailua area of Hawaiʻi Kona. It consisted of eight ahupuaʻa, and was approximately 13 kilometres long. Kamehameha also had lands in the fertile Waipiʻo Valley of Hāmākua district, and his family estate in Kohala district.[61] While Hawaiian dietary staples could be preserved in a relatively compact, transportable form to feed the substantial armies that were brought together for war, for most of the year warriors remained dispersed among the various chiefly retinues of the polity. The staggering of crop harvests to ensure reasonable production for much of the year reduced the need to maintain stores of preserved food for the lean months of the harvest cycle.[62]

---

60 Kamakau (1961), pp. 135, 159.
61 Thrum vol. 5 (1918–1919), p. 478.
62 Hommon (1976), pp. 115–18; Peebles & Kus (1977), pp. 425, 426; and Kirch & Sahlins (1992), p. 28.

Excessive expropriation of stored food for military campaigns endangered the community's ability to cope with natural disasters, such as droughts, and risked alienating the population. Much of the surplus production beyond subsistence needs was reserved as offerings to the gods. Propriety demanded that such offerings were not blatantly used for other purposes. The mōʻī maintained his own retinue through the production of his own lands and from specific rights to other resources. His retinue included expert fishermen whose sole job was to provide the court with fish. The court could call upon the produce of kōʻele lands and fishponds that were used solely to feed aliʻi and chiefly retinues. Part of the harvest from the lands farmed by makaʻāinana households was set aside as tribute to their overlords. Most tribute from the more remote holdings of chiefs consisted of pigs, dogs and salted fish rather than vegetable staples. The ruler reserved a portion of the first fruits offered to Lono during the makahiki for later redistribution. These rights and resources seem to have allowed mōʻī to maintain retinues of a few thousand men at most. Such retinues did not confer enough of a relative advantage upon the ruler to allow him to govern without the consent of the majority of his aliʻi vassals. Ultimately, the most important bond between the ruler and his vassals was probably their perception that it was in their own interests to support him or her.[63]

Indeed, the political coherence of the moku rested upon the diffusion of power. Powerful constraints operated to curtail the consolidation of power in the hands of one individual, or even one coherent group within a moku. Makaʻāinana obedience to the mōʻī rested upon the latter's perceived sacred status and the expectation of benefits, in return for contributions of produce and labour. The loyalty of vassal aliʻi to their mōʻī rested heavily upon the expectation of rewards for services rendered. Logistical and political considerations limited the potential to concentrate armed forces in one body and meant that the threat of punitive action alone would not ensure compliance.

These internal constraints acted as powerful incentives for the pursuit of mana outside one's own moku. Battle against the forces of rival mōʻī and the conquest of enemy lands were preferable to contests over the division of limited resources within the moku, or the application of pressure on one's own makaʻāinana to increase production. The same forces that

---

63 Valeri (1985a), p. 159; Beckwith (1932), p. 150; Malo (1951), pp. 145 ff.; and King, in Beaglehole (1967) 3:1, pp. 517–18.

pressured those in power to look beyond their own territory also served, however, to limit their ability to convert the spoils of war into enhanced power bases. Nevertheless, relations between moku were an important part of the structure of power. It is to these relations that we now direct our attention.

The nature of warfare

Hawaiians fought for a variety of reasons. Fornander asserts that a ruler attacked rivals 'as much for the purpose of keeping his warriors and fleet in practice and acquiring renown for himself, as with a view of obtaining territorial additions to his kingdom'.[64] He also cites the desire to control resource areas as a cause of war. The need to avenge insults and injuries to maintain mana played a prominent role in aliʻi actions. The desecration of ancestral bones was particularly offensive. Grudges might be harboured for generations. The Maui mōʻī Kahekili's decimation of Oʻahu aliʻi who revolted against him in the 1780s was partly driven by a desire to avenge the abuse of the bones of his ancestor Kauhi by Oʻahu aliʻi. Peleiʻōhōlani of Oʻahu slaughtered many of the chiefly elite of Molokaʻi for the killing of his daughter there. When Vancouver sought to punish the killers of two Europeans on Oʻahu in the 1790s, local chiefs were hesitant to hand over the culprits for fear that their killer's relatives would seek revenge.[65]

Hawaiians seldom commenced hostilities without first seeking supernatural sanction. Kahuna would pray and sacrifice to the gods and seek omens. The construction of a luakini heiau preceded most hostilities. This activity served to forewarn rivals of aggressive intent, although not the precise timing of attacks. Sometimes formal embassies were sent to announce the intention to attack and arrange a mutually acceptable place of battle. This was not always the case. Kahekili's invasion of Oʻahu in 1783 seems to have caught its ruler Kahahana by surprise and forced him to give battle before he was fully mobilised.[66] The mobilisation of a rival's

---

64 Fornander (1969), pp. 280–81.
65 Fornander (1969), p. 300. See also Kamakau (1961), pp. 215–18, 232–33. On the desecration of bones, see Fornander (1969), p. 208. On revenge, see Vancouver (1801) bk 3, pp. 343 ff.; and Dening (1988), p. 19.
66 Ellis (1969), pp. 150–52; Fornander (1969), pp. 223, 334; and Kamakau (1961), p. 135.

forces was always cause for concern, as rival polities were never more than a few days' march or a day's sail away in good weather, and the loyalty of subordinates could not always be relied on.

When war was imminent, messengers would travel around the mokuʻ to inform subordinate aliʻi of the number of men they were required to mobilise. This would vary depending upon the nature of the threat posed or enterprise envisaged. Those called up were expected to arm and supply themselves and assemble at designated places. These calls to arms were generally rapidly responded to. Evasion of the call to arms carried the threat of severe punishment. Ellis claimed that those caught evading the call up had their ears slit and were led to camp by ropes tied around their waists. In May 1791 European merchants witnessed the power of the call to arms while trading off Waikiki on Oʻahu. When a single canoe arrived with news of war, the Hawaiians present left immediately and some did not even wait to receive payment for the trade goods they had brought out to the European vessel.[67]

Hawaiian armies were equipped with a variety of wooden weapons. Although battles usually began with an exchange of projectiles, the issue was generally decided at close quarters. The polulu, a long hardwood pike of up to six metres in length, was a favoured weapon. Another popular weapon was the pahoa, a hardwood dagger measuring up to 60 centimetres long. The Hawaiian arsenal also included various types of short wooden clubs that were used as bludgeons. Some clubs were edged with shark's teeth and could inflict vicious wounds. Finally there was the ihe, a short spear measuring from two to 2.5 metres long that could be used to thrust or parry, and could also be thrown like a javelin.[68]

The sling was the main projectile weapon. Made of plaited twine, Hawaiian slings could hurl stones the size of hens' eggs with great force. A number of traditional accounts mention aliʻi being disabled by slingstones. These accounts imply slingstones wounded or stunned opponents rather than killed them outright. With enemy warriors in hand-to-hand combat range, however, being momentarily stunned or distracted by injury could have fatal consequences for individuals hit by slingstones. Sometimes stones were thrown by hand. One type of club, known as a pikoi, was used

---

67 Ellis (1969), pp. 152–53; and Ingraham, in Kaplanoff (1971), p. 89.
68 See Clerke, in Beaglehole (1967), 3:2, p. 1322; Cook, in Beaglehole (1967), 3:1, p. 282; Samwell, in Beaglehole (1967), 3:2, p. 1182; Malo (1951), p. 194; Ellis (1969), p. 156; and Buck (1964), pp. 417–64.

as a throwing club to bring down fleeing enemy. The bows possessed by Hawaiians were flimsy devices made from slender reeds and tipped with bird or human bone, which were used by aliʻi to shoot rodents for sport. Kamakau refers to Kahekili's army including experts with the bow and arrow in 1783, but there is no reference to the use of the bow in battle.[69]

It was relatively easy to equip large armies with this military technology. Slingstones were available from a number of sources, such as streambeds, while the koa and kauila wood preferred for spears and clubs was found in the upper reaches of the dry forest that covered the lower slopes of the islands' mountains. Indeed, koa was the predominant tree of the forest zone. Koa was also the wood preferred for the hulls of war canoes.[70] Hawaiian fleets contained hundreds or even thousands of double- and single-hulled canoes. Double-hulled canoes were a major investment in resources, exceeded only by luakini heiau in terms of the commitment of manpower and raw materials required for their construction. Only important aliʻi could commission and own double-hulled canoes.[71] They consisted of two parallel hulls of equal size, connected by crosspieces that supported a central platform. They were paddled or propelled by a light triangular sail made of matting connected to a mast and boom. Some were up to 21 metres long. The trader John Turnbull witnessed canoes being paddled at speeds of 17 to 19 kilometres per hour. Cook and his officers were impressed with both the sailing skills of the Hawaiians and the quality of their canoes.[72]

Warfare was also a major undertaking in terms of the effort required to feed an army. The large size of Hawaiian armies has already been noted. In addition, their ranks were often further swelled by non-combatants.[73] Between January 1778 and December 1797 open conflict occurred in 13 out of 20 years. Even when fighting did not break out, the threat of attack forced the mobilisation and concentration of sizeable armies for

---

69 Kamakau (1961), p. 135.
70 Malo (1951), pp. 20–22; Kirch (1985), p. 29.
71 Malo (1951), pp. 20–21, 125–29; King, in Beaglehole (1967), 3:1, pp. 522–23; Clerke, in Beaglehole (1967), 3:1, p. 593; Samwell, in Beaglehole (1967), 3:2, p. 1167.
72 Clerke, in Beaglehole (1967), 3:1, p. 598; King, in Beaglehole (1967) 3:1, p. 626; Samwell, in Beaglehole (1967), 3:2, pp. 1183–84; Clerke, in Beaglehole (1967), 3:2, p. 1321; Hommon (1975), pp. 149–50; and John Turnbull, *A Voyage Round the World in the Years 1800, 1801, 1802, 1803 and 1805* (Philadelphia: Benjamin and Thomas Kite, 1810), pp. 165–67.
73 Ellis (1969), pp. 103–04, 124.

substantial periods, particularly in the early 1790s on Maui and Hawai'i. Most mobilisations, however, seem to have lasted only a matter of a few weeks or a few months (see Appendix 1).

Armies must be fed enough to perform effectively. There have been virtually no studies of the diet of non-Western chiefly armies, despite a wealth of anthropological and archaeological studies of subsistence patterns. Modern nutritional studies can also shed light on this topic. A healthy diet requires a balance of organic compounds. The four main classes of organic compounds found in living matter are carbohydrates, lipids, proteins, and nucleic acids. Carbohydrates are the source of energy for the body. Digested carbohydrates are converted into a usable form known as glucose, and circulated through the bloodstream to various parts of the body. Glucose excessive to immediate needs is converted into glycogen in the liver and muscles. If there is too much glucose present for storage as glycogen it is synthesised into body fats. Fats and fat-like substances are known as lipids. Proteins are the building blocks of the body, and consist of complex combinations of amino acids. The body is built up from the amino acids it obtains digesting food proteins. Nucleic acids control the process of heredity by which cells reproduce their proteins and themselves. An adequate diet must, therefore, include not only enough carbohydrates to fulfil energy needs, but also sufficient proteins to provide the amino acids needed for growth and maintenance, as well as all the required minerals, vitamins and liquid intake for good health.[74]

The most suitable food for troops in the field is one that is compact, portable and durable. It must answer nutritional needs and preferably not require cooking, as fuel and water are often not available in the field. Grain crops, such as wheat, maize and rice, fit many of these requirements. When eaten in their wholegrain form, they are rich in protein, minerals and the B-vitamin group. With the exception of rice, however, grain crops do not grow well in wet, tropical areas. Root crops, such as taro, thrive in damp tropical conditions and can produce prolific yields with very little cultivation. They tend to be low in proteins, however, do not store well once removed from the ground, and are

---

74 Konrad B. Krauskopf & Arthur Beiser, *The Physical Universe* (5th edn) (New York: McGraw Hill, 1985), pp. 419–26.

bulky to transport. While 28 grams of polished rice will provide 100 calories of energy for the body, it takes 70 grams of taro to provide the equivalent amount of energy.[75]

Nutritional needs vary in accordance with energy expended. While battle and forced marches require a great deal of physical exertion, warfare also involves a great deal of inactivity. The US National Academy of Sciences' recommended energy intake for healthy males between the ages of 15 and 50 with an average weight 70 kilograms is between 2,700 and 2,900 calories. The human body can, however, function on much less than this caloric intake. A study of famine-stricken Ethiopian villagers suggested that a reduced work rate could be sustained on an average caloric intake of only 1,475 calories for adult males, and 1,950 calories for adult females. The villagers concerned displayed none of the usual symptoms of victims of starvation victims, such as significant weight loss, increased death rates, or physical and mental lethargy.[76] As little as 56 grams of protein a day will suffice for an individual, providing that it contains all the necessary amino acids. Meat, fish, eggs and milk are good, well-rounded sources of protein, while humans have traditionally relied on grain or root crops for their bulk carbohydrates to provide daily caloric requirements. Unlike animal products, plant proteins do not usually contain all the body's required amino acids.[77]

Well-nourished humans can sustain short periods of undernourishment by breaking down existing skeletal muscle to provide the amino acids needed to process essential proteins from foods. When skeletal muscle is lacking or used up, lean body tissue must be resorted to. Weight loss and a marked decrease in resistance to disease and infection soon result. A clinical experiment using well-nourished subjects recorded a 24 per cent reduction in body weight over a six-month period on a diet of 1,578 calories. Most famine victims die as a result of their reduced resistance to diseases such as pneumonia and dysentery, rather than undernourishment.[78]

---

75 Smith (1976), pp. 85–87; Alland (1980), pp. 329–30; and Massal & Barrau (1956), p. 9.
76 National Academy of Sciences, 'Recommended Dietary Allowances', in D. A. Wenck et al., *Nutrition* (2nd edn) (Reston Publishing Co., 1983), pp. 630–34; D. S. Miller & J. Rivers, 'Seasonal Variations in Food Intake in Two Ethiopian Villages', *Proceedings of the Nutritional Society*, vols 31, 32A, 33A, 1972.
77 Krauskopf & Beiser (1985), p. 426; and Wenck et al. (1983), p. 630.
78 Nevin S. Scrimshaw, 'The Phenomenon of Famine', *American Review of Nutrition*, 7, 1987, 7–13.

The main staples of the Hawaiian diet were taro (*Colocasia esculenta*), 'uala (sweet potato, *Ipomoea batatas*) and fish. Irrigated taro fields tended to dominate in areas with permanent streams, while dry-field taro and 'uala prevailed elsewhere. The only exception to this pattern was reliance on 'ulu (breadfruit, *Artocarpus altilis*) in a few limited areas, like Puna in Hawai'i. Although all three crops are highly perishable and it is necessary to stagger plantings and practice preservation to ensure year-round supply. While there was seasonal variation in diet, the quantity of food available at any time of the year seems to have been reasonably regular, and ample for the needs of a population dispersed to suit localised production regimes.[79]

Irrigated taro is an extremely productive and useful crop. Mature wet taro can be kept in flooded taro patches for months without rotting. When steamed, mashed and pressed into hard dry cakes (pa'i'ai) it can be kept 'almost indefinitely'.[80] Pa'i'ai was a compact, durable food for armies, which simply required mixing with water to form edible poi (cooked and mashed corm of taro with water added). Dry-field taro is more seasonal than wet taro. In areas of heavy rainfall, such as Hilo on Hawai'i, dry taro can be planted at any time but, in drier areas like Ka'ū on Hawai'i, it was generally planted at the beginning of the rainy season to reduce the possibility of desiccation through drought. Tests on modern variants of the types of taro used by Hawaiians produced 1.23 to 2.46 tonnes of edible tubers per acre per year. Under optimum, irrigated conditions, output can be as high as 3.28 tonnes per acre per year or more. Kirch cites even higher yields – 40 tonnes plus per hectare per year for irrigated taro compared to only 10 tonnes per hectare per year for dry-field taro. Unprocessed taro weighing 2.495 kilograms would be needed to provide the average daily requirement of 2,800 calories for one man. Kirch notes that 100 grams of edible taro produces 153 calories.[81]

Hawaiian 'uala can tolerate drier conditions than taro and generally matures much faster – in three to six months as opposed to nine to 15 months for most varieties of taro. Minimum requirements tie it to areas of at least seasonal rainfall. At the other extreme, wet soil tends to cause 'uala to rot and heavy rain could force an early harvesting of the crop. In drier areas it was advisable to wait until the ground had received

---

79 Handy & Handy (1972), pp. 75, 101, 134, 276; Malo (1951), p. 206; and B. Currey, 'Famine in the Pacific: Losing the Chances of Change', *Geojournal*, vol. 4 (5), 1980, 457.
80 Handy & Handy (1972), p. 75.
81 Handy & Handy (1972), pp. 75, 104; Massal & Barrau (1956), pp. 7–9; Purseglove (1972a), p. 64; Kirch & Sahlins (1992), p. 28; and Kirch (1994), pp. 92–93.

several good showers of rain at the start of the rainy season before planting, while in areas of higher rainfall it was advisable to plant at the end of the rainy season and hope for a relatively dry summer. Cook noted that ʻuala obtained at Kauaʻi in 1778 lasted only 10 days at sea in an unpreserved state. The drying of harvested ʻuala helped stave off deterioration. ʻUala could also be cooked and mashed to form poi (poi ʻuala), although it tended to ferment after only a few days. Some ʻuala fields produced prolific yields. Cook's expedition was particularly impressed with the productivity of the fields above Kealakekua Bay on the leeward coast of Hawaiʻi. King noted that ʻuala were so plentiful here 'that the poorest natives would throw them into our ships for nothing'.[82] Studies by French medical specialist Emile Massal and ethnobotanist Jacques Barrau suggest an acre of sweet potato produces approximately 60 per cent of the caloric value of an acre of taro.[83]

The productivity of breadfruit groves and fishing expeditions was also impressive. Breadfruit trees can bear 50 to 100 fruit a year, which equates to 60 to 177 kilograms of fruit annually. Kirch suggests that average densities for breadfruit per hectare would produce between three to five tonnes of fruit per hectare per year.[84] Marine resources were abundant, despite winter storms and seasonal kapu restricting offshore fishing. Schools of aku (bonito or skipjack (*Katsuwonus pelamis*)) could contain up to 1,000 fish. Nineteenth-century Hawaiian sources imply that it was not unreasonable to expect a catch of 100 aku in a day. In 1810, a European resident of Honolulu knew of a day's expedition that produced 10 to 12 canoes deeply loaded with fish caught in nets. As a generalisation 2,400 calories roughly equates to 2.722 kilograms of fish. Small aku weigh between 2.268 and 5.433 kilograms, while some can weigh up to 9.979 kilograms. Even allowing for weight reduction due to gutting and drying, a moderate catch of aku represented a significant food resource.[85] The fishponds of the aliʻi represented a highly concentrated and easily accessible marine resource. A study of Hawaiian fishponds at the turn of

---

82   King, in Beaglehole (1967), 3:1, p. 618.
83   Handy & Handy (1972), pp. 75, 127–34; Kirch (1985), p. 51; Malo (1951), p. 205; Cook, in Beaglehole (1967), 3:1, p. 277; Beaglehole (1967), 3:1, p. 618, n. 1; and Massal & Barrau (1956), pp. 7–9. I am indebted to Marie Toussaint of the Ecole des Hautes Etudes en Sciences Sociales, Centre Norbert Elias – Marseille for the information on Massal's disciplinary background and training.
84   Kirch (1994), p. 92.
85   Campbell (1967), pp. 140–42; Hommon (1975), p. 142; and Patricia Price Beggerly, 'Hawaiian Initial Settlement – A Possible Model', in *Micronesian and Polynesian Voyaging – Three Readings*, Pacific Islands' Program – Miscellaneous Work Papers (Honolulu: 1976), p. 99.

this century found average yields of 166–365 kilograms of fish per acre. Cured fish, preserved by drying and salting, were obtained by Cook at Ni'ihau in 1778 and found to keep well and to be very good to eat.[86]

Massal and Barrau put the annual production of one acre of dry-field taro at 5,200,000 calories, one of irrigated taro at 6,930,000 calories, and one acre of sweet potato at 5,800,000 calories. According to these figures, the annual production of around 6.47 hectares of dry taro, 5.36 hectares of wet taro, or just over 5.67 hectares of 'uala could sustain 1,000 men for a month.[87] These figures were arrived at by multiplying 1,000 (men) x 2,800 (daily caloric intake) x 30 (average days in a month), divided by each crop's annual caloric output per hectare. Archaeological measurements of the dry-field system of the South Kona area of Hawai'i suggest it measured around 139 square kilometres.[88] In other words, the main logistical problem for waging war was not growing enough food to feed armies, but rather ensuring that enough food was available at a specific locality at a specific time.

While ali'i maintained storehouses of food, Ellis implies that those who were called up were expected to bring their own provisions. The main provisions carried were various types of poi and dried fish and calabashes of water. Poi and fish were often wrapped in edible taro leaves. Accounts of campaigns reveal that armies also lived off the land. Just prior to the battle of Moku'ōhai in 1782, for example, ali'i sent their men into nearby uplands to collect taro. The degree to which armies relied on preserved food stores as opposed to food taken in the field is uncertain. The evidence suggests that the latter played a more significant role. Stockpiles of preserved food needed to be partially maintained as a safeguard against famine. In Ka'ū, rat damage to stored provisions was a problem. Rats could devastate an entire crop and have been recorded in American Samoa as eating 117.27 kilograms of a 362.874-kilogram sweet potato harvest. Although preserved food was compact, the amount of food and water combatants could carry with them was limited. Canoes could carry considerable loads but there were no beasts of burden. Women sometimes accompanied husbands to war, and were probably weighed down with provisions on the march. Ellis mentions that they often waited at the

---

86 Kirch (1985), p. 213; Cook, in Beaglehole (1967), 3:1, p. 279.
87 Massal & Barrau (1956), pp. 7–9.
88 Kirch (1985), p. 225.

rear of battlefields with food and water to boost their husbands' strength during combat. The women of Maui and Hawai'i carried heavy loads of food and water from upland fields during peacetime.[89]

Supplies were occasionally sent between islands to armies based beyond their own territory. The longer an army remained in the field, the more the war zone was stripped of provisions. Any mobilisation that lasted more than a few months placed severe strains on the economy. After a prolonged siege of Ka'uiki Head in east Maui, the besieging force had to withdraw from the devastated neighbourhood to another locality and plant a food crop. In 1793, the Maui ali'i Komohomoho told Vancouver that Maui, Moloka'i and Lāna'i were suffering under the strain of supplying an army on Maui for the last two years to guard against the threat of invasion by Kamehameha. Famine occurred on O'ahu in 1796 because of the continued presence of Kamehameha's 10,000-man army situated there from 1795.[90]

The problems of maintaining an army in the field, and the danger of rebellions at home while the ruler was absent, meant most mobilisations soon resulted in armed clashes. Nineteenth-century ethnographies suggest battles were rather formal affairs. There is some support for this in Hawaiian traditions and eyewitness accounts. In 1790, Kamehameha sent a messenger to his rival Kahekili to arrange a mutually suitable place of landing and field of battle for Kamehameha's intended invasion of O'ahu. It is uncertain whether this was more of a taunt than a serious proposal, for Kamehameha was forced to return to Hawai'i before he could launch his attack.[91] In February 1796, the trader Captain Charles Bishop witnessed two armies on Kaua'i encamped on opposite sides of a valley with only a small stream separating them. By mutual agreement a temporary kapu on fighting was in place. Bishop noted that:

---

89   Ellis (1969), pp. 124, 153; Malo (1951), pp. 195, 219; Kamakau (1961), pp. 238–39; Handy & Handy (1972), pp. 133–34, 276; Currey (1980), p. 447; and Peter S. Bellwood, *A Settlement Pattern Survey, Hanatekua Valley, Hiva Oa, Marquesas Islands*, Pacific Anthropological Record no. 17 (Honolulu: Bernice P. Bishop Museum 1972), p. 27.
90   Handy & Handy (1972), p. 491; Fornander (1969), pp. 216–17; Vancouver (1801), bk 3, pp. 295–96; Broughton (1967), pp. 40, 71; and R.C. Schmitt, 'Famine Mortality in Hawaii', *Journal of Pacific History*, vol.5, 1970, 111.
91   Malo (1951), pp. 196–97; Ellis (1969), pp. 155–56; and Fornander (1969), p. 237.

4. THE HAWAIIAN MILITARY TRANSFORMATION FROM 1770 TO 1796

As Soon as the Taboo is Proclaimed in one camp, for one, two, or three days, it immediately takes place in the other for the like time – In this time, these intervals of war, they sit on the opposite banks of the stream conversing with each other as friends.[92]

When terrain allowed, troops were usually drawn up in a crescent-shaped formation known as kahului with the crescent's horns pointing towards the enemy. Sometimes the opposing forces would simply be drawn up in line facing each other. This formation was known as kukulu. According to Ellis, slingers and javelin men were distributed along the whole battleline. In a battle exercise witnessed by Vancouver, many in the remainder of the battleline were armed with polulu. When broken terrain ruled out these formations, armies fought in small, flexible groups. Such a battle order was known as makawalu. The 1782 battle of Moku'ōhai was fought in such a manner on rough lava fields dissected by deep gulches.[93]

The Hawaiian Islands had relatively few sites suitable for unimpeded large-scale manoeuvring prior to the rise of European plantation agriculture in the late 19th century. Much was virgin forested uplands or lava flows, and most of the flat land around the coasts was settled and covered with dwellings, flooded taro fields and dry-field systems. In a description of a council of war, related by Kamakau, advisers expressed their preference for a battlefield with enough open ground unimpeded by cultivations to manoeuvre their troops; and where any advantage of high ground lay with them.[94] Battle sites from this era were generally not suited to unimpeded movement by large bodies of men. Most were also very narrow, suggesting that Hawaiian armies were reasonably small, especially for battles fought in open order.

Ali'i usually led their own contingents into battle, unless prevented by old age or illness. The mō'ī was usually stationed in the centre of the battleline. Leading from the front was necessary for chiefly mana and also served to stiffen the resolve of followers, but diminished the role of generalship in battle. Tactical plans needed to be agreed on beforehand. The use of reserves in battle suggests, however, that some degree of behind-the-lines coordination occurred during combat. The battlefield role of the

---

92   Bishop, in Roe (1967), p. 146.
93   Ellis (1969), p. 155. On makawalu, see Malo (1951), p. 109. On Moku'ōhai's terrain, see Kamakau (1961), pp. 120–22; and Fornander (1969), pp. 309–11.
94   Kamakau (1961), p. 50.

kalaimoku and other war councillors is uncertain. There may have been sub-commanders within each retinue in the form of the ka'a-kaua, which are mentioned in passing by Malo.[95]

Battles were preceded by appeals to the gods for support, and the search for favourable omens in front of the assembled forces. Ali'i encouraged their followers with speeches, while orators, brandishing spears in front of the battleline, spurred their side on to deeds of valour. Important ali'i were accompanied into battle by images of their war gods carried by kahuna.[96] Ellis was led to believe that Hawaiian battles 'were most commonly a succession of skirmishes, or partial engagements'.[97] Battles often began with single combat between champions. Much importance was placed on drawing first blood, and then securing the corpse for immediate sacrifice on the field of battle. This was seen as an indication of divine favour, and could have a decisive effect on the morale of both sides. The impression of battle as a series of individual duels is consistent with Ellis's observation that the wives of warriors were present to provide food and water for their husbands. For this to occur, individual contestants had to be able to temporarily disengage and move to the rear, or the women had to be free to move around the battlefield without disrupting the battle. Group formations acting in unison would have prevented these actions.

Some fights were decided by the clash of massed battlelines, however, as at Aiea in 1794. A hail of projectiles generally preceded the collision of the two sides. On at least one occasion a heavy barrage of projectiles was enough to cause one side to break and flee. Unless one side dissolved rapidly, combat probably broke into a series of individual duels. Gavan Daws vividly portrays this type of battle as 'a war of daggers and clubs and even bare hands' where 'life or death depended on swiftness of hand and foot, and, in the last moments spine-breaking brute strength'.[98] Most casualties probably occurred when one side broke and fled, exposing their backs to their antagonists close at hand.

Fighting did not only consist of set battles. The Hawaiians had terms for ambushes (poi-po) and night attacks (moemoe). I'ī relates how Kalani'ōpu'u concealed his forces in dense vegetation alongside a narrow

---

95   Ellis (1969), pp. 155, 159; and Malo (1951), pp. 59, 196.
96   Ellis (1969), pp. 155, 157–58; Kamakau (1969), p. 211; Fornander (1969), p. 236; and Valeri (1982), p. 16.
97   Ellis (1969), p. 159.
98   Daws (1968a), p. 31; Kamakau (1961), p. 87; and Clerke, in Beaglehole (1967), 3:1, p. 594.

4. THE HAWAIIAN MILITARY TRANSFORMATION FROM 1770 TO 1796

trail through the forest of Paiei and ambushed the forces of Alapaʻi as they came along the trail. Alapaʻi's men were surrounded and slaughtered. Some years later, Kalaniʻōpuʻu's forces fell victim to a similar tactic. In 1775, a special unit known as the alapa advanced too far ahead of the main body of Kalaniʻōpuʻu's forces and was ambushed and all but wiped out in sandhills south-east of Wailuku on Maui.[99]

Naval operations were usually restricted to transporting troops and supplies, but there are also scattered references to other types of naval activity. In a comprehensive survey of Hawaiian traditions, Robert Hommon found three references to naval battles, one to a battle on Molokaʻi where an Oʻahu force was attacked from the sea and mountains simultaneously, and one to the successful repulse of an attempted naval landing on Oʻahu. Double-hulled canoes were not modified for fighting at sea until the introduction of cannon. Naval engagements consisted of exchanges of projectiles, followed by attempts to board opponents' canoes. Hawaiians spent much time training in canoes and were extremely skilled in their use.[100]

Battle dress was the same for battles on land and sea. Aliʻi usually wore distinctive capes and feathered caps. While Ellis doubted their practical value, Cook believed they were capable of absorbing the impact of projectiles and spear thrusts. They also served to distinguish aliʻi, possibly to preserve the general kapu on aliʻi–makaʻāinana interaction in the heat of battle. The grisly fate of the makaʻāinana who accidentally injured an aliʻi in a spear exercise has already been noted, although such propriety may not have extended to enemy aliʻi. Differences in cloaks distinguished aliʻi status. According to King, the longer the cloak the greater its wearer's rank. The shorter cloaks of the lesser aliʻi were also less colourful than the magnificent yellow and red cloaks of aliʻi nui.[101] Most other combatants wore little more than a piece of cloth, known as a malo, around their waists. Hawaiians used wetted mats as shields against the musket fire of British marines at Kealakekua Bay in 1779. Mats were more awkward and cumbersome than chiefly cloaks, and were used by 'inferior people' only.[102]

---

99   Malo (1951), p. 196; Iʻī (1959), pp. 3–4; Kamakau (1961), pp. 85–88; and Thomas G. Thrum, 'Some Noted Battles of Hawaiian History', in Thomas G. Thrum (comp.), *Hawaiian Almanac and Annual for 1889* (Honolulu: Press Publish Co, 1889), pp. 59–60.
100   Hommon (1975), pp. 176 ff.; and Ellis (1969), p. 155; and Vancouver (1801), bk 3, pp. 211–12; and Iʻī (1959), pp. 130–31.
101   Clerke, in Beaglehole (1967), 3:1, pp. 594–95; Ellis (1969), pp. 156–57; Sahlins (1985), pp. 130–31; and Linnekin (1988), p. 276.
102   Clerke, in Beaglehole (1967), 3:1, pp. 594–95; and Malo (1951), p. 251.

The main defensive asset of Hawaiians was their ability to dodge and parry blows and projectiles. In February 1787, for example, the trader Nathaniel Portlock was given an exhibition on board his vessel during which an ali'i had spears hurled at him 'with the utmost force' from only 10 metres range. The first spear was:

> avoided by a motion of the body, and caught it as it passed him by the middle: With the spear he parried the rest without the least apparent concern; he then returned the spears to his adversary, and armed himself with a Pa-ho-a; they were again thrown at him, and again parried with the same ease.[103]

Kamehameha was also observed by the Frenchman Pierre Francois Peron dodging spears thrown in quick succession, confirming Hawaiian sources' praise of his exceptional ability. Kamehameha's instructor, Kekūhaupi'o won renown for his duel with the Maui slinger Oulu when he avoided all his adversary's slingstones despite the fact that they were only 11 metres apart.[104] These skills served ali'i well as long as Hawaiian warfare remained centred on individual prowess. Battle provided a dramatic stage for the exhibition of the courage and skill on which so much chiefly status rested. Indiscriminate, mass volleys of projectiles and the use of drilled formations acting in unison could, however, undermine this system. It was exactly these two tactical trends that signalled the beginning of modern warfare in Europe in the late medieval period. Accounts of battles, drills witnessed by Vancouver and the formation of units of specialists demonstrate that a similar transformation was underway in Hawai'i in the late 18th century. The old ways still predominated but, in the atmosphere of intense rivalry that prevailed, the temptation to bend conventions and improve fighting effectiveness must have been great.

This suggestion of a tension between old and new ways is supported by a comparison of information on casualties and the duration of engagements. Information on casualties is limited. Hawaiian traditions tend to mention prominent figures killed in battle rather than total casualties. Ellis and Dibble claimed Hawaiian battles were usually only prolonged skirmishes with few casualties. In February 1779, Captain Charles Clerke learnt that a recent battle in Kaua'i had cost the victors only one man, while they had killed 26 of their rivals, including three ali'i. In 1793, Vancouver was told that a revolt on Kaua'i had just been

---

103 Portlock (1968), pp. 188–89.
104 Peron (1975), p. 6; and Thrum, vol. 5 (1918–19), pp. 452–56, esp. 454.

4. THE HAWAIIAN MILITARY TRANSFORMATION FROM 1770 TO 1796

crushed in a battle involving no losses to the victors and the death of two rebel aliʻi and five of their followers. Some others had been wounded, but had managed to escape into a nearby forest.[105] The fact that both battles involved internal disputes on Kauaʻi means, however, that caution must be used in generalising from their example.

Traditions mention at least three occasions when the vanquished were virtually wiped out. These occasions were the two ambushes cited above, and Kahekili's execution of the garrison of Kaʻuiki Head after their surrender to him following a long siege. Actual numbers killed are unclear beyond the fact that the Alapa unit ambushed in 1785 numbered 800 men. Kamehameha's greatest victory, the battle of Nuʻuanu in 1795, cost the vanquished somewhere between 300 and 500 men.[106] Their total strength is unknown, but it probably numbered many thousand given that it was the last stand of the Maui line against Kamehameha's 10,000-man army.

While naval battles seem to have been decided on the same day as conflict was joined, fighting on land could last for several days before one army retreated or was routed. Both the battle of Kawela on Molokaʻi in the middle of the 18th century and the battle of Mokuʻōhai on Hawaiʻi in 1782 were decided on the fifth day, after four days of indecisive skirmishing.[107] This coincidence may indicate the use of a standardised expression to designate a hard or long struggle, as is common in oral traditions. But it is supported by Ellis and Dibble's comments on warfare, and by Hawaiian traditions. The destruction of the alapa in 1775 was just one incident in fighting that ranged over many kilometres in the course of a number of days. The battles of ʻĪao in 1790 and Aiea in 1794 were also the culmination of days of fluid skirmishing and smaller engagements. Although no definite conclusions can be drawn, it appears that Hawaiian battlefields were not yet the concentrated killing grounds that the triumph of drill and discipline over individuality and discretion has caused elsewhere. Missionary Hiram Bingham was told that, between 1780 and 1795, Kamehameha's losses numbered 6,000, while his opponent's had lost double this. Many of these casualties were the result of starvation and sickness in the wake of the depletion of local food resources rather than due to direct violence.[108]

---

105 Clerke, in Beaglehole (1967), 3:1, pp. 577–78; and Vancouver (1801), bk 7, pp. 369–70 (Mar. 1793).
106 On Kaʻuiki, see Stokes (1937), pp. 35–36; and Fornander (1969), pp. 215–16.
107 On Kawela, see Kamakau (1961), p. 71. On Moluʻohai, see Kamakau (1961), pp. 120–21.
108 Stokes (1937), pp. 36–39.

The consequences of defeat in battle varied. Logistical problems and the ever-present threat of internal factionalism restricted the degree to which victory could be exploited. If the vanquished could evade their pursuers for long enough, they stood a good chance of rallying unmolested, providing sufficient confidence remained in chiefs seeking to revive their fortunes. The rate of recovery for localities serving as war zones varied according to the damage inflicted, local environmental circumstances, and subsequent involvement in political and military affairs. Armies passing through enemy territory generally plundered local resources and destroyed what they could not use or carry off. Invaders burned dwellings, wrecked canoes, cut down tree crops, destroyed fishponds, wells and irrigation ditches, uprooted crops and killed livestock.[109] The destruction of tree crops, such as breadfruit and coconut trees, were major losses as new trees take from six to eight years to produce fruit. Taro, however, if ruined by drought or deliberately uprooted can remain alive for months when kept in a damp place and cut with a generous portion of the crown intact. Both taro and ʻuala produce crops in a matter of months rather than years. In the interim, famine foods in the forest might sustain the local population.[110]

Rainfall and respite from invasion were crucial to recovery. In the 1790s, arid Lānaʻi was still recovering from a raid by Kalaniʻōpuʻu in 1778 that had stripped the island of food.[111] In 1790, Kamehameha's forces moved through the Lahaina area on Maui, plundering or destroying cultivations and livestock. When Vancouver visited Lahaina in 1793 he found only limited taro cultivation in the immediate vicinity of the settlement. He wrote that 'By far the larger portion of the plain was in a ruinous state; the small part that was in a flourishing condition, bore the evident marks of very recent labour'.[112] This was despite the fact that the rulers of Maui were straining to feed troops who had been mobilised on the island for some years to counter the threat of another invasion by Kamehameha. By February 1796, European visitors were remarking on the excellent state of Lahaina's cultivation and the large area that was under cultivation.[113] Kamehameha's victory over the Maui ruling family in 1795 had ended Maui's role as a battle zone, enabling local cultivators around Lahaina to rebuild their field

---

109 Kamakau (1961), pp. 51, 66, 70, 108; and Fornander (1969), pp. 133, 137, 141, 240.
110 Malo (1951), p. 43; Handy & Handy (1972), p. 94; Massal & Barrau (1956), p. 20; J. W. Purseglove, *Tropical Crops*, vol. 2: *Monocotyledons 2* (London: Longmans, 1972b), pp. 464–65; and J. W. Purseglove, *Tropical Crops, Dicotyledons 2* (London: Longmans, Green and Co., 1968), p. 382.
111 Hommon (1976), p. 157; and Schmitt (1970), pp. 110–11.
112 Vancouver (1801), bk 3, pp. 332–33.
113 Broughton (1967), p. 37.

systems and draw on the rainfall of the nearby mountains of west Maui. Table A1 in Appendix 1 demonstrates that most localities were not invaded frequently in this period. During the period covered in this study, Lahaina seems to have been pillaged only in 1790 and the previous time that it had suffered war damage was around 1750. The fact that Lahaina's coconut and breadfruit trees escaped destruction in 1790 suggests Kamehameha may have been confident of retaining control of the area.[114]

Victors attempting to occupy conquered territory might proclaim an amnesty to get the land back into production again. Maka'āinana were more useful as cultivators than as fugitives. Although Ellis claims they were enslaved and treated cruelly, such oppression ran the risk of alienating a population with uncertain loyalties, while their previous ruler might still be capable of mounting an effort to regain lost lands. There are hints that the Hawai'i ruler's control of the Hana and Kipahulu districts of east Maui in the 1770s and 1780s involved the retention of some local ali'i in administrative posts. With the rest of the island still controlled by the Maui mō'ī Kahekili, the support of local inhabitants was important.[115]

Lesser ali'i might have a role in the conqueror's new administration, but prominent enemy ali'i would always pose a threat as potential rallying points for dissent. For prominent ali'i, defeat and capture meant death or a loss of mana. Kin ties or respect for high status saved some like Keawemauhili, who was released after being captured at Moku'ōhai in 1783.[116] Victory was often emphasised by the construction of a new heiau on the ruins of enemy heiau and, occasionally, by the incorporation of the enemy's god images into the new heiau's pantheon.[117] The fate of a dead ali'i's retinue is uncertain. They were either hunted down and killed, or sought a new lord. Victorious and ambitious chiefs were always looking to bolster their retinues to control new territory and strengthen their position for internal power struggles. Kahekili, for example, left the governing of Maui to others while he moved to newly conquered O'ahu to personally oversee what turned out to be a troublesome consolidation.[118]

---

114 Vancouver (1801), bk 3, p. 295; and Cordy (1972), p. 398.
115 Ellis (1969), p. 152; and Hommon (1975), pp. 98–100.
116 Kamakau (1961), p. 122.
117 Valeri (1982), p. 6.
118 Fornander (1969), pp. 223–25.

Fortresses were rare in Hawai'i, despite the potential benefits as bulwarks against invasion and for consolidating conquest. Most fortified positions served merely as temporary refuges. If fugitives could not flee and hide in the forested uplands, or to the territory of sympathetic friends, their only means of evading capture was to reach a fortified refuge or sanctified places of refuge known as pu'uhonua. The most famous pu'uhonua was at Hōnaunau on the South Kona coast of Hawai'i. After appropriate rituals of purification, those who reached such sanctuaries were allowed to leave unmolested. Most fortified sites consisted of steep ridges modified by fosses, and occasionally strengthened with fighting platforms. Interestingly, the fortified ridge at Kawela on Moloka'i ended in a pu'uhonua. In some localities, fortified caves served as refuges, as possibly did a peninsula in Puuloa (Pearl Harbour) on O'ahu.[119]

The most prominent stronghold in Hawaiian traditions was Ka'uiki Head, a small steep-sided volcanic hillock on Hana Bay, east Maui. In the latter part of the 18th century, east Maui intermittently served as a battlefield between the forces of Maui and Hawai'i. Ka'uiki Head facilitated the occupation of the area by Hawaiian forces by providing a refuge in times of defeat until help could be sent. Ka'uiki's summit was reached by means of a ladder made of trees and vines. References to sorties by its besieged defenders and to the head being fortified suggest that another, more accessible passage to the summit also existed. Ka'uiki Head was not, however, an ideal position. It lacked defensible, sheltered anchorages and had limited space on its summit. Reliance on rainfall and springs at the base of the hill for drinking water was perhaps its greatest weakness. These shortfalls suggest it was more a refuge in desperate times than a stronghold from which to dominate the country around it.[120]

There are scattered references to the construction of field fortifications. With one exception, all are associated with firearms. On 14 February 1779, Hawaiians at Kealakekua Bay threw up several stone breastworks in expectation of retaliation for the death of Cook. When Kamehameha invaded Maui in 1790, he encountered a fortified position at Pu'ukoae, probably in response to his firearms and cannon. Earthworks and trenches were constructed at Kāne'ohe on O'ahu in 1794 specifically to counter

---
119 Kirch (1985), p. 273; Kamakau (1961), pp. 110–11; Pogue (1978), pp. 36–38; I'ī (1959), p. 97; McAllister (1933), pp. 35–36; and Ellis (1969), pp. 103–04.
120 Handy & Handy (1972), pp. 502–04; Fornander (1967), pp. 98–99, 108, 215–16; and Kamakau (1961), pp. 80, 115, 154.

the impact of firearms. In a battle on Hawai'i in 1791, warriors from Ka'ū squatted in small holes to avoid enemy musket fire. The one instance in which the construction of fortifications did not involve firearms is a reference to the forces of the Maui ali'i Kukeawe fortifying themselves strongly at Kapuoa in response to attacks from local forces. As was suggested earlier, this may have been a response to indigenous firepower.[121]

The distinction between war and peace was not always clear. Some conflicts ended in a formal peace ceremony sanctified with prayers and sacrifices, and celebrated through feasts and games. At other times, however, open hostilities were followed by uneasy stand-offs that sometimes lasted for years. In such circumstances, peaceful visits between ali'i were potentially tense affairs. Visitors might be treated with respect and courtesy, as the Maui ali'i Kahahawai was when he called on Kamehameha soon after defeating him in battle in 1782. At other times, their lives were endangered. When Kamehameha sent two of his most senior councillors, Keaweaheulu and Kamanawa, to make overtures for peace with his enemy Keōua, Keōua's advisers recommended killing them. They were only spared because Keōua rejecting his councillors' advice, and accepted Kamahameha's overture. Keōua was struck down and sacrificed to Kū'kā'ili-moku when he arrived to meet Kamehameha. When Vancouver attempted to mediate between Kahekili and Kamehameha in 1793 and 1794, he found his efforts blocked by each party's fear that they would be killed if they went to talk with the other.[122]

The tension noted by Vancouver needs, however, to be placed in perspective. It occurred at the height of a prolonged military struggle for power between Kamehameha and Kahekili that was more intense than anything experienced before in Hawai'i. Outside of such times of elevated tension, the importance of high-status marriage partners meant that ties among the upper echelons of the ali'i extended between districts and islands. Visits to relatives and the search for status marriages took ali'i out of their own polities. All chiefly dynasties traced their ultimate origins to the same divine ancestors, resulting in a fixed, archipelago-wide status hierarchy. Generally the oldest and most senior lines were found on the western islands of Kaua'i and O'ahu. Chiefs from Maui and Hawai'i

---

121 Samwell, in Beaglehole (1967), 3:2, p. 1205 (1779); Fornander (1969), p. 236 (1790); Menzies (1920), p. 193 (1791); and Kamakau (1961), p. 168 (1794).
122 Vancouver (1801), bk 3, pp. 261, 317–19; bk 5, p. 82; Fornander (1969), pp. 319, 331; and Kamakau (1961), pp. 155–58.

sought to enhance their status by seeking unions with members of the older lines of the western islands.[123] Inter-district and inter-island travel by aliʻi seems to have been reasonably frequent, as the following passage from Fornander implies:

> Following the custom of the times, Lonokahaupu set out from Kauaʻi with a suitable retinue of men and canoes, as became so high a chief, to visit the islands of the group, partly for exercise and practice in navigation, an indispensable part of a chief's education, and partly for the pleasures and amusements that might be anticipated at the courts of the different chieftains where the voyagers might sojourn.[124]

On this particular trip, Lonokahaupu visited Keawe, ruler of Hawaiʻi, and became one of the husbands of Keawe's wife Kalanikauleleiaiwa.

Most fighting in the late 18th century took place between moku rather than within them. Victory vindicated the mana of a ruler. External wars might also stifle or divert internal dissent. In 1794 Kaʻeokulani, the ruler of Kauaʻi, diverted an oncoming rebellion by proposing that his army immediately attack his Oʻahu counterpart rather than return to Kauaʻi.[125] Prolonged periods of peace created domestic restlessness among ambitious aliʻi and retinue members anxious to display their worth in battle. Wars did not occur every year, however, and some polities saw no fighting for years on end. Yet, outside of succession disputes, most polities experienced limited open dissent. This suggests a higher degree of political acumen than has generally been allowed for.

Warfare was an integral part of chiefly relations by 1770 and provided an important means of enhancing status for some but not all aliʻi nui, kaukau aliʻi and makaʻāinana. Consideration of the logistical and morale requirements to keep an army functioning in the field for any length of time, however, meant that the arts of peace – notably agricultural production and political consensus-building to maintain coherence, and a shared sense of identity and purpose – mattered as much as the arts of war. The next chapter details how Kamehameha's military victory and successful unification of Hawaiʻi in the last two decades of the 18th century rested on this vital combination of the arts of war and the arts of peace.

---

123 Sahlins (1985), pp. 20–21; and Kirch & Sahlins (1992), p. 23, citing Thrum, vol. 6 (1919–20), p. 244; and Fornander (1969) endpaper.
124 Fornander (1969), p. 296.
125 Fornander (1969), pp. 263–64; and Kamakau (1961), p. 168.

5
The Pursuit of Power in Hawai'i from 1780 to 1796

This chapter introduces the third main theme of this book – that historical details matter and unification of the Hawaiian Islands was not inevitable simply because the necessary structural conditions were in place. The structural features proposed as essential prerequisites for unification were all in place in Hawai'i well before the 1790s. Specific events and decisions influenced the course of history. Hawaiian traditions place limited emphasis on settlement patterns, carrying capacity and other structural characteristics of Hawaiian society. They focus on battles fought, rivals slain and marriage alliances successfully concluded. Environmental factors, political and social organisation may have set limits on action, but they could not dictate the specific course of events. That was a matter for the gods and ali'i.

A detailed examination of Hawaiian traditions suggest that events in the 1780s and 1790s allowed the relatively young and militarily weak chief Kamehameha to seize power through fortuitous circumstances and conciliatory practices pursued initially through his weak position but later, as his power consolidated, through choice. The 1780s saw the foremost military tactician and military innovator Kahekili expand his realm, while Kamehameha was preoccupied with consolidating his political heartland against older, more established subordinates. Kahekili overextended himself and alienated his new subjects with repressive measures, thereby weakening his realm and fatally dividing his polity into warring factions upon his death. Their fighting undermined their cohesive strength and allowed Kamehameha to achieve a relatively easy victory over their remnants in 1795. Detailed accounts of the battles of the 1790s, accompanied by battle maps, reveal that firearms and cannon did not and could not have been as decisive as many modern commentators suggest. The chapter concludes by noting that victory was relatively easy: Kamehameha's real struggle lay in consolidating this temporary ascendancy into sustained control.

Two paths to power: Political consolidation versus territorial expansion in the 1780s

In recent decades, European historiography's traditional focus on the lives and clashes of political elites has lost ground to analysis of the social and economic structures around which societies are organised. Without attention to historical narratives, however, there is a danger that structures are seen to determine events. Historical trajectories then take on an air of inevitability. The chaos and randomness of human activity is lost. While the general pattern already outlined holds true for this period, the following detailed account of events shows the influence on history of specific events and decisions.

When Captain James Cook's expedition arrived in the archipelago in 1778, the islands were divided between four mōʻī. Kalaniʻōpuʻu ruled over Hawaiʻi and had also established a presence in east Maui. His main protagonist was Kahekili, who controlled the rest of Maui, Lānaʻi and Kahoʻolawe. Peleiʻōhōlani, the ruler of Oʻahu, had recently conquered Molokaʻi. Beyond Oʻahu, Kāneoneo presided over Kauaʻi and Niʻihau.[1]

Kalaniʻōpuʻu was probably the most powerful of the four mōʻī in the late 1770s. As well as maintaining the unity of Hawaiʻi, he had preserved the foothold he secured in east Maui during the reign of Kahekili's predecessor, his brother Kamehamehanui. His recent attempts to invade west Maui had been repulsed, however, Kahekili suffered heavy losses in the process of preserving his territory. Although he still accompanied his army to war, Kalaniʻōpuʻu was ageing. Ship's surgeon on the Cook expedition David Samwell estimated that he was over 60 and described him as 'very tall and thin, seemingly much emaciated by debauchery, tottering as he walks along, his skin is very scurfy and his eyes sore with ava [kava]'.[2]

---

1   King, in Beaglehole (1967), 3:1, pp. 500, 614; and Thrum, vol. 5 (1918–19), p. 310.
2   Samwell, in Beaglehole (1967), 3:2, p. 1162; King, in Beaglehole (1967), 3:1, p. 512; Clerke, in Beaglehole (1967), 3:1, pp. 597–98; and Fornander (1969), p. 214.

Kahekili had become the ruler of Maui relatively late in life, after the death of Kamehamehanui. Abraham Fornander dates this succession to the mid-1760s, but it may have been a decade later, as Kalaniʻōpuʻu and Peleiʻōhōlani's attacks on Maui lands in the mid-1770s may have been an attempt to exploit the death of Kamehamehanui. Samwell described Kahekili as 'a middle aged man ... of rather mean appearance'. He proved to be a skilled military tactician. In his later years he was described as a stern, resolute man, with a cold, calculating manner.[3] Peleiʻōhōlani was also a formidable opponent who successfully maintained the unity of Oʻahu, which was forged by his immediate predecessor, Kūaliʻi. When he invaded Molokaʻi, he killed or exiled most of the local aliʻi in revenge for the murder of his daughter by aliʻi from windward Molokaʻi.[4] Kāneoneo became mōʻī of Kauaʻi by marrying his cousin, Kamakahelei. Both were of very high rank. Unlike his three counterparts, Kāneoneo did not launch any expeditions against rival rulers. Kamakahelei exerted much influence on Kauaʻi, and the young Kāneoneo's hold on power at Wailua was to prove tenuous.[5]

Cook was able to learn little about the balance of power in the chain when he arrived at Kauaʻi in January 1778. By the time he returned to the islands in November of that year, Kalaniʻōpuʻu and Kahekili were at war in east Maui. After raiding Lānaʻi and parts of Maui, Kalaniʻōpuʻu had been confronted by the forces of Kahekili in Hāmākualoa. A battle was fought and, when Cook arrived off east Maui, Kalaniʻōpuʻu's forces were retiring in good order towards Hana through Koʻolau. Kalaniʻōpuʻu remained in east Maui until January 1779, when he returned to Kealakekua Bay with part of his force. His return seems to have been prompted by Cook's presence at Kealakekua Bay rather than internal dissent elsewhere in the island. Gananath Obeyesekere proposes that Kalaniʻōpuʻu returned to Kealakekua Bay to try and recruit Cook as his foreign priest to counter the influence of Kahekili's priest, Kaleopuʻupuʻu of Oʻahu, who came from a lineage of foreign priests. Fornander makes it clear that Kaleopuʻupuʻu's religious ability was believed to be the reason behind Kahekili's recent victory on Maui.[6]

---

3   Samwell, in Beaglehole (1969), 3:2, p. 1151; Fornander (1969), pp. 214–15; and Kamakau (1961), pp. 166–67.
4   Thrum, vol. 5 (1918–19), p. 310; and Handy & Handy (1972), p. 278.
5   Fornander (1969), p. 297; Valeri (1985a), p. 166.
6   Obeyesekere (1992), p. 81; Cook, in Beaglehole (1967), 3:1, pp. 476 ff.; King, in Beaglehole (1967), 3:1, p. 511; Dibble (1909), p. 22; Kamakau (1961), p. 91; Fornander (1969), pp. 146–79; and Pogue (1978), p. 71.

TRANSFORMING HAWAI'I

On 14 February 1779, followers of Kalaniʻōpuʻu killed Cook when he tried to take the old mōʻī hostage to secure the return of the ship's cutter, which was stolen the previous night. The effect of the confrontation between Kalaniʻōpuʻu's people and Cook's party on the old mōʻī's rule is unclear. A number of Hawaiians were killed by British punitive measures in the days following Cook's death and before peace was restored.[7] Kalaniʻōpuʻu and his followers were left with an early insight into the power of European cannon and muskets, and mana from their possession of most of the bones of the great captain. Samwell and James King were led to believe that Kalaniʻōpuʻu received the legs, thighs and arms of Cook, while his great warrior-chief Kekūhaupiʻo received his head. Kalaniʻōpuʻu's nephew, Kamehameha, was given Cook's hair. The rest of the body was burnt.[8]

As the British expedition made one last journey through the islands, they discovered two more conflicts. On 27 February 1779, King learned that the fires they had seen on Molokaʻi were probably due to the fighting between Peleiʻōhōlani and Kahekili. The fact that Kahekili later sought Halawa Valley on Molokaʻi from Peleiʻōhōlani's successor suggests Kahekili's attack was unsuccessful.[9] The British learnt that Kaʻeokulani, the half-brother of Kahekili, had recently supplanted Kāneoneo as Kamakahelei's consort on Kauaʻi. Only days before the British arrival on 28 February, Kāneoneo had been defeated in battle by the combined forces of Kamakahelei, her son Keawe, and Kaʻeokulani. Kāneoneo had escaped, but his remaining support on Kauaʻi was uncertain. Keawe was installed as mōʻī, although it soon became apparent that the real influence lay with Kaʻeokulani and Kamakahelei.[10]

Peleiʻōhōlani died of natural causes sometime in 1779 or 1780, and was succeeded by his son Kumahana. There is no record of any succession disputes, although an unspecified number of Oʻahu aliʻi deposed Kumahana soon afterwards in response to his increasingly despotic rule. A council of Oʻahu aliʻi 'elected' Kahahana, the young son of the powerful ʻEwa aliʻi Elani, as the new mōʻī. Kumahana was allowed to return to Kauaʻi with his family, where relatives of his mother and sister at Waimea

---

7   King, in Beaglehole (1967), 3:1, pp. 549 ff.; and Clerke, in Beaglehole (1967), 3:1, pp. 531 ff.
8   Samwell, in Beaglehole (1967), 3:2, p. 1215; King, in Beaglehole (1967), 3:1, p. 566; and Kamakau (1961), p. 103.
9   King, in Beaglehole (1967), 3:1, pp. 584–85.
10 Clerke, in Beaglehole (1967), 3:1, p. 577; Valeri (1985a), p. 166; and Stokes (1937), pp. 36–37.

5. THE PURSUIT OF POWER IN HAWAI'I FROM 1780 TO 1796

took them in. Kumahana's son Kāneoneo was probably here also after his recent overthrow in Puna. There is no indication that their line posed a serious threat to the new power clique at Wailua.[11]

Although the new mō'ī of O'ahu had blood links with Kaua'i, his ties with Maui had the greatest influence on the future of O'ahu. Kahahana was closely related on his mother's side to Kahekili of Maui and had been raised in Kahekili's household. Fornander claims that Kahekili made Kahahana promise to cede the sacred O'ahu site of Kualoa in Ko'olaupoko to him before allowing him the leave for O'ahu. Kahekili also requested palaoa pae, the right to whalebone washed up on shore, for O'ahu. This right was usually reserved to the mō'ī of the land. Kahekili increased his leverage over the O'ahu mō'ī by keeping his wife Kekuapoiula at his court. Fornander asserts that the only reason Kahekili did not invade O'ahu to take advantage of the disruption created by Kumahana's overthrow was the threat that Kalani'ōpu'u posed to Maui through his continued presence in Hana.[12]

Time was on Kahekili's side. Kalani'ōpu'u was ageing and, with each passing month, Kahahana became increasingly at odds with his subject ali'i over Kahekili's demands. Kahahana's announcement of Kahekili's demands had caused divisions in the O'ahu ali'i. The kahuna nui Kaopulupulu was particularly critical, claiming the handing over of sacred Kualoa was disrespectful to the gods and the granting of palaoa pae was tantamount to recognition of Kahekili's right to rule O'ahu. Kahekili created a rift between Kahahana and Kaopulupulu by claiming the O'ahu kahuna nui had twice offered the government of O'ahu to him behind Kahahana's back. On the second occasion, Kahahana was already ruling as mō'ī. In the wake of Kaopulupulu's continued criticism of his rule, this was apparently enough to convince Kahahana to summon his kahuna nui and have him killed. The slaying of Kaopulupulu and his son Kaholupue alienated many on O'ahu.[13]

---

11   Kamakau (1961), pp. 128–29; Fornander (1969), pp. 217, 297–98; Thrum, vol. 5 (1918–19), pp. 282–83; and Kirch & Sahlins (1992), p. 36, n. 1.
12   Fornander (1969), pp. 218–19; Thrum, vol. 5 (1918–19), p. 282; and Kamakau (1961), pp. 128–29.
13   Fornander (1969), pp. 221–22; Thrum, vol. 5 (1918–19), pp. 287–88; and Kamakau (1961), pp. 133–34.

Kalaniʻōpuʻu confined his activities to touring his moku with a sizeable court. The tour was perhaps a response to restlessness among his people over the prospect of his declining health and imminent death. Sometime in 1780 or 1781 the Puna aliʻi ʻĪmakakaloa rebelled against Kalaniʻōpuʻu. The rebellion received much support from aliʻi and makaʻāinana, who were disgruntled at the excessive demand for provisions from their mōʻī's large touring party. The rebellion, however, seems to have been confined to Puna. After consecrating a heiau to his war god at Ohele in Hilo, Kalaniʻōpuʻu attacked ʻĪmakakaloa in Puna. The rebellious aliʻi was defeated after a long struggle. Kalaniʻōpuʻu went on to neighbouring Kaʻū and built another heiau at Pakini in preparation for the capture and sacrifice of ʻĪmakakaloa to Kūkāʻili-moku as thanks for victory. ʻĪmakakaloa avoided capture for upwards of a year before Kalaniʻōpuʻu lost patience and ordered Puna ravaged until the vanquished leader was handed over. Loyalty had its limits: ʻĪmakakaloa was soon betrayed and killed.[14]

Signs that Kalaniʻōpuʻu's death would result in a succession struggle emerged at the ceremony of sacrifice in Pakini heiau. While Kalaniʻōpuʻu's son Kīwalaʻō was conducting the preliminary rituals, Kamehameha boldly usurped his role and offered up the body of ʻĪmakakaloa himself. Kalaniʻōpuʻu had signalled his recognition of Kamehameha through the division of Cook's remains, and Kamehameha's close friendship with Kalaniʻōpuʻu's greatest warrior-chief Kekūhaupiʻo was well known. But, by this action, Kamehameha stepped beyond the bounds of acceptable behaviour. Much anger resulted among the assembled aliʻi and, on Kalaniʻōpuʻu's advice, Kamehameha left the court and retired to his estate at Halawa in Kohala.[15]

It is uncertain when aliʻi began committing themselves to the contending successors to Kalaniʻōpuʻu. It is also uncertain if Kalaniʻōpuʻu had declared Kīwalaʻō as his heir and Kamehameha as the guardian of his war god at Waipiʻo in Hāmākua prior to the Puna rebellion or on his deathbed, or whether he had clearly indicated his wishes at all. Whatever the case, it would be the alignment of the moku's aliʻi and not the will of a dead mōʻī that would decide the issue.[16]

---

14 Fornander (1969), pp. 200–01; and Kamakau (1961), pp. 105–08.
15 Fornander (1969), pp. 202–03; and Kamakau (1961), p. 109. On Kekūhaupiʻo, see S. L. Desha, *Kamehameha and his Warrior Kekūhaupiʻo*, F. N. Frazier (trans.) (Honolulu: Kamehameha Schools Press, 2000).
16 Fornander (1969), p. 299; Kamakau (1961), p. 107; Iʻī (1959), p. 13; and Dibble (1909), p. 42.

Kalaniʻōpuʻu died in Kaʻū in January 1782. Kīwalaʻō succeeded his father. Tension mounted as the time for the new mōʻī's announcement of land redistribution approached. Many aliʻi brought their retinues to the site of the announcement. The aliʻi assembled at Hōnaunau in South Kona, where Kīwalaʻō deposited the bones of his father in the Hale o Keawe mausoleum. Kīwalaʻō's uncle, Keawemauhili of Hilo, pressured the young mōʻī into ensuring that he did well out of the redistribution. Keawemauhili and his windward allies did indeed benefit at the expense of leeward aliʻi, and even to the detriment of Kīwalaʻō's brother, Keōua Kuahuʻula, and Kīwalaʻō himself. The result was just what the leeward aliʻi had feared and prompted them to mobilise their forces behind their chosen leader, Kamehameha, to mount a challenge to Kīwalaʻō's party. Their forces gathered in the vicinity of Kealakekua Bay a few miles north of Hōnaunau.[17]

The fighting began when Keōua attacked some of Kamehameha's allies. Skirmishing continued for the next few days while the aliʻi aligned themselves with one or other party and forces were assembled. The resulting coalitions were more marriages of convenience than coherent entities, reflecting a complex interaction between self-interest, opportunism, blood ties and personal rivalries. Kamehameha headed a coalition centred on the forces of five powerful Kona chiefs: Kekūhaupiʻo, Keʻeaumoku, Keaweaheulu, Kameʻeiamoku and Kamanawa. Other blood ties bonded this group together. Kamanawa and Kameʻeiamoku were twins. Keaweaheulu lost out to Keawemauhili in seeking the hand of Ululani and, through her, the control of Hilo. They were supported by some Kohala chiefs and Kamehameha's brothers: Kalaimamahu, Kawelookalani and Kalanimalokuloku-i-Kapoʻokalani. Kīwalaʻō, Keōua and Keawemauhili were the most prominent aliʻi in the other coalition. Their forces were numerically superior and were drawn predominantly from Hilo, Puna and Kaʻū. Some Kona and Kohala aliʻi sided with them, however, the most notable being Kamehameha's paternal uncle Kānekoa and his brother Kahai.[18]

---

17   Fornander (1969), pp. 204, 302–06; Kamakau (1961), pp. 118–19; and Kahananui (1984), p. 198.
18   Fornander (1969), pp. 307–09; Kamakau (1961), p. 120; and Valeri (1985a), p. 167.

After three or four days of skirmishing, matters came to a head when Kīwalaʻō encountered Keʻeaumoku on the battlefield among the rough lava country of Mokuʻōhai. The terrain forced the combatants to fight in small groups. The fighting was open and fluid, with aliʻi to the fore. The crucial moment came when warriors accompanying Kīwalaʻō failed to finish off Keʻeaumoku after he became isolated and was badly wounded. A warrior rushing to Keʻeaumoku's rescue struck Kīwalaʻō with a sling stone, allowing Keʻeaumoku to crawl over to the disabled mōʻī and dispatch him with a shark's tooth dagger. The death of Kīwalaʻō triggered the rout of his forces. Keōua and his men fled to their canoes and sailed to Kaʻū. Others fled into the mountains and eventually made their way back to their homes on the other side of the island. A large number of prisoners were taken, including Keawemauhili. He managed to escape, and fled to Hilo. Kamehameha only arrived at the battlefield late in the day after conducting religious observances, but participated in the fighting and killed at least one enemy aliʻi.[19]

Kalaniʻōpuʻu's moku was now effectively divided between three rulers: Kamehameha, Keawemauhili and Keawe. Kamehameha controlled Kona, Kohala, northern Hāmākua and eastern Maui. Keawemauhili declared himself mōʻī over the rest of Hāmākua, Hilo, and part of Puna. As a nīʻaupiʻo aliʻi, Keawemauhili was the highest ranking aliʻi of the three and, perhaps, the most powerful given the resources of his power base and the fact that he had governed Hilo since well before the death of his brother Kalaniʻōpuʻu. Keōua was acclaimed as Kīwalaʻō's successor by the Kaʻū aliʻi.

Keōua was prepared for now to acknowledge the superior rank of his uncle Keawemauhili, and to align himself with him against the threat of Kamehameha. Kamehameha's family estate in Kohala and his personal retinue were probably small compared to his rivals. Rather, his power seems to have derived from his willingness to rule in accordance with the wishes of the more established Kona aliʻi, the so-called Kona uncles. Fornander describes this relationship as an 'open and tacit partnership'.[20]

---

19   Fornander (1969), pp. 309–11; Kamakau (1961), pp. 120–22; and Dibble (1909), p. 43.
20   Fornander (1969), pp. 315, 311–12; and Kamakau (1961), p. 122.

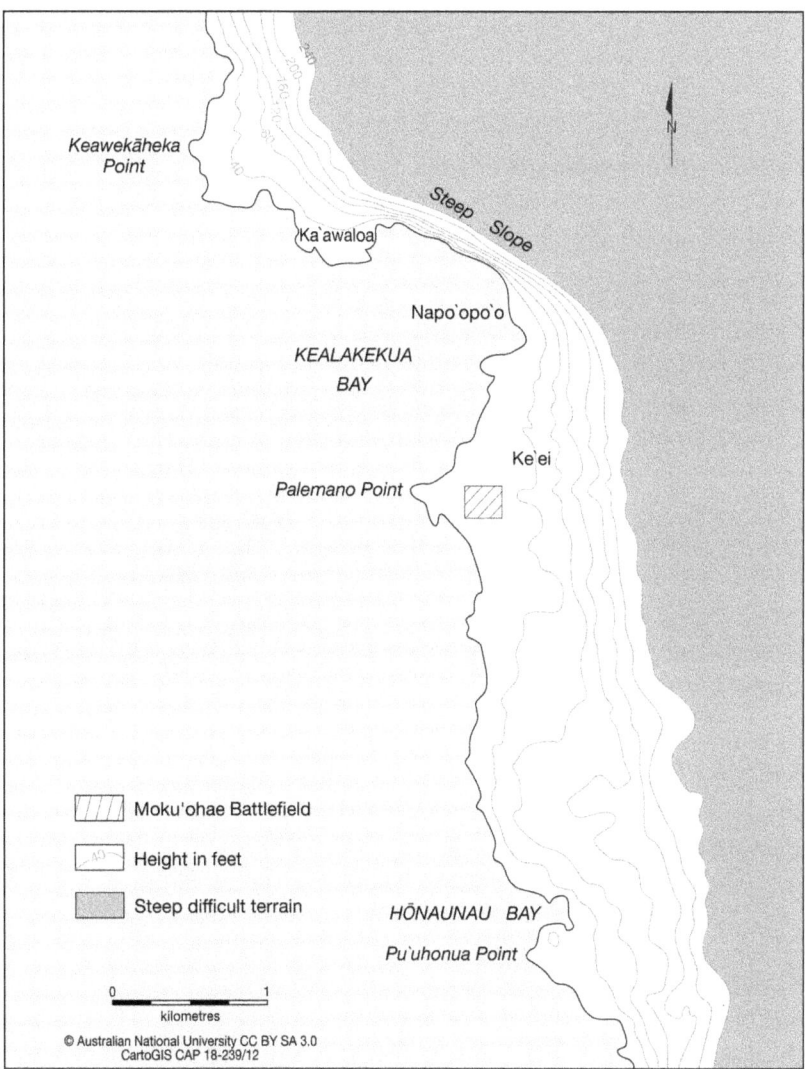

Figure 9: The battle of Mokuʻōhai, 1782
Source: CartoGIS, The Australian National University.

Kamehameha's relatives Kānekoa and Kahai fled to Hilo with their followers after the defeat at Mokuʻōhai. Keawemauhili granted them refuge and gave them lands. For unknown reasons the two aliʻi soon rebelled against Keawemauhili. They were soundly defeated and fled to the lands of Keōua where they were again granted refuge. Yet again they rebelled and were defeated. Kānekoa was slain and Kahai fled to Kamehameha and threw himself upon his mercy. He was forgiven and does not figure in Hawaiian traditions again.[21] It is unclear how many aliʻi moved between mōʻī like this. They seem to have represented a small minority, and such movements were probably more pronounced during succession disputes. The fortunes of Kānekoa and Kahai suggest no mōʻī was powerful enough at this stage to ignore the opportunity to increase their fighting strength, regardless of the risk involved in taking on people who had already deserted other mōʻī.

Kahekili was not slow to exploit the divisions that arose after Kalaniʻōpuʻu's death. He offered an alliance to Kamehameha after hearing of his victory at Mokuʻōhai. It is unclear whether this was a genuine offer. There were rumours that Kahekili was Kamehameha's true father. Kamehameha refused the offer, and found himself confronted by an alliance of Kahekili, Keawemauhili and Keōua. Kahekili moved against the Hawaiʻi forces that still occupied east Maui. Confronted by a two-pronged attack through Kaupo and Koʻolau, and probably outnumbered, the defenders retired to the sanctuary of Kaʻuiki Head, without attempting to block Kahekili's progress. Kaʻuiki Head was invested and a long siege ensued. Kahekili also sent a contingent of Maui warriors under Kahahawai to Hilo to assist Keawemauhili.[22]

Kamehameha and his main aliʻi met at Kawaihae to decide how to counter the powerful coalition arrayed against them. It was agreed to strike before the enemy could launch a concerted attack. While Keʻeaumoku distracted Keawemauhili with a fleet of canoes off the Hilo coastline, Kamehameha and the main army marched over the Humuula Saddle to the Kilauea area. From here Kamehameha could prevent Keōua's and Keawemauhili's forces joining, and defeat them in detail.[23] The two leeward forces reached their destinations, despite rough seas off the windward coast, and rain and cold foggy conditions in the mountains. According to Samuel Kamakau, Kamehameha's army encountered elements of Keawemauhili's forces near Kilauea crater in cold, rainy conditions. The engagement was thereafter referred to as Kau-ua-ʻawa, the battle of the bitter rain.[24] Another council of war was held and it was decided to combine with Keʻeaumoku's forces and move against Keawemauhili. Kamehameha's forces were met five to six kilometres from Hilo Bay at Puaʻaloa. The leeward forces were routed

---

21 Fornander (1969), p. 316; and Kamakau (1961), p. 124.
22 Fornander (1969), pp. 216, 315–17, 220 n. 1; Kamakau (1961), pp. 115–16; and Dibble (1909), pp. 40–41.
23 Fornander (1969), pp. 220–22; and Kamakau (1961), p. 124.
24 Kamakau (1961), p. 125; and Fornander (1969), p. 317.

after a fierce contest at close quarters. Kahahawai and his Maui contingent played a decisive role in the victory. The fact that Kamehameha's forces were able to seek sanctuary on Keʻeaumoku's canoe fleet lying just offshore raises questions about the extent of their defeat and rout. The leeward forces retired up the Hāmākua coast to Laupāhoehoe to recover.[25]

The windward coalition did not follow up the victory, as Kahekili recalled the Maui forces for a more important enterprise. Locked in a stalemate deep in enemy territory, Kamehameha withdrew to Kohala. Kamehameha's retreat was also spurred by news that Kaʻuiki Head had fallen to Kahekili after a long siege. Kahekili had recently discovered that the stronghold's main water source lay beyond its defences and had moved to cut access. When a desperate sortie by the defenders failed to recover access to it, they were left with no choice but to surrender. Most were put to death. Only a few escaped.[26]

Kahekili was now free to direct his forces elsewhere. With Hawaiʻi divided into hostile camps, he felt secure to exploit Kahahana's troubled reign on Oʻahu. After assembling his forces at Lahaina, the Maui mōʻī sailed for Oʻahu, touching briefly at leeward Molokaʻi on the way. Keawemauhili and Keōua supplied several canoes for the fleet. Kahekili's invasion seems to have taken Kahahana by surprise. He was at Kawananakoa in the upper Nuʻuanu Valley when the Maui forces landed at Waikiki at the beginning of 1783. Kahekili sent his forces in three columns towards Nuʻuanu from Waikiki by way of Puowaina, Pauoa and Kapena. Kahahana gave battle near the small stream of Kaheiki in the Nuʻuanu Valley with the forces he had been able to hastily assemble (see Figure 12 for locality). He was routed and fled into the Koʻolau Mountains. Kahahana led a precarious life as a fugitive during the two years he evaded capture. The Oʻahu aliʻi did not rally behind him, and he was eventually captured and killed after being betrayed by a relative.[27]

The victory at Kaheiki did not secure Oʻahu for Kahekili. The island was divided among his aliʻi after the battle, but many of the Oʻahu aliʻi had not fought at Kaheiki and remained undefeated. A coordinated island-wide rebellion was attempted sometime around 1785. While Kahahana's

---

25 Kamakau (1961), pp. 125–26; Fornander (1969), pp. 220–22, 311–12, 317–19; and Dibble (1909), pp. 45–46.
26 Fornander (1969), p. 216; Kamakau (1961), p. 116; and Dibble (1909), p. 44.
27 Fornander (1969), pp. 222, 324; Kamakau (1961), pp. 135–36; and Thrum, vol. 5 (1918–19), pp. 474–76.

father Elani was to lead an uprising in ʻEwa, the Oʻahu chiefly supporters of Kahahana Makaioulu and Pupuka were to surprise and kill Kahekili and other Maui aliʻi at Kailua, and two other Oʻahu chiefs supporting Kahahana, Konamanu and Kalakioonui, were to lead an attempt against Kahekili's man in Waialua, Kiko Hueu. Kahekili was forewarned of the rebellion and was able to alert the majority of aliʻi because they were concentrated in Koʻolaupoko, Kona and ʻEwa. Only Kiko Hueu, in distant Waialua, could not be warned in time. He and most of his retinue were wiped out. Kahekili moved rapidly and decisively against the rebellion. The main fighting centred on Kona and ʻEwa. Kahekili crushed all resistance, killing many non-combatants in the process. Most of the important Oʻahu aliʻi were killed and their bones used to adorn a house near Moanalua in Kona. It is even claimed that some female aliʻi of kapu moe status were killed or mutilated.[28]

The instability of Hawaiian polities was demonstrated by the fact that a number of prominent Maui aliʻi sided with the rebels just as Kona aliʻi had sided with the windward coalition at Mokuʻōhai. Kahekili's nephew, Kalaniulumoku, for example, was the son of the previous Maui mōʻī Kamehamehanui, and met his death fighting for the rebels. Other Maui aliʻi who supported the rebellion managed to escape to Kauaʻi. They included Kaʻiana and his two younger half-brothers Nahiolea and Namakeha. Their reasons for changing sides are not mentioned. Possibly they had been excluded from the upper echelons of power or fared poorly in Kahekili's redistribution of Oʻahu lands. Kāneoneo had come from Kauaʻi to join the rebels just prior to the uprising. Denied rule over Kauaʻi, he was possibly seeking to re-establish his family's name on Oʻahu after his father's overthrow there a few years earlier. He was killed during the fighting at Maunakapu on the descent to Moanalua on Oʻahu.[29]

It took time to stamp out the remaining embers of resistance on Oʻahu, although the core of resistance was now broken. Kahekili remained on Oʻahu overseeing the subjugation, while his son, Kalanikūpule, returned to restore order on Maui where there had been an uprising against abuses

---

28 Fornander (1969), pp. 225–27; Kamakau (1961), pp. 135–40; and Thrum, vol. 5 (1918–19), p. 478.
29 Thrum, vol. 6 (1919–20), pp. 288, 290–91, 298; Kamakau (1961), p. 140; and David G. Miller 'Kaʻiana, the Once Famous "Prince of Kauaʻi"', *Hawaiian Journal of History*, vol. 22, 1988, 1–9.

by the aliʻi Kukeawe. The death of Kukeawe ended the fighting before Kalanikūpule arrived and his sympathetic pronouncement on the just nature of the grievances against Kukeawe was enough to restore order.[30]

There is no record of fighting on Hawaiʻi in 1783 and 1784. While Kahekili expanded his domains, Kamehameha worked to consolidate his power. He married Kaʻahumanu, the daughter of Keʻeaumoku, one of his main supporters. She soon became his favourite wife and a valued political adviser. Kamehameha also put some effort into building up his logistical base, spending much time developing the agricultural capacity of the leeward districts. His fortunes suffered a setback in 1784 when Kekūhaupiʻo was fatally wounded during a training exercise with spears.[31]

In 1785, Kamehameha moved against his enemies. He invaded Hilo and was met by the combined forces of Keawemauhili and Keōua. After a long, indecisive campaign he withdrew to Kohala.[32] The next year Kamehameha sent his younger brother Kalanimalokuloku-i-Kapoʻokalani to retake eastern Maui. This was soon achieved, although all the gains were soon lost when Kalanikūpule dispatched a force from Wailuku under Kahekili's brother Komohomoho to meet this threat. In a fierce battle near Lelekea Gulch in Kipahulu, the Hawaiian forces were driven back to Maʻulili, where Komohomoho again emerged victorious. The defeated forces fled back to their island in disarray.[33]

Kahekili dominated the Hawaiian political scene at the end of 1786. He ruled over Maui, Lānaʻi, Kahoʻolawe, Molokaʻi, and Oʻahu and he was on good terms with his half-brother Kaʻeokulani, the mōʻī of Kauaʻi. His warriors seemed invincible in battle. The remnants of the Oʻahu and Kauaʻi aliʻi, who might oppose them, posed little threat from their refuge in Kauaʻi Kona. Hawaiʻi remained divided between three mōʻī, none of whom was able to conquer the others. Kamehameha was the only one of the three who had been able to launch offensive campaigns.

Kahekili's ascendancy was built on shaky foundations. Internal coherence mattered as much as territorial size. While Kamehameha worked to consolidate his existing power, Kahekili was pushing his to the limit. The rapidity of the conquest of east Maui, Molokaʻi and Oʻahu stretched his

---

30 Fornander (1969), pp. 227–28; and Kamakau (1961), pp. 142–43.
31 Kamakau (1961), pp. 126–27; Fornander (1969), p. 319; and Kameʻeleihiwa (1987), pp. 107–08.
32 Fornander (1969), pp. 319–20; and Kamakau (1961), p. 126.
33 Fornander (1969), pp. 228–29; and Kamakau (1961), pp. 143–44.

Maui contingents thinly and meant local loyalty could not yet be assured. Oʻahu forces were serving in his army by 1791 but only at the price of wiping out much of the island's fighting core between 1783 and 1786. The remainder of the population lived with the memory of Kahekili's brutal repression. Prior to the fall of Kaʻuiki Head in 1782, much of Hana and Kipahulu had been outside of Kahekili's sphere since at least the mid-1770s. He had to be informed of Kaʻuiki's vulnerable water source by locals. His long siege of Kaʻuiki exhausted local resources while, prior to 1782 and during their invasion in 1786, Hawaiʻi aliʻi treated the local population and their livelihood with respect. Kalanikūpule was given charge of Maui after 1783 so that Kahekili could turn his attention to Oʻahu. Much of his effort was spent building up the devastated Kona district. The trader George Dixon found that the plain behind Waikiki was crowded with new plantations when he visited Oʻahu in September 1787.[34] Kahekili's relocation to Oʻahu is perhaps explained by the concentrated wealth of the Kona–Koʻolaupoko area, but the need to be on hand to consolidate his new lands must also have figured in his considerations.

From late 1787, the Hawaiian Islands played host to increasing numbers of European trade vessels seeking provisions for their operations in the north-west Pacific fur trade. Among the items traded were metal cutting weapons, other metal that could be moulded into weapons, and small amounts of firearms and ammunition. Although visiting vessels tended to favour Kealakekua Bay, Waikiki, and Waimea on Kauaʻi as ports of call, no mōʻī appears to have gained a decisive advantage in European weaponry over his rivals in the early years of this trade.[35]

There appears to have been a relative lull in hostilities between moku in the late 1780s. The only significant fighting was a 1788 rebellion against Kaʻeokulani on Kauaʻi. The rebels were based in Waimea, although there are no indications that access to trade influenced their move against the Kauaʻi mōʻī. The rebellion failed.[36] Nahiolea's involvement in the rebellion prevented his brother Kaʻiana returning to Kauaʻi in December 1788 after a trip to China on board a European trading vessel. Kaʻiana sought refuge with Kamehameha when the vessel touched at Kealakekua Bay. Kamehameha realised the value of the small cache of weapons and

---

34   Dixon (1968), p. 266.
35   Fornander (1969), pp. 229–30; Kamakau (1961), p. 144; Pogue (1978), p. 77; and Kahananui (1984), p. 176.
36   Fornander (1969), p. 321; and John Meares, *Voyages Made in the Years 1788 and 1789 from China to the North-West Coast of America* (New York: Da Capo Press, 1968), p. 335.

knowledge of firearms that Kaʻiana had acquired on the trip, and accepted him into his moku. Kamakau claims that Kamehameha soon gave Kaʻiana command of a force to attack Keōua in Kaʻū. This appointment angered his other aliʻi, who felt that they were being passed over. There are, however, doubts about this incident. Fornander does not mention the campaign, and Kamakau's description of Kaʻiana's victory over Keōua reads suspiciously like a campaign between the two that occurred in 1791, for which there is agreement between sources. In Kamakau's narrative, this campaign is placed after events in 1790.[37] This lull in hostilities may be explained by two observations made by Captain James Colnett at Kailua in 1791. He noted a resurgence of volcanic activity in leeward areas of Hawaiʻi between 1788 and 1791, and the appearance of a previously unknown sickness among the population. This was almost certainly the result of renewed European contact after 1786.[38]

The virtues of moderation: Kamehameha I's road to military victory, 1790–96

The relative peace between moku ended in 1790. In March of that year Kamehameha received a windfall of European military equipment when Kameʻeiamoku seized a small trading vessel in North Kona. Kameʻeiamoku attacked the schooner *Fair American* to avenge the beating and abuse he had suffered at the hands of a previous visiting ship's captain. Only one of the six crew members survived the attack. The sole survivor was an Englishman named Isaac Davis, who was only spared on the personal intercession of another aliʻi. When Kamehameha learnt of the attack, he marched to Kameʻeiamoku's lands with a sizeable force and took Davis, the schooner and the small cannon and firearms on board.[39] Meanwhile another vessel, the *Eleanora*, arrived at the Kona coast and anchored at Kealakekua Bay. To prevent news of the attack of the *Fair American* reaching the *Eleanora*, Kamehameha put a kapu on the bay. When the ship's boatswain, John Young, came ashore he was detained until

---

37 Vancouver (1801), bk 1, p. 403; Kamakau (1961), pp. 153–54; and Ellis (1969), pp. 209–10.
38 Sahlins (1989), p. 379, citing James Colnett, *Colnett's Journal Aboard the Argonaut* (New York: Greenwood Press, 1968), p. 220.
39 Fornander (1969), pp. 231–34; Kamakau (1961), pp. 146–47; and Vancouver (1801), bk 3, pp. 227, 230; bk 5, p. 59.

the *Eleanora*'s captain tired of waiting for him to return and sailed away.[40] Kamehameha's caution was more justified than he realised. The captain of the *Fair American* was the son of the *Eleanora*'s captain, and the latter had just come from Olowalu in Maui where he had massacred hundreds of locals by opening fire on their canoes with his cannon for a perceived grievance.[41]

In a few days Kamehameha had gained a cannon, firearms and two Europeans to assist in their use. Whether this good fortune changed the actual balance of power is debatable. Kamehameha had already obtained a small swivel cannon and muskets by 1790 without enhancing his military position. The swivel had been mounted on a double canoe, but there is no record of it being used prior to 1790. The *Fair American*'s small crew cannot have carried many firearms. The captured vessel, its cannon and two Europeans to operate it were, however, potentially valuable assets for Kamehameha.

Despite the poor showing of Hawaiian armies against the forces of Maui in the previous decade, Kamehameha now decided to attack Maui. Memories of the damage inflicted by trained gun crews in the wake of Cook's death, and tales of the recent carnage at Olowalu against exposed canoes, possibly raised expectations of the effect that cannon would have in local warfare. A recent reconciliation with Keawemauhili also influenced Kamehameha's decision. Keawemauhili sent canoes for the expedition against Maui as a sign of his good faith. Keōua remained defiant, but now Keawemauhili could watch him while Kamehameha pursued his ambitions elsewhere.[42]

Kamehameha crossed over to Hana with a force of 8,000 men in a fleet of 2,000 canoes. The landing seems to have been uncontested. Fornander mentions some preliminary raids prior to the main invasion,[43] but the first mention of fighting on which all sources agree was a battle in Hāmākualoa, where Kamehameha encountered a force sent from west Maui by Kalanikūpule under the command of Kapakāhili. An initial engagement

---

40 Fornander (1969), pp. 233–34; Kamakau (1961), p. 146; Daws (1968a), p. 34; Henry B. Restarick, 'John Young of Hawaii, an American', *21st Annual Report of the Hawaiian Historical Society for the Year 1912* (Honolulu: 1913), p. 29; and C. H. Barnard, *A Narrative of the Sufferings and Adventures of Captain Charles H. Barnard in a Voyage Round the World During the Years 1813, 1814, 1815 and 1816* (New York: J. Lindon, 1829), pp. 224–29.
41 Kamakau (1961), pp. 143–46; Pogue (1978), pp. 83–84; and Daws (1968a), p. 34.
42 Fornander (1969), p. 235; Kamakau (1961), p. 147; and Westervelt (1922), pp. 28–29.
43 Thrum, vol. 5 (1918–19), p. 470 n. 18.

between the two vanguards at Puʻukoaʻe near Hanawana ended in favour of the forces from Hawaiʻi. The main forces met in the same area a few days later. Despite promising omens, Kamehameha's men fared badly and looked like being defeated. They were saved by reinforcements, who helped turn the day and rout the enemy. Kamehameha led from the front throughout. The Maui forces were pursued vigorously to prevent them from rallying and, when the exhausted fugitives turned and attempted to make a stand near Kokomo, the issue was decided by single combat between Kamehameha and the Maui commander. Kamehameha slew his rival and the enemy's resistance crumbled. The road to Wailuku lay open.[44]

Kamehameha regrouped his forces before moving against west Maui. Kalanikūpule prepared to meet him at Wailuku with the fugitives from Kapakāhili's forces and whatever other combatants he could assemble. With the canoe fleet accompanying it, Kamehameha's army advanced to the eastern end of Kahului Bay (see Figure 10). From there they moved overland to Wailuku on the banks of the ʻĪao stream. Accounts of the battle are vague. It seems that the Maui forces offered prolonged resistance over a number of days, and were only gradually driven back towards the ʻĪao stream. The local topography suggests that a small ridge between the stream and Kahului Bay may have served as a focal point for the defenders to make a stand, with sand hills and marshes around the bay impeding the attacker's advance. Eventually the Maui forces retired or were driven into the upper ʻĪao Valley. Here the valley narrowed between steep mountains, allowing the defenders to make a stand on a narrow front that could not be outflanked. They were broken when Lopaka, the *Fair American*'s cannon, was brought up and fired at them with great skill by Davis and Young. Its effect on the Maui forces as they stood, packed between the steep valley walls, was devastating. The ʻĪao became choked with bodies. Resistance crumbled. Many more were killed as they tried to flee up the cliff faces lining the valley.[45]

Traditions remember the battle as kaʻuwaʻu pali (clawed off the cliff) and ka pani wai (the damming of the waters). Casualties are unknown although it has been noted that the upper ʻĪao could be dammed by as few as 100 bodies. Significantly, no Maui aliʻi of any consequence was killed or captured. Kalanikūpule and his main aliʻi and advisers were able

---

44 Kamakau (1961), pp. 147–48; and Fornander (1969), p. 236.
45 Fornander (1969), p. 236; Kamakau (1961), pp. 148–49; Dibble (1909), pp. 48–49; and Stokes (1937), p. 37.

to flee over the mountains and sail to Oʻahu. The lack of noteworthy aliʻi casualties may mean that, after the reverses of Hāmākualoa, much of Kalanikūpule's force consisted of hastily assembled makaʻāinana levies from west Maui. Kahekili's expansion into Molokaʻi and Oʻahu may have forced a watering down of the aliʻi fighting core on Maui even before Kamehameha's invasion. It may also mean that Lopaka was only directed against a blocking force made up predominantly of makaʻāinana or lesser aliʻi.

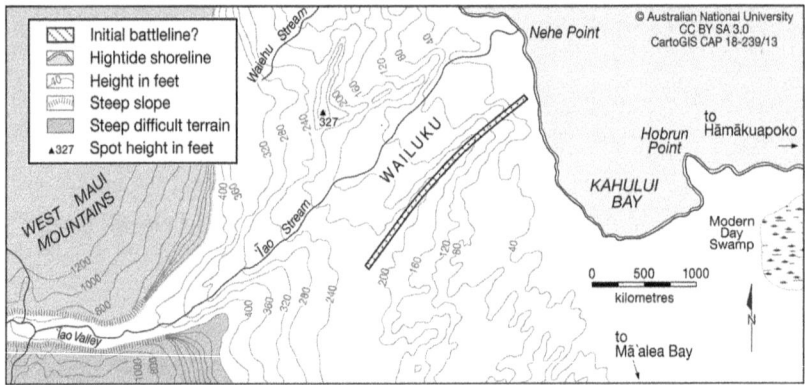

Figure 10: The battle of ʻĪao, 1790
Source: CartoGIS, The Australian National University.

The battle gave Kamehameha control of Maui, which he divided among his followers before going on to secure Molokaʻi, apparently without opposition. On Molokaʻi he sought to enhance his family's future status by seeking the hand of the niʻaupiʻo aliʻi Keōpūolani. This was also an attempt to bring about reconciliation with Kīwalaʻō's family, the older branch of the powerful Keawe dynasty. Keōpūolani was the daughter of Kīwalaʻō and also had connections with the Maui ruling dynasty. The overture was accepted. Kamehameha sent word to Kahekili that he intended to attack Oʻahu and challenged him to set a place of battle. But he showed that his mind was also concerned with securing control of Hawaiʻi when he sought advice from the respected Kauaʻi soothsayer Kapoukahi on how best to achieve this goal. Kapoukahi advised him that, once he had built a large heiau to his god at Puʻukoholā near Kawaihae, he would gain control of the whole island without further loss of life.[46]

---

46 Fornander (1969), pp. 238–40; Iʻī (1959), p. 70; Kamakau (1961), pp. 149–51, 208; and Kameʻeleihiwa (1986), pp. 60–61.

Kamehameha was forced to return to Hawai'i when news arrived that Keōua had attacked Hilo and defeated Keawemauhili in battle near Alae. Keawemauhili had been killed in the battle and resistance in Hilo had collapsed. Keōua had moved on to Hāmākua and ravaged Waipi'o. As the news reached Kamehameha, Keōua was already moving against the Waimea Saddle. There was no time to lose. Kamehameha hastened back to Kawaihae and set out for Waimea at the head of an army accompanied by Lopaka. Keōua withdrew to Pa'auhau and prepared to give battle. Kamehameha's forces approached and battle was joined. Lopaka did not intimidate Keōua's forces. Neither side would give ground. The stalemate was broken when two of Keōua's warriors, Ka'ia'iaiea and Uhai, led a charge against Lopaka while it was being reloaded and captured it. The battle continued without either side being able to gain an advantage. Fighting ended when fire from Kamehameha's foreign musketeers persuaded Keōua to withdraw from the field. No clear victor had emerged despite heavy casualties on both sides.[47]

Battle was renewed again the next day a short distance away at Koapapa. The battlefield consisted of a broad, open plain with a small grove at its southern end. Hawaiian accounts of the battle make no mention of Lopaka, however, muskets were prominent. As at Pa'auhau, neither side was prepared to give ground. Descriptions of the battle imply Kamehameha's musketeers skirmished between the two armies and did enough damage to cause Keōua's side discomfort. Lacking firearms, Keōua's men rushed forward and seized enemy muskets. When the gunpowder they had been able to seize began to run out, Keōua's forces retired from the field. Neither side had gained a decisive advantage. Kamehameha retired to Kohala and Keōua continued his withdrawal towards Hilo.[48] While Lopaka and muskets were a focal point of the battle narratives, they do not seem to have been numerous enough or deadly enough to supplant the influence of personal bravery on the final outcome.

After dividing up Hilo among his followers, Keōua set out for Ka'ū with the rest of his forces. Kilauea crater erupted while they were in the vicinity. Clouds of poisonous gases from the volcano enveloped the middle section of Keōua's army and the division was wiped out, with sources putting the loss of life anywhere between 80 and 2,000 people.[49] Perhaps seeking

---

47 Fornander (1969), pp. 240–41, 323–24; Kamakau (1961), p. 151; and Dibble (1909), p. 50.
48 Kamakau (1961), p. 152; and Fornander (1969), p. 324.
49 Fornander (1969), p. 324; Kamakau (1961), p. 152; and Stokes (1937), p. 38.

to capitalise upon Keōua's misfortune, Kamehameha launched a two-pronged attack upon his lands sometime in the later part of 1790 or early 1791. Although sorely pressed, Keōua held out. Keʻeaumoku attacked his lands in Hilo while Kaʻiana led a force against Kaʻū. Little is known about the operations in Hilo, but traditions pertaining to the Kaʻū theatre suggest that, despite Kaʻiana's advantage in firearms, the honours were once again even. A number of battles were fought. In some battles, Kaʻiana was forced to fall back to his fleet while, in others, he was victorious. Kamakau claims that the outcome of the battles was influenced by the generalship of Keōua and his two commanders, Kaʻiana's personal bravery, and the latter's use of firearms. Some years later, Archibald Menzies was shown a battle site where Keōua's men had countered Kaʻiana's advantage in firearms by digging small holes to squat into when they saw the flash of the musket's ignition powder. The campaign ended with Kaʻiana withdrawing from Keōua's territory.[50]

Kaʻiana's withdrawal from Kaʻū was possibly a response to events in the leeward islands. During the makahiki season of 1790–91, Kahekili and Kaʻeokulani concluded an alliance against Kamehameha. The potency of Kamehameha's mana after his victories on Maui could not remain unchallenged without eroding their own mana. Kaʻeokulani joined Kahekili on Oʻahu soon after the makahiki season ended in 1791. Their combined forces then sailed for Maui. Kalanikūpule was left as Kahekili's regent on Oʻahu, while Enemo ruled Kauaʻi on Kaʻeokulani's behalf. Faced with this powerful new coalition and continued defiance from Keōua, Kamehameha abandoned Maui and Molokaʻi without a fight in favour of defending his Hawaiʻi heartland. Kahekili valued Kaʻeokulani's assistance enough to offer him the sovereignty of Maui in return for his support. When Kaʻeokulani began to divide up Maui between his followers, however, Kahekili's sons and other Maui aliʻi were enraged. The Kauaʻi and Maui aliʻi came to blows near Waiehu. The rift was somehow patched up and the two forces proceeded on towards east Maui, but they now sailed separately. Kahekili was paying the price for overextending himself across a multi-island polity.[51]

The coalition now moved against Kamehameha on Hawaiʻi. Kaʻeokulani's forces sailed from Hana to Waipiʻo in Hāmākua and proceeded to ravage the valley. Meanwhile Kahekili sailed from Mokulai and landed

---

50   Menzies (1920), p. 110; Fornander (1969), pp. 245, 326–27; and Kamakau (1961), pp. 153–54.
51   Fornander (1969), p. 242; and Kamakau (1961), pp. 159–60.

5. THE PURSUIT OF POWER IN HAWAI'I FROM 1780 TO 1796

at Halawa in Kohala where he fought a series of inconclusive skirmishes with Kamehameha's forces. He then moved onto Waipi'o and joined Ka'eokulani.[52] Kamehameha was in Kona when these attacks were launched. He soon mobilised a large fleet and moved against his enemies. The two fleets encountered each other off the windward Kohala coast near the Waimanu valley. Kamehameha's fleet now included the *Fair American* and a number of double canoes on which cannon were mounted. Davis and Young accompanied the fleet and probably assisted with the firing of the cannon. Ka'eokulani's force also included cannon and a foreign sharpshooter known as Mare Amara (Murray the Armourer?). Little is known about the battle except that no significant ali'i lost their lives. The fact that the battle became known as Kepuwaha'ula'ula (the battle of the red-mouthed gun) suggests that cannon played a prominent role. The battle ended with Kahekili and Ka'eokulani disengaging their forces and retiring to Maui. Sheldon Dibble claims that they lost the greater part of their fleet in the action, but this is not in keeping with the lack of important ali'i among the casualties. On the other hand, it was to be the last offensive action by Kahekili and Ka'eokulani against Kamehameha. It is unclear if the previous rift between the Maui and Kaua'i forces affected the outcome of the fighting and the subsequent defensive outlook of the Maui–Kaua'i coalition.[53]

Kamehameha also achieved final victory over Keōua around this time, although sources are divided on whether this occurred just before or just after the victory over Kahekili and Ka'eokulani. The heiau at Pu'ukoholā was completed and Keōua was invited to attend. Keōua accepted the offer and arrived at the heiau with only a small escort. He was promptly killed and sacrificed to the Kū'kā'ili-moku. Thus, the prophecy of Kapoukahi was fulfilled. While Gavan Daws and Greg Dening hint at treachery on the part of Kamehameha, Kamakau and Fornander suggest that Keōua realised the fate that awaited him. Before sailing into Kawaihae Bay, he prepared his body for sacrifice and chose a small body of men to accompany him to the heiau as his moe-pu (companions in death).[54] The preceding events seemed to suggest that the gods were abandoning

---

52 Kamakau (1961), pp. 160–61.
53 Fornander (1969), pp. 243–44; Kamakau (1961), pp. 161–62; Dibble (1909), p. 51; Thrum vol. 5 (1918–19), p. 474; and Hiram Bingham, *A Residence of Twenty-One Years in the Sandwich Islands* (2nd edn) (Hartford: Hezekiah Huntington, 1849), p. 40.
54 Fornander (1969), pp. 327–35; Kamakau (1961), pp. 155–58; Dibble (1909), p. 53; Daws (1968a), p. 36; Valeri (1985a), p. 162; and Dening (1988), p. 89.

Keōua in favour of Kamehameha. Keōua had been forced to constantly defend his own lands in the recent campaign against Kaʻiana. At one stage of the campaign he had to abandon Kaʻū for Puna. The Kilauea disaster must also have affected his morale, especially in light of the fact that Kamehameha had already begun construction of the Puʻukoholā heiau as the prophecy of Kapoukahi demanded. These recent misfortunes and Kamehameha's victory off Waimanu seem to have convinced Keōua that resistance was hopeless.

The fate of Keōua's followers is unclear. Keōua left his fleet under the command of his half-brother, Pauli Kaʻoleioku, before sailing into Kawaihae Bay. Kamehameha was rumoured to be the father of Kaʻoleioku.[55] The traditions are silent on whether Kaʻoleioku's genealogy tempered Kamehameha's treatment of Keōua's people and it is unclear whether Keōua's followers peacefully submitted to Kamehameha's rule after the death of Keōua. Given the longstanding animosity between windward and leeward aliʻi on the island, it seems reasonable to assume that Kamehameha needed time to consolidate his rule over his new subjects in Hilo, Puna and Kaʻū. Certainly, Kamehameha did not wage campaigns against other islands in the chain over the next few years.

An uneasy stand-off now developed between Kamehameha and his leeward island rivals, with neither side willing to attack. George Vancouver found both sides professed a desire for peace, but neither could overcome deep suspicion of the other and agree to Vancouver's offer to mediate between them.[56] Vancouver noted that firearms were in great demand. Although Vancouver refused to supply weapons, some of the increasing number of trading vessels calling at the islands had no such qualms. No one knows for certain how many firearms came into the islands during these years. While one second-hand account claimed that Kamehameha's forces possessed 5,000 muskets by 1795, confirmed sightings by visitors and accounts of battles in the mid-1790s suggest the figure of 600 muskets, which was given to Urey Lisiansky in 1804, is probably closer to the mark. Visiting ships' captains never reported seeing more than 20 to 30 muskets in any one place during the 1790s.[57]

---

55   Fornander (1969), p. 335; and Kamakau (1961), p. 153.
56   Vancouver (1801), bk 3, pp. 261, 306, 313, 317, 319, 321, 357 (Feb.–Mar. 1793); and bk 5, p. 83 (Feb. 1794).
57   Contemporary accounts of muskets are listed in Appendix 2, and Vancouver (1801) bk 2, pp. 353, 355, 391; bk 3, p. 224; bk 5, p. 49.

5. THE PURSUIT OF POWER IN HAWAI'I FROM 1780 TO 1796

The influence of European technology should not be overemphasised. The maintenance of internal coherence in moku continued to be the crucial issue for the pursuit of power. After his triumph over Keōua, Kamehameha divided the districts of Hawai'i between his trusted followers and he continued to rely on his original supporters, the Kona uncles. By February 1794, Ke'eaumoku governed Kona, Kame'eiamoku presided over Kohala, Keaweaheulu saw to Kamehameha's interests in Ka'ū, and Kamanawa ruled over Hilo. Kamehameha's half-brother, Kalaimamahu, was given the relatively unimportant district of Hāmākua, and Ka'iana was given charge of Puna. At the beginning of 1793, Vancouver was told the most powerful vassal ali'i of Kamehameha was 'Kahowmotoo' (Ke'eaumoku), followed by 'Commanow' (Kamanawa) and 'Kavaheero' (Keaweaheulu).[58] It may be significant that Kamehameha's most troublesome subordinate, Ka'iana, was placed in Puna between two of the most powerful and loyal ali'i. Their districts had also been the heartlands of Kamehameha's last two rivals, Keōua and Keawemauhili.

Vancouver noted tensions between Kamehameha and Ka'iana on a number of occasions, including one instance involving an affair between Ka'iana and Ka'ahumanu. Ka'iana was linked to Kamehameha's old windward rivals, the I and Keawe families of Hilo, through his parents' blood lines. In February 1793, Vancouver was told a rift had developed between the leading ali'i on Hawai'i. The malcontents did not openly challenge Kamehameha, however, as he retained the support of the majority of ali'i. Kamehameha had the support of Ke'eaumoku, Kalaimamahu and Keaweaheulu, while Ka'iana had the backing of his brother 'Nomatahah' (Namakeha) and 'Tamaahmottoo' (Kame'eiamoku). Vancouver described Kame'eiamoku as the proudest man on the island.[59] When he had massacred the crew of the *Fair American* for an affront to his mana by the crew of a preceding vessel, Kamehameha had deemed it judicious to take a large force with him to recover the vessel for himself. It may not have been coincidental that Ka'iana and Kame'eiamoku were put in charge of districts at opposite ends of the island. The power of Kamehameha's close collateral kin was also restrained. Kalaimamahu governed Hāmākua, the weakest district on the island. Another of Kamehameha's half-brothers,

---

58 Vancouver (1801), bk 3, p. 235, bk 5, pp. 26, 50–53; and Sahlins (1981), p. 62.
59 Vancouver (1801), bk 3, pp. 215–17 (Feb. 1793); bk 5, p. 10 (Jan. 1794) and pp. 40–46, 59; Thrum vol. 6 (1919–20), p. 288; and Miller (1988).

Kalaiwahi had no significant territorial holdings. Kalanimalokuloku-i-Kapoʻokalani fades from prominence in the traditions after his defeat on Maui in 1786.[60]

The alliance of Kahekili and Kaʻeokulani also had problems in the years following their repulse from Hawaiʻi. The two mōʻī kept their forces mobilised on Maui from 1791 through until at least 1793 to guard against invasion from Kamehameha. The task of feeding this large force caused severe hardship on Maui. By 1793 supplies were also being sent from Lānaʻi and Molokaʻi, and these islands were beginning to struggle under the strain. Vancouver also found it difficult to obtain supplies on Oʻahu in 1792 and 1793.[61] No further conflict is noted between the Kauaʻi and Maui contingents, but future events suggest that tensions persisted. Kaʻeokulani's aspirations on Maui may also have been an influence on the continued mobilisation of his forces there.

Kaʻeokulani's prolonged absence from Kauaʻi weakened his influence there. In his absence, Enemo had become increasingly despotic and increasingly frail. His ageing frame was no longer able to support his body and he bore the signs of excessive ʻawa consumption. A rebellion soon took place in 1793 when the rebels mobilised on a small hill near Enemo's residence at Puna. Enemo was warned of the impending attack and moved decisively to pre-empt the rebel plans. He assembled his supporters and marched to the hill. While the seven Europeans in his service gave covering fire with muskets from the base of the hill, Enemo's warriors attacked. Three rebel aliʻi fell, along with four of their men. The rest of the insurgents fled. A number of the surviving ringleaders and other suspects were taken prisoner. These included Kaʻeokulani's half-sister, who was one of his favourite wives and had borne him a child. Enemo sent the captive rebels to Kaʻeokulani for judgment. One of the Europeans in Enemo's service told Vancouver that the rebellion had been provoked by Enemo's excesses, and that the people were still loyal to Kaʻeokulani and his son, Kaumualiʻi, on whose behalf Enemo governed.[62]

Enemo declared his independence from his mōʻī a year later in February 1794. As they tried to land, the contingent sent by Kahekili to investigate was met by local warriors and Europeans armed with muskets.

---

60 Vancouver (1801), bk 5, pp. 90–91; and Sahlins (1981), p. 62.
61 Fornander (1969), p. 244; Vancouver (1801), bk 2, pp. 352, 361–63; and bk 3, pp. 296, 301, 342, 359–60.
62 Vancouver (1801), bk 3, pp. 367–70, 375–76; and Menzies (1920), p. 134.

The Europeans opened fire and drove off the approaching party with much slaughter. Kahekili reacted with uncharacteristic restraint and political skill. He persuaded Captain William Brown of the *Butterworth* to take him to Kauaʻi from Oʻahu and used his vessel as a neutral venue for talks with Enemo. The meeting on board ended with Enemo agreeing to revert to being merely regent in Kaʻeokulani's absence and Kahekili would return back to Oʻahu. In his younger days Kahekili would not have been so forgiving.[63]

Kahekili was now over 60 years old and only had a few months to live. Like many other elderly aliʻi, he was increasingly debilitated by ʻawa.[64] Kahekili's interaction with Enemo raises the question of Kaʻeokulani's position and aspirations at this time. In March 1793, Vancouver was under the impression that Kaʻeokulani was subordinate to Kahekili rather than being an equal ally. An aliʻi named 'Tamahanna' (Namahana) seemed to be in command on Maui, and appeared second only to Kahekili in consequence. Kalanikūpule continued to rule Oʻahu on his father's behalf. Subsequent events suggest that Kaʻeokulani kept his forces with him from 1791 to 1794. He spent these years on Maui and Molokaʻi. His absence from Kauaʻi in the wake of its internal troubles suggests that he harboured ambitions elsewhere. By the middle of 1794, Kaʻeokulani was in effective control of Maui, Molokaʻi and Lānaʻi. His position was strengthened in February 1794 when the main powder magazine on Maui exploded and killed Namahana while he was inside it.[65]

Kahekili died at Waikiki in July 1794.[66] Kaʻeokulani and Kalanikūpule were the obvious contenders to inherit his mantle. While Kaʻeokulani, who was about 50 years old, was beginning to show signs of ʻawa consumption, he retained his sharp mind.[67] Kauaʻi may have been his in name only by this stage. The degree to which he was able to supplement the Kauaʻi followers accompanying him with Maui, Molokaʻi and Lānaʻi personnel by this time is unclear. Their loyalty may have been inclined towards Kalanikūpule, who was technically the successor to the Maui

---

63   Fornander (1969), p. 260; and Vancouver (1801), bk 5, pp. 125–26.
64   Vancouver (1801), bk 3, p. 305; and Menzies (1920), p. 104.
65   Vancouver (1801), bk 3, pp. 304–05 (Mar. 1793); bk 5, p. 118 (Feb. 1794); Kamakau (1961), p. 168; and Fornander (1969), pp. 214, 244.
66   Fornander (1969), p. 260.
67   Fornander (1969), p. 262; Kamakau (1961), p. 168; and Vancouver (1801), bk 3, p. 314 (Mar. 1793).

dynasty as Kahekili's oldest son. Ka'eokulani's occupation of Maui denied Kalanikūpule access to its manpower and resources should the two come to blows.

Kalanikūpule's position on O'ahu was also uncertain. He possessed high genealogical status, but defeat at 'Īao had eroded his mana. On O'ahu, he represented a recently imposed alien dynasty with a bloody record against the local population. The core of his support continued to be transplanted Maui ali'i and their retinue. He had the advantage, however, of benefiting from trade with the vessels that began to frequent Pu'uloa in the 1790s, although this contact had probably also brought disease. In 1793 Kalanikūpule suffered a puzzling illness that had left him emaciated and temporarily unable to use his legs.[68]

In November 1794, Ka'eokulani sailed from Maui with his ali'i and warriors, ostensibly to make a long overdue visit to Kaua'i. An attack on Maui by Kamehameha was apparently no longer his most pressing concern. Subsequent events suggest that a number of Ka'eokulani's men increasingly resented their long absence from Kaua'i. Ka'eokulani must also have realised the value of securing the resources of Kaua'i for future power struggles. On learning of the approach of his uncle's fleet, Kalanikūpule took the precaution of fortifying the Ko'olaupoko coast with trenches and earthworks. The fact that he knew which coastline the fleet would sail down suggests he had been forewarned of the route, and perhaps of Ka'eokulani's true intentions. An attempted landing soon followed Ka'eokulani's arrival off Kukui in Ko'olaupoko. This was repulsed in a severe battle during which a prominent ali'i was shot and killed by Ka'eokulani's gunner, Mare Amara. The fleet remained just offshore for the next two days and nights, exchanging shots with those on shore. Kalanikūpule then made overtures to his uncle to end the fighting. The two met at Kalapewai in Kailua and parted a few days later with the goodwill between them restored.[69]

Ka'eokulani continued his journey up the windward coast of O'ahu to Waimea. Here he discovered a plot to throw him overboard during the crossing to Kaua'i. The conspiracy was serious enough to involve his close adviser Kai'awa and a number of other ali'i. Uncertain of his support, Ka'eokulani chose not to confront the ringleaders and instead sought to

---

68 Vancouver (1981), bk 3, pp. 357–58 (Mar. 1793); and Daws (1968a), pp. 37–38.
69 Fornander (1969), pp. 262–63; and Kamakau (1961), p. 168.

divert the conspiracy by proposing war against Kalanikūpule. His gamble worked. To stiffen the resolve of the combatants, the canoes were hauled on shore and dismantled: there would be no turning back. As they marched overland towards 'Ewa, their ranks were swelled by warriors from Waialua and Wai'anae.[70] These districts had never taken kindly to the imposition of rule from Kona–Ko'olaupoko, regardless of whether the instigators were from Maui or O'ahu.

Kalanikūpule advanced from Kona to meet the threat at 'Ewa. He concluded an agreement with vessels reprovisioning at Pu'uloa for them to provide him with a contingent of musket-armed sailors in return for 400 hogs.[71] The two sides first encountered each other at Punahawele in 'Ewa. Details are sketchy. It appears that the two sides contented themselves with skirmishing, until Kalanikūpule's forces retreated after Mare Amara picked off some of the sailors accompanying them. Kamakau states that some Hawaiians were killed also. Fighting continued over the next few days as Ka'eokulani's forces gradually advanced through 'Ewa. Kalanikūpule only committed part of his forces to these encounters and gathered the rest at Aiea near the boundary of 'Ewa and Kona.[72]

Kalanikūpule occupied a strong position at Aiea (see Figure 11). His battlefront was probably little more than 2 kilometres long. Its left flank rested on the shores of Pu'uloa and its right flank merged into the steep foothills of the Ko'olau Mountains. The Kalauao Stream ran in front of his battleline. Kalanikūpule commanded the centre of his line. His brother, Koalaukani, led the right wing that occupied the heights of Kuamo'o, Kalauao and Aiea. The left flank rested firmly against the harbour at Malei Beach and was commanded by Kalanikūpule's uncle, Komohomoho. The contracted sailors were to provide flanking fire from long boats just offshore. The narrow coastal plain beyond the Kalauao Stream was covered in irrigated taro fields that would impede movement. Further inland the Kalauao's steep-sided ravine ruled out any chance of being outflanked.

The battle took place on 12 December. With his canoes dismantled and a quick victory as the only way to avoid open dissent, Ka'eokulani had no option but to assault Kalanikūpule's strong defensive position.

---

70 Fornander (1969), pp. 263–64; and Kamakau (1961), p. 168.
71 Kamakau (1969), pp. 168–69.
72 Fornander (1969), p. 264; and Kamakau (1969), p. 169.

A fierce and bloody struggle raged for most of the day, despite the hail of musket and cannon shot fired into Kaʻeokulani's flank from the harbour. The decisive blow came late in the day. Koalaukani led his men in a determined charge down from the heights and drove into the flank of Kaʻeokulani's forces. The flank buckled and Kaʻeokulani's forces were in danger of being hemmed against the shoreline. They panicked and fled, despite their leader's attempts to rally them. Kaʻeokulani was forced to flee as his army disintegrated. As he hid from his pursuers in a small ravine near the shoreline of Puʻuloa, his bright battle cloak betrayed him to the sailors offshore. While they pinned him down with musket fire, Kalanikūpule's men closed in on him. He died, fighting bravely, together with his wives and the aliʻi and warriors still with him.[73] The fate of the survivors from Kaʻeokulani's forces is unknown. There is no reference to punitive measures being taken against Waiʻanae and Waialua. Nor is it certain if the survivors were able to escape to Kauaʻi or elude capture on Oʻahu.

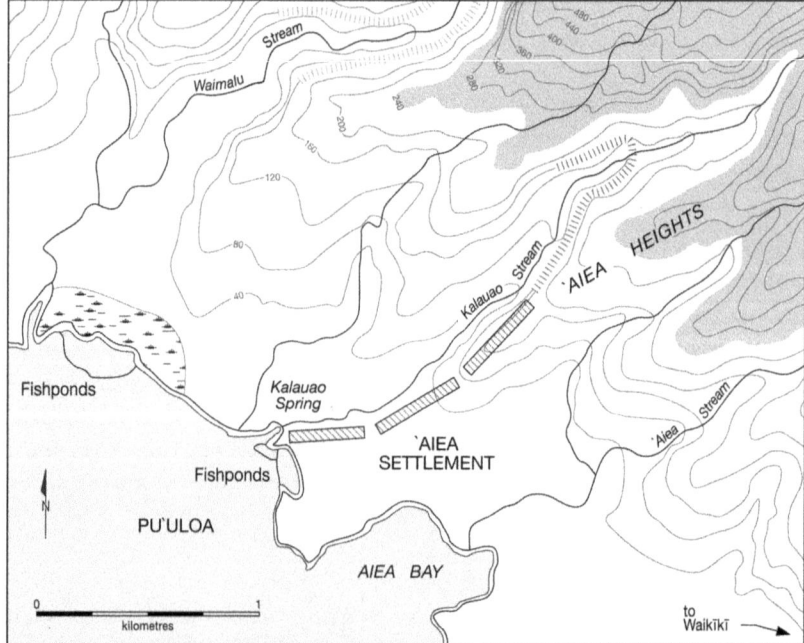

Figure 11: The battle of ʻAiea, 1794
Source: CartoGIS, The Australian National University.

---

73 Fornander (1969), pp. 264–65; and Kamakau (1961), p. 169.

5. THE PURSUIT OF POWER IN HAWAI'I FROM 1780 TO 1796

Kalanikūpule's success at Aiea seems to have encouraged him to contemplate extending his rule beyond Oʻahu. On 1 January 1795, he suddenly turned on his European allies and seized their vessels, the *Prince Lee Boo* and the *Jackal*, as they lay anchored in Puʻuloa. Only a few of the crew were spared to help sail the vessels, and probably also to assist in manning the ship's cannon. The seizure of the two vessels also provided a supply of muskets and ammunition. Instead of satisfying themselves with filling the vacuum created by Kaʻeokulani's defeat, Kalanikūpule and his advisers decided to move directly against Kamehameha. Three weeks later their forces set sail for Hawaiʻi in their newly acquired vessels and a fleet of canoes. Just off Oʻahu, the surviving crew managed to seize some firearms and drive their captors overboard. Kalanikūpule was among the passengers expelled. The Oʻahu mōʻī had now lost his European vessels and most of his firearms and ammunition. Contrary to the advice of Komohomoho, Kalanikūpule had stored all his guns and ammunition on board the two ships instead of distributing them among his followers. The invasion was aborted and the surviving crew of the two ships proceeded to Hawaiʻi and informed Young and Davis of Kalanikūpule's loss. They may even have traded or given their former captor's arms to Kamehameha.[74]

Kalanikūpule was now particularly vulnerable. Although he may have been able to concentrate his remaining supporters from Maui, Molokaʻi and Lānaʻi on Oʻahu before Kamehameha attacked, he had not had time to consolidate his hold over the multi-island moku since defeating Kaʻeokulani. His control beyond Oʻahu was tenuous and, even on that island, the shaky loyalty of many aliʻi had been demonstrated by their recent support of Kaʻeokulani. On Kauaʻi, Kaumualiʻi had succeeded his father and could hardly be relied on for support.[75] To make matters worse, Kalanikūpule was now at a serious disadvantage to Kamehameha in European military technology.

Kamehameha wasted little time in organising an attack on Kalanikūpule. Messengers were dispatched all over Hawaiʻi to mobilise men and canoes. Kamehameha set sail for Maui at the head of a large force. The fleet now also included a small schooner with 12 cannon that Vancouver had helped Kamehameha to construct. There is no mention of any resistance on Maui. The traditions imply Kamehameha merely stopped briefly at Lahaina and

---

74 Kamakau (1961), p. 170; Fornander (1969), pp. 267–68; Dibble (1909), pp. 55–56; and Daws (1968a), p. 240.
75 Kamakau (1961), p. 169.

moved on to the Kona coast of Moloka'i.[76] The sheer size of his fleet may have been enough to intimidate these islands into submission, or to persuade those opposed to Kamehameha to flee to O'ahu.

At Moloka'i, Ka'iana resolved to join Kalanikūpule. There had been tension between Ka'iana and Kamehameha for some time, and most of Kamehameha's main ali'i were now antagonistic towards him. He began to suspect the worst when he was excluded from the war councils on Moloka'i. As the fleet crossed over from Moloka'i to O'ahu, Ka'iana and his supporters separated from the main fleet and headed for Ko'olaupoko instead of the intended landing place at Waikiki in Kona. Ka'iana's breakaway does not seem to have been contested. From Ko'olaupoko, Ka'iana proceeded over the Ko'olau Mountains to join Kalanikūpule in the Nu'uanu Valley.[77]

The main fleet landed at Waikiki. Kamehameha's force numbered around 10,000 men. Although some sources claim that 5,000 of these had firearms, the figure was probably closer to the 600 firearms of Kamehameha's army in 1802. The army also possessed 12 cannon that were commanded by Europeans. Even allowing for Ka'iana's defection and forces left on Hawai'i, Maui, Lāna'i and Moloka'i, Kamehameha's army almost certainly outnumbered its opponents, and definitely outgunned them.[78] Kalanikūpule did not contest their landing on the open coastal plain, and made his stand in the Nu'uanu Valley (see Figure 12). Kalanikūpule had chosen his ground well. A gradual slope led up to his battlefront, giving him the advantage of the high ground. The steep valley walls meant that, as at Aiea, his battlefront was relatively narrow and hard to outflank. After spending a few days at Waikiki, Kamehameha moved against Kalanikūpule's position. One source claims the battle was preceded by a brief delaying action, but most simply refer to the main battle in the valley. The defenders resisted with great determination but, according to Fornander, were gradually worn down as:

> the superiority of Kamehameha's artillery, the number of his guns, and the better practice of his soldiers, soon turned the day in his favor, and the defeat of the O'ahu forces became an accelerated rout and a promiscuous slaughter.[79]

---

76 Fornander (1969), pp. 343–44; Kamakau (1961), pp. 170–71; and Bishop, in Roe (1967), pp. 141–42.
77 Fornander (1969), p. 347; and Kamakau (1961), p. 172.
78 Boit (n.d.), p. 5; and Bishop, in Roe (1967), p. 141.
79 Fornander (1969), pp. 347–48.

The broken forces of Kalanikūpule were pushed into the increasingly narrow confines of the heavily forested upper Nuʻuanu Valley, where they were hemmed in by its steep slopes. The valley ended at the Nuʻuanu Pali, a 304-metre cliff on the windward face of the Koʻolau Mountains. A narrow trail leading down the slope beside it linked Kona with Koʻolaupoko. According to some accounts the retreating forces attempted to make a stand at Laʻimi behind a stone wall on top of a steep slope. Cannon were dragged up the valley and used to dislodge them. In one account, this stand ended when Kalanikūpule was wounded, and splinters resulting from a cannonball hitting the wall killed Kaʻiana. Young later told Lisiansky that Kaʻiana was killed by a spear, and Fornander claims Kaʻiana and his brother Nahiolea were killed early in the battle. The stone wall referred to was possibly at the original battleline further down the valley.[80]

Most of Kalanikūpule's forces seem to have escaped up the valley's slopes and along the ridges of the Koʻolau Mountains, or down the trail into windward Oʻahu. Given the length of the valley and the tree cover of its upper reaches, it is possible that the pursuers did not reach the Pali by nightfall. Some defenders were trapped against the Pali and condemned to a grisly death on the rocks at the foot of its steep cliffs. A fortified ridge-top position at the head of the valley[81] may have served as the location for a final stand by those that could not, or would not escape. The reference to Kaʻiana being struck down by a spear suggests that firearms and cannon did not dominate the fighting. The following year the trader Bishop was told that Kamehameha's side lost only 20 men and inflicted at least 500 casualties on the enemy. William Broughton was told the defenders' losses were 300 men. William Ellis's claim that 400 men were driven over the Pali is, therefore, probably an exaggeration.[82]

---

80 Kamakau (1961), pp. 171–72; Fornander (1969), pp. 347–48; Thrum, vol. 5 (1918–19), p. 474; Campbell (1967), p. 97; Lisiansky (1967), p. 132; Jarves (1872), pp. 84–85; and Thomas G. Thrum, 'The Battle of Nuuanu', in Thomas G. Thrum (comp.), *Hawaiian Almanac and Annual for 1899* (Honolulu: Press Publishing Co., 1899), pp. 111–12.
81 Kirch (1985), pp. 116, 273.
82 Bishop, in Roe (1967), p. 180; Broughton (1967), p. 71; and Ellis, cited in Stokes (1937), p. 38.

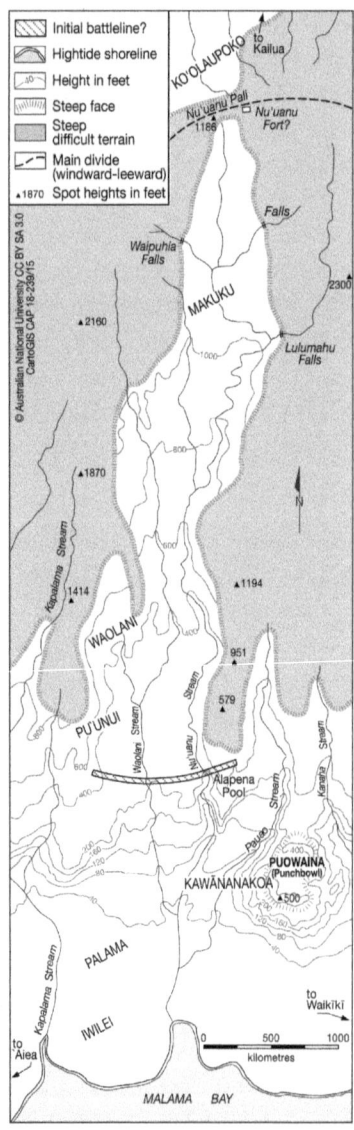

Figure 12: The battle of Nu'uanu, 1795

Source: CartoGIS, The Australian National University.

Kalanikūpule escaped into the Ko'olau Mountains and hid there for some months, until he was finally captured and killed. His body was brought to Kamehameha and offered as a sacrifice to Kū'kā'ili-moku. Ka'iana and other prominent enemy ali'i killed at Nu'uanu had been sacrificed straight after the battle and their heads stuck on the palings of the heiau. Kalanikūpule's brother Koalaukani is the only member of the vanquished side's leadership that seems to have escaped to Kaua'i.[83]

The Hawaiian army remained on O'ahu for over a year while Kamehameha prepared to invade Kaua'i. Part of the preparations included the construction of a 36-tonne European-style vessel by his foreign carpenters at Honolulu.[84] The consolidation of his recent territorial acquisitions also had to be attended to. Many of the female ali'i nui of O'ahu were married off to Kamehameha's supporters. Young, for example, was married to Namokuelua of O'ahu in 1795.[85] The prolonged stay of Kamehameha's forces on O'ahu (which probably increased the island's population by 25 per cent) severely strained local food resources and produced famine.

---

83 Kamakau (1961), p. 172; Fornander (1969), p. 348; and Lisiansky (1967), p. 132.
84 Kamakau (1961), pp. 172–73; and Broughton (1967), p. 71.
85 Westervelt (1922), p. 26; and John F. G. Stokes, 'Nationality of John Young, A Chief of Hawaii', *47th Annual Report of the Hawaiian Historical Society for the Year 1938* (Honolulu: 1939), pp. 15–16.

5. THE PURSUIT OF POWER IN HAWAI'I FROM 1780 TO 1796

Visitors to O'ahu reported the population to be in a desperate state by 1796. No mention is made of food being brought in from other islands under Kamehameha's control. No leader emerged on O'ahu to encourage an uprising, as had happened in the 1780s. Agricultural production was stepped up after the disruption of war and, by 1798, O'ahu seemed to be recovering from its ordeal.[86]

Kamehameha was ready to invade Kaua'i in the summer of 1796. His attempt was thwarted when much of his fleet was capsized by strong winds during a night crossing of the channel between O'ahu and Kaua'i. Many more canoes would have been lost if the fleet not been close enough to O'ahu to reach the safety of shore.[87] Kamehameha remained in O'ahu waiting for another opportunity. He probably used the time to replace his losses. In the meantime, Kaumuali'i had faced a serious challenge from his half-brother, Keawe, on Kaua'i. Keawe was based in Waimea and had Europeans serving with him. When Broughton visited Kaua'i in July 1796, Keawe was also in control of Wailua and Kaumuali'i was his prisoner. Keawe died soon after taking power, however, and Kaumuali'i was restored as mō'ī of Kaua'i.[88]

Kaumuali'i was spared the danger of a second attempt on Kaua'i later in the year by divisions within Kamehameha's domains. News arrived from Hawai'i that Ka'ū, Puna and Hilo had rebelled against Kamehameha. The rebellion was led by the ali'i nui Namakeha. In the absence of Kamehameha and his army, they were encountering little opposition and were threatening the Kona heartland. There had been some skirmishes involving the loss of life, but most of Kamehameha's subjects seemed lost without their ali'i to lead them. Davis found it necessary to send to Kamehameha for help. Kamehameha returned to Hawai'i in September 1796 and marched against Namakeha, crushing the rebels in battle at Hilo. In January 1797, Kū'kā'ili-moku once more received the body of one of Kamehameha's opponents as Namakeha was offered up as a sacrifice.[89]

---

86   Kirch & Sahlins (1992), p. 41, citing Bishop, Journal, 21 Feb. 1796; Townsend (1888), p. 72; Broughton (1969), pp. 40, 71; and Schmitt (1970), p. 111.
87   Kamakau (1961), p. 173; Broughton (1967), p. 71; and Daws (1968a), p. 41.
88   Broughton (1967), p. 44; Bishop, in Roe (1967), p. 145, n. 1; and Stokes (1937), p. 41.
89   Kamakau (1961), pp. 173–74; Thrum, vol. 5 (1918–19), p. 476; Broughton (1967), pp. 69–70; Daws (1968a), p. 41; and Sahlins (1983), pp. 535–36.

While Hilo was Kamehameha's last battle, it did not secure lasting control of Hawai'i any more than the battle of Nu'uanu ensured his rule over O'ahu. Just as Kahekili had felt the need to remain on O'ahu to consolidate his victory over Kahahana, so Kamehameha's advisers had cautioned against Kamehameha leaving O'ahu to deal with Namakeha in 1796. His old enemies might be dead, but the prospect of new challengers loomed once the army was broken up and power decentralised in the usual way among district ali'i. In February 1796, Broughton noted dissent among Kamehameha's ali'i over the proposal to invade Kaua'i.[90] When considering who to put in charge of O'ahu while he was absent attempting to quell Namakeha's rebellion, Kamehameha was reputedly advised:

> Do not appoint a chief over O'ahu, for during your absence in Hawaii he would rebel against you. The best thing to do is to leave none but commoners on O'ahu and take the young chiefs with you.[91]

Heeding this advice:

> Kamehameha therefore put his steward Ku-i-helani in charge of O'ahu, and Ka-lani-moku appointed his man Ka-hanau-makai'i, to collect taxes. Ke-kua-manoha', although among those who fought for Ka-lani-ku-pule and plotted against Kamehameha, was left on O'ahu because many of his relatives were among Kamehameha's followers.[92]

It was a move that contained both compromise and innovation. With it, the seeds for a new order were planted.

---

90 Broughton (1967), p. 144.
91 Kamakau (1961), p. 173.
92 Kamakau (1961), pp. 173–74, 182.

6
Creating a Kingdom: Hawai'i from 1796 to 1819

Kamehameha followed up his victory with a cautious and conciliatory policy of power sharing with his key long-term chiefly supporters, rather than power monopolisation. This maintained the coherence of his support base. United, they increased their coercive advantage by monitoring all localities in the realm to anticipate and stifle rebellious sentiment before it developed into a serious challenge. A devastating epidemic on the island of O'ahu in the early 1800s decimated many of those trained in warfare, while each year of peace and the cessation of widespread training for warfare after 1796 reduced the military capacity of the population. Kamehameha's clique monopolised firearms and demilitarised the islands, including their own capacity once their relative coercive advantage was assured. In the decade before his death in 1819, Kamehameha showed himself to be a cultural conservative in adhering to the old gods and leaving much of the day-to-day running of the kingdom to a bureaucracy that combined old offices and the new practices that responded to and were influenced by the increasing visits from Western vessels. He left a secure and peaceful kingdom, but one in which a powerful clique – centred on his wife Ka'ahumanu – sought a greater embrace of Western ways and an erosion of traditional religious beliefs, in the face of the looming prospect of more direct Western interference in the kingdom's affairs. Life for most Hawaiian commoners, away from a few ports frequented by Westerners, continued to exhibit much continuity with past beliefs and ways, beyond the periodic arrival of new diseases and increasing demands from chiefs for labour and produce with which to purchase luxury items for their own consumption.

The transition of societies from advanced chiefdoms to early states is generally seen as a process involving the centralisation, secularisation and institutionalisation of power. The creation of a permanent administrative body and an effective full-time military force, both of which are loyal to the state, is usually seen as essential to the success of this transition. The state needs access to income sufficient to maintain these institutions and retain their loyalty. The ability of the ruler to appoint candidates to offices within these bodies is an important yardstick with which to measure the consolidation of a monarch's power.

From 1796 until his death in 1819, Kamehameha made much progress in ensuring that the necessary conditions for centralisation existed. In Samuel Kamakau's list of Kamehameha's reforms after the crushing of Namakeha's rebellion, the implication is that reform was initiated rapidly in a relatively coherent package. No significant opposition is mentioned. Modern commentators have not questioned this representation, despite the limited detail Kamakau provides on events during the crucial years immediately following the cessation of hostilities. The lack of open confrontations in this period obscures the fact that Kamehameha's power was by no means unassailable, even after reforms to the structure of power. On closer examination, it appears that his consolidation of power was a gradual and, at times, fragile, process. This process can be broadly divided into three relatively distinct phases: 1776–1804, 1804–12, and 1812–19.

1796–1804: Oligarchy

The four Kona uncles continued to be crucial to Kamehameha's power in this period. With a large, multi-island moku to hold together, and temporarily weakened by their losses in the Kaua'i channel, it made sense for the Kona clique to share the burden of controlling the newly conquered lands. Keaweaheulu, Ke'eaumoku, Kamanawa and Kame'eiamoku were given charge of the islands under Kamehameha's control. Each also received large tracts of land throughout the islands. It was specified that Kamehameha could not alienate these lands from them.[1]

---

1   Kamakau (1961), pp. 175–76; and Kame'eleihiwa (1986), p. 103.

Power within the ruling clique was carefully balanced and restricted. Land grants that were scattered throughout different localities on different islands inhibited the development of local power bases. John Papa Iʻī's description of Kamehameha's division of lands on Oʻahu among his important followers is typical:

> The ʻiliʻaina land of Kaneloa in Waikiki and the ahupuaʻa of Punaluu in Koʻolauloa to Keliimaikai; Hamohamo and the ahupuaʻa of Kaaawa to Keawe a Heulu; Kaluaokau and Pau and the ahupuaʻa that includes the two Laie's to Kalaimamahu; Kalaepohaku and a part of Halawa for an ahupuaʻa to Isaac Davis; Pahoa and the other part of Halawa for his ahupuaʻa to John Young; Kanewai and a Kalana land division of Moanalua to Keeaumoku; Kapunahou and Moanalua for his ahupuaʻa to Kameeiamoku; Waialae together with all the large iliʻi kupono within the lands of the King to Kaʻahumanu.[2]

Iʻī also mentions that all prominent chiefs were given parcels of land in Waikiki, as it was a site favoured by aliʻi. Kamehameha's lands included rich agricultural tracts at Nuʻuanu, Puaaliʻiliʻi, Kapalomo, Keoneʻula, Puʻupueo, and a residence at the increasingly busy port of Honolulu. Kamehameha's full brother, Keliʻimaikai, his half-brother, Kalaimamahu, his favourite wife, Kaʻahumanu, and his two closest European advisers, John Young and Isaac Davis, also did well out of the land redistribution. The mōʻī's sons, however, do not appear to have been granted significant landholdings.[3] The fragmentation of landholdings increased the number of overseers on the land as chiefs increasingly became absentee landlords and settled junior kin to see to their interests on their scattered fragments.

Chiefly power was not only diminished by the fragmentation of landholdings but also counterbalanced by the establishment of an independent administrative structure. The aliʻi Kalanimoku was particularly powerful within this structure. He was designated pukaua (commander in chief) as well as puʻuku nui (chief treasurer). As puʻuku nui, he was given the task of dividing the lands among Kamehameha's followers, and his consent was required for any gifts Kamehameha wished to bestow upon his supporters.[4] Land and gifts were two crucial tools for securing loyalty in the traditional system. Kalanimoku's powers, therefore, represented a major concession by Kamehameha as mōʻī.

---

2 Iʻī (1959), p. 70; see also Kamakau (1961), pp. 175–76.
3 Iʻī (1959), pp. 26, 69–70; Kameʻeleihiwa (1986), pp. 98–99, 101; and Kirch & Sahlins (1992), p. 49.
4 Kamakau (1961), p. 175.

In another passage, Kamakau notes 'Kamehameha appointed men to serve under the different chiefs as stewards. There were several hundred of these, all well-educated for the position, alert and strong'.[5] The only existing groups that could have fulfilled this function were possibly lesser aliʻi within retinues or the priesthood. In 1810 Archibald Campbell claimed that 'The principal duties of the executive were, however, entrusted to the priests, by them the revenues were collected, and the laws enforced'.[6]

In an undated passage, Kamakau mentions that Kamehameha appointed commoners to govern the islands 'lest a chief stir up rebellion'.[7] This conflicts with his earlier statement that the four uncles were made kuhina (governors) of the islands. The only kuhina who was not one of the four Kona uncles in this period was Young, who administered Hawaiʻi from 1802 onwards. But this may have been because Kamehameha launched another expedition against Kauaʻi in 1802 that presumably involved all four uncles and their contingents. Marshall Sahlins makes a convincing argument that these so-called 'commoners' were in fact kaukau aliʻi (the children of unions between mōʻī and women of lesser rank). It was this group that David Malo described as the backbone of the king from which the aliʻi nui chose his executive officers and advisers.[8]

The checks and balances within the ruling clique appear to have been a mutually agreed-on attempt to preserve their power by reducing the potential for fission. Kamanawa suggested the idea of fragmenting landholdings to avoid the danger of chiefly rebellion. The strategy worked and there are no accounts of tension within the ruling group. Kamehameha continued to rule with his uncles' approval. His powers were restricted by the functions of Kalanimoku's office. Kamehameha maintained a large court with the usual kahuna, craftsmen, fishermen and retinue of warriors, but this alone was insufficient to maintain his rule. The fledgling bureaucracy would eventually enhance the ruler's power relative to his vassal aliʻi. The restriction of Kamehameha's power and the granting of land in perpetuity was enough to secure the Kona uncles' approval for the formation of a bureaucracy, particularly as it also enhanced their

---

5   Kamakau (1961), p. 178.
6   Campbell (1967), p. 123.
7   Kamakau (1961), p. 184.
8   Campbell (1967), p. 97; Kamakau (1961), p. 184; Lisiansky (1967), p. 100; Sahlins (1981), p. 57; and Malo (1951), pp. 54–55.

control over the rest of the aliʻi. Kamehameha's council was enlarged to include more advisers who were experienced in the old ways of warfare and government, such as Kai, Kapalaoa and the kahuna Kalaikuahulu.[9]

The ruling clique had a large enough power base to ensure that, as long as it remained united, it could dominate the islands. There was a significant coercive gap between their power base and that of other aliʻi. According to the testimony of Kekuanioʻa during land hearings after Kamehameha's death, each one of the four uncles received 60 to 80 'lands', while lesser aliʻi, such as Kekuanioʻa, received only one or two 'lands' each. The previously cited reference in Iʻī to the division of land in Oʻahu suggests that the lands Kekuanioʻa refers to were probably ahupuaʻa or even smaller units. Furthermore, those outside of the ruling clique were not guaranteed hereditary rights to the lands.[10]

The new bureaucracy served as Kamehameha's eyes and ears, ensuring that his orders were obeyed, and notifying him of any aliʻi gathering men about them with rebellious intent. Kamehameha is also said to have scattered informers and female spies throughout his domains to watch for signs of trouble.[11] Crews of paddlers headed by skilled canoe masters conveyed Kamehameha's messengers between islands.[12] In this way, rebels had no secluded haven within the realm in which to mobilise without attracting the attention of their overlord. The main aliʻi were required to accompany the mōʻī and his court so that he could keep a close watch over them. Removed from a personal landed base, these aliʻi depended upon Kamehameha for sustenance, and could not feed and maintain large retinues themselves. Campbell noted that these aliʻi numbered between 20 and 30 in 1810.[13]

The economic power of the ruler was also enhanced by the formation of a bureaucracy. As in the past, all land grants carried the obligation of providing tribute, corvée labour and military service when needed. Kamakau states that the level of tribute was set at one-tenth of the hogs and crops raised, as well as a proportion of manufactured goods, such as nets, mats, tapa and fishing lines. Kamehameha used his officials to

---

9   Kamakau (1961), pp. 175, 177–78; Westervelt (1922), pp. 25–26.
10   Kameʻeleihiwa (1986), p. 80; Iʻī (1959), p. 116.
11   W. D. Alexander, *A Brief History of the Hawaiian People* (New York: American Book Co. 1891), pp. 149–50.
12   Kamakau (1961), pp. 177–78.
13   Campbell (1967), pp. 92–93; Turnbull (1810), p. 141; and Kamakau (1961), p. 178.

tighten up the collection of tribute. Instead of imposing a head tax on households, tribute was now correlated with productivity. Tax assessors were appointed to fix individual tenants' tribute according to the size of their holdings. Others collected and recorded tribute once a year at a location nominated by Kamehameha. While it is unclear what form the payment took, Campbell's observation that priests made up much of the bureaucracy could mean that the collection was in the form of the annual makahiki offerings. Samuel Kamakau, however, refers to these payments as taxes, implying that they were distinct from religious offerings.[14]

It is unclear whether the mōʻī's traditional kōʻele lands and stock herds were sufficient to maintain the new structure of government. Kamakau quantifies kōʻele lands as 10 per cent of all cultivated land. The old problem of utilising production was addressed by improving the transport of produce between localities and islands by canoe. In 1801, for example, Young sent canoes to Maui for supplies when no fish were to be had off Kawaihae on Hawaiʻi. European trading ships were also occasionally commissioned into service for this task.[15] This may have been enough to ensure that kōʻele lands alone could support the new government structure. There is also reference to Kamehameha not setting seaward and upland boundaries to ahupuaʻa so that they were not 'hemmed in'.[16] The implication is that rights of access to offshore fishing and upland resources were loosened.

Kamehameha's political and economic innovations contrasted sharply with his religious conservatism. He remained a strong supporter of traditional religion until his death. Makahiki and annual fishing kapu were maintained. The first fish caught and the first fruits continued to be reserved for the gods. Kamehameha retained his strong devotion to Kūʻkāʻili-moku, as well as his other personal gods, Kalaipahoa and Pele. In 1801, for example, Kamehameha attempted to stem the flow of lava from Hualalai by appeasing Pele, the volcano goddess, by throwing hogs into the lava followed by cuttings of his own hair. Many heiau were restored and others constructed to gods such as Kūʻkāʻili-moku, Ku ke oloʻewa and Kū hoʻoneʻenuʻu. Luakini heiau continued to be built and human sacrifice persisted. Both, however, diminished in frequency after the ending

---

14   Kamakau (1961), pp. 176–77, 192; and Westervelt (1922), p. 26.
15   Kamakau (1961), pp. 177, 190–91; Kirch & Sahlins (1992), p. 42; and Young, *Manuscript Journal* (Hawaiʻi State Archives, n.d.), f1.5.
16   Kahananui (1984), p. 202.

of hostilities in 1796.[17] A number of important kahuna were included among his valued advisers, including Puʻou and his son Hewahewa of the Paʻao priesthood, Kuaiwa and Halo io lena of the Nahulu class, and Ka pou kahi of the Hulihonua class. New laws issued by Kamehameha continued to be framed in terms of kapu, with kahuna prominent in ensuring compliance.[18] Kamehameha groomed his son, Liholiho, to be his successor by teaching him the correct procedure for heiau ceremonies and other religious events. The declaration of Liholiho as heir apparent was formalised by bestowing the kapu of the heiau upon him.[19]

During this period, Kamehameha issued decrees that were designed to reinforce traditional kapu, and to preserve the civil peace brought about by the end of wars between mōʻī. Murder, theft, destruction of property, disobeying the kapu of the gods and sorcery were all prohibited. Perhaps the most celebrated decree was the so-called law of the broken paddle, by which it was forbidden to rob or murder the defenceless and the innocent. The law was prompted by a meeting between Kamehameha and a fisherman who some years earlier, had injured Kamehameha with a paddle near Laupāhoehoe in Hilo when the fisherman sought to defend himself against raiders seeking sacrificial victims. Instead of seeking revenge, Kamehameha is said to have criticised his own actions as an unjustified move against a weaker party who had done him no previous harm. The man was pardoned and an edict issued forbidding such actions in the future.[20] These decrees seem to have generally been adhered to without need for punitive measures and, for example, only one account of a murder occurs in the pages of Iʻi and Kamakau. This was an incident where the aliʻi Kāne i halau killed Mokuhia at sea in an attempt to win the governorship of Hawaiʻi.[21]

Certain events between 1796 and 1804 suggest, however, that Kamehameha's consolidation of power was by no means complete or smooth. While Kamakau and Iʻi do not mention any rebellion in this period, William Westervelt claims that there were rebellions, and that

---

17   Kamakau (1961), pp. 175–76, 179–80, 183–88; Iʻi (1959), pp. 70, 72–76, 115; Campbell (1967), pp. 95, 128–29; Westervelt (1922), pp. 33–34; and Alexander (1891), pp. 151–52.
18   Kamakau (1961), pp. 187, 191–92; and Campbell (1967), p. 123.
19   Kamakau (1961), p. 188, 221; and see, for examples, Iʻi (1959), pp. 56–59.
20   Kamakau (1961), pp. 175–76, 181–83; Westervelt (1922), pp. 24–25; and Alexander (1891), p. 151.
21   Kamakau (1961), p. 191.

Kamehameha left his kuhina to deal with them.[22] Much of Kamehameha's efforts were directed towards preparations for another attempt at conquering Kaua'i. One of the reasons Kamakau gives for Kamehameha's desire to subdue Kaua'i was the need to 'satisfy the clamour of his chiefs and warriors who had endured so many privations to make him ruler, [to satisfy them] in their desire for more lands to conquer'.[23] This was a legacy of the past emphasis on martial prowess. Such ingrained attitudes would not die out overnight. The retinues of old rivals might be disbanded, but a large number of ali'i and kanaka still remained skilled in the arts of war. Their presence necessitated the continued maintenance of Kamehameha's own forces, and the age-old problem of diverting their restlessness in times of inactivity remained.

After crushing Namakeha's rebellion, Kamehameha remained on Hawai'i until 1802. The troublesome windward districts of that island may have required Kamehameha to personally oversee a lengthy period of incorporation, as Kahekili had done on O'ahu in the 1780s. Much of Kamehameha's efforts during this time seem to have been directed towards ensuring that the 1796 disaster in the Kaua'i channel was not repeated. He ordered his ali'i to construct larger, sturdy canoes called peleleu. According to 19th-century Hawaiian educator and historian William Alexander, most of the fleet was constructed on Hawai'i, particularly from trees felled in the interior of the district of Hilo. The fleet was five years in the making and, eventually, may have numbered as many as 800 peleleu. Several small European-style vessels were also constructed by Hawaiian carpenters under the direction of foreigners, particularly James Boyd, who had been in the islands since the early 1790s.[24]

When the trader Ebenezer Townsend visited Hawai'i in 1798 he saw a 55-tonne schooner being constructed at Kawaihae under the supervision of Young. A large peleleu was also under construction there. Its twin hulls were 21 metres long, 1.8 metres deep and 60 centimetres wide. The sides of the hulls tumbled inwards to avoid taking in water. The hulls were lashed

---

22 Westervelt (1922), p. 25.
23 Kamakau (1961), p. 187.
24 Kamakau (1961), p. 187; Ebenezer Townsend Jr., *Extracts from the Diary of Ebenezer Townsend Jr* (Honolulu: Hawaiian Historical Society, n.d.), pp. 71–72; Alexander (1891), pp. 150–51; Daws (1968a), p. 42; R.S. Kuykendall, *The Hawaiian Kingdom*, vol. 1: *1778–1854, Foundation and Transformation* (Honolulu, University of Hawai'i Press, 1938), pp. 48–49; Thomas Bargatzy, 'Beachcombers and Castaways as Innovators', *Journal of Pacific History*, 15 (1), 1980, 95; and Kirch & Sahlins (1992), p. 43.

together with a 1.5-metre space between them. This gap was covered by a platform at the stern, which made the vessel more seaworthy. They were also equipped with a mast (kia), mainsail (peʻa ihu) and a jib (kiakahi) similar to those on European-style sloops. Townsend also noticed a large number of single canoes of various sizes.[25] The construction of the fleet may have served to satisfy the competitive spirit of the aliʻi and to occupy the attention of their followers.

By 1802 Kamehameha was ready to move against Kauaʻi. Young informed the Russian explorer Urey Lisiansky that the force assembled numbered 7,000 Hawaiians, 50 Europeans and an artillery train of 14 cannon, 40 swivel guns and six mortars with large quantities of powder and shot. Lisiansky also found that Kamehameha controlled trade and had all the firearms and other European military technology he needed. Cloth was now the trade item most in demand.[26] The composition of this force is uncertain. Training with traditional weapons continued and the obligation of military service still existed for makaʻāinana. John Turnbull noted that the supplies were transported to the warriors on each island, implying that each kuhina had his own forces.[27]

Kamakau mentions that Kamehameha divided the 'warrior-chiefs' into companies. His description suggests that this process may have been used to incorporate former enemies and replacements. He states that the companies were decided according to certain classes and that Kamehameha:

> put every man into one of these classes: the Keawe, the Mahi, the I, the Ahu, the Pulena, the Luahine, and the Paia. For young stranger chiefs he made three classes: the Okaka, the 'Ai 'ohiʻa, and the Uouo.[28]

Some of the first group bears the names of families that had been traditional rivals of Kamehameha. The same practice is attributed to Kalaniʻōpuʻu on Hawaiʻi. In both cases, it is unclear if there was a central force loyal to the ruler, or if those combatants were distributed amongst his followers. A reference to the invasion force on Oʻahu in 1804 suggests that forces were still drawn in large part from a number of chiefly retinues – Kamakau refers to the whole company as including:

---

25 Townsend (n.d.), pp. 23–29; and Kamakau (1961), p. 187.
26 Lisiansky (1967), pp. 11, 133.
27 Kamakau (1961), p. 178; Iʻī (1959), p. 189; Lisiansky (1967), p. 116; Turnbull (1810), p. 226.
28 Kamakau (1961), p. 176.

Kamehameha's sons and daughters with their households and those of his brothers and sisters, his councilors and chiefs, over a hundred in each household, running into a thousand.[29]

Kaumuali'i, the mōʻī mōʻī of Kaua'i, told Lisiansky that his own forces consisted of five Europeans, three cannon, 40 swivel guns, a large number of muskets with an ample supply of powder and shot, and 30,000 warriors.[30] While the figure of 30,000 is probably an exaggeration, it may indicate that the gravity of the situation caused Kaumuali'i to call up the maka'āinana, while Kamehameha's force of 7,000 represented a force of trained warriors only.

The only indication of any break with tradition patterns is Lisiansky's reference to the large stocks of firearms possessed by Hawaiians, and his mention of a small bodyguard within Kamehameha's retinue who wore blue European-style coats and drilled in European style. The reference to drill presumably means that they at least used firearms, although Lisiansky also noted that they were said to be the best warriors in the islands.[31] The pursuit of power was beginning to increasingly involve the use of European goods during this time. There was a noticeable increase in agricultural production during these years, particularly on O'ahu and, to a lesser extent, around Kealakekua Bay, Kailua and Kawaihae. All were ports of call for European vessels and the new fields developed tended to cater to the visitors demands for yams and potatoes as well as taro and 'uala. As Ross Cordy has noted, chiefly power stood to be enhanced through arming retainers with firearms and maintaining loyalty through the redistribution of European trade goods.[32]

By the end of this period Kamehameha had also collected an impressive fleet of European vessels. Turnbull notes that Kamehameha had upwards of 20 European-style vessels ranging between 22 and 63 tonnes. Some were even copper-bottomed like the best European vessels, although there was a shortage of naval stores in general. The largest of these vessels were used as men-of-war and some mounted a few light guns. Most vessels seemed to be used solely to transport provisions between the islands to Kamehameha's forces. These vessels were ideal for this task because of their

---

29 Kamakau (1961), p. 189.
30 Lisiansky (1967), p. 113.
31 Lisiansky (1967), p. 116. See also Turnbull (1810), pp. 160–62.
32 Kamakau (1961), p. 190; Cordy (1972), pp. 407, 411–12; and Kirch (1985), pp. 235–36, 310 ff., esp. 313.

6. CREATING A KINGDOM

relatively large holds and ability to cope with rough seas. Soon afterwards, Lisiansky noted a similar number of European vessels and commented that some were armed with swivel guns and commanded by Europeans.[33]

The impressive force gathered for the invasion of Kaua'i never saw action. After leaving Young to govern Hawai'i and formally declaring Liholiho to be his chosen successor before his assembled councillors and kuhina, Kamehameha sailed to Maui at the head of the peleleu fleet. The fleet touched at Kipahulu and Kaupo before stopping at Lahaina. Heiau were consecrated in all three landing places. They were probably luakini heiau, given Kamehameha's intentions. Alexander implies this was the case when he refers to the 'usual cruel rites'[34] which attended their consecration. As guardian of the kapu of the heiau, Liholiho now presided over these ceremonies.

The expedition remained at Lahaina for a year 'feeding and clothing themselves with the wealth of Maui, Moloka'i, Lāna'i and Kaho'olawe, and worshipping the gods'.[35] It is unclear why Kamehameha remained on Maui for so long. He may have been disturbed by a prophecy that warned against undertaking the expedition uttered by one of his diviners before the fleet left Hawai'i. Perhaps the mobilisation was intended to intimidate Kaumuali'i into submission and deter potential rebels within Kamehameha's domains. When Turnbull visited Kaua'i in 1802, he found Kaumuali'i, gloomy and fearful of the prospect of the invasion, constructing a European-style vessel in which to flee. During the expedition's stopover on Maui, one of the Kona uncles, Kame'eiamoku, died at Lahaina, and was replaced by his son Hoapili.[36]

Towards the end of 1803 the expedition moved to O'ahu. Again they settled down for a lengthy stay. They were camped on O'ahu in 1804 when an epidemic struck the island. Offerings of hundreds of hogs, coconuts and bananas failed to stem its ravages. The sacrifice of three kapu-breakers at a Waikiki heiau also failed to satisfy the gods. The disease has not yet been identified. Kamakau described it as:

---

33 Turnbull (1810), p. 160; and Lisiansky (1967), p. 133.
34 Alexander (1891), p. 152. See also Kamakau (1961), p. 188; and Lisiansky (1967), p. 100.
35 Kamakau (1961), p. 188; and Turnbull (1810), pp. 141, 158.
36 Turnbull (1810), p. 149; Kamakau (1961), p. 188; and Alexander (1891), p. 152.

a very virulent pestilence, and those who contracted it died quickly. A person on the highway would die before he could reach home. One might go for food and water and die so suddenly that those at home did not know what had happened. The body turned black at death. A few died a lingering death, but never longer than twenty-four hours. If they were able to hold out for a day they had a fair chance to live. Those who lived generally lost their hair, hence the illness was called 'Head stripped bare' (poʻokole).[37]

Lisiansky was told the epidemic 'destroyed the flower of his [i.e., Kamehameha's] army'.[38] Hawaiian traditions suggest that the epidemic may have killed up to two-thirds of the army gathered there. Patrick Kirch and Marshall Sahlins dispute this figure, and imply that most of the army survived and later settled on Oʻahu. It is unclear what the death toll for the civilian population was and whether the epidemic spread throughout the chain. While the epidemic may not have killed as many as some claim, it still dramatically altered power relations in the islands. The army would have suffered many more deaths than ever occurred in indigenous warfare, and a number of politically influential aliʻi died, including the three remaining Kona uncles. Kamehameha barely escaped with his own life.[39]

1804–12: From oligarchy to autocracy?

Kamehameha moved decisively to reconstitute his power base after the 1804 disaster. The sons of the three dead kuhina took their places and Kamehameha conferred their fathers' privileges upon them. Koahou replaced Kamanawa, Kahekili Keʻeaumoku replaced Keʻeaumoku, while Naihe replaced Keawe a Heulu. With Hoapili, these men formed the new backbone of the king's power. All proved to be loyal supporters of Kamehameha. A particularly close relationship developed between

---

37 Kamakau (1961), 189.
38 Lisiansky (1967), p. 133.
39 Kirch & Sahlins (1992), p. 44. See also Alexander (1891), p. 152; Westervelt (1922), p. 29; Daws (1968a), pp. 42–43; Stannard (1989), pp. 55–57; Bushnell (1993), pp. 115–61, 149–51; and A.W. Crosby, 'Hawaiian Depopulation as a Model for the Amerindian Experience', in Terence Ranger & Paul Slack (eds), *Epidemics and Ideas: Essays on the Historical Perception of Pestilence* (Cambridge University Press, 1992), p. 190.

6. CREATING A KINGDOM

Kamehameha and Hoapili. The young ali'i was allowed to take Kamehameha's wife Keōpūolani as a wife and was given the future honour of hiding Kamehameha's bones to protect them from enemies.[40]

Kamehameha remained on O'ahu until 1810, from where he administered the affairs of the whole realm with a firm hand. Young continued to act as his administrator on Hawai'i. Ke'eaumoku was made kuhina of Maui.[41] With Kamehameha's approval, kuhina appointed tax collectors, district heads and other local officials. On Hawai'i at least, old established chiefly families were increasingly marginalised from influence by the kuhina and the lesser ali'i who made up his local officials. Campbell describes how the tenants paid 'rent' to ali'i four times a year. The payments were made in kind, usually in pigs, cloth or mats. The lack of agricultural produce in the tribute and frequency of payment implies the mō'ī's lands were sufficient to provide for government needs, and that this rent or tax was distinct from makahiki tribute. The produce of Kamehameha's estates, ho'okopu (offerings) and levies ('auhau) satisfied his logistical needs.[42]

Sacred authority continued to be a key aspect of Kamehameha's power. Human sacrifice and execution for kapu violations still took place, but rarely. Most of the population seemed to adhere to the kapu, if Campbell's observations at Honolulu are representative. Campbell heard of no sacrifice during his 13-month stay on O'ahu, but did note the execution of one ali'i for violating a kapu that Kamehameha had placed on others having sexual relations with Ka'ahumanu. Alexander claims three men were sacrificed at Leahi heiau on O'ahu in 1807 because their eating of kapu coconuts was thought to be responsible for the illness of the ali'i nui Keōpūolani. Others were willing to risk the consequences of breaking kapu. Campbell noted that women took advantage of the presence of European vessels to swim out to them at night and eat forbidden foods away from the eyes of other Hawaiians. Campbell once encountered Ka'ahumanu breaking a kapu in this manner. She asked for him to keep it a secret, implying that a revelation would endanger her life.[43]

---

40   Kamakau (1961), pp. 189–90; Westervelt (1922), pp. 29–30; and Kame'eleihiwa (1986), pp. 103, 106.
41   Kamakau (1961), pp. 184, 191; and Campbell (1967), p. 97.
42   Alexander (1891), p. 150; Campbell (1967), p. 118; and Kirch & Sahlins (1992), p. 44, 50–51.
43   Sahlins (1981), p. 64; Campbell (1967), pp. 128–29, 136, 155; and Alexander (1891).

Kamehameha was well aware of the benefits of his traditional sacred status to his position as ruler. With Davis acting as interpreter, Kamehameha told a European visitor:

> I should be afraid to adopt such a dangerous expedient as Christianity, for I think no Christian King can govern in the absolute manner in which I do, and yet be loved by his subjects as I am by mine: such a religion might perhaps answer very well in the course of a few generations; but what chief would sanction it in the beginning, with risk of its subverting his own power, and involving the islands in war? I have made a fixed determination not to suffer it.[44]

Campbell and other European visitors to the islands during these years found Kamehameha to be popular with his subjects.[45]

European interactions with Hawaiians suggested peace and prosperity reigned. But tensions loomed beneath the surface. Trade was booming in part because many aliʻi were using trade to enhance their power base. Kamakau noted that it was from these visiting vessels that:

> the chiefs and people bought arms and gunpowder. Kamehameha had several storehouses well stocked with foreign arms, but nobody wanted money or clothing. On the part of the foreigners potatoes and yams were in great demand. The chiefs accordingly went into the cultivation of these foods, and grew potatoes on the hill of ʻUalakaʻa between Manoa and Makiki, and yams at Kaʻakopua, and sold them to the foreigners.[46]

Kamehameha's impressive supply of munitions seems attributable more to his considerable trading skills and ability to meet European requirements than his capacity to exclude other aliʻi from trade.[47] Despite the increasing concentration of most European trade at Honolulu after 1805, Kamehameha was still unable to halt the diffusion of firearms. His continued residence on Oʻahu was probably in large part due to his desire to exercise influence over trade after the disruption of his power base in the 1804 epidemic.

---

44   John Martin, *Tonga Islands: William Mariner's Account* (4th edn) (Tonga: Vavaʻu Press Ltd, 1981), p. xxxiv.
45   Campbell (1967), p. 131; H.W. Bradley, *The American Frontier in Hawaii: The Pioneers 1789–1843* (Stanford University Press, 1942), p. 10.
46   Kamakau (1961), p. 190; Iʻi (1959), pp. 68–69; and Cordy (1972), pp. 406–07.
47   Daws (1968a), p. 44; Howe (1984), p. 161; and Turnbull (1810), p. 159.

6. CREATING A KINGDOM

The coercive gap between the power of the Kamehameha's supporters and other aliʻi now became weak enough for some of the latter to contemplate challenging the ruling clique. Much of the opposition to Kamehameha seems to have centred upon his favourite wife Kaʻahumanu. She had always refused to devote herself entirely to her husband, either emotionally or politically. She had a significant power base, controlling considerable landholdings, and possessing genealogical links with the old ruling line of Maui as well as important families on Hawaiʻi. As the senior member of her generation, Kaʻahumanu exercised much influence over her close relatives. Her brother Kahekili Keʻeaumoku was now kuhina of Maui, while she was inducted into Kamehameha's council. Although she bore Kamehameha no children herself, Kaʻahumanu sought to increase her influence over Liholiho by declaring him to be her hanai (adopted child).[48]

Before he died, Kaʻahumanu's father warned Kamehameha to be wary of his daughter, and suggested that she was the only aliʻi in the realm who posed any real threat to his rule. Kamehameha declared it a capital offence for anyone but himself to sleep with her, probably fearing that dissidents might coalesce around such a union. In 1809 Kanihonui, a nephew of Kamehameha, was discovered to have defied this edict. While drunkenness may have accounted for his defiance of Kamehameha's prohibition, Kamehameha feared the worst and had Kanihonui executed. Kaʻahumanu was furious. She attempted to organise a revolt to overthrow her husband and install Liholiho in his place. Kamehameha mobilised his supporters and prepared for trouble. Liholiho refused to endorse the revolt in front of the assembled malcontents. With Kamehameha displaying a determination to contest the issue, Liholiho's action was enough to dissuade the assembled aliʻi from openly challenging their ruler. The gathering disbanded and conflict was avoided for the meantime.[49]

Tensions simmered until September 1811, when Kamehameha moved to quell trouble on Oʻahu. It had come to his attention that aliʻi in Koʻolaupoko, Koʻolauloa, Waialua and ʻEwa were gathering men around them. At the same time they were increasing their agricultural production and storing guns and powder. Heeding the advice of his councillors, he announced that he was returning to Hawaiʻi and that he required the aliʻi

---

48 On Kaʻahumanu's power and influence, see Kamakau (1961), pp. 313, 315; Iʻi (1959), pp. 26, 53; Sahlins (1981), p. 58; Daws (1968a), p. 56; and Kameʻeleihiwa (1986), p. 109.
49 Kamakau (1961), pp. 189, 194; and Iʻi (1959), pp. 50–51.

to turn over their guns and ammunition and go with him to his home island accompanied by no more than two men each. The conspirators were faced with the prospect of either declaring their intentions by mobilising prematurely or allowing themselves to be disarmed. None seem to have resisted.

According to Hawaiian sources, the accumulated weapons were loaded onto one of Kamehameha's European vessels, the *Keoua*. A carefully stage-managed leak saw the *Keoua* return to Honolulu and disembark its passengers but not its cargo of munitions. The leak was fixed and Kamehameha sailed to Hawai'i. Here the confiscated military hardware was stored with two trusted men: Young at Kawaihae and Kamakau at Kealakekua Bay. However, a European resident of Honolulu claimed that the initial confiscation of the firearms was sufficient to diffuse the situation, and that the confiscated weapons were not transported to Hawai'i until almost a year later. I'ī also mentions that, just prior to returning to Hawai'i, Kamehameha closed the schools of combat that had been set up.[50]

The ease with which Kamehameha was able to disarm his potential enemies suggests that he had a decisive coercive advantage over them. This advantage probably occurred as a result of a general reduction of military forces rather than through a major build-up of Kamehameha's forces. Many of his forces must have perished at sea in 1796 and in the epidemic on O'ahu in 1804. This was also where the armies of Ka'eokulani and Kalanikūpule had last been assembled. Certainly there may have been some movement from the island after 1795, and garrisons would have been maintained on other islands during the attempted assault on Kaua'i, but the epidemic was still a major blow to the military forces concentrated there.

There is no indication that Kamehameha's regular forces on O'ahu numbered more than 500 men in this period. These men were described as 'disciplined native soldiers',[51] by a visitor to Honolulu in 1806. The

---

50   Kamakau (1961), pp. 197–98; I'ī (1959), p. 103; Alexander (1891), pp. 157–58; and Ross H. Gast & Agnes Conrad (eds), *Don Francisco de Paula Marin – A Biography with the Letters and Journals of Francisco de Paula Marin* (Honolulu: University of Hawai'i Press, 1973), pp. 201, 206, 207.
51   Fitzsimmons (1969), p. 171, citing missionaries visiting from Tahiti in 1806. See also Kirch & Sahlins (1992), p. 45, citing William Shaler, 'Journal of a Voyage Between China and the North-Western Coast of America Made in 1804', *American Register*, no. 3, 1808, 164; and Alexander Ross, *Adventures of the First Settlers on the Oregon and Columbia River* (London: Smith, Elder, 1849), p. 147.

only body of full-time troops witnessed by Campbell during his stay in Honolulu in 1809 and 1810 was a guard of approximately 50 men stationed at Kamehameha's residence in Honolulu. They had no uniform beyond a malo. Each man carried a musket, a bayonet and a cartridge box.[52] It is unclear if this guard formed all or part of the body of troops that I'ī watched practicing gun drill when he was a boy in Honolulu. I'ī's description of the drill suggests that European tactics now accompanied the adoption of European weapons also:

> Drilling in those days was not quite like that of today, for they had only half of the present knowledge. Their soldiers stood in line from the front all the way to the back, and so it was with each line. At the proper command, those in the front row, which extended from one end of the field to the other, raised their guns in unison and fired. Then they placed the guns on their shoulders, turned left about face, marked time, and began to advance. So it went until the drilling period was over.[53]

Campbell's observations on the drill practices confirm I'ī's assertion that the troops were still learning to use their weapons. He noted that:

> rapidity, and not precision seemed to be their great object. The men stood at extended order, and fired as fast as they could, beating the butt upon the ground, and coming to the recover without using the ramrod, each man gave the word 'fire' before he drew the trigger.[54]

Campbell describes these men as guards, implying they were the same men he saw stationed at Kamehameha's residence. I'ī noted that the troops he watched were the successors to an earlier company of troops, organised by Kamehameha and known as the kulailua ('knocked down') in reference to the ramifications of a musket discharge when not held tightly against the shoulder. This evidence of poor handling of muskets casts doubts on the degree to which they were used prior to this. It is unlikely that the 1804 epidemic entirely wiped out Kamehameha's veterans and required a totally new intake of recruits for training. I'ī claims that Kamehameha's warriors were still unequalled in their ability with traditional weapons. Such skills took more than a few years of drills to achieve.

Other forces existed besides Kamehameha's troops. Davis had a company of warriors who protected him. The ali'i Kuakini had his own European vessel and was given six cannon for it by Liholiho. Quality, rather than

---

52 Campbell (1967), pp. 149–50.
53 I'ī (1959), p. 54.
54 Campbell (1967), p. 158.

relative numbers, may have been the decisive factor in giving Kamehameha a coercive advantage. Iʻī states that, while Kamehameha's fighting schools were not the only ones, they were the best of the schools. Kamehameha's men not only drilled regularly with firearms but also trained with spear points exposed in a much more rigorous manner than anyone else. While no descriptions of other schools of fighting remain, Iʻī's reference to Kamehameha's schools implies the other schools practised with the spear points covered over.[55] Campbell mentions that throwing and catching sugarcane stalks was a popular pastime and that the general population trained for war from youth.[56] A mock battle described by Iʻī suggests, however, that most of the population was poorly prepared for battle and the only weapons used appear to have been stones. The passage is worth quoting in full:

> Two chiefs who had gone from Honolulu to Puuloa with some chiefs of that locality landed at Aioloolo in Waikele, and the battle was staged between them and residents of Waikele that very afternoon. The two sides gathered at a place above Aioloolo on the slope of the hill leading down to Kupapaulau.
>
> The spectators noticed that both sides were equally skilled in stone throwing and in dodging the stones that flew back and forth. No one was hurt or harmed, and the skill of the participants and the chiefs who arranged the sham battle was praised. It seems that the chiefs watched to see how skilled their people were in battle.[57]

It is possible that the most proficient participants were inducted into the fighting schools as their predecessors had been into chiefly retinues. The relationship between these schools and chiefly retinues is unclear. During the 1809 crisis, supporters were called up, only to be dismissed when the anticipated confrontation did not arise.[58] Kamehameha kept important chiefs at his court and moved against the outer districts of Oʻahu only when aliʻi there began to gather supporters and arms. Keʻeaumoku may indeed have been right when he asserted that the only danger to Kamehameha came from Kaʻahumanu.

---

55 Iʻī (1959), pp. 30, 54, 66, 69, 83.
56 Campbell (1967), pp. 149–50.
57 Iʻī (1959), p. 76.
58 Iʻī (1959), p. 51.

Kamehameha's power rested upon more than just manpower. In 1806 he was reported to have 2,000 stands of arms stored in a fortified residence that dominated the Honolulu foreshore. A palisade protected its land approaches, while a battery of 16 cannon faced out to sea. These guns were from Kamehameha's ship the *Lily Bird* (*Lelia Byrd*) that lay unrigged in the harbour. Within the enclosure were situated the king's and queen's huts, a store, a powder magazine and a guardhouse. Two storehouses brimming with European trade items, including munitions, stood nearby.[59] As most European trade now came through Honolulu, Kamehameha's compound provided a means of controlling or at least monitoring the flow of arms into the realm. The 1811 crisis may have been more of a pre-emptive strike by Kamehameha than a reaction to a serious challenge. It was one thing to acquire firearms, but quite another to maintain and replenish one's stock, and to drill followers in their use before the government noticed and took action.

Rival ali'i might attempt to match Kamehameha's strength in muskets, but they could not hope to compete against his naval strength. By 1810 Kamehameha possessed over 40 European vessels. Most were scoops and schooners weighing under 36 tonnes that had been constructed by Kamehameha's carpenters. These carpenters were now highly skilled boat builders and operated from his naval yard at Honolulu. European captains were generally still used to command Hawaiian crews. No naval threat existed within the archipelago and, by 1810, Kamehameha seems to have abandoned his plans to invade Kaua'i. As a result, Campbell found most of Kamehameha's European vessels hauled up on Waikiki beach in boat sheds, with their spars laid alongside and their riggings and cables under cover. Only 10 to 12 of his vessels were moored in Honolulu harbour and only one scoop was in regular use, sailing between O'ahu and Hawai'i. The peleleu fleet lay drawn up on Waikiki beach, exposed to the elements, and slowly falling into a state of disrepair.[60]

The problem of Kaua'i was resolved diplomatically, without need for naval or military action. While Kamehameha never publicly declared an end to his campaign to invade Kaua'i, he had been sending conciliatory signals to Kaumuali'i since 1804 in the form of gifts and embassies inviting him to visit O'ahu. Kaumuali'i received the embassies hospitably but was

---

59 Campbell (1967), pp. 91, 149–50.
60 Campbell (1967), pp. 111, 144; I'ī (1959), pp. 103, 105, 109, 113; Ross (1849), pp. 38–39; Daws (1968a), p. 43; and Kirch & Sahlins (1992), p. 43.

understandably reluctant to travel to Oʻahu to visit the slayer of Keōua. Eventually he agreed to meet with Kamehameha through the mediation of Nathan Winship, an American trader. Although Kaumualiʻi had a body of musket-armed Europeans and continued access to European trade at Waimea, he could not hope to match Kamehameha's military resources. Reasonable peace terms were preferable to the constant threat of invasion. The meeting went well and ended with an agreement by which Kaumualiʻi would rule Kauaʻi as a tributary 'King' acknowledging Kamehameha as his sovereign. There was also a veiled reference to Liholiho becoming heir to Kaumualiʻi's lands as well as those of Kamehameha.[61]

While the arrangement satisfied Kamehameha, it did not please some of his aliʻi. Perhaps angered at the prospect of missing out on the spoils that would follow the conquest of Kauaʻi, they attempted to sabotage the meeting of the two leaders by trying to poison Kaumualiʻi. Davis learnt of the plot and warned Kaumualiʻi in time, only to be poisoned by the conspirators. The idea of killing Kaumualiʻi had actually been raised in Kamehameha's council, but had been rejected after Kamehameha and Kalaikuahulu had argued persuasively against it. Iʻī names the main conspirator as Naihe. Naihe's fate is unclear, as is the degree of support for him. It may be significant that, soon after this event, Kamehameha moved to disarm the aliʻi on Oʻahu and sailed for Hawaiʻi.[62]

1812–19: Sacred kingship and bureaucracy?

Sahlins suggests that Kamehameha's move back to Hawaiʻi may have been an attempt to preserve his sacred power by insulating himself from increasing exposure to foreign influences on Oʻahu. Foreigners and their goods were outside the kapu system and did not usually conform to its needs and expectations. For all of his political innovations and military reforms, Kamehameha remained a religious conservative until his death. After his return to Hawaiʻi he continued to worship his personal gods and to rebuild heiau. Liholiho's sacred role as intermediary between the gods and his people to ensure successful harvests continued to be emphasised. The makahiki remained an important event. Kamehameha

---

61   Kamakau (1961), pp. 195, 196; Iʻī (1959), p. 83; and Daws (1968a), pp. 42–43. See commentaries in Daws (1968a), p. 42; John M. Lydgate, 'Ka-umu-alii, the Last King of Kauai', *24th Annual Report of the Hawaiian Historical Society for the Year 1915* (Honolulu: 1916), pp. 26–27.
62   Iʻī (1959), p. 83; Kamakau (1951), p. 196; and Daws (1968a), pp. 43–44.

incorporated a number of his own gods into the makahiki procession, and used the offerings to them as de facto taxes. Although his storehouses were soon brimming with makahiki offerings, they mostly consisted of tapa, skirts and malo rather than assets he could use to pay or feed to his administration.[63]

It has been suggested that Kamehameha moved away from Kū'kā'ili-moku and towards other gods during this period. In particular, there seems to have been an increasing association with sorcery gods. With warfare now a distant memory, protection from sorcery seems to have become a more prominent aspect of Kamehameha's worship. Evidence in I'ī supports this contention. Liholiho was entrusted with the care of Kū'kā'ili-moku for the return voyage to Hawai'i from O'ahu. When Kamehameha's council met in 1812 to discuss the loyalty of his subjects, it was suggested that the help of the Ololupe god be sought 'to bring hither the spirits of the rebellious to be destroyed'.[64] Kamehameha's faith was apparently more intense than a number of his subjects. The Russian naval captain Otto Von Kotzebue's observations of ali'i behaviour during his expedition's visit to Hawai'i in 1816 reveal apparent inconsistency in their attitude towards the kapu system. A female maka'āinana was killed for breaking an eating kapu, yet ali'i of both sexes openly ate together on board the Russian vessel and drank alcohol. On shore the expedition's naturalist was surprised to find religious ceremonies in a heiau observed with little reverence.[65]

Apart from meeting with his council, Kamehameha left much of the business of government to his administrators. He remained on Hawai'i until his death, and spent much of his time fishing and gardening. He was always consulted on important decisions by his officials, but rarely intervened personally in affairs of state. Kamehameha's withdrawal from political affairs opened the way for other ali'i to enhance their power. Sahlins labels this group the Ka'ahumanu group because their political alignments and kinship relations centred on her. Sahlins bases the group on the ali'i who came to control the government after Kamehameha's death, including Ka'ahumanu's brothers Kahekili Ke'eaumoku, and Kuakini, and

---

63 Sahlins (1981), p. 46; Sahlins (1995), pp. 218–19; Kamakau (1961), pp. 200, 203; and I'ī (1959), p. 104.
64 I'ī (1959), p. 123. On sorcery, see Valeri (1982); and I'ī (1959), p. 124. On Liholiho and Kū, see I'ī (1959), p. 104. Ololupe was an 'aumakua associated with conveying the dead ali'i to their 'aumakua. I am indebted to Jon Osorio for providing this information.
65 Daws (1968a), p. 58.

her collateral brothers Kalanimoku and Boki. Kaʻahumanu's relations were prominent in government because Kamehameha continued the traditional Hawaiʻi practice of denying collateral kin power bases by using affinal kin for important offices. By the time of Kamehameha's death, Keʻeaumoku governed Maui, Kuakini governed Hawaiʻi, Boki administered Oʻahu while Kalanimoku continued to serve as pukaua and puʻuku nui. They all controlled significant landholdings as well. In contrast, Kamehameha's collateral kin were mainly entrusted with sacred aspects of government, such as the upholding of the ruler's kapu and his gods.[66]

The Kaʻahumanu group identified by Sahlins may not have had a common purpose prior to 1819. Blood ties were no guarantee of cooperation in Hawaiian politics. Although rumours were rife that this group intended to seize power as soon as Kamehameha died, there is no indication that they used their offices to put their interests ahead of Kamehameha's before 1819. Even if they had been united in purpose they would not have monopolised secular power. The designation of Liholiho as Kamehameha's successor must have enhanced his chances of securing the loyalty of the royal administration and army that had taken the place of vassal aliʻi and their retinues as the source of secular power. The demilitarisation of the islands continued in this period, consolidating the royal forces' advantage in coercive power.[67]

While martial prowess ceased to be encouraged in the majority of the population, Kamehameha began to create a substantial standing army on Hawaiʻi. In January 1816, German employee of the Russian American Company Doctor George Scheffer visited Kamehameha's military camp, 8 kilometres south of Kailua. Here he noted that Kamehameha 'taught military discipline to about 1,000 men, two-thirds of who had wooden arms'.[68] Scheffer subsequently went on to scheme against Kamehameha without Russian Government consent so that, when Von Kotzebue visited the Kona coast in November, he found 400 soldiers armed with muskets waiting to see what his intentions were. The force that was mobilised to counter Scheffer's provocative actions in Honolulu came largely from Hawaiʻi and consisted of 'chief and fighting men who had joined the

---

66   Daws (1968a), p. 44; Sahlins (1981), p. 60; Kirch & Sahlins (1992), pp. 2, 60. On Kamehameha's distancing himself from government, see Alexander (1891), p. 158; and Iʻi (1959), p. 117. On Kalanimoku's duties, see Iʻi (1959), p. 112. On Boki's duties, see Iʻi (1959), p. 145.
67   Iʻi (1959), p. 123; Kamakau (1981), p. 208.
68   Cited in Richard A. Pierce, *Russia's Hawaiian Adventure, 1815–1817* (Berkley, University of California Press, 1965), p. 164.

King (Okaka), and others besides'.[69] This seems to imply that the royal forces formed the full-time core of Kamehameha's army, which was supplemented by others in times of crisis. When Vasili Golovin touched at Kailua in October 1818, he was given the impression that Kamehameha could arm 6,000 men. The European resident Portuguese physician Juan Elliot d'Castro told Golovin the figure was 8,000 men, but Golovin chose to believe the lower number, which was given him by another resident, the Spaniard Don Francisco de Paula Marin (known as Manini to the Hawaiians). The difference between these figures and those observed by Scheffer and Von Kotzebue may represent the difference between the full-time army, and the total number of men that could be called up.[70]

Most of the regulars seemed to have used firearms and been subject to European-style drill. European observers were not impressed with these forces. Golovin noted that many of their arms were rusty and that they used 'many peculiar, amusing and strange methods'[71] in their drills. In 1819 the French explorer Louis Freycinet expressed similar views about the appearance of these troops at Kawaihae:

> A fairly large number of soldiers scattered here and there lent an air of great variety to this strange picture of the odd and irregular fashion of their uniforms. No order, no uniformity of appearance and movement existed amongst them; each one carried his gun as it was convenient to him or as it was most comfortable. All of them wore a loincloth, but most of them wore in addition an enormous cape of a brownish color and rather coarse material; proud of this odd equipment, they paraded past us quite complacently, not having the least idea that their appearance was to us highly grotesque.[72]

Despite their appearance, these forces acted as an effective deterrent to challenges from both internal and external sources. Few, if any, within the islands could match them. After Kamehameha ended the fighting schools when he left Oʻahu, mock battles between communities lost any sense of being training exercises. Sugarcane stalks were used instead of spears and sling stones, to avoid real battles amongst participants erupting as the

---

69 Kamakau (1961), p. 206.
70 Otto von Kotzebue, *Voyage of Discovery in the South Sea undertaken in the Years 1814, 16, 17 and 18* (London: Sir Richard Phillips and Co., 1821), p. 84; and V. M. Golovin, *Around the World on the Kamchatka, 1817–1819*, Ella L. Wisnell (trans.) (Honolulu: Hawaiian Historical Society and University of Hawaiʻi Press, 1979), pp. 191–92, 200.
71 Golovin (1979), p. 200.
72 Kelly (1978), p. 14.

result of serious wounds and deaths during the sparring. In some instances, musket-armed soldiers stood by to preserve order. Golovin found the participants in the mock battles he witnessed to be unenthusiastic, although a few fistfights did break out afterwards. Americans he met told him that the Hawaiians had lost their traditional martial skills and the warlike, brave spirit that had characterised earlier generations.[73]

Incidents immediately before and after Kamehameha's death suggest that he not only attempted to monopolise the supply of firearms in the islands, but also restricted the number of firearms issued. Kamakau relates that, when a war of succession seemed inevitable soon after Kamehameha's death, 'Arms and ammunition were given out that evening to everyone who was trained in warfare, and feathered caps and helmets distributed'.[74] The reference to trained forces suggests only the regular forces were given the privilege of carrying firearms. Firearms may have been distributed more widely, just prior to Kamehameha's death, in preparation for possible conflict, however, as Don Francisco de Paula Marin noted on 2 May 1819, 'the King is a little better and Cajumanu [Ka'ahumanu] took all the muskets of the chiefs'. This implies that Kamehameha's demilitarisation had not been total, or that firearms had been reluctantly distributed by those in power as the prospect of a leadership struggle arose, and were re-collected as soon as signs of Kamehameha's recovery occurred.[75] Kamakau's reference to the issue of capes and helmets suggests that traditional weapons were also still in use. An 1819 painting that depicts the bodyguard of the king illustrates him with a cape and helmet, and armed with a spear.[76] (Scheffer's reference to two-thirds of the troops he watched training in 1816 carrying wooden arms could either refer to traditional weapons or wooden replicas of firearms.)

The only serious disturbance in this era occurred in 1815–16 when Scheffer exceeded his instructions to recover property from a vessel wrecked off Waimea on Kaua'i. He sought trade concessions on Kaua'i from Kaumuali'i in return for Russian naval and military assistance. Both made these moves without consulting their superiors, and Scheffer lacked the ability to fulfil his promises. Scheffer set up a trading post at Waimea.

---

73 James Jackson Jarves, *History of the Hawaiian or Sandwich Islands* (Boston: Tappan and Dennet, 1843), p. 96; and Golovin (1979), p. 187.
74 Kamakau (1961), p. 227. See also Dibble (1909), p. 133.
75 Gast & Conrad (1973), p. 230.
76 The painting, which depicts a Hawaiian chief in his feathered cloak and helmet, by the French artist Jacques Arago in 1819, is held in the Bancroft Library, University of California, Berkeley.

Soon after the Russian sealing ship *Discovery* arrived at Waimea and left 30 Kodiak Indians from its crew with Scheffer. Then, in November 1815, a vessel sent by the Russian governor of Alaska arrived in Honolulu and its crew proceeded to erect a blockhouse. Cannon were placed in the blockhouse and the Russian flag was hoisted.

Young and resident American traders, who saw Scheffer as a threat to their interests, had earlier driven him out of Honolulu. They then followed him back to Kaua'i, where he had to be protected by Kaumuali'i's guards. This new Russian move called for a more organised response. Kamehameha sent Kalanimoku and an armed force from Hawai'i to Honolulu to ascertain the Russians' intentions. If they meant no harm, they were to be supplied with vegetables and pork. If not, Hawaiian forces might once more engage in battle. As it was, the Russians withdrew almost immediately to Kaua'i.[77]

This incident was enough to persuade Kalanimoku to construct a large fort to guard the harbour against similar incursions. Construction began in January 1816. The fort was completed early in 1817 using corvée labour from O'ahu. Sited on the Honolulu waterfront, it measured 103 by 91 metres. Its walls, which were 3.5 metres high and 7 metres thick at the base, were constructed of coral blocks faced with an adobe mix of clay, sand and dry grass. At least 40 cannon were mounted on the walls, ranging in size from four to 18 pounders with the heaviest pieces facing out to sea. Adobe embrasures protected those on the wall on the seaward side, while a parapet protected the landward sides. The fort was called kapapu (the gun wall) and kakuanohu (the thorny back) because of the guns bristling along its horizon.[78]

In the meantime, Scheffer had constructed a fort at Waimea with help from Kaumuali'i's subjects. By 1817, however, information from visiting Russian vessels revealed to both Kaumuali'i and Kamehameha that Scheffer had neither the financial or military backing he claimed. When Kamehameha ordered Kaumuali'i to expel Scheffer, the order was obeyed with little resistance from either Kaumuali'i or Scheffer. Kaumuali'i remained in charge of Kaua'i and Kamehameha's control of Honolulu was now stronger than ever. A garrison trained and drilled by a resident Englishman George Beckley permanently manned the fort at Honolulu.

---

77 Kamakau (1961), pp. 205–06; Alexander (1891), pp. 159–61; Westervelt (1922), pp. 35–36; Lydgate (1916), pp. 31–32; Daws (1968a), pp. 49–53; and Pierce (1968), esp. pp. 20–21.
78 Kelly (1978), pp. 90–91; Golovin (1979), pp. 185–86; Alexander (1891), p. 160; and Westervelt (1922), p. 36.

Strict discipline was observed with a regular watch maintained throughout the night. Inside the fort were chiefs' houses and barracks for the garrison, all arranged around a central flagpole flying the Hawaiian flag.[79]

Kamehameha's naval strength continued to be based on a number of European vessels armed with cannon. He re-established the naval yards at Kailua when he returned to Hawai'i in 1812. Golovin reported that Kamehameha's navy included two or three brigs and several schooners and large decked vessels, all of which were armed with cannon or falconets. Most of the crew and many of the captains were now Hawaiians. The majority of the ships were used only to transport goods between islands. Kamehameha derived great pleasure from acquiring European vessels, right up until his death. In 1819 Freycinet noted that he possessed five brigs of 81 to 90 tonnes each, five schooners of 54 to 63 tonnes, and approximately 10 18-tonne cutters. The king's 170 Hawaiian carpenters constructed some of these vessels, while others were bought. Batteries of cannon were noted at Kealakekua Bay, Kailua and Kawaihae. Golovin was told that, in all, Kamehameha had 100 cannon.[80]

Kamehameha's fort, cannon and vessels served more as pillars of his domestic power base than as ramparts against outsiders. The Hawaiian Islands did not face the prospect of a serious external challenge in Kamehameha's time. Kamehameha's attempts to align himself with Britain met with British unwillingness to risk involvement, while the European powers with a presence in the region tended to counterbalance each other. As long as their European rivals did not move into Hawai'i, they were content to leave matters as they were.[81]

The mounting interest in European goods and ideas became more pronounced after 1810 with the opening up of the Hawaiian sandalwood trade. Ka'ahumanu and her clique were particularly enthusiastic about what they could acquire through such trade.[82] A number of prominent ali'i dressed in European clothing and also began learning English. Liholiho, Ke'eaumoku, Kuakini and Kaumuali'i were among this group.

---

79 Peter Corney, *Voyages on the Northern Pacific: Narrative of Several Trading Voyages from 1813 to 1818* (Honolulu: Thos G. Thrum, Publisher, 1896), p. 98.
80 Golovin (1979), pp. 182, 191–92, 200; Kelly (1978), pp. 86–87, 90, 91, 114 n. 49; citing Kuykendall (1938), p. 96 n. 94; and Kirch & Sahlins (1992), p. 60. On cannon numbers, see Fitzsimmons (1969), p. 202. On Kamehameha's purchases, see I'ī (1959), pp. 103–04, 128, 129; Kamakau (1961), p. 207; Bradley (1942), pp. 55–56; and Alexander (1891), pp. 161–63, 169.
81 Daws (1968a), pp. 50–51; and Kamakau (1961), p. 209.
82 I'ī (1957), p. 128; Kamakau (1961), p. 204; and Sahlins (1981), pp. 60–62.

Denied the thrill of battle, and shut out of military and political power by Kamehameha and a small clique, the aliʻi took to the trade in sandalwood with a passion. The accumulation of European trade goods now became the medium for chiefly competition. Liquor, silk cloth and other luxury items were more sought after than metal tools and military hardware. Breaking with tradition, most of these goods were stored away rather than redistributed among followers.[83]

The new chiefly competition brought suffering to the makaʻāinana. Aliʻi sent their tenants into the mountains to seek sandalwood for months on end. It was hard physical work and their prolonged absences in the mountains resulted in less manpower to grow crops for domestic needs and to provision visiting ships. The use of women in agriculture offered a partial solution. Women were already part of the agricultural workforce in leeward Maui, and Kona and Kohala on Hawaiʻi. Thus, the diversion of manpower into the sandalwood trade does not seem to have seriously threatened food production. The only famine recorded between 1810 and 1819 occurred on the leeward side of Hawaiʻi in 1811–12, and European visitors were told the famine was due to low rainfall over the last three years rather than human agency.[84]

Kamehameha moved quickly to try and control the sandalwood trade. He declared a royal monopoly on the trade under which aliʻi had to give 60 per cent of the wood collected to the government. Ostensibly this was to deter exploitation of makaʻāinana and the neglect of agriculture. According to the chief Kanaʻina in the 1820s, however, aliʻi kept 60 per cent of the proceeds from the sale of sandalwood while Kamehameha received only 10 per cent.[85] Whatever the division of proceeds was, the trade was so lucrative that aliʻi continued to send commoners out to cut sandalwood. One picul of sandalwood, a measure equating to around 61 kilograms of sandalwood, sold for eight to 10 United States dollars.[86]

---

83   Kamakau (1961), pp. 231–32; Alexander (1891), p. 156; Sahlins (1981), pp. 30–31; Howe (1984), p. 162; Ralston (1984), pp. 26–29; Levin (1968), p. 422; and Golovin (1979), p. 210.
84   Kamakau (1961), p. 231; Cordy (1972), p. 412. On Anahulu, see Kirch (1985), p. 314. On leeward Kohala, see Kirch (1985), p. 178. On sandalwood-induced famine, see Ralston (1984), p. 26 versus Cordy (1972), pp. 409–10. On drought-induced famine, see Levin (1968), p. 422; Schmitt (1970), p. 113; Iʻī (1959), p. 114; Alexander (1891), p. 158; and Kamakau (1961), pp. 205–06.
85   Kirch & Sahlins (1992), p. 59, citing Robert Crichton Wylie, *Supplement to the Report of the Minister of Foreign Relations*, (Honolulu: Government Printer, 1856), p. 25.
86   Kamakau (1961), p. 207. See also Cordy (1972), pp. 409, 412; Theodore Morgan, *Hawaii: A Century of Economic Change, 1778–1876* (Cambridge, Mass.: Harvard University Press, 1948), pp. 63, 66; Bradley (1942), pp. 55–59; and Alexander (1891), p. 161.

Chiefly demand for European items continued to rise, despite inflated prices. Kamehameha was one of the most enthusiastic collectors of European goods. His storehouse in Kona was crammed full of silverware, crystal, shoes and other manufactured items, as well as more practical items of government such as munitions and foreign cash. His sandalwood revenue was such that he was enabled to engage in major expenditure. His purchases of European vessels went well beyond his commercial and defence needs and, between 1816 and 1818, he purchased six vessels. In 1816, for example, he bought the 150-tonne *Albatross* for 400 piculs of sandalwood. In 1818 he paid the same price in sandalwood for a package of assorted items including nails, olive oil, paint oil, brushes, flour, rice, sugar, pitch, kettles and old copper.[87]

Kamehameha's administration closely supervised all trade and imposed a variety of taxes. By 1819, Kamehameha had imposed a one-Spanish piaster tax on his subjects for any transactions with foreigners. When the Hawaiian crews of three of Kamehameha's vessels returned to the islands with European hats and clothing in 1812, government officials confiscated all their possessions. By the middle of the decade it was usual for visiting vessels to direct their business through Kamehameha's representatives. These were usually lesser aliʻi with some proficiency in English. They ensured the smooth progress of provisioning and repairs, and even accompanied ships to other islands in the chain away from Honolulu. At the same time, they provided Kamehameha with details of crew needs and ship's trade goods, so that he had an edge over the visitors in setting the terms of trade. All items traded to vessels carried a royal sales tax. In addition, visitors had to pay various dues before they could enter port and conduct their business. The various revenues collected by Kamehameha's government placed its finances in a healthy state. As well as an impressive array of Hawaiian goods collected as payment in kind, by 1819 the state coffers are said to have contained a sizeable amount of foreign currency.[88]

Kamehameha also kept a tight rein on the behaviour of foreigners onshore. While he was on Oʻahu, the number of beachcombers at Honolulu had risen to around 100. Many spent much of their day drinking alcohol.

---

87 See Kelly (1978). See also Golovin (1979), p. 196; Alexander (1891), p. 161; Bradley (1942), p. 56; Kirch & Sahlins (1992), p. 60.
88 On foreign currency, see Kelly (1978), p. 90. On the system for dealing with visiting vessels, see Golovin (1979), pp. 203–05; Iʻi (1959), p. 88; Daws (1968a), p. 44; and Howe (1984), p. 161.

6. CREATING A KINGDOM

Kamehameha encouraged visiting vessels to recruit from amongst their ranks and, as a result, most of these itinerants did not stay long and, by 1810, their numbers were down to around 60. Those with desired skills, such as carpenters and blacksmiths, were encouraged to work for Kamehameha and were often given small grants of land as incentives. Honolulu avoided the notorious lawlessness that characterised other Pacific ports such as Kororareka (modern day Russell) in the Bay of Islands, New Zealand. Ships' crews were made to adhere to a system of harbour rules and the waterfront was policed by government forces to control brawling within the foreign community, and incidents between foreigners and Hawaiians. On 5 June 1812, for example, a man was placed in irons and given 24 lashes for wounding his captain. On another occasion, Hawaiian officials imprisoned two sailors in the fort for striking their first mate.[89] Government forces also controlled relations between locals and visitors. Golovin provides the following description of a shore patrol at Kealakekua Bay:

> About ten o'clock at night several people with torches and crying something out in a singsong passed from Kaawaroa to Karekekooa along the beach close to the cliff. Later we learnt that his was the patrol walking through the settlements and proclaiming by the King's orders that the inhabitants were not to approach the Sloop in the night and were not to harm us in any way.[90]

Kamehameha also attempted to control the use of alcohol. While Kamehameha was still on O'ahu, rum and distilled ki (*Cordyline terminalis*) had become notable agents of social disruption among European and Hawaiian alike. Ali'i and maka'āinana of both sexes partook. Many of the ali'i who drank regularly also advocated freeing up the kapu system. Eventually Kamehameha ordered all stills destroyed and prohibited the future manufacture of liquor in the islands. Stills continued to be built, however, which only served to confirm their danger to social order.[91]

The royal administration also maintained its control over those areas away from points of European contact. Kamehameha's stores at Kailua still brimmed with tribute in the form of hard poi, dried fish, tapa, malo,

---

89   On beachcombers, see Daws (1968a), pp. 46–47; Maude (1968), pp. 139–40; Bargatzy (1980), p. 95; I'ī (1959), pp. 86, 87; and Campbell (1967), pp. 118–19, 144, 154. On the enforcement of shore regulations, see Gast & Conrad (1973), pp. 206, 225.
90   Golovin (1979), p. 176.
91   Westervelt (1922), p. 37; Alexander (1891), p. 157; Kamakau (1961), pp. 193–94; and I'ī (1959), pp. 84–86.

fishnets and fibrous ropes. In 1818, Golovin was told that European resident Juan Elliot d'Castro paid an annual tax of 40 piasters for land upon which he had 10 to 20 people working. In addition a one-piaster tax existed for seasonal inshore fishing.[92] It is uncertain whether these were part of the taxes on production imposed after 1796 or new head taxes. Kamakau does state that the system devised in the 1790s was designed specifically to avoid head taxes.

By 1816 the tax collecting bureaucracy had been centralised, or at least a centralised structure had been imposed over existing local officials. Charles Barnard relates how he sailed from Hawai'i to O'ahu:

> having on board between fifty and sixty natives, who were collectors of taxes and receivers of rents ... On the second day after sailing, we arrived at Woahoo, landed the unwelcome visitors, who began collecting the exactions, consisting of tapa, a kind of cloth made of the fine inner bark of a particular kind of tree, and bunches of dried fish. When all was collected, the ship was nearly full betwixt decks.[93]

This passage implies that both taxes and rent were collected.

Europeans were now playing an important role in government. Golovin described Juan Elliot d'Castro as Kamehameha's minister of foreign affairs and secretary of state. Juan Elliot d'Castro assisted in meetings with visiting naval officers and any other interactions with representatives of foreign governments. For this he received the land grant referred to above as well as an annual salary of 800 piasters worth of sandalwood that he sold to visiting traders. Others, such as Marin and the American Oliver Holmes played an important supervisory role in the government's trade with vessels at Honolulu. Marin had come to the islands from Spain in 1791. Fluent in Spanish, English and French, he acted as an interpreter for Kamehameha and as his agent to vessels visiting Honolulu. By the second decade of the 19th century, he had been granted lands on O'ahu and Moloka'i. He resided at Honolulu with 180 people living on his lands. Young continued his close association with Kamehameha and remained a respected adviser as well as becoming a prominent landowner. The writing skills of some of the Europeans in Kamehameha's service facilitated government administration. Golovin noted that, as well as

---

92 I'ī (1959), pp. 120–22; Kelly (1978), p. 90; and Golovin (1979), p. 205.
93 Barnard (1829), pp. 219, 221.

sending messengers to transmit instructions verbally, a written version bearing Kamehameha's seal was also sent. In this way the recipient could check the seal and then compare the written and verbal messages.[94]

It remained to be seen whether the structure of the new kingdom could outlive its founder. Institutional positions had been introduced to replace reliance on powerful vassal aliʻi, but the degree to which Kamehameha's mana held the whole edifice together was uncertain. Kaʻahumanu sought to extend her influence over the young heir, Liholiho, from the early 1800s. Kamehameha's actions laid the foundations for a succession struggle between Liholiho and Kekuaokalani, the son of Kamehameha's younger brother Keliʻimaikai. Kekuaokalani was Kamehameha's favourite among his collateral kin and was entrusted with Kūkāʻili-moku as Liholiho was increasingly brought into the running of the kingdom.[95] It was a division of responsibility that echoed the one between Kamehameha and Kīwalaʻō in 1782. It has been suggested that this division of responsibilities was intended to ensure that Liholiho would have to prove his worthiness to rule in the pit of battle.

This was not, however, to be a competition between equals. The conferring of the guardianship of Kūkāʻili-moku may not have been as significant as it had been in 1782. Worship of Kūkāʻili-moku had declined in importance as peace reigned in the islands. Many of Kamehameha's political and military reforms were designed to minimise the possibility of challenges to central rule. Kamehameha might tell the two young men that, in times past, the god and the government were of equal importance, but he gave his European arsenal to Liholiho alone. Guns, not gods, would secure Liholiho's succession. Kamehameha seems to have expected trouble, as he purchased $8,000 worth of munitions in March 1819. His attitude to complaints from aliʻi about the haughty and provocative behaviour of Kekuaokalani is instructive in this regard. According to Kamakau he replied:

> It is well if he robs the chiefs and not the common people; that would be a real fault. He is a fatherless child and can do these things only while I am alive. When I am gone you will not pay any attention to him![96]

---

94   Golovin (1979), pp. 177, 192, 205. On prominent Europeans in general, see Daws (1968a), p. 47. On Holmes, see Kamakau (1961), p. 174. On Marin, see Alexander (1891), p. 154.
95   Iʻī (1959), pp. 139–40; and Kamakau (1961), p. 209.
96   Kamakau (1961), p. 209; and Sahlins (1981), p. 76 n. 19.

1819: The question of succession

Kamehameha died at Kailua, Kona, on 8 May 1819, after a lengthy illness. The main aliʻi were summoned to Kailua from Oʻahu, where they had been cutting sandalwood. Only Boki and a few other notable aliʻi were left on Oʻahu to see to matters of government administration. In accordance with Kamehameha's wishes, there were no sacrifices to solicit the gods for his recovery, nor were human sacrifices a part of the mourning ceremonies. While kahuna kuni (sorcery priests) sought to ascertain if Kamehameha's death had been caused by sorcery, Keʻeaumoku disturbed proceedings with his drunken behaviour. The kahuna promptly declared that Kaʻahumanu and her family were behind Kamehameha's death.[97]

The assembled aliʻi were divided over the future division of power within the kingdom. A week after Kamehameha's death, Marin noted that the chiefs were in an uproar, prompting him to begin cleaning and repairing his own neglected firearms.[98] Most aliʻi wanted the royal monopoly on sandalwood overturned to increase their profits. A division of opinion soon emerged over the question of land distribution. Those who felt they were poorly rewarded under Kamehameha's division of his conquests argued that land should be redistributed by Liholiho, as was customary for an incoming ruler. But those who had occupied important posts under Kamehameha and held significant tenure rights argued that they had been granted hereditary rights to their lands. They naturally sought to preserve their privileged position by maintaining the political status quo.[99]

At the same time, the powerful clique gathered around Kaʻahumanu now sought to overthrow the kapu system. Stephanie Levin argues that this was because the kapu system threatened the status quo by requiring rulers to prove their continued mandate from the gods through successful actions. These included defeating attempts to unseat them from power. The abolition of the kapu system would effectively make political succession hereditary. Davenport has argued that the abolition of the kapu, and all the state ritual surrounding it, may also have been seen as a way of freeing

---

97   Kamakau (1961), pp. 212–14; and Kahananui (1984), pp. 207–10. On Marin, see Gast & Conrad (1973), p. 230.
98   Gast & Conrad (1973), p. 231 (15 May, 18 May 1819).
99   Kamakau (1961), p. 219.

6. CREATING A KINGDOM

up the makahiki produce and other religious offerings for use by the state. On a more personal level, it would free the aliʻi nui from the very real restrictions that the kapu imposed upon their daily activities.[100]

Kaʻahumanu was able to gain the support of Liholiho's mother, Keōpūolani, in her attempt to end the kapu. Keōpūolani was one of the highest ranking kapu chiefs in the islands. Kaʻahumanu also succeeded in winning over Hewahewa, the kahuna nui of the Holoaʻe priestly order. In return, the priestly orders were promised the retention of their landholdings and their position within the aliʻi.[101] These terms suggest that the outcome of the succession was already apparent to Hewahewa, and that he was aligning the priesthood with a force he felt he could not block. During the mourning period, Liholiho and Kekuaokalani left Kailua and went to Kawaihae for 10 days to avoid the ritual pollution present at Kailua while Kamehameha's body lay there. Kekuaokalani suspected Kaʻahumanu's intentions and tried to persuade Liholiho not to return to Kailua. Liholiho characteristically compromised. He answered the summons to return to Kailua, but promised Kekuaokalani that he would boycott any ai noa (free eating), or any other attempt to subvert the kapu system.[102]

The hiding of Kamehameha's bones by Hoapili in the vicinity of the lava-strewn plains of Puʻuotaroa in North Kona signalled the end of the ritual state of pollution at Kailua. Liholiho was officially recognised as his father's successor on 21 May. The council of chiefs, the kuhina, war leaders, and lesser aliʻi all assembled at Kailua to witness the event. Armed soldiers were also present. Kaʻahumanu was given the honour of announcing Kamehameha's political will. Instead of declaring Liholiho as the successor, she declared that it had been Kamehameha's will that Liholiho and she rule together. She created the post of kuhina nui for herself. This move made her the senior executive officer in the kingdom and firmly placed her at the centre of power alongside Liholiho.[103]

---

100 Levin (1968), p. 423; William H. Davenport, 'The "Hawaiian Cultural Revolution": Some Political and Economic Considerations', *American Anthropologist*, vol. 71, 1969, 19; Howe (1984), pp. 166–67; Ralston (1984), pp. 29–30.
101 Levin (1968), p. 423; Kamakau (1961), p. 224.
102 Kamakau (1961), p. 224.
103 Kamakau (1961), pp. 215–20. See also Daws (1968a), pp. 55–56; Howe (1984), pp. 162–63; and Kameʻeleihiwa (1986), p. 110.

There was no immediate backlash against Kaʻahumanu's initiative. Kamehameha had never declared such a role for Kaʻahumanu publicly, but few influential aliʻi were willing or able to oppose her. She represented the interests of the main power group within the aliʻi as well as her own interests. While Liholiho refused a request from his mother to join her in a meal to break the food kapu, he would not openly move against the ai noa lobby.[104] As long as Liholiho and his father's top office holders remained in this tense association, the rest of the aliʻi proceeded cautiously. There was vigorous pressure for a decision over reform of the royal monopoly on sandalwood and existing land tenure, but no open hostility. While the ruling clique was able to maintain their coherence, the war leaders and royal army had no conflict of loyalty to divide them. None of the other aliʻi was capable of mounting a serious challenge to the status quo. Kaumualiʻi was probably the only vassal with a sizeable force of his own, but he seemed to have remained on Kauaʻi, unwilling or unable to influence events at Kailua.

The future direction of the Kingdom was still uncertain when Freycinet arrived at the leeward coast of Hawaiʻi in August. Liholiho had delayed making any policy decisions, and most leading aliʻi were still assembled there. Freycinet described how several of the principal chiefs of the island had raised claims to which there was still not perfect agreement. There existed a certain vagueness and indecision in the political situation towards which efforts at settlement were being made.[105]

Freycinet's main informant was Young, who was concerned enough to urge the Frenchman to declare his support for Liholiho to deter rebellion. He was particularly worried about Kekuaokalani, who remained apart from the assembled aliʻi and was threatening to march against Liholiho and overthrow him because of his wavering attitude towards preserving the kapu system. Kekuaokalani was now openly talking about killing all Europeans to ensure the preservation of the old ways.[106]

Liholiho summoned the council of chiefs to Kawaihae in August. Faced with the threat of Kekuaokalani, he agreed to the aliʻi's desire to control all sandalwood on their own lands to secure their support. But he stopped short of agreeing to a redistribution of land rights. It might be desirable

---

104 Kamakau (1961), p. 224; Alexander (1891), pp. 166–67.
105 Kelly (1978), p. 5.
106 Kelly (1978), pp. 20–23.

6. CREATING A KINGDOM

to avoid driving lesser ali'i into Kekuaokalani's camp, but it was essential to retain the support of the dominant clique, who controlled most of the land in the existing set up. Liholiho made a show of upholding the old ways by attempting to consecrate a heiau at Honokahou, in Kona, Hawai'i. But he did so without enthusiasm and in a drunken stupor. In this state he failed to achieve the faultless rendition of his ceremonial duties that the heiau ritual demanded.[107]

After the meeting at Kawaihae, Ka'ahumanu returned to Kailua and continued to press for the ending of the kapu. In November, Liholiho finally agreed. He was now politically and socially isolated. Already his real and adopted mothers, Keōpūolani, Ka'ahumanu and Kaheiheimalie, and his wives Kamokau and Kekauluohi were pressing him to give in. Kalanimoku, Naihe, Hoapili and most other powerful ali'i also supported Ka'ahumanu. Short of the desperate option of joining Kekuaokalani, Liholiho had little choice in the matter. He delayed the issue one last time by cruising off the Kona coast, drinking heavily with friends. After a few days he came back into Kailua. At a public feast he sat down and ate with high-ranking female ali'i. The ai kapu was then declared overturned and, to reinforce the point, images of gods in local heiau were destroyed. Messengers were sent to proclaim the abolition of the kapu throughout the archipelago. Few resisted.[108]

Only Kekuaokalani and his supporters attempted to defend the old ways. Kekuaokalani refused to join in the feast at Kailua and now retired to Ka'awaloa to make his stand. Here he was joined by those prepared to risk all to uphold the kapu system – the kahuna Kuaiwa and Holoialena, and members of the priestly lines of Kauahi and Nahulu. They urged Kekuaokalani to take up arms. To men who still believed in the old ways, Liholiho's failure to perform the temple rituals at Honokahou indicated that the gods had deserted him.[109] Kekuaokalani, on the other hand, was the guardian of Kū'kā'ili-moku, a god who had rarely failed his supplicants when appealed to through human sacrifice. Kū'kā'ili-moku might once more vanquish all his worshipper's enemies. The odds were against Kekuaokalani, who may have hoped his stand would galvanise others into action. According to Kamakau, '[M]any commoners and

---
107 Levin (1968), p. 424; Alexander (1891), p. 167; and Sahlins (1981), p. 64.
108 Kamakau (1961), pp. 221–25; Kahananui (1984), pp. 216–18; and Alexander (1891), p. 169. See also Sahlins (1981), p. 55; Daws (1968a), pp. 56–57; and Howe (1984), pp. 163–64.
109 Kamakau (1961), p. 226; Levin (1968), p. 424; Alexander (1891), p. 170; and Sahlins (1981), p. 64.

chiefs, even those who had practiced free eating, and the brothers of Ka'ahumanu's themselves, wanted tabu eating. Few of the chiefs were in favour of free eating'.[110]

Liholiho and Ka'ahumanu tried to avoid open conflict by offering Kekuaokalani the freedom to observe the kapu if he would return to Kailua. But they insisted that those who chose to do so could also observe ai noa. Kekuaokalani refused the offer.[111] A partial kapu was no kapu at all. Such terms would still leave him in the political wilderness, with Ka'ahumanu's party retaining its grip on the effective sources of power in the kingdom: the army and the administrative infrastructure. With their overture rejected, Ka'ahumanu and Liholiho decided to move against Kekuaokalani before he became a rallying point for other malcontents.

The only other revolt against Liholiho was a local uprising in Hāmākua. When Liholiho sent a lesser ali'i named Lonoakahi to investigate, he and two of his men were killed in a skirmish at Mahiki. The bones of the slain enemy were then taken to Kekuaokalani, presumably as offerings to Kū'kā'ili-moku.[112] Refusing to be distracted by the disturbance in Hāmākua, Kalanimoku advised Liholiho to strike directly against Kekuaokalani and his supporters in Kona. Liholiho agreed.[113]

Kalanimoku marched out of Kailua at the head of the royal army to confront the rebels. The evidence suggests that the royal force numbered in the thousands, although the exact size is uncertain. Hiram Bingham writes that Kalanimoku raised a regiment, while Dibble claims that the army was arranged in nine battalions. Nine war canoes accompanied the army, along with food and water bearers. Kamakau implies that others, who were trained in the use of weaponry, reinforced the regular forces under arms at Kailua. Large supplies of firearms were collected at Honolulu in December in response to the crisis. Marin noted in his journal that, on 2 December, Ke'eaumoku II, the son and successor of the original Ke'aumoku, arrived at Honolulu on board the brigantine *Bordeaux Packet* to collect cannon, muskets, powder and flints. Marin's entry for 12 December notes that 900 more muskets were brought ashore from a Captain Luis's ship. The rebels' possession of firearms suggests that they had powerful supporters with access to European trade. Nevertheless,

---

110 Kamakau (1961), p. 226; and Kahananui (1984), p. 219.
111 Kamakau (1961), pp. 226–27.
112 Kamakau (1961), p. 226; Alexander (1891), p. 170; and Sahlins (1981), p. 75 n. 18.
113 Kamakau (1961), pp. 227–28; Dibble (1909), p. 131.

although Alexander claims Kekuaokalani attracted a large body of priests, chiefs and commoners to his cause, accounts of the battle that followed suggest the rebels were outnumbered and outgunned. Freycinet's expedition had noted 40 to 60 cannon and several thousand muskets belonging to the government. Only the royal force had continued to train for warfare in the last decade of Kamehameha's rule,[114] and it had been many years since Hawaiians had been to war. Both sides' determination was probably tinged with a sense of apprehension.

The first encounter took place at Lekeleke, when the royal forces encountered a rebel scouting party. Kalanimoku's men were unsettled by the loss of some of their men to rebel musket fire and retired to regroup behind a stone wall. When it was realised how few rebels opposed them, the royal forces resumed their advance and the enemy scouts retreated. Kalanimoku came on the main rebel force at Kuamo'o between Keauhou Bay and Kealakekua Bay. Kekuaokalani's battle line seems to have run at right angles to the coastline. The royal forces outflanked his right flank and drove the rebels towards the seashore. Here they were exposed to flanking fire from the double canoes accompanying the royal army. The firepower on board the canoes included an artillery piece manned by an unnamed foreign gunner. Inspired by the example of their leader, the rebels resisted stubbornly until Kekuaokalani fell after being hit several times. His wife Manona was struck down beside him in a hail of musket balls. Rebel resistance then crumbled. In 1823 Ellis walked over the battlefield from Lekeleke to Kuomo'o. He noticed piles of stone marking the graves of the dead. These steadily increased as he approached the site of Kekuaokalani and Manona's last stand. The rebel's graves were particularly concentrated around those of their leaders. Alexander dates the battle to 20 December 1819, but it may have been later as Marin wrote that news of the victory only arrived in Honolulu on December 30.[115]

Jarves was told that 10 royalists had been killed as opposed to around 50 rebels. Most of the rebel leaders were killed at Kuomo'o.[116] The survivors hid in fear of their lives until Liholiho eventually announced

---

114 Compare Bingham (1848), p. 76 with Dibble (1909), p. 135. See also Thrum, vol. 5 (1918–19), p. 480; Kamakau (1961), p. 227; Gast & Conrad (1973), pp. 235–36; and Alexander (1891), p. 170.
115 Alexander (1891), p. 171; and Gast & Conrad (1973), p. 236. On Lekeleke, see Kamakau (1961), p. 228; Alexander (1891), pp. 170–71; and Dibble (1909), p. 133. On Kuamo'o, see Kamakau (1961), p. 228; Alexander (1891), p. 171; Dibble (1909), pp. 132–33; Ellis (1969), pp. 122–25; Kahananui (1984), pp. 231–32; and Fitzsimmons (1969), pp. 171–72.
116 Jarves (1843), p. 219. On casualties, see Kamakau (1961), p. 228; and Alexander (1891), p. 172.

a pardon for all surviving rebels. The insurrection in Hāmākua was put down soon after the battle of Kuomoʻo. Hoapili and the royalist forces had little trouble defeating the rebels in Waipiʻo valley after marching against them from Kawaihae by way of the Waimea Saddle.[117]

The overthrow of the kapu consolidated the influence of those who were already in power. Kaʻahumanu continued to have a strong influence over Liholiho. With the freeing up of the royal share of the sandalwood trade, the aliʻi turned their attention towards increasing the exploitation of their lands by demanding more from their makaʻāinana tenants. The aliʻi became, in the words of one visiting European, 'a united corps of peaceful merchants'[118] who saw their lands and tenants as merely a means of gaining access to European trade goods. The long-term viability of this commercial focus, however, remained uncertain. It was based on a rapidly declining stock of sandalwood and depended on the demands of distant markets over which Hawaiian aliʻi had little control. In time, mercantile power might rise to rival more traditional forms of power – as it had in Europe centuries before – but, for now, it enhanced the position of those controlling the administrative and coercive resources of government and the landed elite. While the position of many aliʻi improved, conditions for the makaʻāinana declined. There was little opposition to the increasingly skewed exchange of services between aliʻi and makaʻāinana. As Caroline Ralston notes: 'The awe and respect inculcated over generations were not to be effaced by four or five decades of chiefly refusal to respect customary ideas of reciprocity.'[119]

Some commentators have interpreted the overturning of the kapu as a cultural revolution that was heavily influenced by contact with Europeans, whose exotic behaviour brought into question hitherto accepted beliefs. Kamakau and others describe it as an action taken by a handful of powerful chiefs for political as much as religious reasons. Golovin was told that observation of kapu was most lax among the more important chiefs.[120] Kaʻahumanu and her chiefly supporters, in particular, had a long history of challenging accepted norms and admiring European ways. The majority of the population was less enthusiastic and merely

---

117 Kamakau (1961), p. 228; and Kahananui (1984), p. 220.
118 Howe (1984), p. 168; citing Kuykendall (1938), p. 89. On the reign of Liholiho, see Howe (1984), pp. 168 ff.; and Daws (1968a), pp. 49 ff.
119 Ralston (1984), p. 37.
120 Golovin (1979), p. 209.

followed their lead. What disappeared from their lives was state ritual that had usually been remote from the daily routine and domestic religious activities of most maka'āinana.

Decades of European contact may have eroded the coherence of the Hawaiian worldview, but it did not overwhelm it. The potency of Kū and his fellow gods may have been brought into question, but they did not disappear from the thoughts of Hawaiians. Traditional beliefs continued to be widely held well into the following period of missionary proselytising. Idols were still worshipped secretly, as were the bones of dead ali'i, while offerings continued to be made to numerous gods to seek their assistance for a variety of undertakings.[121] For most Hawaiians, the supernatural world continued to mingle with that of humans, sorcerers continued to pray enemies to death, and Pele still displayed her displeasure through the awesome grandeur of volcanic activity.

By 1819, significant European influence was probably still largely confined to the immediate vicinity of the main ports. Despite its importance to the ali'i, Honolulu was then still only a settlement of a few hundred huts and most Hawaiians continued to live in agricultural communities in the countryside. Their world was very different from that which European observers witnessed in ports. Gavan Daws speculates that for most:

> As long as the passing seasons were observed in the old way and the makahiki festival guaranteed good times to come any exchanges brought in at the ports could be seen as superficial, perhaps curious and entertaining, but easily put off like European clothes, not touching at the heart of things, which was as carefully planted in the soil as the buried navel strings and dead bones of centuries of Hawaiians.[122]

---

121 Howe (1984), p. 168, citing Ellis (1967), p. 287; and Bingham (1848), p. 79.
122 Daws (1968a), p. 49. On 'urbanisation' in Hawai'i, see Cordy (1972), pp. 406–07.

7

The Hawaiian Achievement in Comparative Perspective

This chapter draws on historical patterns on the impact of Western contact observed elsewhere in the non-Western world to reinforce the contention of this study that the Hawaiian achievement of political centralisation was at best enhanced rather than triggered or wholly created by newly introduced Western elements and ideas. The evidence assembled in this chapter is directed towards answering the question of how Hawaiian society reacted to new elements in a time of internal transition. Three aspects of change are studied and three general propositions articulated. The first relates to the fact that new ideas and objects are confronted by existing ideas and ways of viewing the world – Marshall Sahlins's powerful conception of the structure of the conjuncture. I argue that the structure was much more fluid, mobile and varied than has generally been allowed for. As the fluidity of Hawaiian structures of power has been dealt with in detail in Chapters 3 and 4, this first section focuses on more general observations on the nature of change and continuity. The second focus is on the campaigns towards unification of the Hawaiian Islands, and it is argued that, in the Hawaiian context, the type of Western firearms and cannon introduced were incapable of producing the decisive military impact that archaeologists claim, as has been shown in numerous, detailed historical studies around the globe. The last point is that consolidation of unified rule was achieved by adherence to institutions of consensus-building and peacemaking accumulated over centuries in the context of rulers who lacked decisive coercive advantages over the populations they ruled. This process was assisted by depopulation caused by introduced diseases that allowed a demilitarisation of the islands. Demilitarisation was, however, a choice. The same circumstances could also have facilitated the accumulation and consolidation of coercive advantage by the state as occurred, for example, in parts of Europe.

Political transformation: New seeds in old soil

As a well-documented late transition from chiefly fragmentation to a centralised kingdom and period of culture contact with Europeans, Hawai'i provides an ideal insight into the processes of political consolidation, culture contact and the dynamics of power. As a small, intimate society, it also provides an ideal comparative study for those of larger, better known societies, where processes may not be as apparent as in Hawai'i because of the sheer scale and size of the societies under review. The Hawaiian example offers lessons on the dangers of perceiving state formation as ultimately about the consolidation and centralisation of power in circumstances of diverse and highly localised identities. Greater consolidation came from the exercise of moderation and accommodation by Kamehameha, particularly in circumstances where new realities on the ground moved ahead of old mindsets. These lessons on how external weapons and attitudes change circumstances faster than they alter local attitudes, and that military victory is as much psychological as material, have a chilling resonance in the current era of state formation and failed state discourse, which is emanating largely from the Western developed nations, but directed at the non-Western world.

The efficacy of Pacific historian the late Jim Davidson's idea persists that culture changes round the edges as a result of cultural interaction and changed circumstances, but the core remains intact, changing only gradually, if at all. External influences and their impact are likened to the fluid intertidal zone at water's edge – eroding the margins, but rarely altering the island interior in any significant way.[1] The form might vary and alter, but underlying beliefs persist. In her classic account of religious syncretism in colonial Papua New Guinea, 'Sunday Christians, Monday Sorcerers', anthropologist Miriam Kahn makes the point that Pacific Islanders saw no contradiction in continuing to worship traditional spirits to enhance crop fertility while also adhering to Christian churches

---

1   Davidson (1970), p. 267.

7. THE HAWAIIAN ACHIEVEMENT IN COMPARATIVE PERSPECTIVE

or, more correctly, Islander-modified forms of Christian worship and doctrine.[2] Kahn's analysis is the norm in Pacific Studies' interpretations of religious conversion and adaptation among both anthropologists and historians, with strong emphasis on ongoing continuity in religious beliefs and practices, but eventual modification through the gradual incorporation and adaptation of new belief systems. This blending of old and new resulted in multiple forms of belief existing side by side in a fluid and evolving form of interaction. This acceptance of, and search for, syncretism has not, however, taken root in other areas of study. This is most noticeable in the fields of legal beliefs and governance, which were intimately connected to religious legitimacy in Pacific societies. A profound sense of political pluralism also prevailed in the Pacific.

This study has suggested a different reading of the relationship between power and authority in Hawai'i to that noted by Gavan Daws and Sahlins, in which power is always violent and external, but in which rule is ultimately needed to be considered legitimate to endure, and this authority was always conveyed from within.[3] Usurping outsiders who defeated rulers usually then married the highest born local women to gain legitimacy, as they rarely had sufficient numbers to sustain their position without local cooperation.[4] Relations might be tense and filled with suspicion, but there was little alternative. Rulers who offended their people could not rely on their support when the next usurper arrived, and might even face a challenge from within.[5] Kamehameha ruled powerful chiefs whose retinues were of a similar magnitude to his and other powerful chiefs. Marriage links and loyalties to sisters extended blood alliances across moku boundaries. Kanalu Young has shown that even kaukau ali'i could draw on extensive networks of allies. Mō'ī lacked significant coercive advantage over the alliance networks within their lands and so needed to be conciliators and mediators as much as fighters to succeed – a lesson Kahekili and his son neglected to learn, to Kamehameha's profit. External power and internal legitimacy were as much moral cultural categories that rulers moved between through their actions as geographical designations.

---

2   Miram Kahn, 'Sunday Christians, Monday Sorcerers: Selective Adaptation to Missionization in Wamira', *Journal of Pacific History*, vol. 18, 1983, 96–112.
3   Daws (1984), p. 16.
4   Sahlins (1994), pp. 63–65, 69.
5   On Pohnpei, see Ward H. Goodenough, 'Sky World and This World: The Place of Kachaw in Micronesian Cosmology', *American Anthropologist*, vol. 88 (3), 1986, 553; Fornander (1969), pp. 201–02, 229; and Kamakau (1961), p. 143.

We need to move away from debates about change versus continuity, and towards recognition that change was a constant for most Pacific peoples. What mattered was how societies coped with change. As anthropologist Alexander Spoehr noted:

> Change of itself need not imply instability. Change is always present in greater or lesser degree in every culture and society. Stability is not. Stability lies in orderly change and finds expression in a continuing successful adaptation to habitat and in non-violent shifts in the pattern of social organisation.[6]

The degree of internally generated change between 1770 and 1796, and 1796 and 1819 that is described in Chapters 3 to 6 has important implications for archaeology, anthropology and history. Archaeologists and anthropologists cite few works by Pacific historians. The degree of short-term, internally generated change noted by Kānaka Maoli historians Kanalu Young, Jonathan Kay Kamakawiwoʻole Osorio and Lilikalā Kameʻeleihiwa suggests that sources and methodologies employed by Pacific historians could significantly enhance Pacific archaeology and anthropology. This work has portrayed Hawaiian communities as highly localised in their affinities, with local polities and leaders capable of pursuing dramatically different paths within a single generation from broadly similar, internally generated institutions and structures also subject to rapid and significant changes resulting from external influences. Such issues of cultural construction and cultural resilience require collaboration between archaeologists, anthropologists *and* historians.[7] The Hawaiian example argues for greater resilience and continuity in local traditions and attitudes in circumstances of increasing Western presence and influence, but also for the need to combine archaeological structures of the long durée and anthropological structural, institutional approaches to non–Western history with historical approaches to historical processes that suggest the timing of events and individual choices can significantly alter history within the bounds set by environmental and cultural structural constraints.

---

6   Spoehr (1954), p. 210.
7   These issues are discussed in more detail in Paul D'Arcy, 'Cultural Divisions and Island Environments Since the Time of Dumont d'Urville', *The Journal of Pacific History*, vol. 38 (2), 2003b, 217–35. This article was part of a special issue on the legacy of d'Urville involving archaeologists, anthropologists and historians and which demonstrated the potency of such collaboration.

7. THE HAWAIIAN ACHIEVEMENT IN COMPARATIVE PERSPECTIVE

There is still no comprehensive account of European influences on the unification process in Hawai'i. Particular European influences have, however, been addressed. Most studies conclude that Europeans had a significant influence on the political process and most scholars claim that European military technology was a decisive factor in Kamehameha's military successes in the 1790s. European transport technology and concepts of government have been suggested as central pivots in Kamehameha's post-conquest centralised administration. Others note that the pursuit of trade goods provided a crucial alternative to the conquest and distribution of land at this time, thereby helping to maintain the peace that followed Kamehameha's campaigns of unification. At the same time, European actions and ideas often conflicted with Hawaiian beliefs, and challenged many of the religious assumptions that supported chiefly rule. Finally, David Stannard's upward revision of the demographic impact of European diseases carries with it sociopolitical implications that are germane to the issue of unification.

This study argues that Kamehameha gained victory because his opponents overextended themselves logistically, and were weakened at crucial times by internal divisions. Battles were important but, in most cases, European military technology was not crucial to the outcome. Military success came at the end of a process of attrition rather than in a dramatic confrontation on a particular day. Military victory alone was not enough to secure power. Many mō'ī had triumphed in battle before Kamehameha. What distinguished him from those before was his method of consolidating victory off the battlefield. Centralisation was a victory of the arts of peace over the arts of war. Kamehameha had already demonstrated skill at building and maintaining coalitions before John Young and Isaac Davis were on the scene to advise him. His political reforms after 1796 were a blend of old and new.

The conquest phase: Muskets versus mana

Visitors to the Hawaiian archipelago during the wars of unification were often told that European weapons had been a decisive factor in Kamehameha's success. Davis claimed his much-valued knowledge of firearms had 'proved of essential service' to Kamehameha.[8] Revisionist

---

8   Campbell (1967), p. 97.

military historians' emphasis on the importance of logistical and organisational factors calls for a re-evaluation of the significance of European weaponry and mercenaries in Kamehameha's wars of unification. While battles were important, European military technology was not crucial to the outcome in most cases. Military success came at the end of a process of attrition, rather than in a dramatic confrontation on a particular day. This study also supports the idea that weapons are used according to cultural values and priorities rather than simply to maximise the casualties inflicted. It also suggests that competition and fear of an eroding position can undermine such cultural values in favour of ultimately self-destructive arms races and increasingly pyrrhic victories. These assertions find a great deal of support from around the globe.

Traders and beachcombers left few records about the Hawaiian gun trade between 1786 and 1795. Hawaiians were generally visited by at least three ships a year during this time.[9] Several captains traded arms and ammunition for provisions and Hawaiians also obtained weapons as a result of attacks on shore parties or vessels. There is no evidence to suggest that Kamehameha or his rivals had any more than five or six artillery pieces and a handful of muskets until 1794. The few ships' inventories noted in this study suggest visiting traders carried 100–200 muskets for trade (see tables in Appendix 2). Visiting ships' captains never reported seeing more than 20 to 30 muskets in any one place during the 1790s.[10] Historians give no indication that anything more than a few cannon and small squads of musketeers were involved in the combat that occurred before 1795.[11] Hawaiians' large-scale accumulation of European weapons may have occurred only in 1794–95 or later. Young, Kamehameha's trusted friend, informed visitors that Kamehameha's 10,000-man army of 1795 had 5,000 muskets and an impressive artillery train. In 1804, however, Young told Urey Lisiansky that Kamehameha's forces possessed only 600 muskets, which raises doubts about his earlier claim.[12]

A number of chiefs recruited European beachcombers for their knowledge of firearms. According to George Vancouver, there were 14 beachcombers spread among the chiefs on Hawai'i in 1794. Kalanikūpule of Maui had

---

9 Bernice Judd, *Voyages to Hawaii before 1860* (Honolulu: University of Hawai'i Press, 1974), pp. 1–8; Pogue (1978), pp. 77 ff.; and Kahananui (1984), p. 176.
10 Vancouver (1801), bk 2, pp. 353, 355, 391; bk 3, p. 224; bk 5, p. 49.
11 Campbell (1967), p. 97.
12 Boit (n.d.), p. 5; Broughton (1967), p. 34; Lisiansky (1967), p. 133; and Bishop, in Roe (1967), p. 141.

around five beachcombers in his territory, while Kauaʻi was home to up to seven beachcombers during the 1790s. In 1796, white residents told Captain Charles Bishop that Kamehameha's army had one or more Englishmen in the vanguard of each division. Hawaiians considered them to be good warriors. Kaʻeokulani's Kauaʻi forces used Mare Amara and his regent Enemo used foreign musketeers to support his assault against rebel forces on Kauaʻi in 1793. In 1794, Kalanikūpule temporarily hired sailors from vessels anchored in Puʻuloa to assist him in his war against Kaʻeokulani. The sailors fared badly against Mare Amara in the initial skirmishes. Their role in the deciding battle at Aiea was limited to firing into the flank of Kaʻeokulani's army from the safety of longboats offshore, while the two battlelines collided and the issue was decided at close quarters.[13]

Although Hawaiians faced risks in adopting firearms, some embraced the new technology. In 1792, Archibald Menzies, for example, noted that the *aliʻi* Kaʻiana and his followers were proficient in the use of firearms. Kaʻeokulani keenly observed European armourers forge metal and strip and clean their firearms.[14] Not all Hawaiians were as enthusiastic about firearms, and often with good reason. The great Maui warrior Peʻapeʻa died a slow, painful death around this time as a result of severe burns acquired when sparks from his musket's firing mechanism fell into a nearby powder keg.[15] Vancouver and Menzies commented on the poor condition of many of the muskets traded to Hawaiians. Menzies dressed the hand of a young aliʻi after it had been badly damaged when his musket exploded on firing. He was told that his hosts were reluctant to use a shipment of muskets as many had burst open on their first firing.[16]

Most muskets traded in Hawaiʻi came from the east coast of the United States or Britain. The flintlock musket was the main military firearm in use in Europe and North America during this time. The poor quality of some muskets suggests that some firearms introduced into Hawaiʻi were not standard military-issue flintlock muskets. Studies of the gun trade with West Africa distinguish between army-issue 'Tower' muskets and trade muskets. Tower muskets were smoothbore flintlocks that had been

---

13   Bishop, in Roe (1967), pp. 177–78; Kamakau (1961), p. 169; Vancouver (1801), bk 3, pp. 381, 386; bk 5, p. 112; Fornander (1969), p. 159; Maude (1968), pp. 139–40; and Bradley (1942), pp. 33–34.
14   Menzies (1920), pp. 14, 109–10.
15   Kamakau (1961), p. 161.
16   Vancouver (1801), bk 5, p. 49; Menzies (1920), p. 72.

tested with charges of powder by government inspectors at the Tower of London, and thus had a minimum guaranteed standard barrel strength. Until the establishment of commercial proof houses for testing trade guns towards the end of the Napoleonic Wars, trade guns carried no guarantee that they would not burst if fired. Most of these trade guns were manufactured for West Africa, and often had not been fired by their manufacturers to check for imperfections. Trade muskets were cheaper, lighter and less mechanically complicated than Tower muskets. They were not intended for rapid firing or for the rigours of campaigning.[17]

Trade muskets continued to be of dubious quality after the establishment of commercial testing houses. Many gun barrels made of substandard iron still passed through the tests, and many barrels were thinned down after they had passed the proofing tests. The counterfeiting of proofmarks flourished.[18] Exploding gun barrels may also have resulted from improper gunpowder charges. The higher the saltpetre component of gunpowder, the greater its explosive force. Obviously the strength of the gunpowder should match the strength of the gun barrel, however, it was common to increase profits by diluting gunpowder with charcoal or other substances that could not be distinguished in the mix. This resulted in powder of varying quality and strength, so that charges could not be gauged with any consistency. Powder could also be damaged by exposure to dampness. Failure to turn powder barrels regularly resulted in the powder clogging and the saltpetre accumulating at the bottom of the barrel, creating an uneven consistency. Humidity and high rainfall added to the deterioration of firearms and gunpowder.[19]

Military-issue firearms did not necessarily confer an advantage to their possessors over opponents armed with traditional Hawaiian weapons. Although traditional projectile weapons travelled much slower than musket balls and, therefore, generally did less damage when they struck, they were more reliable and accurate than muskets within each weapon's

---

17   The whole issue of the *Journal of African History*, vol. 12 (2), 1971, deals with firearms in Africa. For the export of firearms out of Britain see Gavin White, 'Firearms in Africa: An Introduction', *Journal of African History*, vol. 12 (2) 1971, 175–82. Another interesting insight into the gun industry around this time is found in Smith (1976).
18   See White (1971), p. 181.
19   White (1971), pp. 174–75; F. Clunie, *Fijian Weapons and Warfare* (Suva: Fiji Museum, 1977), p. 79; R.A. Kea, 'Firearms and Warfare on the Gold and Slave Coasts from the Sixteenth to the Nineteenth Centuries', *Journal of African History*, vol. 12 (2), 1971, 204–05.

effective range.[20] The flintlock musket was unreliable at any range over 90 metres and was preferably used at ranges of 45 to 65 metres, or less, against massed targets. Tests conducted by the Prussian army in the late 18th century bear witness to this fact. In the tests, an infantry battalion fired volleys into a canvas target 30 metres long and 1.8 metres tall, which was the average height and frontage of an infantry unit. At 205 metres, only 25 per cent of the musket balls fired hit the target; at 137 metres, 50 per cent hit; while, at 68 metres, 60 per cent of the shots found their mark.[21] Such strike rates required the enemy to be tightly packed together, which was often not the case in Hawaiian warfare.

Although soldiers could fire up to four or five times a minute under test conditions, the average soldier usually loaded and fired at a rate of only twice a minute. The residue of the powder burnt to propel the musket ball tended to clog the musket barrel after prolonged use. The faster the rate of fire, the more prone the barrel was to fouling. Tests conducted by the British army in 1834 showed that, although flintlocks could be loaded and fired every 20 seconds, the rate of misfires at this speed was one in every 6.5 shots. In the field, the rate of misfires increased significantly. Damp powder prevented the musket from firing and powder on an open priming pan was particularly prone to damage by rain and dispersal by wind.

When a flint became chipped or blunted, it was less likely to generate sufficient sparks into the priming pan to ignite the charge. Flints could last up to 60 shots but most had a much shorter lifetime. US army regulations stated that a flint should be replaced after 20 rounds. It was not easy to change a flint in mid-battle, and the musketeer was extremely vulnerable until the new flint was installed. Without a local manufacturing industry, gun maintenance was also a problem, particularly for worn-out firing mechanisms and defective metal gun barrels. Maintenance was only possible because the guns were handmade. Surrogates for flints and

---

20 The discussion of the technical capabilities of flintlock muskets is based primarily on the following sources: H.C.B. Rogers, *Weapons of the British Soldier* (London: Seeley Service and Co., 1960), pp. 154–63; H.L. Blackmore, *British Military Firearms 1650–1850* (London: Herbert Jenkins, 1961), p. 45; T.H. McGuffie, 'Musket and Rifle', *History Today*, vol. 7 (4), 1957, 2157–63, and vol. 7 (7), 1957, 473–79; and Clunie (1977), p. 83.
21 David Chandler, *The Campaigns of Napoleon* (London: Weidenfield and Nicholson, 1966), p. 342, cited in Dyer (1985), p. 62.

musket balls could be found, but they diminished the consistency of ignition and the accuracy of fire. Young attributed one of Kamehameha's minor reverses to a loss of firepower brought about by deficient flints.[22]

Hawaiian musketeers were vulnerable in battle because of the general failure to adopt the bayonet. When fighting at close quarters, warriors armed with unloaded muskets without bayonets would find their weapons of little use for clubbing, thrusting, or parrying – the British standard military-issue Short Land Pattern musket (the Brown Bess) for example, was 1 metre long and weighed only 6 kilograms. There are many examples throughout the Pacific of musketeers being overcome when their opponents anticipated their musket discharges after observing the ignition of the powder charges just beforehand, and then rushed in while the guns were being reloaded.[23] The limited range of flintlock muskets meant that warriors could cover the effective shooting range in well under the average reloading time of 30 seconds. This may have been the case at the battle of Koapapa in the early 1790s where the forces of Keōua rushed forward and seized the guns of Kamehameha's musket men. John Young claimed that Davis and he had to be carried on the backs of strong warriors to keep up with the flow of Hawaiian battles because of the time it took them to reload.[24]

In a comparison of the battle of Waterloo in 1815 and Alexander the Great's victory at Gaugamela in 331 BC, John Keegan points out that edged-weapon fighting and battles in the flintlock era had much in common. The effective range of firearms meant that the decisive fighting in 18th-century European warfare still took place at close range and depended on the steadiness of the combatants. Keegan notes that, because of the close proximity of the antagonists in both modes of fighting, battles were 'noisy, physically fatiguing, nervously exhausting and, in consequence of that physical and nervous strain they imposed, narrowly compressed in time'.[25] In both cases each side attempted to extend its line of battle to maximise

---

22   Barnard (1829), pp. 230–32, referring to a battle in Hawai'i Kohala. Kamakau, however, does not mention this battle, and claims Kamehameha was in neighbouring Kona at the time.
23   R.A. Cruise, *Journal of a Ten Month Residence in New Zealand* (2nd edn) (Christchurch: Capper Press, 1974 (1824)), p. 68; S. Percy Smith, *Maori Wars of the Nineteenth Century* (2nd edn) (Christchurch: Whitcombe and Tombs Ltd, 1910), p. 144; Duperrey, in C.A. Sharp (ed.), *Duperrey's Visit to New Zealand in 1824* (Wellington: Alexander Turnbull Library, 1971), p. 61; and Marsden, in J.R. Elder, (ed.), *The Letters and Journals of Samuel Marsden 1765–1838* (1st edn) (Dunedin: Coulls Somerville Wilkie Ltd, and A.H. Reed, 1932), p. 284.
24   Barnard (1829), p. 229.
25   Keegan (1987), p. 115.

the number of weapons that could be brought to bear against the enemy, without the risk of overextending themselves. Each side either sought to outflank the other or, failing that, to break some point of the enemy's line by 'superior savagery',[26] where the issue would be decided at speaking, if not spitting distance.

Cannon were more intimidating weapons than muskets. Hawaiians received dramatic demonstrations of the destructive power of cannon in the British response to the death of Captain James Cook at Kealakekua Bay in 1779. While the British were impressed with the Hawaiians' courage under fire, they also noted that they sustained many casualties. On 14 February 1779 alone, at least 25 Hawaiians were killed, including several prominent aliʻi. Many more were badly wounded. Most fell to ships' cannon as they crowded along the shoreline. Kamehameha was among the wounded. He was hit in the face by a splinter when a British cannon ball struck a nearby stone.[27] When trading contacts began in 1786, Kamehameha eagerly sought European artillery. He had at least four artillery pieces by 1790 and his artillery train had risen to 12 by 1796. Little is known about the number of cannon his rivals possessed (see Table 2A.1 in Appendix 2).

Pogue recorded the reaction of Hawaiians to bombardment by ship's cannon at Waimea on Oʻahu in 1792. As the cannon opened fire:

> 'The Natives wondered what is this thing which makes a continuous noise?' Said one of them: 'it is powder, a death-dealing substance, they light it and the people are no more. It is well that we save ourselves from death at the hands of these demons. If we stay here, we will all be killed.'[28]

Mary Pukui and Samuel Elbert's Hawaiian dictionary lists four terms pertaining to cannon: Pu kuni ahi (gun burning fire) and olohao (iron noise) refer to the two most noticeable features of their firing action. Two others allude to their role in land warfare: Pu kuʻa (rolling gun) refers to cannon mounted on wheels to facilitate overland movement; Pu kaua refers not only to artillery, but also commanders, champions, and war leaders, suggesting cannon were highly valued battlefield assets.[29]

---

26 Keegan (1987), p. 116.
27 King, in Beaglehole (1967) 3:1, pp. 562, 565.
28 Pogue (1978), p. 87.
29 Mary Kawena Pukui & Samuel H Elbert, *Hawaiian Dictionary* (Honolulu: University of Hawaiʻi Press, 1986).

Cannon were capable of inflicting great damage, even against troops in open formation. They could fire either solid iron balls or masses of small projectiles. The former ploughed its way through all obstacles until it lost momentum. Although the ball's momentum declined markedly at distances over a kilometre, it was still capable of shattering limbs at this range. Cannon packed with smaller projectiles had an effect similar to that of a sawn-off shotgun. The projectiles spewed out over a wide arc along the line of trajectory after leaving the cannon barrel. Each projectile was capable of killing or disabling a person. Cannon could only fire such ammunition up to ranges of 400 metres.[30]

The robust nature of cannon meant that supplies of ammunition were less of a problem than for muskets. If conventional ammunition was unavailable, local substitutes could be used. In particular, almost any small object could be used for close range scatter shots. But the substitution of rounded boulders for round shot did reduce accuracy and range considerably. Prolonged use might also damage the barrel, and imported gunpowder was still needed as the igniting agent.[31]

Almost all of the artillery pieces obtained by Hawaiians in this period were naval guns. Naval captains required artillery that was much heavier than artillery used on land, as its tactical function required hitting power rather than mobility. Naval warfare in this period was based on the manoeuvring of sail-powered warships to deliver broadsides, or cannon barrages from cannon lining either side of the ship, against the sturdy timber of opposing vessels. Cannon were classified by the weight of the shot they fired. For example, a three-pounder cannon fired a three-pound shot. While land artillery ranged from three to 12 pounders, naval cannon generally consisted of 12, 16, 24 and 32 pounders, which were designed for stationary firing. Even the three-pounder field gun of the late 18th century still weighed around 350 kilograms.[32] Two smaller naval cannon were in use by Kamehameha's time. The carronade was a shorter cannon with a stubby, thinner barrel. Its thin barrel limited its range, but within that range it was more destructive than long cannon of the same bore. The swivel gun was even smaller and lighter, so that it could even

---

30   P. Griffith, *Forward into Battle: Fighting Tactics from Waterloo to Vietnam* (Chichester, Great Britain: Anthony Bird, 1981), p. 145; Robert Leckie, *Warfare* (New York: Harper and Row, 1970), pp. 115–17; and Keegan & Holmes (1985), p. 107.
31   Smith (1976), pp. 110 ff.
32   Clunie (1977), p. 78.

be mounted on rowboats.³³ The fluid nature of Hawaiian land battles reduced the impact of cannon. Without beasts of burden, Hawaiians were dependent on human muscle and dry and unimpeded terrain to move artillery. They needed to mount naval cannon on mobile carriages if they were to be of any use in warfare on land. Henry Restarick claims that John Young mounted a small cannon from the *Fair American* on a carriage for use on land. This was almost certainly the gun named Lopaka in Hawaiian traditions.³⁴

The first use of cannon in battle occurred in 1790 at 'Īao, when Kamehameha attacked neighbouring Maui after securing a cannon, firearms and two Europeans to assist in their use.³⁵ Memories of the damage inflicted by trained gun crews in the wake of Cook's death, and tales of the recent carnage at Olowalu inflicted by ship's cannon on canoes possibly raised expectations of the effect that cannon would have in local warfare. At Olowalu, Hawaiians came out in canoes to trade with the *Eleanora*, unaware that the ship's captain blamed them for a previous attack and was intent on revenge. Hundreds died or sustained horrific injuries as they attempted to flee the hail of musket balls and nails packed into the ships' cannon. The corpses were later retrieved from the sea and laid out on the beach. Hawaiian accounts mention that many of the victims had badly battered skulls whose contents seeped out over the beach. A number almost certainly had shattered torsos and limbs.³⁶

The impact of cannon in battle varied. In the two of the three land battles known to have involved cannon, the able handling of artillery by foreigners, especially John Young and Davis, is cited as an important factor in deciding the outcome. At 'Īao and Nuʻuanu, cannon fire exacted a heavy toll on Kamehameha's enemies. The effect at Paʻauhau is less certain. These relatively immobile weapons required troops to stand firm and protect them in battle. Obviously this did not happen at Paʻauhau. Artillery was most effective against stationary, mass targets, such as the Maui forces hemmed into the 'Īao Valley on the last day of fighting, and Kalanikūpule's

---

33   William Reid, 'Carronades', *War Monthly*, vol. 8, 1974, pp. 44–45, 47; and Clunie (1977), p. 79.
34   Restarick (1913), p. 29.
35   Fornander (1969), pp. 231–34; Kamakau (1961), pp. 146–47; and Vancouver (1801), bk 3, pp. 227, 230; and bk 5, p. 59.
36   Kamakau (1961), pp. 145–46; Jarves (1843), p. 70; Kahananui (1984), pp. 177–78; Vancouver (1801), bk 3, pp. 227–31; and S.J. Odgers, 'Early Western Contact with Hawaii', BA Hons Thesis, The Australian National University, 1977, p. 43, citing *Frothingham's Long Island Herald*, vol. 1 (n.d.).

initial battleline in the lower Nuʻuanu valley in 1795. No mention of cannon is made in the fighting around Wailuku that preceded the carnage in ʻĪao, nor in the fighting in the upper Nuʻuanu valley in 1795. Once Lopaka had stung Keōua's forces into action at Paʻauhau, it became more of a prize to fight over than a weapon to decide the battle. The use of cannon at ʻĪao and Nuʻuanu were not so much decisive turning points as the culmination of longer processes of attrition that saw large armies kept in the field for lengthy periods of inactivity that were occasionally punctuated by battles settled by hand-to-hand combat.

Cannon were more suited to Hawaiian naval warfare where canoes and European vessels provided suitable platforms for firing and movement. The one naval battle involving cannon, Kepuwahaʻulaʻula, remembered afterwards as the battle of the red-mouthed gun, involved Kamehameha's *Fair American* and its cannon. Both sides probably also deployed war canoes modified to carry smaller cannon, such as swivel guns. Both sides used foreign gunners in this battle. Too little is known about the battle, however, to allow any firm appraisal of the role of cannon. The battle's title may owe more to the novelty of cannon than to their decisive nature. At a time when Hawaiian fleets numbered hundreds, even thousands of canoes, there is nothing to suggest that any more than a handful of cannon were present.

Cannon used by Hawaiians were out of their element culturally as well as physically. Hawaiian traditions continue to emphasise the individual acts of valour that occurred in the 1790s. It may not be coincidence that no aliʻi of any consequence were among the victims of cannon fire at ʻĪao or the naval engagement of Kepuwahaʻulaʻula. How should we explain Kaʻiaʻiaiea and Uhoi's assault against the cannon Lopaka at Paʻauhau? Were they enhancing their mana by challenging such a fearsome adversary, or did their bold charge merely reflect a more sanguine tactical necessity? Did Kamehameha's slaying of his opposite number at Kokomo in single combat ultimately enhance his cause more than Lopaka's firepower in the ʻĪao Valley a few days later? In these initial decades of European influence, the supplanting of the old with the new was by no means a foregone conclusion.

The importance placed on personal encounters between skilled warriors in Hawaiian battles was threatened by Western weaponry. By substituting the chemical energy of exploding gunpowder for physical strength, firearms threatened to diminish the importance of traditional fighting skills. Although the flash of the priming pan's ignition provided warning of an impending projectile, no amount of personal skill in dodging traditional weapons could protect warriors from projectiles they could not see. The more firearms used in battle, the greater the chance of being struck. Hawaiian warfare was not only a vehicle for the pursuit of political power and economics resources but also a stage for the maintenance and advancement of social status. Worthy opponents of equal status were difficult to seek out and challenge while trying to avoid musket and artillery fire. The indiscriminate hail of lead that characterised battles involving firearms was no respecter of rank or prowess, knew no code of conduct, and feared no sanctions for breaking social norms.

Firearms brought about some changes to Hawaiian warfare, but generally traditional tactics and attitudes continued. This was possible because only limited numbers of firearms were introduced into Hawaiian warfare before unification. Battlefields continued to be stages for the display of personal bravery. Although the inability of wetted mats and feathered cloaks to fend off musket balls had been made apparent on 14 February 1779, Hawaiians continued to act 'in a most daring and resolute manner'.[37] On 15 February, James King noted that, 'a man had the audaciousness to come almost within Musket Shot ahead of the Ship & twirl about Captn Cooks hat in defiance and heave stones, whilst those on the N. Side were exalting him & encouraging his boldness'.[38] The importance of individual bravery continued into the 1790s. At the battle of Koapapa in 1790, warriors of Keōua's forces, armed with traditional weapons, charged Kamehameha's musketeers and seized their guns.

Ultimately, however, guns did begin to modify tactics, as at the battle of Koapapa when Keōua's men constructed shallow pits in which to crouch when they saw the flash from the musket priming pans of Ka'iana's forces. Chiefs were pinned down by musket fire from Europeans in their enemies' ranks on Kaua'i in 1793 and at 'Aiea in 1794, while their opponents closed in and routed them with traditional weapons. Mare Amara's shooting of a prominent O'ahu war chief at Kukui in 1794 perhaps vindicated the O'ahu forces decision to fight from the shelter of trenches and earthworks on this occasion.

---

37 Thomas Edgar, 'Extracts from Journal', 14 Feb. 1779, copy of MS, Hocken Library, Dunedin.
38 King, in Beaglehole (1967), 3:1, p. 561.

Hawaiians appear to have also begun experimenting with European tactics. A number of sources state that Kamehameha was influenced by discussion over military tactics with Vancouver. The 1838 *Mooolelo Hawaii* claims Vancouver taught Kamehameha how to drill soldiers. Vancouver makes no reference to this in his journal, however, portraying himself as a man intent on ending the fighting.[39] Bishop's reference to Englishmen being attached to 'divisions' might mean organisational reforms were instituted, although there is no indication that this was the case. The only other suggestion of military reform in the 1790s is Restarick's reference to John Young having trained a small body of men in the use of muskets. This was possibly Kamehameha's 30-man bodyguard armed with muskets, who Bishop noticed in 1796.[40] There is no direct evidence that firearms or European tactics dramatically altered Hawaiian tactics in the wars of unification. Battle formations used in the 1790s all had indigenous precedents.

The old ways still predominated among mōʻī but, in the atmosphere of intense rivalry that prevailed, the temptation to bend conventions and improve fighting effectiveness must have been great. Hawaiian leaders seem to have considered using indigenous weapons that threatened to undermine chiefly prowess in close quarter fighting on the eve of the introduction of firearms. Although there is no record of the use of bows in battle, Kahekili's army included expert archers by 1783.[41] If firearms had not been introduced, it was perhaps only a matter of time before Hawaiians used the bow in warfare. Political rivalry between chiefs also led to the formation of specialist military units on Maui and Hawaiʻi by the 1770s. These units could also undermine the significance of individual chiefs in battle, particularly when they employed tactics such as the massed drills witnessed by Vancouver in the 1790s.[42]

---

39 Pogue (1978), p. 90; Kahananui (1984), p. 183; and Freycinet, in Kelly (1978), p. 103 n. 3.
40 Restarick (1913), p. 13; Bishop, in Roe (1967), p. 144.
41 Kamakau (1961), p. 135.
42 Vancouver (1801), bk 3, pp. 252–58.

The consolidation phase: Coercion and consent revisited

The consolidation of the Hawaiian Kingdom under Kamehameha I involved changes to the ideological, economic, military and organisational aspects of power. In each of these spheres, the presence of Europeans provided potential new tools for the exercise of power, or brought about modifications to existing practices. The extent of European influence should not be overstated. European vessels continued to restrict their visits to a handful of ports and Europeans residents also tended to remain around the ports. While a few beachcombers overindulged in rum and occasionally caused trouble around Honolulu, European residents generally assimilated into their host society and adhered to its rules.[43] Although Hawaiian mobility increased after unification, most Hawaiians continued to live within a highly localised world that was predominantly rural and conservative.

Kamehameha carefully monitored and regulated trade of the unified kingdom through his bureaucracy. The king used his administrative and military strength to ensure that potential rivals were not able to utilise access to European trade to build up independent power. With the fragmentation of landholdings, subordinate aliʻi were also denied the chance to develop local power bases. The kingdom based its domestic security as much on the denial of resources to rivals as increasing the capacity of the kingdom.

This was especially true of the military sphere. The 1804 epidemic allowed Kamehameha to consolidate military power by demilitarising Hawaiian society. Actual fighting strength declined markedly, but the relative coercive advantage of the ruler over his subjects became greater than ever before. The 1804 epidemic on Oʻahu decimated Kamehameha's army assembled there to invade Kauaʻi. Many warriors from the armies of Kamehameha's old rivals, Kalanikūpule and Kaʻeokulani, were probably also still resident on Oʻahu at the time. It is not until 1815 that there is any indication of armed forces numbering over 1,000 being present in the islands.

---

43   Howe (1984), p. 103; Maude (1968), pp. 139–40.

Royal forces largely monopolised European military hardware after 1804. In addition, the main threat to Kamehameha in this period was perceived to be attempts by aliʻi on Oʻahu to obtain firearms and raise followers to use them against the king. The validity of Kamehameha's fears is open to question. As it was, the challenge never eventuated and the king was able to collect his subjects' firearms and remove them from circulation. This emphasis on firearms would at first seem to be at odds with their technical capabilities and utilisation in the 1790s. Perceptions may have been more important than realities. Without regular training, the issue of muskets to royal supporters would do little to enhance their military effectiveness. As it was, most of Kamehameha's muskets seem to have remained in storage.[44] Archibald Campbell had not been overly impressed with the ability of those troops who did drill regularly with firearms at Honolulu.

The longer that peace was maintained, the greater the government's coercive advantage over possible challengers became. Regular drilling with firearms and traditional weapons maintained the organisational coherence, discipline and esprit de corps, as well as the martial prowess of troops. Without regular practice the skills of others could not have been maintained. With no justification for retraining, and the kings' men observant throughout the land, any move to reconstitute military retinues by other aliʻi faced the prospect of swift countermeasures before an effective fighting force could be organised. Bravery was no substitute for training, as Kekuaokalani and his followers found in 1819. Also, by 1819, the ending of the Napoleonic wars in Europe freed up vast stocks of army-issue muskets that were eagerly purchased by traders as items of trade.[45] Tower muskets, not trade muskets, may have been the weapons that Kekuaokalani faced at Kuamoʻo.

The perception of European military technology could only be enhanced the longer it remained unchallenged in battle. The public musket drills at Honolulu, the impressive batteries of cannon that guarded Hawaii's main ports of call, and the fleet of European vessels may have drawn much of their effect from their association with Kamehameha's victories in the 1790s. That most guns faced out to sea was a reminder that the

---

44   Similar processes occurred in 16th-century Japan and Tudor England; see Noel Perrin, *Giving up the Gun: Japan's Reversion to the Sword, 1543–1879* (Boulder, Colorado: Shambala Productions, 1979), pp. 45–47, 58–59; and Dyer (1985), p. 58.
45   Clunie (1977), p. 82; Rogers (1960), p. 154; and White (1971), p. 181.

7. THE HAWAIIAN ACHIEVEMENT IN COMPARATIVE PERSPECTIVE

military served to guard the king's subjects from outsiders as much as to preserve the domestic peace. The threat posed by George Scheffer, late in Kamehameha's reign, seemed to bear out this conviction.

The maintenance of peace and unity in the later part of Kamehameha's reign owes much to the workings of the royal administration. The King's officials served as intermediaries and, to a certain extent, buffers between Hawaiian society and the outside world. They ensured that their ruler, not his rivals, controlled the trade with visiting vessels. Kamehameha also built up a reservoir of artisans who were skilled in European crafts such as shipbuilding and metalworking. Europeans were used within the royal bureaucracy as artisans and administrators. Such artisans usually taught their skills to Hawaiians while practicing their crafts in the service of the king.[46] Other Europeans were valued for their knowledge of writing and financial matters, both of which were important tools in dealing with foreign traders and government representatives. European vessels soon supplanted Hawaiian canoes as the chief mode of inter-island transport and communications for government business. Their large holds and ability to handle heavy seas allowed for the rapid movement of men, supplies and messages throughout the kingdom, although traditional canoes remained in use among the general populace.

Old administrative practices persisted. The lesser ali'i and kahuna who formed the majority of officials at the local level were part of an indigenous tradition that stretched back for centuries. Most of the royal administration remained concerned with relations between the king and his subjects. The existing system was modified rather than changed. The features of the royal administrative structure concerned with government away from the ports were present in the pre-existing system, and all that changed was that the scale was larger and the ruler was able to exercise more control over his administrators, now that his nominees had replaced the semi-autonomous and powerful vassal ali'i who governed localities under the old system.[47] These nominees did not have a local support base of their own; rather, their authority rested on their association with the king. This move may owe its implementation to the advice of Europeans that was based on their experience of European monarchies. But it is equally possible that the reason it was introduced was that only now were the powerful interests opposed to centralisation able to be

46 Campbell (1967), pp. 99, 118–19, 144, 154; Daws (1968a), p. 46; and Bargatzy (1980), p. 94.
47 Howe (1984), p. 158.

overcome. Attempts by Hawaiians to integrate large regions or whole islands into unified politics date back to the 1600s at least. It is only when Kamehameha's unification is placed within this longer timescale that the dynamic of his state-building efforts in Hawai'i can be truly understood.

The mere presence of outsiders in ports of call such as Honolulu and Kealakekua Bay did not necessarily ensure change, even at these cultural interfaces. Europeans visiting Hawai'i during Kamehameha's reign were in no position to force change on Hawaiians. Increasing exposure to European goods and ideas went hand in hand with changes that stemmed largely from indigenous factors, particularly the cessation of open warfare. Some transformations that occurred in Kamehameha's lifetime were the climax of processes begun centuries before. What particularly distinguished Kamehameha from other mō'ī was his method of consolidating military victory. Kamehameha mastered the art of building and maintaining coalitions. The early Hawaiian Kingdom was more of a chiefly federation that acknowledged Kamehameha's primacy than a monarchy with power concentrated in the hands of the ruler. Kamehameha's administrative reforms after unification combined Hawaiian practice with European ideas. Most commentators have noted the significance of these administrative changes, but few acknowledge that demilitarisation of the islands was central to the unification process. Hawaiian demilitarisation was assisted by epidemics, natural disasters and isolation from external threats after unification. Kamehameha may not have been able to implement his political reforms without this demilitarisation.

Hawaiian beliefs were challenged before 1819 simply by the non-adherence of foreigners to Hawaiian norms. At the time of Cook's arrival, chiefly power was becoming more secular, but still rested partly on a belief system that closely associated ali'i with gods. The gods affected the fortunes of men. If kapu were adhered to and mō'ī conducted their duties correctly, the gods looked after their community of human worshippers. Although worship varied across the archipelago, the underlying assumptions were generally accepted. The situation was aided by the archipelago's relative isolation from communities with differing worldviews. While the few Europeans who crossed the cultural divide and lived in Hawaiian society could be made to adhere to its rules, less control existed on board visiting vessels. Sailors broke kapu by allowing women to eat with them, others manhandled aliʻi. The fact that European sailors did not receive supernatural or chiefly sanction for disobeying kapu was also noted.[48]

Kamehameha realised the danger that Europeans posed to the kapu system. Any system of beliefs needs to conceal new ideas from the population, contain them, or incorporate them to continue to work as a means of social conditioning.[49] Kamehameha chose to contain the European threat to the kapu system. In the 1790s, Vancouver's men were requested to stay away from heiau. As transgressors of kapu, the entry of the crew into these sacred places threatened to defile them. When Vancouver left Hawaiʻi in 1793, Kamehameha went into seclusion to purify himself because he had been in contact with foreigners who had eaten and drunk with Hawaiian women. Kamehameha continued this policy throughout his reign. When the Scheffer entered a heiau near Honolulu in 1816 during a kapu period, the heiau was declared desecrated and was burned down.[50] Kamehameha also sought to restrict ship visits largely to Honolulu and to regulate visits through government officials.

Aliʻi were divided over the extent to which European influence should be controlled. As early as 1793, Keʻeaumoku's favourite wife, Namahana, had argued that Europeans and their vessels stood outside of the kapu system as it applied only to things Hawaiian.[51] A number of Hawaiian aliʻi were attracted to European ways and openly imitated them. Kaʻahumanu's brother, Kahekili Keʻeaumoku, told a European visitor that the white man's god was the only true god.[52] Faced with such beliefs, Kamehameha's religious conservatism became a crucial pillar for the old system of beliefs in the final years of his rule.

Aliʻi in regular contact with Europeans stood uneasily between two systems of belief. Inconsistencies in the behaviour of many aliʻi inevitably occurred. Female aliʻi dined with sailors in 1815 on board a ship anchored nearby to the corpse of a female makaʻāinana who had been killed for eating kapu food. When sailors traded with Hawaiians, aliʻi used kapu to restrict makaʻāinana access to European trade goods and then accumulated large quantities for themselves. Such kapu had dubious religious justification

---

48 Sahlins (1981), pp. 53–55; and Daws (1986a), pp. 57–58.
49 Galbraith (1985), p. 129.
50 Sahlins (1981), p. 54; and (1985), pp. 85–89.
51 Vancouver (1801), bk 3, p. 195.
52 Corney, cited in Sahlins (1989), p. 415 n. 6.

and therefore ran counter to the reciprocal basis of the Hawaiian social contract between aliʻi and makaʻāinana. Straying from traditional forms of kapu threatened to undermine the legitimacy of the whole kapu system.

With the exception of labour demanded for harvesting sandalwood, most of the compromising behaviour associated with interaction with Europeans remained confined to a few ports. Makaʻāinana secular and ritual life continued to revolve around localised agricultural production. Kamehameha's departure from Honolulu in 1810 may have been prompted by his desire to avoid the compromises that Honolulu's role as a port imposed upon his ritual efficacy. The Hawaiʻi he returned to, with its celebration of agricultural fertility, sense of local community and belief in supernatural potency was probably still the Hawaiʻi of the majority in 1819. The willingness of makaʻāinana to break kapu imposed on trade with Cook's vessels shows kapu were contested. The fact that these transgressions occurred from the moment of contact, and did not develop over a period of time after the arrival of Europeans, suggests that such contests were already an ongoing part of Hawaiian society and did not arise solely as a result of contact with the opportunities that outsiders presented.

The major change to state religion in Kamehameha's time, as the prospect of war faded, was the decline in the worship of Kū. Hawaiian sorcery gods rose to prominence to fill the void. While sorcery gods were associated with war gods as a milder form of the aggressive, violent aspect of kingship, Valerio Valeri proposes that their increasing emphasis undermined royal power. Whereas the worship of Kū centred on public ritual closely associated with the ruling chief, sorcery 'tended to "internalise" the conceptualisation of social processes and consequently to devalue their objectified, ritual expression'.[53] Sorcery was, therefore, in keeping with the 'incipient individualism' that Valeri detects as aliʻi began to compete with each other in accumulating commercial wealth.

The European influences that found the most enduring place in the popular consciousness were the memory of Cook and the ravages of introduced diseases. Cook's visit triggered a genuinely spontaneous and widespread celebration among the makaʻāinana in both Maui and Hawaiʻi in late 1778 and early 1779. A large crowd followed his circuit of Hawaiʻi, culminating in the massive crowd that greeted him at Kealakekua

---

53   Valeri (1982), p. 30.

Bay. Cook was clearly associated with Lono, the most popular god in the family shrines of commoners as well as the focus of the makahiki.[54] While there has been debate on whether Cook was viewed as Lono or a dangerous rival chief, there is no doubt that the memory of Cook–Lono was incorporated into the Hawaiian world view. Some days after Cook's death, priests of Lono asked when 'Erono' would return.[55] When European contacts were renewed in 1786, the belief in the imminent return of Cook as Lono makua remained. Evidence from the 1790s and 1800s shows that Cook was incorporated into the Hawaiian pantheon and formally worshipped as a royal cult. His worship echoed that given to Lono makua during the makahiki.[56] The English seaman William Mariner learnt from Hawaiians in Tonga during his forced residence there that:

> His bones (the greater part of which they still have in their possession!) they devoutly hold sacred. They are deposited in a house consecrated to a god, and are annually carried in a procession to many other consecrated houses, before each of which they are laid on the ground, and the priest returns thanks to the gods for having sent so great a man.[57]

This passage implies that Cook was perceived as an agent of Hawaiian gods. All great gods were foreign. European goods may also have been rationalised within the existing order as Mariner was also told that gods sent Cook 'to civilise them'.[58] Cook–Lono also seems to have been perceived as acting like a Hawaiian god. Over a decade after Cook's death, Captain James Colnett found that two recent volcanic eruptions in the Kailua area of Hawai'i Kona and a new illness were attributed to divine anger for the death of Cook. The association with volcanism relates to Lono's association with lightning. As fire in the sky, lightning was a manifestation of Lono's association with the family of Pele.[59]

Colnett's observations are also interesting for his informants' association of introduced diseases with the gods. Kamehameha's consolidation of power was aided by natural hazards and introduced disease, which resulted in an unplanned demilitarisation of the islands. His attempted invasion of Kaua'i in 1796 was thwarted when much of his fleet was capsized between O'ahu and Kaua'i. By 1804 Kamehameha was ready to attack

---

54   Sahlins (1989), p. 413; and Kahananui (1984), p. 173.
55   King, in Beaglehole (1967), 3:1, pp. 560–61.
56   Sahlins (1989), pp. 377–86, 389.
57   Mariner, in Martin (1981), p. 280.
58   Mariner, in Martin (1981), p. 280.
59   Sahlins (1989), p. 379.

Kaua'i again, however, his 7,000-strong force[60] never saw action due to the ravages caused by the 1804 epidemic. Kamehameha's reconstituted power base after the 1804 epidemic fell well short of its previous level.

The magnitude of the decline of the Hawaiian population in Kamehameha's time can never be accurately known. Samuel Kamakau's assurance that 'Many of the old chiefs were still alive in Liholiho's day' is supported only by a partial list of surviving members of important lineages. Only with Ke'eaumoku's offspring are we given any indication of the impact of disease. Five of his six children are said to have survived into Liholiho's reign, with only Kuakini falling victim to disease.[61] Such evidence can hardly be considered sufficient for any generalisation. It contrasts dramatically with Hawaiians' claims to William Ellis in 1823 that their population was only one quarter of what it had been 45 years earlier.[62]

Despite David Malo's statement that all islands were badly depopulated,[63] the possibility remains that the impact of introduced disease varied between localities. Islands playing host to visiting vessels may have suffered disproportionately more losses due to disease than their neighbours. Given the limited mobility between communities, outside of the ali'i nui, it is possible that ahupua'a communities away from ports like Honolulu may have suffered less than those in closer proximity. Certainly Kamakau noted that country districts were still thickly populated with chiefs at the arrival of missionaries a few years after Kamehameha's death.[64]

Stannard suggests that it was normal for 50 to 90 per cent or more of Pacific populations to be struck down by exotic disease in the first few generations after European contact. Donald Denoon is more circumspect, noting that rates of depopulation varied, and concludes that 50 per cent in the first generation after of exposure to exotic disease is a more reasonable figure. For both, the key demographic factor was the post-epidemic recovery rate.[65] The level of nutrition, frequency of epidemics, fertility rates and the ability to maintain economic and social patterns influenced recovery. Stannard emphasises that a side effect of many exotic diseases was infertility in women. It seems probable that venereal

---

60 Lisiansky (1967), pp. 11, 133.
61 Kamakau (1961), p. 221.
62 Stannard (1989), pp. 53–54.
63 Malo, cited in Stannard (1989), p. 57.
64 Kamakau (1961), p. 236.
65 Denoon (1994), pp. 332–34; and Stannard (1990), pp. 325–50.

disease, for example, was introduced early and caused infertility, which contributed to population decline. Hawaiian histories attribute most of the population decline to loss of fertility from sexual diseases acquired in liaisons with sailors. They rank infertility ahead of epidemics, wars and infanticide as the leading cause of their population's decline in the 50 years following Cook's arrival.[66] Stannard notes that, even in the period 1834–41 when no major epidemics occurred, the median birth rate of Hawaiians was only 19.3 per thousand, compared to a median crude death rate of 47.3 per thousand. Stephen Kunitz is less certain, noting that the best evidence is from New Zealand, where a decline in Māori fertility from 1769 to the 1850s was followed by an increase in fertility from 1850 to 1880, during a time when the overall Māori population continued to decline.[67]

Alfred Crosby also emphasises the significance of factors suppressing Pacific Islanders' ability to recover from epidemics. In addition to infertility, he lists a raft of less dramatic, but persistent diseases and infections, like tuberculosis, that chipped away at the population by overloading immune systems so that they were less able to resist more serious pathogens.[68]

The details concerning the social impact of exotic diseases remain far from resolved. Judd's observation was not untypical, and many contemporary European observers attributed this behaviour to despair. Infertility was so widespread by the 1850s that Hawaiians began to wonder if their race would become extinct.[69] Yet, they continued to resist European inroads until the 1893 coup and beyond, just as Māori mounted sustained military resistance in the 1840s and 1860s as their population also plummeted. There is little evidence of a crisis of confidence, even in the immediate aftermath of the most devastating epidemics. At the time of the 1804 oku'u epidemic, for example, agricultural production in Hawai'i increased in some areas in response to Western trade,[70] and Europeans found the population of the island of Hawai'i numerous and industrious.[71] Hawaiians launched themselves into the construction of a Western fleet after 1800 and successfully repelled a Russian attempt to establish themselves on Kaua'i in 1816. Religious adherence among

---

66   Kahananui (1984), pp. 232–33.
67   Stannard (1990), pp. 331–35; and Kunitz (1994), p. 51.
68   Crosby (1992), p. 193.
69   Daws (1968a), pp. 168–69.
70   Cordy (1972), pp. 408–09; and Kirch (1985), pp. 178, 314.
71   Campbell (1967), p. 87.

chiefs did slacken in the last decade of Kamehameha's reign, however, and the new political elite overturned the old religious system after his death in 1819. Most Hawaiians continued to make offerings to their local gods for bountiful harvests on the land they had farmed for generations, even after Christianity became the official religion in the 1820s. The real disruption to their lifestyle came in the 1840s with the legal change to land ownership.[72]

The colonial experience of epidemics in the Pacific supports the proposition that dispossession rather than depopulation was the key disruption to indigenous life. Samoans suffered the highest mortality of any community in the world during the 1918–19 influenza epidemic – 30 per cent of adult males, 22 per cent of adult females and 10 per cent of children. European settlement and control of land remained limited, however, and Samoans made a quick recovery. Within a decade, the Samoan population's growth rate averaged over 3 per cent. Fijians' birth rate also increased in the years immediately following the measles epidemic that struck their islands in 1875. This was followed by a 20-year decline that coincided with the introduction of a new form of economic production as British authorities sought to develop a plantation economy.[73]

Access to European manufactured goods during Kamehameha's reign provided new possibilities for the formulation of economic power. Hitherto, the Hawaiian political economy had focused on the control and allocation of land and the distribution of its largely perishable production. Both processes were used to secure and maintain followers. In terms of traditional formulations of power, European goods had two possible uses. As exotic, locally unavailable items, they might serve as prestige possessions. Some had potentially more functional uses. In particular, European firepower might enhance military capabilities, especially if accompanied by tactical reform, and iron tools held the promise of improvements in farming and indigenous manufacturing.

The ali'i seemed more determined to accumulate large stores of European goods than to encourage their use among their subjects, moving early to shut maka'āinana out of the trade in European goods through regulatory kapu and the appropriation of any items that found their way into the hands of their lesser subjects. For example, although ali'i soon satisfied

---

72 Daws (1968a), pp. 49–60.
73 Denoon (1994), p. 332.

their desire for iron tools and moved on to accumulate other items of trade, there remained a general shortage of iron tools in the community at large into the 19th century.[74]

European items that did find their way into the wider economy seem to have had a limited impact prior to 1819. Crafts involving the working of wood were enhanced by the use of metal adzes. By 1809 they had almost totally replaced traditional stone adzes.[75] Introduced crops and livestock did not find favour among Hawaiians and traditional food sources continued to dominate the Hawaiian diet. While metal tools may have aided the breaking in of raw ground, there was little to be gained from their adoption in the Hawaiian agricultural system, dominated as it was by the labour-intensive work of mulching and weeding agricultural plots.[76] The adoption of metal fishhooks and sinkers and European cast nets that occurred over the course of the 19th century did little to alter fishing techniques or the size of harvests.[77]

Most items of European trade were used primarily to enhance the status of their individual chiefly owners. Whereas traditional status items, such as feathered cloaks, acquired their value through their association with the mana of their possessor, the value of European goods seems to have been more associated with the quantity of the item as an indication of the owner's economic wealth. The sale of feathered cloaks and chiefly headdress to European trade may indicate that the flood of introduced goods devalued traditional status items, although Jocelyn Linnekin suggests that those items sold were usually not associated with important ali'i.[78]

To acquire European goods, the ali'i had to meet the demand of visiting vessels. Initially this consisted of agricultural provisions. Later this was supplemented by a demand for sandalwood. To accommodate these demands, the ali'i drew upon their traditional right to a proportion of their maka'āinana tenants' produce and labour. Prior to unification, it would appear that the Hawaiian economy was able to meet the demand for provisions from visiting vessels without being overextended.[79] Ships' complements ranged from five on the *Fair American* to just over 50 on the

---

74 Sahlins (1981), p. 44; Ralston (1984), pp. 25–26.
75 Campbell (1967), p. 143; Malo (1951), p. 52.
76 Cordy (1972), pp. 403–06; Kirch (1984), pp. 189–90.
77 Hommon (1975), p. 116.
78 Linnekin (1988), pp. 275–76.
79 Cordy (1972), pp. 400–03.

Eleanora.[80] Considering that the retinues of individual aliʻi were usually much more numerous than this, early European demand may in fact have been able to have been met from the agricultural production and free-ranging herds of pigs of koele lands. After 1800, agricultural production seems to have increased to allow the aliʻi greater access to European trade. This was particularly true of ahupuaʻa around the main ports. Around Honolulu, for example, new fields were planted in yams and potatoes, and even a limited number of sheep and goats were raised to satisfy the European palate.[81]

The extent to which production was also increased away from the ports is uncertain. During the sandalwood period, there is archaeological evidence that production may have declined in certain areas such as leeward Kohala on Hawaiʻi.[82] The fact that military garrisons were supplied by inter-island ship voyages at this time shows that the Hawaiian Kingdom had the ability to mobilise resources archipelago-wide. After 1810, demands on residents of ahupuaʻa away from ports certainly increased as aliʻi sent makaʻāinana into the mountains to harvest sandalwood.

Any loss of makaʻāinana support that aliʻi demands may have caused was not compensated for by the formulation of new support bases through the distribution of European goods. The kingdom's healthy currency reserves and the stores of material possessions did not translate into domestic political influence. Currency was useful in dealings with European visitors and for paying European officials in the kingdom's government but, elsewhere, the agriculture-based economy predominated. Most of the king's local officials were paid from a proportion of their administrative area's production through which the king's subjects acknowledged the monarchy's spiritual and secular protection. Presumably the royal army was also supported by agricultural tribute. There are certainly no indications that they were paid in currency or goods, as the kingdom's European officials were. Overall, the newly unified Hawaiian Kingdom still exhibited more continuity with past practices than Western-influenced innovation.

---

80 Vancouver (1801), bk 3, p. 227.
81 Cordy (1972), pp. 402, 407, 411–12; and Kamakau (1961), p. 190.
82 Kirch (1985), pp. 178, 314.

Conclusion

Timing mattered. The initial formation of the Hawaiian Kingdom was affected as much by specific events and individuals as by structural features. Archaeologists and anthropologists correctly emphasise economic modes of production, coercive capacity and ideological hegemony as the key structures of political power in the pre-unification period. By emphasising general structures of power over the enactment of power, however, they are unable to explain why unification occurred, when and as it did, without recourse to European influences. Western influences did alter the configuration of the kingdom, but were not necessarily essential for its foundation. Marshall Sahlins moves towards combining general structures and specific enactments with his structure of the conjuncture, but emphasises ideological schemes and neglects coercion in his assessment of Hawaiian chiefly power in Kamehameha's time. Hawaiian chiefs were testing and extending the limits of their secular power from the 1770s. A number of futures are possible within any combination of longer term structural parameters. Would Kamehameha still have become the first unifier of the islands if he emulated Kahekili's less conciliatory policies? Would he have been able to seize the islands if Kahekili had died five years earlier or five years later? The historiography of Hawai'i in Kamehameha's time demonstrates the potential of interdisciplinary approaches, particularly the value of constructing detailed narratives to supplement analysis of underlying environmental features and cultural structures, and to test more general theories.

The experience of Hawaiian society between 1782 and 1812 is an example of the exercise of power in a time of transition. The formation of a centralised polity that transcends local kin-based loyalties is invariably a watershed in social evolution. The potential for unification was in place before Western influences became a permanent feature of the political landscape. Kamehameha's administrative reforms after unification combined existing Hawaiian practice with European ideas, personnel and technology. The written word and Western vessels facilitated inter-island communication, while residents such as John Young and Isaac Davis proved to be loyal lieutenants when entrusted with senior administrative posts and regulation of commercial interactions with visiting trade vessels. Kamehameha also drew upon centuries of political practice and accumulated knowledge about the construction and maintenance of chiefly coalitions and the administration of moku, which lay at the heart of power within a decentralised polity. Coercion also played a role. Kamehameha forged the Hawaiian Kingdom in battle in the early 1790s. His military gains may have been diminished, however, if they had not been followed by the astute political compromises that took place in the decade following the battle of Nuʻuanu.

Kamehameha lived in a society that underwent major transformations over the previous few hundred years. Spurred on by increasing population pressure and status rivalry between aliʻi, the relationship between humans and the environment and rulers and subjects had been altered dramatically. Cultivation in favoured locations was intensified, while settlement expanded into more marginal agricultural zones. Both processes required a degree of coordination beyond family and local community organisation. In drought-prone leeward areas, the threat of famine exerted a powerful influence on communities to concede greater powers to their rulers. Hawaiʻi traditions record the rising influence of leeward chiefs relative to those of older windward communities with larger populations. The defining of fixed landholdings, which was inherent in the demarcation of ahupuaʻa boundaries, created new functions for rulers as administrators, and as defenders of frontier boundaries. Even without these pressures, competition between chiefs for status provided a powerful incentive for waging war. Leaders developed sizeable retinues and used their sacred status to further their administrative and military activities. Feeding retinues and making offerings to the gods required a share of agricultural production beyond subsistence needs.

These factors gave rise to the structures of power that were witnessed by Captain James Cook in the 1770s. By 1778, polities encompassed many ahupuaʻa, and some consisted of a number of islands. The political coherence of these polities rested on the diffusion of power. Makaʻāinana obedience to the mōʻī and his aliʻi was based to a large extent on the latter group's sacred status. Produce and labour were given with the expectation that the ruler would protect his subjects from external enemies and attract divine favour to ensure prosperity within the realm. The existence of secular sanctions for transgressions of chiefly and divine kapu suggests that ideology alone did not ensure makaʻāinana obedience. The relative coherence of chiefly retinues provided leaders with a coercive advantage over the fragmented makaʻāinana communities that made up the overwhelming majority of the population. The system also held together because chiefly demands did not intrude too deeply into the worlds of local makaʻāinana communities.

Mōʻī lacked the necessary coercive advantage to dominate their vassal aliʻi. Most mōʻī inherited powerful, well-established aliʻi families as vassals from their predecessors. The selection of mōʻī often owed much to concerns for the preservation or balancing of existing power blocs within the aliʻi, rather than the relative strength of the candidates. Personal power bases had to be built up by mōʻī through time. The support of powerful vassal aliʻi remained a necessity for the maintenance of any moku's coherence. Entrenched power, logistical problems and the importance of individual prowess in battle for the enhancement of mana all worked against the formation of a full-time, centralised army that was drilled to fight in unison and loyal to a central ruler.

The two moku that were most associated with attempts at military reform in this period included the leeward districts of Maui and Hawaiʻi within their domains. The dangers of drought may have allowed mōʻī to justify increased chiefly powers in terms of demands made on their subject's labour and on agricultural production to create a more militarily efficient, magazine economy. This process may have been behind the relatively late and rapid rise of leeward areas to political prominence, detected by Patrick Kirch, and the challenge they posed to older, windward centres of power. Relations between moku in Kamehameha's time, however, raise doubts about this theory. The centre of power for the Maui line was on the windward coast at Wailuku. Hawaiʻi's windward chiefs were as aggressive as their leeward counterparts throughout the late 1700s. Ecologically based theories of the evolution of Hawaiian power understate the importance of individual ability among mōʻī and specific historical configurations. Was Maui the most powerful moku in the 1780s because of its ecological base or the tactical ability and aggressiveness of its ruler Kahekili, combined with the temporary weakness of their rivals while new, young mōʻī sought to consolidate power?

Kamehameha's success in unifying the Hawaiian chain cannot be understood merely in terms of these generalised structural characteristics. The economic structures described by Kirch, Earle and others were in place long before unification. They provided a foundation for unification, but do not explain why unification occurred when and as it did. Within these sociopolitical and environmental parameters, the decisions and actions of leading figures decisively shaped the course of events. Prior to becoming mōʻī of the leeward coast of his home island, Kamehameha was a rather impetuous young man who was more of a warrior than a leader. He developed into a mōʻī whose success was based as much on consent as coercion. Kamehameha's rise owed a great deal to the support of the four Kona uncles. His respect for this clique, and their continued coherence, ensured the security of Kamehameha's rule against possible threats from within the moku. The induction of Kaʻiana into this ruling group in 1789 and the occasional dissent of Kameʻeiamoku never seriously challenged this unity. Shielded behind Hawaiʻi's rugged interior, the moku's Kona heartland prospered in the absence of external intruders or serious natural disaster.

Whether through choice or circumstance, the early years of Kamehameha's rule involved little territorial expansion. Kamehameha's career as mōʻī can be seen in contrast with that of his main rival, Kahekili. While superior to Kamehameha as a tactician, Kahekili's military expansionism and harsh treatment of rivals weakened his moku's coherence. His bloody conquest of Oʻahu ensured a legacy of animosity among many of the island's inhabitants. His expansion on to Oʻahu also diverted resources away from east Maui, which was only loosely integrated into Kahekili's moku after over a decade of Hawaiʻian control. Kahekili's extermination rather than integration of much of the Oʻahu aliʻi meant his resources were merely stretched, rather than expanded, over a multi-island polity.

In the wake of Kalanikūpule's defeat on Maui in 1790, Kahekili and Kaʻeokulani of Kauaʻi allied to protect their realms from the rising star of Kamehameha. Kamehameha's naval victory against this coalition in 1791 put his many rivals into a defensive frame of mind. Kahekili and Kaʻeokulani maintained a standing army on Maui for the next few years in anticipation of an invasion by Kamehameha. Kamehameha was left free to move against his enemies on Hawaiʻi. Once Keōua was removed, Kamehameha was able to consolidate his hold on Hawaiʻi without fear of attack. Meanwhile, the strain of maintaining a coalition formed to counter a possible invasion began to tell on the political coherence and economic capabilities of Kahekili and Kaʻeokulani's domains.

The open rupture of this coalition followed soon after Kahekili's death in 1794. Kalanikūpule's victory over Kaʻeokulani at ʻAiea later that year was not enough to salvage the erosion of the Maui line's power base over the preceding three years. During this time, the dynasty's old heartland of west Maui had been presided over by Kaʻeokulani rather than Kalanikūpule, and bled dry by unprecedented logistical demands. Kalanikūpule's victory did not even secure all of Oʻahu for him. Aliʻi from Waiʻanae and Waialua fought for Kaʻeokulani at ʻAiea, in a continuation of their districts' traditional resistance to rule from mōʻī based in the Kona–Koʻolaupoko area. Kauaʻi remained independent and in no mood to ally with the slayer of its deceased mōʻī, Kaʻeokulani. Kalanikūpule's loss of his European arsenal in early January of 1795 was enough to persuade Kamehameha to attack. Kalanikūpule was denied the chance to consolidate his position. He probably went into battle against Kamehameha at Nuʻuanu with his core of support reduced to the chiefly retinues based on Oʻahu's Kona and Koʻolaupoko districts.

Contemporary military historiography's emphasis on the importance of logistical and organisational factors calls for a re-evaluation of the significance of European weaponry and mercenaries in Kamehameha's wars of unification. Cannon may have secured an advantage for Kamehameha at sea, which served to protect the heartland of his moku and to threaten that of his enemies. Traditional accounts of land warfare in this era, however, suggest victories were gained by the steady accumulation of advantage over a number of days or weeks. Individual battles were significant as part of a wider process. The two most noted instances of the use of cannon on land, at ʻĪao and Nuʻuanu, occurred only at the end of such processes. Nowhere in the traditions is there any clear indication of the widespread or decisive use of firearms. The available muskets were generally of poor quality, and an indiscriminate hail of lead threatened the individual martial prowess on which so much Hawaiian chiefly status rested.

Each passing year after the ending of hostilities in 1796 may have enhanced the reputation of firearms. Past myths rather than contemporary performance might well have ensured the future of firearms as tools of coercion. The prolonged peace from 1796 to 1819 probably had more impact on Hawaiian society than the mounting European presence. European influence remained largely confined to a few ports of call and trade in European goods was mainly the preserve of aliʻi. The vast majority of the population continued to live a traditional, rural life. Traditional obligations arising from Kamehameha's sacred status still formed the basis of his dealings with his makaʻāinana subjects. The continued coherence of the ruling clique of Kamehameha and the four Kona uncles enabled Kamehameha to hold onto his much-expanded realm in the crucial years immediately following 1796.

To preserve their coherence, the ruling group agreed to fragment their landed power base and create an independent administrative structure to counter their own power. As long as they remained coherent, the ruling clique could preserve their near monopoly on coercion by keeping the islands demobilised. The administrative bureaucracy could detect attempts to rearm and retrain well before potential rebels could mount an effective challenge. Demobilisation was aided by military losses in the Kauaʻi channel disaster of 1796 and the 1804 epidemic on Oʻahu. General military training declined with each year of continued peace, as did the ability of those outside the ruling clique to mount an effective military challenge. Denied access to administrative and coercive power the lesser aliʻi increasingly focused their energies on the competitive accumulation of European goods. Even in this sphere, the ruling group's grip on other avenues of power allowed them to control and regulate European trade.

Kamehameha's kingdom is perhaps best described as a centralised monarchy in the form of an oligarchy. Like mōʻī prior to 1796, Kamehameha's rule rested on the support of a group of powerful aliʻi families within his moku. After 1796, however, the ruling clique became smaller, and the balance of power within it was reinforced and institutionalised by the creation of designated offices and a bureaucracy. This, in turn, allowed the demilitarisation of the islands to be preserved, with the retention of only a small standing army. The pursuit of power remained distant from the day-to-day life of the vast majority of the population. Whether or not the embryonic kingdom's government could keep the outside world equally distant remained to be seen.

Appendix 1: Hawaiian Military Activity 1778–97

Key for Table 1A.1

	Makahiki Season
2	Source (list follows table)
▬	Period of datable mobilisation
①	Known, datable battle
▪▪▪▪	Mobilisation implied, but not directly states in sources
k	Kauaʻi
o	Oʻahu
m/m	Molokaʻi/Maui
hl	Leeward Big Island
hw	Windward Big Island

TRANSFORMING HAWAI'I

Table 1A.1: Military activity by month and locality, 1778–97

Year	General events (month uncertain) / Source (see list)	Jan	Feb	Mar	Apr	May	Jun	Jul	Aug	Sep	Oct	Nov	Dec	
		Makahiki Season									Makahiki Season			k / o / m/m / hl / hw
1778	1										— — — ① —			
1779	2, 3	— —	③ —	— —										
1780	4													
1781	5													
1782	6, 7, 8, 9	———————————————— ⑥ — — — ———————												
1783	10, 12?	⑩ — — — — — — .?. . .												
1784	11, 12?													
1785	12?, 13				— — — — — — — — — — — — — — — — — — —									
1786	14				— — — — ——— — — —									
1787	15													
1788	16											— — — —		
1789	17?													
1790	18, 19, 20					———————— — — — ? . . . . ———			....?═════ ....?═					
1791	21, 22, 23, 24	——————— —												
1792	24	———————————— —												
1793	25, 26	— — — ㉖ —												
1794	27, 28, 29, 30	— — — — — — — — — — ———————— — — — — — — — — — — — ?												
1795	31, 32, 33, 34	═══ — — — ? — — — — — — — — — — :.?												
1796	35, 36							...? ?						
1797	37													

Key to symbols
- k — Kaua'i
- o — O'ahu
- m/m — Moloka'i/Maui
- hl — Leeward Hawai'i
- hw — Windward Hawai'i
- ① — Known, datable battle
- ——— Period of datable mobilisation
- — — — Mobilisation implied, but not directly stated in the sources

APPENDIX 1

Table 1A.2: Areas Experiencing Hostile Armies, 1778–96

Generalised Locality	1778	1779	1780	1781	1782	1783	1784	1785	1786	1787	1788	1789	1790	1791	1792	1793	1794	1795	1796
Kona, Hawai'i					■														
Kohala, Hawai'i													■					?	
Hamakua, Hawai'i													■					?	
Hilo, Hawai'i					■		■												
Puna, Hawai'i				?															
Ka'ū, Hawai'i												?							
East Maui	■				■								■						
West Maui	■																		
Lana'i	■																?		
Moloka'i		■																	
Kona, O'ahu							?	?											
Windward O'ahu						?	?	?							■				
Ewa/Waiana'e, O'ahu							?	?											
Waialua, O'ahu							?	?											
Puna, Kaua'i		■								?					■				
Leeward Kaua'i										?									?
Windward Kaua'i																			

References

1. Kalani'ōpu'u raids Maui and Lāna'i (Kamakau (1961, pp. 89–90); and Dibble (1909, p. 22). Cook, in Beaglehole (1967, 3:1, pp. 476 ff.) confirms Kalani'ōpu'u's army was on east Maui Nov. 1778 to Jan./Feb. 1779).
2. Kahekili versus Peleiohalani on Moloka'i (King, in Beaglehole (1967), 3:1, pp. 584–85, 27 Feb. 1779).
3. Kamakeheli defeats Kāneoneo on Kaua'i (Clerke, in Beaglehole (1967), 3:1, p. 577, 28 Feb. 1779).
4. Peleiohalani dies, is succeeded by Kumahama, who is deposed (peacefully?) (Fornander (1969), pp. 217–19, 290).
5. Kalani'ōpu'u defeats rebellion of 'Īmakakoloa in Puna, Hawai'i (Fornander (1969), pp. 200–03. Kamakau (1961, p. 108) is uncertain if this was in 1780 or 1781).
6. Kalani'ōpu'u dies, succeeded by Kamehameha after his slaying of Kīwala'ō at Moku'ōhai (Fornander (1969, p. 311) dates Moku'ōhai to July. See also Fornander (1969), pp. 204, 299–11; Kamakau (1961), pp. 110, 118–21; and Dibble (1909), p. 43).
7. Keawe and Keōua crush revolts (Fornander (1969), p. 316).
8. Kamehameha versus Keawe and Kahahawai in Hilo (Fornander (1969), pp. 220–22, 311–12, 316–19; Kamakau (1961) 124–25; and Dibble (1909) 45–46).
9. Kahekili retakes east Maui (Fornander (1969), pp. 215–17; Kamakau (1961) pp. 115–16; and Dibble (1909), p. 44. It is likely that the siege lasted from January to December 1782 as Kahekili attacked upon hearing of Kalani'ōpu'u's death. The siege lasted one year, and Kahekili attacked O'ahu in early 1783 – 'some say' Jan. 1783 (Kamakau, (1961), p. 136)).

10. Kahekili conquers Oʻahu (Fornander (1969), pp. 220–27; Kamakau (1961), p. 136, 'some say' Jan. 1783).
11. Kahekili consolidates Oʻahu and puts down rebellion sometime from 1783 to 1785 (Fornander (1969, pp. 225–27) claims the Oʻahu revolt occurred in 1785 and he states (p. 298) that Kāneoneo was killed on Oʻahu in 1785. Even if so, the suggestion remains that resistance was not broken until c. 1785?).
12. Rebellion involving Kukeawe on Maui (Fornander (1969, pp. 227–28) is no more specific than to date this revolt to Kukeawe's governorship while Kahekili was on Oʻahu).
13. Kamehameha versus Keawe in Hilo (Fornander (1969, pp. 319–20) describes the conflict as a long and indecisive war).
14. Kalanimalokuloku-i-Kapoʻokalani invades Maui and is repulsed by Kamohomoho (Fornander (1969), pp. 228–29, 320–22. Fornander (p. 320) states that there was a truce on Hawaiʻi. Dixon (1968, p. 51) visited Oʻahu in May and was told that the local aliʻi were at war on another island).
15. No sign of war from November 1786 to October 1787 (Portlock (1958) saw no signs of war during visits to Hawaiʻi, Maui and Oʻahu, Nov. – 20 Dec. 1786 (pp. 149–53), Jan.–Mar. 1787 (pp. 167–73), Sep. – 8 Oct 1787 (pp. 298–308)).
16. Kaʻeokulani challenged by a faction on Kauaʻi (Meares (1968, p. 335, 6 Dec.) was uncertain if the dispute came to blows, but Kahekili's presence on Kauaʻi casts doubts over this possibility. Certainly by Jan. 1779, Meares (1968, pp. 350–51) found Kauaʻi at peace and Kahekili back on Oʻahu).
17. Kamehameha versus Keōua in Kaʻū? (Kamakau (1961), pp. 153–54), and Ellis (1969, pp. 209–10) suggest that Kaʻiana may have conducted operations against Keōua. In March, Meares (1968, p. 354) noted tensions between Kamehameha and a windward chief who was allied to Kahekili. Menzies (1920, p. 10) refers to fighting between Kaʻiana and Keōua in Kaʻū in the recent past, but the two had fought there in 1790–91. Certainly when Menzies returned in July (1968, p. 369–72) there was no sign of war. Nor did the *Felice* (Meares (1968), pp. 272–80) detect signs of war on Hawaiʻi during its reprovisioning between 17 Sep. and 27 Oct.).
18. Kamehameha conquers Maui and Molokaʻi (Fornander (1969), pp. 235–40; and Kamakau (1961), pp. 147–49. The campaign must have occurred after the seizure of the *Fair American* in March 1790 (Kamakau (1961), p. 145; and Fornander (1969), p. 234) as one of its cannon was used at ʻIao. After ʻIao, the army remained mobilised on Maui and Molokaʻi for some time (Fornander (1969), pp. 238–40)).
19. Keōua defeats and kills Keawe in Hilo, and invades Hāmākua and Kohala (Fornander (1969), p. 240; and Kamakau (1961), p. 151).
20. Kamehameha versus Keōua in Hāmākua (Fornander (1969), pp. 323–24; and Kamakau (1961), pp. 151–52).
21. Kamehameha renews attack on Keōua (Kamakau (1961), pp. 153–54. Fornander (1969, p. 326) writes that Keōua held his ground during the spring and summer).
22. Kaʻeokulani and Kahekili attack Kamehameha and are defeated in a naval battle off Waipiʻo (Fornander (1969, p. 241) states that Kaʻeokulani and Kahekili mobilised and reoccupied Molokaʻi and Maui in the winter months of 1790–91. Fornander (1969, pp. 242–43), and Kamakau (1961, pp. 159–62) date the naval battle off Hāmākua to Spring 1791. Colnett (Howay (1940), p. 220) was told that the battle occurred in April or early May. However Ingraham (Kaplanoff (1971), pp. 85–86) witnessed a mobilisation at Oʻahu on 27 May and was informed that Kahekili's fleet was then off Maui, while Kamehameha's was in Kohala (Kaplanoff (1971), p. 71)).
23. Kamehameha kills Keōua (Fornander (1969), pp. 244, 327–35) claims that the naval battle occurred before the sacrifice of Keōua, as does Kamaka (1961, pp. 155–58)).

APPENDIX 1

24. Kaʻeokulani and Kahekili remain mobilised on Maui during 1791 and 1792 (Fornander (1969), p. 244. Vancouver (1801, bk 1, p. 352 (Mar. 1792)) states that Kaʻeokulani and Kahekili met on Molokaʻi in preparation for an expected attack by Kamehameha. He also noted (p. 363) that they had been absent from Kauaʻi and Oʻahu respectively, for 'several' months now. Gooch (Dening (1988), p. 5) noted that Kahekili and his army were still on Maui in May 1792).
25. Continued mobilisation on Maui (and Hawaiʻi?) (Vancouver (1801, bk 3, p. 301) noted that Kamehameha's enemies were still mobilised on Maui in March 1793 to guard against the possibility of attack by Kamehameha).
26. Inamo crushes revolt on Kauaʻi (Vancouver (1801), bk 37, pp. 367–69, 375 (Mar. 1793)).
27. Death of Namahana of Maui (Vancouver (1801, bk 5, p. 118, (Feb. 1794)) and Fornander (1969, p. 214) both agree that Namahana died as a result of the accidental detonation of gunpowder stores. This incident and statements in Menzies (1920, p. 85) imply that forces were still mobilised on Maui).
28. Inamo asserts his autonomy from Kaʻeokulani on Kauaʻi (Vancouver (1801), bk 5, pp. 125–26 (Feb.–Mar.)).
29. Kahekili dies on Oʻahu (Fornander (1969), p. 260).
30. Kaʻeokulani versus Kalanikūpule with the latter emerging victorious (Fornander (1969), pp. 262–65. Kamakau (1961, p. 168–69) dates Kaʻeokulani's landing at Waialua to 16 Nov., and his death in the battle of Aiea to 12 Dec.).
31. Death of Kaʻeokulani and Inamo sees Kaumualiʻi become mōʻī of Kauaʻi (Kamakau (1961), p. 169).
32. Kalanikūpule's seizure and loss of the *Jackal* and *Prince Lee Boo* (Kamakau (1961), pp. 170–71. The ships were seized in late Dec. and recaptured by the surviving crew members on 4 Jan.).
33. Kamehameha conquers Maui, Molokaʻi, and Oʻahu. Kamehameha was on Maui in February. (Fornander (1969), p. 343; and Kamakau (1961), p. 171. From the narrative that follows in Fornander and Kamakau, he seems to have soon moved onto Oʻahu for the decisive showdown. Bishop (in Roe (1967), p. 142), claims that Kamehameha set out from Hawaiʻi in June and landed on Oʻahu in mid-August – but it seems more likely that he would have responded more rapidly to Kalanikūpule's misfortune of 4 Jan. Whatever the case, Kamehameha was in control of Oʻahu when Boit (Judd (1974), p. 8) arrived there on 16 Oct.).
34. Kamehameha remains mobilised on Oʻahu until the failed attempt on Kauaʻi in mid-1796 (Kamakau (1961, p. 173) states that Kamehameha kept his army mobilised on Oʻahu until his fleet was built. The invasion fleet was destroyed by a storm in mid-1796. When Broughton (1967, pp. 70–71) arrived at Oʻahu on 25 Jul., the storm incident had already occurred).
35. Civil war/rebellion on Kauaʻi (Broughton (1967), p. 44 (13 Feb. 1796); and Bishop, in Roe (1967), pp. 145–46. When Broughton returned to Kauaʻi in Jul., Keawe ruled and Kaumualiʻi was his 'prisoner' (Broughton (1967), p. 73)).
36. Kamehameha crushes revolt of Namakeha on Hawaiʻi (Kamakau (1961, pp. 173–74) dates Kamehameha's campaign to Sep.–Nov. Broughton (1967, pp. 69–70) says the rebellion was in progress in Jul.; see also Bishop (in Roe (1967), p. 144). Kamakau (1961, p. 174) states that Namakeha was sacrificed in January 1797).
37. Keawe, the victor of the 1796 rebellion on Kauaʻi, dies of natural causes. Kaumualiʻi becomes mōʻī of Kauaʻi again (Broughton (1967), p. 73; Bishop in Roe (1967), p. 145 n. 1).

Appendix 2: Firearms in Hawai'i, 1786–96

Table 2A.1: From 'Expenditures for the *Columbia*'s Outfit and Cargo', September 1790

		Remarks
John Derby	1 pair of 4 pounders	Ships' armament rather than trade items?
	1 pair of 3 pounders	
	4 pairs of swivels	
	One Iron Cabouse	
	Carting gunns etc	
D. Harthorne	freight of gunns from Salem	
Jos. Callender Senr	135 lb shot at 3d and 1 cartridge box	
Robt. & Joshua Davis	3 doz. handspikes	
John Andrews	nails	In part, for ships' use?
Elisha Sigourney	71 lb. grape shot	
Jos. Coolidge	31 bullet moulds	
	1 doz. common spikes	
Under 'cargo'	a lot of barr iron	In part for ship's use?
	45 quatre cast powder	
	6 1/2 barrels powder	
	20 doz. cuttoe knives	
Listed under individual crew	(1, 8, 4, 4, 3, 4, 5, 3) = 32 musketts	
from 'government'	100 musketts	
	8 blunderbuses	

Source: Howay (1941 pp. 443, 463).

Table 2A.2: Post-voyage inventory of Cptn Charles Bishop after a voyage to the north-west Pacific coast and Hawai'i, March 1796 (Canton)

Expenditure	
a) To purchase furs, includes	23 half-barrels of powder
	64 musketts
	15 pistols
	5,000 flints
	79 1/2 dozen knives
b) To purchase 192 leather war dresses (NW Pacific Coast?)	10 pounds of powder
	4 musketts
	8 silver hilt swords
	3 tin powder flasks
	? cwt muskett ball
c) Provisions (Hawai'i and NW Pacific Coast?)	24 1/2 bars of iron
	2 cwt 3.0 lead balls and shot
	12 half-barrels powder
	2 musketts
	11 dozen knives
	6 bars of steel
d) Breakages	2 pistols (burst)
	1 muskett damaged
e) Goods disposed off at Falklands and Sandwich Islands (not separated in inventory)	1 half-barrel powder
	5 yds cloth
	1 Fowling gun
	2 Hatts
	2 dozen knives
	3 razors
European cargo remaining at Canton, March 1796	16 half-barrels of gun powder
	127 trade guns
	23 pistols
	5,000 flints
	10 cwt 2.0 lead ball and shot
	40 hatchets
	9 dozen Japanese powder flasks

Source: Roe (1967, pp. 162–66).

Appendix 3: A Note on Sources

There is a wealth of material from which to develop a more comprehensive account of the role played by warfare and coercion during the wars of unification. The unification of the Hawaiian archipelago is particularly well documented because of its relatively late date, the large number of European visitors to the chain who left written accounts about the period of unification, and the recording of Hawaiian sources in the 19th century. Seven groups of sources are available for the study of Hawaiian society up until the death of the first king, Kamehameha I, in 1819: the observations of European visitors to the islands from 1778 until 1819, missionary accounts from 1820 onwards, oral traditions and oral testimony recorded by Hawaiian scholars from the 1830s onwards, ethnographic studies by Europeans from the late 19th and early 20th centuries, 19th-century land records, archaeological remains of Hawaiian culture, and modern scientific studies of the physical environment.

The earliest written accounts of Hawaiian society are the journals and logs of various members of Captain James Cook's third voyage of discovery into the Pacific. Cook made three separate visits to the Hawaiian Islands between January 1778 and February 1779. As a number of Cook's officers kept journals, it is possible to crosscheck their accounts for inconsistencies.[1] The expedition only spent three and a half months in the island chain, mostly on board ship. Only Waimea Bay on Kaua'i, and Kealakekua Bay on Hawai'i were visited for any length of time, or described in any detail. Language difficulties added to the problems of comprehending Hawaiian culture. As one of Cook's officers noted, 'There is not much dependence to be placed upon these Constructions that we put upon Signs and Words which we understand but very little of & at best can only give a probable Guess at their Meaning'.[2] Nevertheless, the writings of Cook, James King

---
1 Valeri (1985a), pp. xviii–xxii; and Beaglehole (1967), pp. clxxi ff.
2 Samwell, in Beaglehole (1967), 3:2, p. 1223, cited in Valeri (1985a), p. xix.

and David Samwell stand out for their sensitivity to Hawaiian ways. King was particularly liked by Hawaiians, and was encouraged to remain in the archipelago.

From 1786 until the late 1790s, British and American trade vessels that were shipping furs from the north-west coast of America to China stopped to provision in Hawai'i. They rarely stopped for more than a few days at any location and concerned themselves mainly with matters of commerce.[3] In the early 1790s, another British naval expedition arrived in the Hawaiian Islands. Commanded by George Vancouver, a veteran of Cook's voyages, this expedition visited the chain a number of times from 1792 until 1794. This coincided with Kamehameha's wars of unification, which took place between 1790 and 1795. Vancouver was also able to comment on the long-term changes that had occurred since Cook's time. The expedition spent about four months in total in the archipelago during this time spread over a number of visits.[4] A number of Europeans began to live in the islands in the 1790s, but none left a significant written record of their experiences. This is particularly frustrating in the cases of John Young and Isaac Davis, both of whom participated in important battles of the decade. Young, in particular, became a close adviser and friend to Kamehameha I. The Hawai'i State Archives holds a manuscript listed as *The Journal of John Young*. It consists of only 46 pages of brief administrative details concerning the periods 1801–09, 1821 and 1825. European visitor reports of conversations with Young make it apparent that he was an intelligent and perceptive observer, although at times prone to exaggeration.[5]

The number of European residents steadily increased after Kamehameha secured control over most of the chain with his victory at Nu'uanu in 1795. A number of them left accounts of Hawaiian society in the early 19th century. Visits from European trading vessels and naval expeditions continued for the remainder of Kamehameha's reign. The most valuable accounts from this period are those of Archibald Campbell, Otto von Kotzebue and Louis Freycinet. Campbell was a sailor who spent more

---

3   See Judd (1974) and Valeri (1985).
4   Vancouver (1801). Another excellent account of the Hawaiian Islands, contemporary to Vancouver's, is found in Archibald Menzies (1920).
5   Bradley (1942), pp. 33–34 nn. 129–30; Bruce Cartwright, 'Some Early Foreign Residents of the Hawaiian Islands', *25th Annual Report of the Hawaiian Historical Society for the Year 1916* (Honolulu: 1917), pp. 57–64; and Maude (1968), pp. 134–77, esp. 139 ff.

than a year on Oʻahu in 1809–10. The Russian naval captain Kotzebue touched at the islands in 1816–17, while Freycinet's French expedition arrived in Hawaiʻi just after the death of Kamehameha I in 1819.[6]

The death of Kamehameha I was soon followed by the abolition of the kapu system around which much Hawaiian religious practice was organised. The arrival of Christian missionaries in 1820 served to accentuate the process of cultural transformation. The missionaries left a number of accounts of their work and of what they had learned about Hawaiian society. The most useful are those of Sheldon Dibble, William Ellis and James Jarves. While Dibble revealed a strong European bias and concentrates on the Christian mission, his accounts do include Hawaiian history. He mentions that he received detailed accounts of the Hawaiians' wars but omitted them because he believed that, 'to burden history with a minute account of battles and conquests would be quite unprofitable'. Ellis was more open-minded. He arrived in Hawaiʻi already fluent in Tahitian, and soon learned Hawaiian. He related well to Hawaiians, and was able to collect a great deal of ethnographic and linguistic material during a two-month tour of Hawaiʻi.[7]

In the 1830s, Dibble implemented a program to collect and record Hawaiian lore and traditions. He selected 10 of his best students at the mission seminary at Lahainaluna and formed them into a class of inquiry. Each student went out with a list of 10 questions drawn up by Dibble and recorded all the information they could gather on each subject from the oldest and most knowledgeable informants they could find. The 10 then met and discussed each student's findings to reconcile discrepancies and correct errors. Finally, the various compositions were edited by Dibble and published in 1838 as *Moolelo Hawaii* (*Hawaiian Antiquities*). The published work contained information on Hawaiian culture as well as historical subjects, such as chiefly genealogies and aspects of European contact. Christian elements appear, but are easily detectable and largely confined to moral criticisms of the old ways rather than alterations of them to conform to Christian doctrine.[8]

---

6   Campbell (1967), von Kotzebue (1821) and Kelly (1978).
7   Dibble (1909); Ellis (1969); Jarves (1843) and later enlarged edition(1872).
8   See Ben R. Finney et al., 'Hawaiian Historians and the First Pacific History Seminar', in N. Gunson (ed.), *The Changing Pacific – Essays in Honor of H.E. Maude* (Melbourne: Oxford University Press, 1978), pp. 308–16; and Kahananui (1984), which is based on the 1838 version.

Perhaps Dibble's best student was David Malo, whose *Moolelo Hawaii* was completed in 1839 or 1840. Malo was born in North Kona on Hawaiʻi in 1795. His father had been attached to the court and army of Kamehameha I, and Malo was associated with the high chief Kuakini, the brother of Kamehameha's favourite wife, Kaʻahumanu. Malo also had a close relationship with Auwai, a chief who was well versed in Hawaiian traditions through his role as Kamehameha's genealogist and ritual expert. Valerio Valeri's checking of Malo's original Hawaiian-language manuscript suggests that Nathaniel B. Emerson's English edition distorts and misrepresents the text in places, and that his notes are a misleading mixture of valuable data and falsehoods.[9]

Other Hawaiian historians followed Malo. The most important were Samuel Kamakau and John Papa Iʻī. Kamakau was born at Mokuleia in the Waialua district of Oʻahu in 1815 and entered Lahainaluna in 1833. He based his works on tradition gathered from older people, especially his grandfather. Although Samuel Kamakau was careful to distinguish between the past and his own time, this distinction is blurred in the translations of his ethnographic works. His *Ruling Chiefs of Hawaii* is, however, a chronological narrative. Dorothy Barrere has noted a number of inaccuracies and distortions in Samuel Kamakau's works, but most of these relate to early 'myth history' where he knits biblical references into Hawaiian traditions.[10]

John Papa Iʻī was born in 1800 at Waipiʻo on Oʻahu. He was brought to Honolulu when he was 16 and placed under the supervision of his uncle, Papa, who was an attendant at the court of Kamehameha. Papa placed Iʻī in the household of Liholiho, Kamehameha's son and successor. In his later years, Iʻī was a prominent member of Kamehameha III's court before retiring to ʻEwa, Oʻahu, to work in a Christian ministry until his death in 1870. *Fragments of History* is a collection of his writings for the Hawaiian language newspaper *Kuokoa* between 1866 and 1870. It contains much information on life at the courts of Kamehameha and his successors, as well as accounts of life in Honolulu in the early 1800s.[11]

The other significant Hawaiian sources are Kepelino Keauokalahi, S.N. Haleole, and Kēlou Kamakau. Kepelino was a descendant of the priestly line of Paao on his father's side. His mother was a daughter

---

9   Malo (1951), pp. 1–2.
10 Kamakau (1961). For his more ethnographic work see *Ka Poʻe kahiko: The People of Old* (1964).
11 Iʻī (1959), p. vii.

of Kamehameha I. He was born in Kailua, in the Kona district of Hawai'i around 1830, and began writing in the 1850s. Unlike most Hawaiian historians, he did not attend Lahainaluna as his family was Catholic. Kepelino's family heritage gave him access to Hawaiian priestly and chiefly traditions and the most valuable aspects of his works record chants and details of traditional Hawaiian religion not previously recorded. Haleole wrote a series of articles on Hawaiian religion in the years just prior to his death in 1866 that are based mainly on information he gathered in the 1850s. Translations of these writings were published in a subsequent collection of Hawaiian folklore and traditions. Kēlou Kamakau, a lesser chief of Kaawaloa, in the Kona district of Hawai'i, lived near to the important temple of Hikiau and his writings reveal a detailed knowledge of traditional ritual. He was around 50 years old in 1823.[12]

Most of these Hawaiian historians were associated with Kamehameha's victorious party. Malo, Kepelino and Kēlou Kamakau came from a core area of Kamehameha's support base, while I'ī was closely associated with the court of the Kamehameha dynasty. They came from the leeward coast of Hawai'i and O'ahu. For this reason Samuel Kamakau's *Ruling Chiefs of Hawaii* and volume two of Abraham Fornander's *An Account of the Polynesian Race* are invaluable for their accounts of the political history of each of the main islands in the archipelago. Fornander, a Swede who settled in Hawai'i in 1842, based his writings on information gathered by Hawaiians that he sent to different islands, Europeans familiar with Hawaiian culture, and the works of previous Hawaiian scholars. His works cover mythological, historical and ritual subjects. According to Barrere, most of volume two of *An Account of the Polynesian Race* relies heavily on Samuel Kamakau's writings. Fornander also referred to the work of Malo, Kepelino and S.N. Hakuole (possibly Hale'ole). The information was collected over a three-year period and published in three volumes from 1876 to 1885. After Fornander's death, Thomas G. Thrum edited another three volumes of the traditions Fornander collected and published them between 1916 and 1920 as *The Fornander Collection of Hawaiian Antiquities and Folklore*.[13]

---

12 Valeri (1985a), pp. xxvi–xxvii. Kepelino is discussed in Beckwith (1937, p. 4), and in Valeri (1985a, p. xxvi). Haleole's works are recorded in Thrum (1918–20, pp. 56–59). Some of Kēlou Kamakau's writings were published in Thrum, vol. 6 (1919–20), pp. 2–45.
13 Fornander (1969). See Hommon (1975), pp. 10–12; and Valeri (1985a), p. xxvii.

Hawaiian ethnography continued throughout the late 19th and early 20th centuries. Scholars such as Mary Kawena Pukui, Martha W. Beckwith, E.S.C. Handy and Peter Buck (Te Rangi Hiroa) continued the work of translating Hawaiian texts. Pukui and Beckwith translated the vast collection of Hawaiian language material housed in the Bishop Museum. Handy and Pukui devoted much time to the collection of information on Hawaiian life in the Kaʻū district of the Hawaiʻi. Buck produced a description of Hawaiian material culture, while Kenneth Emory was associated with archaeological surface surveys throughout the Hawaiian Islands and Polynesia.[14]

The proud tradition of mid-19th- and early 20th-century Hawaiian scholars has been carried on and developed by the current generation of indigenous Hawaiʻian scholars, as outlined in Chapter 1 in the work of the late Kanalu G. Terry Young and Jonathan Kay Kamakawiwoʻole Osorio and Lilikalā Kameʻeleihiwa.[15] Kameʻeleihiwa's colleague and contemporary Haunani K. Trask took issue with anthropological and other outsider representations of Hawaiian history in the early 1990s. Subsequently, just prior to his death, Young articulated a powerful vision of Hawaiian historical methodology.[16]

Armies are products of their societies. Information on social and economic organisation can be gleaned from two 19th-century inquiries into landholdings. In 1840 the Hawaiian monarchy replaced the old system of landholding with a new system based on European concepts of land ownership. To obtain land under the new system, commoners had to prove they lived on or cultivated the land in question. The records of this system reveal much about social organisation and land use. Later in the century, a government survey plotted and named all the basic ahupuaʻa land units.[17]

---

14   Valeri (1985a), p. xxvi; and Hommon (1975), p. 10. For example, see Alexander (1891); Buck (1964); Beckwith (1970); E.S.C. Handy & Mary Kawena Pukui, *The Polynesian Family System in Kaʻu, Hawaii* (Tokyo: Charles E. Tuttle Company, 1972); Handy & Handy (1972), and Pukui & Elbert (1986).
15   Haunani-Kay Trask, 'Cultures in Collision: Hawaiʻi and England, 1778', *Pacific Studies* (Laie), vol. 7, 1983, 91–117; Haunani-Kay Trask, 'Natives and Anthropologists: The Colonial Struggle', *The Contemporary Pacific*, vol. 3 (1), 1991, 159–67.
16   Young (1998); and Kanalu G. Terry Young, 'Kuleana: Toward a Historiography of Hawaiian National Consciousness, 1780–2001', *Hawaiian Journal of Law & Politics*, vol. 2, Summer 2006, 1–33.
17   Linnekin (1983), and Kirch & Sahlins (1992).

APPENDIX 3

Studies of warfare need details of the environment to assess impediments to movement and logistics. Archaeological investigations have focused on the structures of day-to-day subsistence. Settlement pattern studies have been conducted in a wide variety of environments throughout the islands and offer valuable contrasts to early European visitors' focus on Waimea and Kealakekua, both populous leeward areas that are not necessarily representative of other ecosystems. Since the mid-1970s, archaeology's subsistence-ecology orientation has been enriched through correlation with Hawaiian political traditions. Initially Robert Hommon led the way but, in recent years, others have followed his lead, most notably Pat Kirch in 2010 and 2012.[18]

The physical environment of Hawai'i remains essentially the same as it was in the 18th century. Human settlement has altered surface features such as vegetation patterns, and volcanic activity has changed Hawai'i, in particular, since the 1700s. Volcanic eruptions are datable, and remnants of unmodified vegetation allow for the reconstruction of original patterns in most localities. Modern scientific methods provide information on physical features such as landforms and soil types, rainfall patterns and vegetation. This information provides a valuable supplement with which to analyse Hawaiian settlement patterns and agricultural activity. A series of detailed maps produced by the United States Department of the Interior in the 1920s and 1950s are particularly useful as they predate the explosion of urban development since the 1960s that has engulfed many important battlefields and settlement sites.[19]

---

18   Hommon (1976), and Kirch (1984).
19   Kirch (1985), pp. 22–33; and Sherwin Carlquist, *Hawaii: A Natural History* (2nd edn) (Honolulu: SB Printers, Inc, 1980). See also US Department of the Interior, *Geological Survey* (Washington D.C.: 1928 and 1953–55).

Bibliography

Alexander, W.D., *A Brief History of the Hawaiian People*, New York, American Book Co., 1891.

Alland, Alexander Jr, *To Be Human: An Introduction to Anthropology*, New York, John Wiley & Sons, 1980.

Allen, J., 'The Role of Agriculture in the evolution of the Pre-contact Hawaiian State', *Asian Perspectives*, vol. 30, 1991, 117–32.

Anderson, Atholl J., *The Welcome of Strangers: An Ethnohistory of Southern Māori A.D. 1650–1850*, Dunedin, Otago University Press in association with Dunedin City Council, 1998.

Anderson, Benedict R., *Imagined Communities: Reflections on the Origin and Spread of Nationalism* (rev. edn), London, Verso, 1991.

Arendt, Hannah, *On Violence*, Orlando, Florida, Harvest Press, 1970.

Atkinson, R.F., *Knowledge and Explanation in History: An Introduction to the Philosophy of History*, New York, Cornell University Press, 1978. doi.org/10.1007/978-1-349-15965-9

Ayalon, David, *Gunpowder and Firearms in the Mamluk Kingdom: A Challenge to a Medieval Society* (2nd edn), London, Frank Cass and Company, 1978.

Bambridge, Tamatoa (ed.), *The Rahui: Legal pluralism in Polynesian traditional management of resources and territories*, Canberra, ANU Press, 2016. doi.org/10.22459/TR.03.2016

Bargatzy, Thomas, 'Beachcombers and Castaways as Innovators', *Journal of Pacific History*, 15 (1), 1980, 93–102. doi.org/10.1080/00223348008572391

Barnard, Charles H., *A Narrative of the Sufferings and Adventures of Captain Charles H. Barnard in a Voyage Round the World during the Years 1813, 1814, 1815 and 1816*, New York, J. Lindon, 1829.

Barrow, Terence, *Art and Life in Polynesia*, Wellington, A.H. and A.W. Reed, 1972.

Bayman, James M., 'The Precious "Middle Ground": Exchange and the Reconfiguration of Social Identity in the Hawaiian Kingdom', in C.D. Dillian & C.L. White (eds), *Trade and Exchange: Archaeological Studies from History and Prehistory*, Springer, 2010, pp. 129–48.

——, 'Technological Change and the Archaeology of Emergent Colonialism in the Kingdom of Hawai'i', *International Journal of Historical Archaeology*, vol. 13, 2009, 127–57. doi.org/10.1007/s10761-009-0076-z

Beaglehole, J.C. (ed.), *The Journals of Captain James Cook on his Voyages of Discovery*, vol. 3: *The Voyage of the Resolution and Discovery*, Cambridge, The Hakluyt Society, 1967.

Beckwith, M.W., *Hawaiian Mythology*, Honolulu, University of Hawai'i Press, 1970.

—— (ed.), *Kepelino's Traditions of Hawaii*, Honolulu, Bernice P. Bishop Museum, 1937.

Beggerly, Patricia Price, 'Hawaiian Initial Settlement – A Possible Model', in *Micronesian and Polynesian Voyaging – Three Readings*, Pacific Islands Program – Miscellaneous Work Papers, Honolulu, 1976, pp. 53–140.

Belich, James, *Making Peoples: A History of the New Zealanders from Polynesian Settlement to the End of the Nineteenth Century*, Auckland, Penguin, 1996.

Bell, Edward, 'Log of the Chatham', *Honolulu Mercury*, Sep. 1929.

Bellwood, Peter S., *A Settlement Pattern Survey, Hanatekua Valley, Hiva Oa, Marquesas Islands*, Pacific Anthropological Record no. 17, Honolulu, Bernice P. Bishop Museum, 1972.

Berg, Gerard M., 'The Sacred Musket – Tactics, Technology, and Power in Eighteenth Century Madagascar', *Comparative Studies of Society and History*, vol. 27, 1985, 261–79. doi.org/10.1017/S001041750001135X

Bergendorff, Steen, Hasager, Ulla & Henriques, Peter, 'Mythopraxis and History: On the Interpretation of the Makahiki', *Journal of the Polynesian Society*, vol. 97, 1988, 391–408.

Bierce, Ambrose, *The Devil's Dictionary*, New York, Sagamore Press, 1957.

Bingham, Hiram, *A Residence of Twenty-one Years in the Sandwich Islands* (2nd edn), Hartford, Hezekiah Huntington, 1848.

Biobaku, Saburi Oladeni, *Sources of Yoruba History*, Oxford, Clarendon Press, 1973.

Black, Francis L., 'Book Review of David Stannard, *Before the Horror*', *Pacific Studies*, vol. 13 (3), 1990, 269–79.

Black, Jeremy, *Rethinking Military History*, London, Routledge, 2004.

Blackmore, H.L., *British Military Firearms 1650–1850*, London, Herbert Jenkins, 1961.

Boit, John Jr, *The Journal of a Voyage Round the Globe 1795 and 1796*, University of Hawai'i microfilm 2890 no. 1, n.d.

Bossen, Claus, 'Chiefs Made War and War Made States? War and Early State Formation in Ancient Fiji and Hawaii', in Ton Otto, Henrik Thrane and Helle Vandkilde (eds), *Warfare and Society: Archaeological and Social Anthropological Perspectives*, Aarhus University Press, 2006a, pp. 237–59.

——, 'War as Practice, Power, and Processor: A Framework for the Analysis of War and Social Structural Change', in Ton Otto, Henrik Thrane and Helle Vandkilde (eds), *Warfare and Society: Archaeological and Social Anthropological Perspectives*, Aarhus University Press, 2006b, pp. 89–102.

Bradley, H.W., *The American Frontier in Hawaii: The Pioneers 1789–1843*, Stanford University Press, 1942.

Braudel, Fernand, *On History*, Sarah Mathews (trans.), University of Chicago Press, 1980.

Broome, Richard, 'The Struggle for Australia: Aboriginal – European Warfare, 1770–1830', in M. McKernan & M. Browne (eds) *Australia: Two Centuries of War and Peace*, Canberra, Australian War Memorial in association with Allen & Unwin, 1988, pp. 92–120.

Broughton, William Robert, *A Voyage of Discovery to the North Pacific Ocean Performed in His Majesty's Sloop Providence, and Her Tender, in the Years 1795, 1796, 1797, 1798*, New York, De Capo Press, 1967 (1804).

Brumfiel, Elizabeth M., 'Aztec State Making: Ecology, Structure and the Origin of the State', *American Anthropologist*, vol. 85 (2), 1983, 261–84. doi.org/10.1525/aa.1983.85.2.02a00010

Buck, Peter, *Arts and Crafts of Hawaii*, Honolulu, Bernice P. Bishop Museum, 1964.

Buick, T.L., *An Old New Zealander, or Te Rauparaha*, Christchurch, Capper Press, 1976 (1911).

Bushnell, Andrew F., '"The Horror" Reconsidered: An Evaluation of the Historical Evidence for Population Decline in Hawai'i, 1778–1803', *Pacific Studies*, 16 (3), 1993, 115–61.

Bushnell, O.A., *The Gifts of Civilization: Germs and Genocide in Hawai'i*, Honolulu, University of Hawai'i Press, 1993.

—— (ed.), *The Illustrated Atlas of Hawaii*, text by Gavan Daws (10th edn), Honolulu, Island Heritage, 1987.

Cachola-Abad, C. Kehaulani, 'Evaluating the Orthodox Dual Settlement Model for the Hawaiian Islands: An Analysis of Artefact Distribution and Hawaiian Oral Traditions', in Michael Graves & Roger C. Green (eds), *The Evolution and Organisation of Prehistoric Society in Polynesia*, New Zealand Archaeological Association Monograph 19, Auckland Museum, 1993, pp. 13–32.

Campbell, Archibald, *A Voyage Round the World from 1806 to 1812*, Honolulu, University of Hawai'i Press, 1967 (1822).

Campbell, I.C., 'European–Polynesian Encounters: A Critique of the Pearson Thesis', *Journal of Pacific History*, vol. 29 (2), 1994, 222–31.

——, *A History of the Pacific Islands*, Christchurch, University of Canterbury Press, 1989.

——, 'Polynesian Perceptions of Europeans in the Eighteenth and Nineteenth Centuries', *Pacific Studies*, vol. 5 (2), 1982, 64–80.

Carleton, H., *The Life of Henry Williams, Archdeacon of Waimate*, vol. 1, Auckland, Wilsons and Horton, 1874.

Carlquist, Sherwin, *Hawaii: A Natural History* (2nd edn), Honolulu, SB Printers Inc., 1980.

Carneiro, Robert L., 'War and Peace: Alternating Realities in Human History', in S.P. Reyna & R.E. Downs (eds), *Studying War: Anthropological Perspectives*, Langhorne, Penn., Gordon and Breach, 1994, pp. 3–27.

——, 'The Chiefdom: Precursor of the State', in Grant D. Jones & Robert R. Kautz (eds), *The Transition to Statehood in the New World*, Cambridge University Press, 1981, pp. 37–79.

——, 'A Theory of the Origin of the State', *Science*, vol. 169 (1970), 733–38. doi.org/10.1126/science.169.3947.733

Cartwright, Bruce, 'Note on Hawaiian Geneologies', *38th Annual Report of the Hawaiian Historical Society*, Honolulu, 1929, pp. 45–47.

——, 'Some Early Foreign Residents of the Hawaiian Islands', *25th Annual Report of the Hawaiian Historical Society for the Year 1916*, Honolulu, 1917, pp. 57–64.

Cary, W.S., *Wrecked in the Feejees*, Nantucket, Mass., The Inquirer and Mirror Press, 1922.

Chandler, David, *The Campaigns of Napoleon*, London, Weidenfield and Nicholson, 1966.

Charlot, John, 'A Note on the Hawaiian Prophecy of Kapihe', *The Journal of Pacific History*, vol. 39 (3), 2004, 375–77. doi.org/10.1080/0022334042000290414

Chinen, J.J., *The Great Māhele: Hawai'i's Land Division of 1848*, Honolulu, University of Hawai'i Press, 1958.

Claessen, Henri J.M., 'War and State Formation: What is the Connection?', in Ton Otto, Henrik Thrane & Helle Vandkilde (eds), *Warfare and Society: Archaeological and Social Anthropological Perspectives*, Aarhus University Press, 2006, pp. 217–26.

Claessen, Henri J.M. & Skalnik, Peter, 'The Early State: Models and Reality', in Henri J.M. Claessen & Peter Skalnik (eds), *The Early State*, The Hague, Mouton Publishers, 1978a, pp. 637–50. doi.org/10.1515/9783110813326.637

——, 'The Early State: Theories and Hypotheses', in Henri J.M. Claessen & Peter Skalnik (eds), *The Early State*, The Hague, Mouton Publishers, 1978b, pp. 3–30.

Clark, Ross, 'Language', in Jesse D. Jennings (ed.), *The Prehistory of Polynesia*, Canberra, Australian National University Press, 1979, pp. 249–70. doi.org/10.4159/harvard.9780674181267.c11

Clunie, F., *Fijian Weapons and Warfare*, Suva, Fiji Museum, 1977.

Colnett, James, *Colnett's Journal Aboard the Argonaut*, New York, Greenwood Press, 1968.

Cook, James & King, James, *A Voyage to the Pacific Ocean … on His Majesty's Ships Resolution and Discovery*, Dublin, Chamberlaine et al., 1784.

Cordy, Ross, *The Rise and Fall of the O'ahu Kingdom*, Honolulu, Mutual Publishing, 2002.

——, *Exalted Sits the Chief: The Ancient History of Hawai'i Island*, Honolulu, Mutual Publishing, 2000.

——, 'The Rise and Fall of the O'ahu Kingdom: A Brief History of O'ahu History', in Janet Davidson, Geoffrey Irwin, Foss Leach, Andrew Pawley & Dorothy Brown (eds), *Oceanic Culture History: Essays in Honour of Roger Green*, New Zealand Journal of Archaeology Special Publication, Dunedin, 1996, pp. 591–613.

——, *A Study of Prehistoric Social Change: The Development of Complex Societies in the Hawaiian Islands*, New York, Academic Press, 1981.

——, 'Cultural Adaptation and Evolution in Hawaii: A Suggested New Sequence', *Journal of the Polynesian Society*, vol. 83, 1974a, 180–91.

——, 'The Tahitian Migration to Hawaii ca. 1100–1300 AD: An Argument Against Its Occurrence', *New Zealand Archaeological Association Newsletter*, no. 17, 1974b, 65–76.

——, 'The Effects of European Contact on Hawaiian Agricultural Systems: 1778–1819', *Ethnohistory*, vol. 19 (4), 1972, 393–418.

Corney, Peter, *Voyages on the Northern Pacific: Narrative of Several Trading Voyages from 1813 to 1818*, Honolulu, Thos. G. Thrum, 1896.

Cromwell, Jarvis, 'Journal of a Trading Voyage Around the World, 1805–1808', *New York Historical Society Quarterly*, vol. 62 (2), 1978, 87–132.

Crosby, A.W., 'Hawaiian Depopulation as a Model for the Amerindian Experience', in Terence Ranger & Paul Slack (eds), *Epidemics and Ideas: Essays on the Historical Perception of Pestilence*, Cambridge University Press, 1992, pp. 175–201. doi.org/10.1017/CBO9780511563645.009

——, *Ecological Imperialism: The Biological Expansion of Europe, 900–1900*, Cambridge University Press, 1986.

Cruise, R.A., *Journal of a Ten Month Residence in New Zealand* (2nd edn), Christchurch, Capper Press, 1974 (1824).

Currey, B., 'Famine in the Pacific: Losing the Chances of Change', *Geojournal*, vol. 4 (5), 1980, 447–66. doi.org/10.1007/BF01795928

D'Arcy, Paul, 'Pacific Islander Culture of War, Including Maori', in Daniel Coetzee & Lee W. Eysturlid (eds), *Philosophers of War: The Evolution of History's Greatest Military Thinkers*, vol. 1: *The Ancient World to Premodern World, 3000 BCE – 1815 CE*, Santa Barbara, Praeger, 2013, pp. 376–79.

——, 'Oceania: The Environmental History of One Third of the Globe', in J.R. McNeill & E.C. Stewart (eds), *A Companion to Global Environmental History*, Oxford, Wiley Blackwell, 2012, pp. 196–221. doi.org/10.1002/9781118279519.ch12

——, *Peoples of the Pacific: the History of Oceania to 1870*, The Pacific World: Lands, Peoples and History of the Pacific, 1500–1900, vol. 3, Aldershot, Ashgate/Valorium, 2008.

——, *The People of the Sea: Environment, Identity, and History in Oceania*, Honolulu, University of Hawai'i Press, 2006.

——, 'Warfare and State Formation in Hawai'i: The Limits on Violence as a Means of Political Consolidation', *The Journal of Pacific History*, vol. 38 (1), 2003a, 29–52.

——, 'Cultural Divisions and Island Environments Since the Time of Dumont d'Urville', *The Journal of Pacific History*, vol. 38 (2), 2003b, 217–35. doi.org/10.1080/0022334032000120549

——, 'Maori and Muskets from a Pan-Polynesian Perspective', *New Zealand Journal of History*, vol. 34 (1), April 2000, 117–32.

Davenport, William H., *Pi'o: An Enquiry into the Marriage of Brothers and Sisters and other Close Relatives in Old Hawai'i*, New York, University Press of America, 1994.

——, 'The "Hawaiian Cultural Revolution": Some Political and Economic Considerations', *American Anthropologist*, vol. 71, 1969, 1–20. doi.org/10.1525/aa.1969.71.1.02a00020

Davidson, J.W., 'Lauaki Namalau'ulu Mamoe: A Traditionalist in Samoan Politics', in J.W. Davidson & Deryck Scarr (eds), *Pacific Island Portraits*, Canberra, Australian National University Press, 1970, pp. 267–99.

Daws, Gavan, *Honolulu: The First Century*, Honolulu, Mutual Publishing, 2006.

——, 'The Death of Captain Cook', *Pacific Islands Monthly*, Apr. 1984, 15–17, and May 1984, 51–53.

——, *Shoal of Time: A History of the Hawaiian Islands*, Honolulu, University of Hawai'i Press, 1968a.

——, 'Kealakekua Bay Revisited: A Note on the Death of Captain Cook', *Journal of Pacific History*, vol. 3, 1968b, 21–23. doi.org/10.1080/00223346808572122

Daws, Gavan, with George Cooper, *Land and Power in Hawaii*, Honolulu, Benchmark Books, 1985.

Dega, M.F. & Kirch, P.V., 'A Modified Culture History of Anahulu Valley, Oʻahu, Hawaiʻi, and its Significance for Hawaiian Prehistory', *Journal of the Polynesian Society*, vol. 111 (2), June 2002, 107–26.

Dening, Greg, *Performances*, Melbourne University Press, 1996, pp. 64–65.

——, *History's Anthropology: The Death of William Gooch*, Lanham, Maryland, University Press of America, 1988.

——, *Islands and Beaches: Discourse on a Silent Land, Marquesas 1774–1880*, Honolulu, University of Hawaiʻi Press, 1980.

Denoon, Donald, 'Pacific Island Depopulation: Natural or Un-natural History?', in Linda Bryder & Derek A. Dow (eds), *New Countries and Old Medicine*, Auckland, Pyramid Press, 1994, pp. 324–39.

Department of Geography, University of Hawaiʻi at Mānoa, *Atlas of Hawaii* (2nd edn), Honolulu, University of Hawaiʻi Press, 1983.

Desha, S.L., *Kamehameha and his Warrior Kekūhaupiʻo*, F.N. Frazier (trans.), Honolulu, Kamehameha Schools Press, 2000.

Dibble, Sheldon, *A History of the Sandwich Islands*, Honolulu, Thos. G. Thrum, 1909.

Dinnen, Sinclair, 'The Twin Processes of Nation Building and State Building', *State, Society and Governance in Melanesia Briefing Note*, no. 1/2007, Society and Governance in Melanesia Program, The Australian National University, 2007.

Dixon, B., Conte, P.J., Nagahara, V. & Hodgins, W.K., 'Risk Minimization and the Traditional *Ahupuaʻa* in Kahikinui, Island of Maui, Hawaiʻi', *Asian Perspectives*, vol. 38, 1999, 229–55.

Dixon, George, *A Voyage Round the World: But More Particularly to the North-West Coast of America – Performed in 1785, 1786 and 1788*, Bibliotheca Australiana no. 37, New York, Da Capo Press, 1968.

Douglas, Bronwen, 'Rank, Power, Authority: A Reassessment of Traditional Leadership in South Pacific Societies', *Journal of Pacific History*, vol. 14, 1979, 2–27. doi.org/10.1080/00223347908572362

Dukas, Neil, *Military History of Sovereign Hawaii*, Honolulu, Mutual Publishing, 2004.

Dunnigan, James F., *How to Make War: A Comprehensive Guide to Modern Warfare*, New York, William Morrow & Co., 1982.

Dupuy, R.E. & Dupuy, T.N., 'Gift Exchange and Interpretations of Captain Cook in the Traditional Kingdoms of the Hawaiian Islands', *The Journal of Pacific History*, vol. 46 (3), 2011, 275–92. doi.org/10.1080/00223344.2011.632895

——, 'Population Trends in Hawai'i Before 1778', *Hawaiian Journal of History*, vol. 28, 1994, 1–20.

——, *The Encyclopaedia of Military History from 3500B.C. to the Present* (rev. edn), London, Jones Publishing Co, 1977.

Dye, Thomas S., 'The Causes and Consequences of a Decline in the Prehistoric Marquesan Fishing Industry', in D.E. Yen & J.M.J. Mummery (eds), *Pacific Production Systems: Approaches to Economic Prehistory*, Occasional Papers in Prehistory, no. 18, Canberra, Department of Prehistory, RSPAS, The Australian National University, 1990, pp. 70–84.

Dyer, Gwynne, *War*, New York, Crown Publishers, 1985.

Earle, Timothy K., *How Chiefs Come to Power: The Political Economy in Prehistory*, Stanford University Press, 1997.

——, 'The Evolution of Chiefdoms', *Current Anthropology*, vol. 30 (1), 1989, 84–88. doi.org/10.1086/203717

——, 'Prehistoric Irrigation in the Hawaiian Islands', *Archaeology and Physical Anthropology in Oceania*, vol. 15 (1), 1980, 1–28.

——, *Economic and Social Organization of a Complex Chiefdom: Halelea District, Kauai, Hawaii*, University of Michigan – Anthropological Paper no. 63, Ann Arbor, 1978.

Edgar, Thomas, 'Extracts from Journal', 14 Feb. 1779, copy of MS, Hocken Library, Dunedin.

Elder, J.R. (ed.), *The Letters and Journals of Samuel Marsden 1765–1838* (1st edn), Dunedin, Coulls Somerville Wilkie Ltd, and A.H. Reed, 1932.

Ellis, William, *Polynesian Researches*, Tokyo, Charles E. Tuttle Company, 1969 (1859).

Elvin, Mark, 'Three Thousand Years of Unstable Growth: China's Environment from Archaic Times to the Present', *East Asian History*, no. 6, 1993, 7–46.

Emerson, Joseph S., 'The Bow and Arrow in Hawaii', *25th Annual Report of the Hawaiian Historical Society for the Year 1916*, Honolulu, 1917, pp. 52–55.

Emory, Kenneth P., 'Warfare', in E.S.C. Handy et al., *Ancient Hawaiian Civilization: A Series of Lectures Delivered at the Kamehameha Schools* (rev. edn), Tokyo, Charles E. Tuttle Company, 1965, pp. 233–40.

Ernst, Thomas M., 'A Comment', in 'A Review Symposium on *The Apotheosis of Captain Cook: European Mythmaking in the Pacific*', *Social Analysis*, vol. 34, Dec. 1993, 66–69.

Farmer, S.S., *Tonga the Friendly Islands, With a Sketch of their Mission History*, London, Hamilton, Adams & Co., 1855.

Feher, J., *Hawaii: A Pictorial History*, Honolulu, Bernice P. Bishop Museum, 1969.

Femia, Joseph V., *Gramsci's Political Thought: Hegemony, Consciousness, and the Revolutionary Process*, Oxford, Clarendon Press, 1981.

Ferguson, R. Brian (ed.), *Warfare, Culture, and Environment*, Orlando, Florida, Academic Press, 1984.

Finney, Ben, et al., 'Hawaiian Historians and the First Pacific History Seminar', in N. Gunson (ed.), *The Changing Pacific: Essays in Honor of H.E. Maude*, Melbourne, Oxford University Press, 1978, pp. 308–16.

Fitzsimmons, James Patrick, 'Warfare in Old Hawaii: The Transformation of a Poleomological System', MA Thesis, University of Hawai'i, 1969.

Fornander, Abraham, *Ancient History of the Hawaiian People to the Times of Kamehameha 1*, vol. 2: *An Account of the Polynesian Race*, Rutland, Vermont, Charles E. Tuttle Company, 1969 (1879).

Fosten, B., *The British Foot Guards at Waterloo, June 1815*, London, Almark, n.d.

Fraenkel, Jon, 'The Coming Anarchy in Oceania? A Critique of the "Africanisation of the South Pacific" Thesis', *Journal of Commonwealth and Comparative Politics*, vol. 42 (1), 2004, 1–34.

Friedman, Jonathan, 'Catastrophe and Continuity in Social Evolution', in C. Renfrew, M.J. Rowlands & Barbara Abbot Segraves (eds), *Theory and Explanation in Archaeology: The Southampton Conference*, New York, Academic Press, 1982, pp. 175–96.

Fry, Greg & Kabutaulaka, Tarcisius Tara, 'Political Legitimacy and State-building Intervention in the Pacific', in Greg Fry & Tarcisius Tara Kabutaulaka (eds), *Intervention and State-building in the Pacific: The Legitimacy of 'Cooperative Intervention'*, Manchester & New York, Manchester University Press, 2008, pp. 1–36.

Fuller, J.F.C., *Armament and History*, London, Charles Scribner's Sons, 1945.

Fussel, Paul, *The Great War and Modern Memory*, Oxford University Press, 1975.

Galbraith, John Kenneth, *The Anatomy of Power*, London, Corgi, 1985.

——, *The Nature of Mass Poverty*, New York, Penguin, 1979.

Galtung, Johan, 'Twenty-five Years of Peace Research: Ten Challenges and Some Responses', *Journal of Peace Research*, vol. 22 (2), 1985, 141–58. doi.org/10.1177/002234338502200205

——, *The European Community: A Superpower in the Making*, London, George Allen and Unwin, 1973.

Gast, Ross H. & Conrad, Agnes (eds), *Don Francisco de Paula Marin: A Biography with the Letters and Journals of Francisco de Paula Marin*, Honolulu, University of Hawai'i Press, 1973.

Gilpin, Robert, 'The Theory of Hegemonic War', *Journal of Interdisciplinary History*, vol. 18 (4), 1988, 591–614. doi.org/10.2307/204816

Glossop, Ronald J., *Confronting War: An Examination of Humanity's Most Pressing Problem*, North Carolina, McFarland, 1983.

Glover, Michael, *The Velvet Glove: The Decline and Fall of Moderation in War*, London, Hodder and Stoughton, 1982.

Godelier, Maurice, 'Infrastructures, Societies, and History', *Current Anthropology*, vol. 19 (4), 1978, 763–71. doi.org/10.2307/204816

Goldberg, Neil J. & Findlow, Frank J., 'A Quantitative Analysis of Roman Military Operations in Britain, Circa A.D. 43 to 238', in R. Brian Ferguson (ed.), *Warfare, Culture and Environment*, Orlando, Florida, Academic Press, 1984, pp. 359–85.

Goldman, Irving, *Ancient Polynesian Society*, University of Chicago Press, 1970.

Goldschmidt, Arthur Jr, *A Concise History of the Middle East* (2nd edn), Boulder, Colorado, Westview Press, 1983.

Golovin, V.M, *Around the World on the Kamchatka, 1817–1819*, Ella L. Wisnell (trans.), Honolulu, Hawaiian Historical Society and University of Hawai'i Press, 1979.

Goodenough, Ward H., 'Sky World and This World: The Place of Kachaw in Micronesian Cosmology', *American Anthropologist*, vol. 88 (3), 1986, 551–68. doi.org/10.1525/aa.1986.88.3.02a00010

Green, R.C., *Makaha Valley: Prior to 1880 A.D.*, Pacific Anthropological Records no. 31, Honolulu, Bernice P. Bishop Museum, 1980.

Griffith, P., *Forward into Battle: Fighting Tactics from Waterloo to Vietnam*, Chichester, Great Britain, Anthony Bird, 1981.

Gunson, Niel, 'The Coming of Foreigners', in Noel Rutherford (ed.), *Friendly Islands: A History of Tonga*, Melbourne, Oxford University Press, 1977, pp. 90–113.

Handy, E.S.C. & Handy, E.G., *Native Planters of Old Hawaii: Their Life, Lore, and Environments*, Honolulu, Bernice P. Bishop Museum, 1972.

Handy, E.S.C. & Pukui, Mary Kawena, *The Polynesian Family System in Ka'u, Hawaii*, Tokyo, Charles E. Tuttle Company, 1972.

Hawkes, C.W., 'Archaeological Theory and Method: Some Suggestions from the Old World', in Morton H. Fried (ed.), *Readings in Anthropology*, vol. 1 (2nd edn), New York, Thomas Y. Crowell Co., 1968, pp. 434–49.

Heath, T., Manuscript, 16 Apr. 1838 (SSL 11) transcribed, typed copy in L. Tallentire, 'Samoa: The Eleven Year War', BA Hons Thesis, University of Otago, Dunedin, 1980.

Heider, Karl G., 'Archaeological Assumptions and Ethnographical Facts: A Cautionary Tale from New Guinea', *Southwestern Journal of Archaeology*, vol. 23 (1967), 52–64. doi.org/10.1086/soutjanth.23.1.3629293

Heilbroner, Robert, *Marxism: For and Against*, New York, Norton, 1980.

Held, Robert, *The Age of Firearms*, Northfield, Illinois, Gun Digest Company, 1970.

Henriques, Edgar, 'Notes Regarding Kamehameha I by Edgar Henriques', *26th Annual Report of the Hawaiian Historical Society for the Year 1917*, Honolulu, 1918, pp. 62–70.

Hodder, Ian, 'The Contribution of the Long Term', in Ian Hodder (ed.), *Archaeology as Long-term History*, Cambridge University Press, 1987, pp. 1–8.

Hole, Frank & Heizer, Robert F., *An Introduction to Prehistoric Archaeology* (2nd edn), New York, Holt, Rinehart and Winston Inc., 1969.

Hommon, Robert J., *The Ancient Hawaiian State: Origins of a Political Society*, New York and Oxford, Oxford University Press, 2013. doi.org/10.1093/acprof:oso/9780199916122.001.0001

——, 'Social Evolution in Ancient Hawaii', in P.V. Kirch (ed.), *Island Societies: Archaeological Approaches to Evolution and Transformation*, Cambridge University Press, 1987, pp. 55–68.

——, 'The Formation of Primitive States in Pre-contact Hawaii', PhD Thesis, University of Arizona, 1976.

——, *Use and Control of Hawaiian Inter-Island Channels: Polynesian Hawaii: A.D. 1400–1794*, Honolulu, Office of the Governor of Hawaii, 1975.

Howard, Alan, 'Review of *Kingship and Sacrifice*', *Journal of the Polynesian Society*, vol. 95 (4), 1986, 530–37.

Howard, Michael, et al., 'What is Military History?', in Juliet Gardiner (ed.), *What is History Today?*, London, Macmillan, 1988, pp. 4–17. doi.org/10.1007/978-1-349-19161-1_2

——, *War in European History*, Oxford University Press, 1976.

Howay, Frederic W. (ed.), *The Journal of Captain James Colnett aboard the Argonaut from April 26, 1789 to November 3, 1791*, Toronto, The Champlain Society, 1940.

Howe, K.R., *Where the Waves Fall: A New South Sea Islands History from First Settlement to Colonial Rule*, Sydney, Allen and Unwin, 1984.

——, 'Firearms and Indigenous Warfare: A Case Study', *Journal of Pacific History*, vol. 9, 1974, 21–38. doi.org/10.1080/00223347408572242

Hui, Victoria Tin-Bor, *War and State Formation in Ancient China an Early Modern Europe*, New York, Cambridge University Press, 2005. doi.org/10.1017/CBO9780511614545

Hunt, Terry L., 'Book Review of David Stannard, *Before the Horror*', *Pacific Studies* (Laie), vol. 13 (3), 1990, 255–63.

Iʻi, John Papa, *Fragments of Hawaiian History*, Honolulu, Bernice P. Bishop Museum, 1959.

Inglis, Kerri A., 'Review of P.V. Kirch, *A Shark Going Inland Is My Chief: The Island Civilization of Ancient Hawaiʻi*', *Journal of Interdisciplinary History*, vol. 44 (2), Autumn 2013, 268–69. doi.org/10.1162/JINH_r_00552

Jarves, James Jackson, *History of the Hawaiian Islands* (4th edn), Honolulu, Henry M. Whitney, 1872.

——, *History of the Hawaiian or Sandwich Islands*, Boston, Tappan and Dennet, 1843.

Jones, Grant D. & Kautz, Robert R., 'Issues in the Study of New World State Formation', in Grant D. Jones & Robert R. Kautz (eds), *The Transition to Statehood in the New World*, Cambridge University Press, 1981, pp. 3–34.

Judd, Bernice, *Voyages to Hawaii before 1860*, Honolulu, University of Hawaiʻi Press, 1974.

Kahananui, Dorothy (ed.), *Ka Moolelo Hawaii*, Honolulu, University of Hawai'i, Committee for the Preservation and Study of Hawaiian Language, Art and Culture, 1984.

Kahn, Miram, 'Sunday Christians, Monday Sorcerers: Selective Adaptation to Missionization in Wamira', *Journal of Pacific History*, vol. 18, 1983, 96–112. doi.org/10.1080/00223348308572461

Kamakau, Samuel M., *Tales and Traditions of the People of Old. Nā Mo'olelo a ka Po'e Kahiko*, Dorothy B. Barrere (ed.), M.K. Pukui (trans.), Honolulu, Bernice P. Bishop Museum, 1991.

——, *The Works of the People of Old: Na Hāna o ka Po'e Kahiko*, Honolulu, Bernice P. Bishop Museum, 1976.

——, *Ka Po'e Kahiko: The People of Old*, Honolulu, Bernice P. Bishop Museum, 1964.

——, *Ruling Chiefs of Hawaii*, Honolulu, Kamehameha Schools Press, 1961.

Kame'eleihiwa, Lilikalā, *Native Land and Foreign Desires*, Honolulu, Bernice P. Bishop Museum Press, 1992.

——, 'Land and the Promise of Capitalism: A Dilemma for the Hawaiian Chiefs of the 1848 Māhele', PhD Thesis, University of Hawai'i at Mānoa, 1986.

Kaplanoff, Mark D. (ed.), *Joseph Ingraham's Journal of the Brigantine Hope on a Voyage to the Northwest Coast of North America 1790–1792*, Barre, Mass., Imprint Society, 1971.

Kea, R.A., 'Firearms and Warfare on the Gold and Slave Coasts from the Sixteenth to the Nineteenth Centuries', *Journal of African History*, vol. 12 (2), 1971, 185–213. doi.org/10.1017/S002185370001063X

Keegan, John, *The Price of Admiralty: War at Sea from Man-of-War to Submarine*, London, Arrow Books, 1988.

——, *The Mask of Command*, London, Penguin, 1987.

——, *The Face of Battle*, London, Penguin, 1976.

Keegan, John & Holmes, Richard, *Soldiers: A History of Men in Battle*, New York, Viking, 1985.

Keesing, Roger M., 'Reply to Trask', *The Contemporary Pacific*, vol. 3, 1991, 168–71.

——, 'Creating the Past: Custom and Identity in the Contemporary Pacific', *The Contemporary Pacific*, vol. 1, 1989, 19–42.

Kelly, M. (ed.), *Hawaii in 1819: A Narrative Account by Louis Claude de Saules de Freycinet*, Honolulu, Bernice P. Bishop Museum Press, 1978.

Kikuchi, W.K., 'Prehistoric Hawaiian Fishponds', *Science*, vol. 193, 1976, 295–99. doi.org/10.1126/science.193.4250.295

Kirch, P.V., *A Shark Going Inland Is My Chief: The Island Civilization of Ancient Hawai'i*, Berkeley, University of California Press, 2012.

——, *How Chiefs Became Kings: Divine Kingship and the Rise of Archaic States in Ancient Hawai'i*, Los Angeles & London, University of California Press, 2010.

——, '"Like Shoals of Fish": Archaeology and Population in Pre-contact Hawai'i', in P.V. Kirch & J.L. Rallu (eds), *The Growth and Collapse of Pacific Island Societies: Archaeological and Demographic Perspectives*, Honolulu, University of Hawai'i Press, 2007, pp. 52–69.

——, *The Wet and the Dry: Irrigation and Agricultural Intensification in Polynesia*, University of Chicago Press, 1994.

——, *Anahulu: The Anthropology of History in the Kingdom of Hawai'i*, vol. 2: *The Archaeology of History*, University of Chicago Press, 1992.

——, 'Regional Variation and Local Style: A Neglected Dimension in Hawaiian Prehistory', *Pacific Studies* (Laie), vol. 13 (2), 1990a, 41–54.

——, 'Review of David Stannard, *Before the Horror*', *The Contemporary Pacific*, vol. 2, Fall 1990b, 394–96.

——, *Feathered Gods and Fishhooks: An Introduction to Hawaiian Archaeology and Prehistory*, Honolulu, University of Hawai'i Press, 1985.

——, *The Evolution of the Polynesian Chiefdoms*, Cambridge University Press, 1984.

Kirch, P.V. & Green, R.C., 'History, Phylogeny, and Evolution in Polynesia', *Current Anthropology*, vol. 28, 1987, 431–43, 452–56. doi.org/10.1086/203547

Kirch, P.V. & Hunt, Terry L. (eds), *Historical Ecology in the Pacific Islands: Prehistoric Environmental and Landscape Change*, New Haven, Yale University Press, 1997.

Kirch, P.V. & Rallu, J.L. (eds), *The Growth and Collapse of Pacific Island Societies: Archaeological and Demographic Perspectives*, Honolulu, University of Hawai'i Press, 2007.

Kirch, P.V. & Sahlins, Marshall, *Anahulu: The Anthropology of History in the Kingdom of Hawaii*, vol. 1: *Historical Ethnography*, University of Chicago Press, 1992.

Knauft, Bruce M., 'Monument of Miscast Error: Obeyesekere Versus Sahlins and Captain Cook', in 'A Review Symposium on *The Apotheosis of Captain Cook: European Mythmaking in the Pacific*', *Social Analysis*, vol. 34, Dec. 1993, 34–42.

Kohl, Phil, 'Force, History and the Evolutionist Paradigm', in Mathew Spriggs (ed.), *Marxist Perspectives in Archaeology*, Cambridge University Press, 1984, pp. 127–34.

Kolb, Michael J., 'The Origins of Monumental Architecture in Ancient Hawai'i', *Current Anthropology*, vol. 47, 2006, 657–65. doi.org/10.1086/506285

Kolb, Michael J., et al., 'Monumentality and the Rise of Religious Authority in Precontact Hawai'i [and Comments and Reply]', *Current Anthropology*, vol. 35 (5), Dec. 1994, 521–47. doi.org/10.1086/204315

Kolb, Michael J. & Dixon, Boyd, 'Landscapes of War: Rules and Conventions of Conflict in Ancient Hawai'i (And Elsewhere)', *American Antiquity*, vol. 67 (3), Jul. 2002, 514–34. doi.org/10.2307/1593824

Krauskopf, Konrad B. & Beiser, Arthur, *The Physical Universe* (5th edn), New York, McGraw Hill, 1985.

Kroeber, A.L., *Anthropology*, New York, Harcourt, Brace and World, 1948.

Kunitz, Stephen, *Disease and Social Diversity: The European Impact on the Health of Non-Europeans*, Oxford University Press, 1994.

Kurtz, Donald V., 'The Legitimation of Early Inchoate States', in Henri J.M. Claesson & Peter Skalnik (eds), *The Study of the State*, The Hague, Mouton Publishers, 1981, pp. 177–200. doi.org/10.1515/9783110825794.177

Kuykendall, R.S., *The Hawaiian Kingdom*, vol. 1: *1778–1854, Foundation and Transformation*, Honolulu, University of Hawai'i Press, 1938.

Ladefoged, T.N., 'Variable Development of Dryland Agriculture in Hawai'i: A Fine-Grained Chronology from the Kohala Field System, Hawai'i Island', *Current Anthropology*, vol. 49, 2008, 771–802. doi.org/10.1086/591424

Ladefoged, T.N. & Graves, M.W., 'The Formation of Hawaiian Territories', in I. Lilley (ed.), *Archaeology of Oceania: Australia and the Pacific Islands*, Oxford, Blackwell, 2006, pp. 259–83. doi.org/10.1002/9780470773475.ch13

Ladefoged, T.N., Kirch, P.V., Gon, S.M. III, Chadwick, O.A., Hartshorn, A.S. & Vitousek, P.M., 'Opportunities and Constraints for Intensive Agriculture in the Hawaiian Archipelago Prior to European Contact', *Journal of Archaeological Science*, vol. 36, 2009, 2374–83. doi.org/10.1016/j.jas.2009.06.030

Lamb, Jonathan, 'Social Facts, Political Fictions and Un-Relative Events: Obeyesekere on Sahlins', in 'A Review Symposium on *The Apotheosis of Captain Cook: European Mythmaking in the Pacific*', Social Analysis, vol. 34, Dec. 1993, 56–60.

Lamb, W. Kaye (ed.), *The Voyages of George Vancouver 1791–1795*, London, The Hakluyt Society, 1984.

Langdon, Robert, 'Benevolent Invaders Among Hawaii's Aborigines', in Donald C. Laycock & Werner Winter (eds), *A World of Language: Papers Presented to Professor S.A. Wurm on His 65th Birthday, Pacific Linguistics, c-100*, 1987, pp. 371–79.

——, *The Lost Caravel*, Sydney, Pacific Publications, 1975.

Latukefu, S., *Church and State in Tonga*, Canberra, Australian National University Press, 1974.

Law, Robin, *The Oyo Empire c.1600 – c.1836: A West African Imperialism in the Era of the Atlantic Slave Trade*, Oxford, Clarendon, 1977.

——, 'The Constitutional Troubles of Oyo in the Eighteenth Century', *Journal of African History*, vol. 12 (1), 1971, 25–44. doi.org/10.1017/S0021853700000050

Leckie, Robert, *Warfare*, New York, Harper and Row, 1970.

Levin, Stephanie Seto, 'The Overthrow of the Kapu System in Hawaii', *Journal of the Polynesian Society*, vol. 77 (4), 1968, 402–30.

Linnekin, Jocelyn, *Sacred Queens and Women of Consequence: Rank, Gender, and Colonialism in the Hawaiian Islands*, Ann Arbor, University of Michigan Press, 1990.

——, 'Who Made the Feather Cloaks? A Problem in Hawaiian Gender Relations', *Journal of the Polynesian Society*, vol. 97 (3), 1988, 265–80.

——, 'Statistical Analysis of the Great Māhele: Some Preliminary Findings', *Journal of Pacific History*, vol. 22 (1), 1987, 15–33. doi.org/10.1080/00223348708572549

——, 'The Hui Lands of Keanae: Hawaiian Land Tenure and the Great Māhele', *Journal of the Polynesian Society*, vol. 92 (2), 1983, 169–88.

Lisiansky, Urey, *A Voyage Round the World in the Years 1803, 4, 5 and 6*, New York, De Capo Press, 1967 (1814).

Lloyd, P.C., 'The Political Development of West African Kingdoms', review article, *Journal of African History*, vol. 9 (2), 1968, 319–29. doi.org/10.1017/S0021853700008902

Luker, Victoria, 'Mothers of the Taukei: Fijian Women and "the Decrease of Race"', PhD Thesis, The Australian National University, 1997.

Lukes, Stephen, 'Power and Authority', in R. Nisbett & T. Baltimore (eds), *A History of Sociological Analysis*, New York, Basic Books, 1978, pp. 633–76.

Lydgate, John M., 'Ka-umu-alii, the Last King of Kauaʻi', *24th Annual Report of the Hawaiian Historical Society for the Year 1915*, Honolulu, 1916, pp. 21–43.

MacIver, R.M., *The Web of Government* (rev. edn), New York, The Free Press, 1965.

Māhina, 'Okusitino, 'The Poetics of Tongan Traditional History, Tala-ē-fonua: An Ecology-Centred Concept of Culture and History', *Journal of Pacific History*, vol. 38 (1), 1993, 109–121.

Makemson, M.W., *The Morning Star Rises: An Account of Polynesian Astronomy*, New Haven, Yale University Press, 1941.

Malo, David, *Hawaiian Antiquities*, Nathaniel B. Emerson (trans.), Honolulu, Bernice P. Bishop Museum, 1951.

——, 'On the Decrease of Population in the Hawaiian Islands', *Hawaiian Spectator*, Apr. 1839, p. 125.

Mann, Michael, *The Sources of Social Power*, vol. 1, Cambridge University Press, 1986. doi.org/10.1017/CBO9780511570896

Martin, John, *Tonga Islands: William Mariner's Account* (4th edn), Tonga, Vava'u Press Ltd, 1981.

Massal, Emile & Barrau, Jacques, *Food Plants of the South Sea Islands*, South Pacific Commission Technical Paper no. 42, Noumea, 1956.

Maude, H.E., 'Beachcombers and Castaways', in H.E. Maude, *Of Islands and Men: Studies in Pacific History*, Melbourne, Oxford University Press, 1968, pp. 134–77.

McAllister, Gilbert J., *Archaeology of O'ahu*, Bernice P. Bishop Museum Bulletin 104, Honolulu, 1933.

McArthur, Norma, *Island Populations of the Pacific*, Canberra, Australian National University Press, 1967.

McCoy, M.D., 'The Development of the Kalaupapa Field System, Moloka'i Island, Hawai'i', *Journal of the Polynesian Society*, vol. 114, 2005, 339–58.

McGuffie, T.H., 'Musket and Rifle', *History Today*, vol. 7 (4), 1957, 2157–63, and vol. 7 (7), 1957, 473–79.

McKinzie, Edith Kawelohea, *Hawaiian Genealogies: Extracts from Hawaiian Language Newspapers*, Ismael W. Stagner (ed.), no. 2, vol. 1, The Institute for Polynesian Studies, Lā'ie, 1983.

McNeil, W.H., *The Pursuit of Power: Technology, Armed Force, and Society Since A.D. 1000*, University of Chicago Press, 1982.

———, *Plagues and People*, New York, Doubleday, 1976.

Meares, John, *Voyages Made in the Years 1788 and 1789 from China to the North-West Coast of America*, New York, Da Capo Press, 1968.

Meleisea, Mālama & Schoeffel, Penelope, 'Discovering Outsiders', in Donald Denoon (ed.), *The Cambridge History of the Pacific Islanders*, Cambridge University Press, 1997, pp. 119–51. doi.org/10.1017/CHOL9780521441957.005

Menzies, Archibald, *Hawaii Nei 128 Years Ago*, Honolulu, T.H. Press, 1920.

Mercer, P.M., 'Oral Tradition in the Pacific: Problems of Interpretation', *Journal of Pacific History*, vol. 14 (2), 1979, 130–53. doi.org/10.1080/00223347908572371

Michon, Cédric, 'State Prelates in Renaissance France and England: New Light on the Formation of Early Modern States', *History Compass*, vol. 9 (11), 2011, 876–86. doi.org/10.1111/j.1478-0542.2011.00809.x

Miles, J., *Infectious Diseases: Colonising the Pacific?*, Dunedin, University of Otago Press, 1997.

Milet-Mureau, L.A. (ed.), *A Voyage Round the World, Performed in the Years 1785, 1786, 1787 and 1788 by J.F.G. de la Perouse*, London, J. Johnson Printer, 1798.

Miller, Daniel & Tilley, Christopher (eds), *Ideology, Power, and Prehistory*, Cambridge University Press, 1984.

Miller, David G., 'Ka'iana, The Once Famous "Prince of Kaua'i"', *Hawaiian Journal of History*, vol. 22, 1988, 1–19.

Miller, D.S. & Rivers, J., 'Seasonal Variations in Food Intake in Two Ethiopian Villages', *Proceedings of the Nutritional Society*, vols 31, 32A, 33A, 1972.

Montgomery, Viscount, *A Concise History of Warfare*, London, George Rainbird Ltd, 1972.

Morgan, Joseph R., *Hawai'i: A Unique Geography*, Honolulu, Bess Press, 1996.

Morgan, Theodore, *Hawaii: A Century of Economic Change, 1778–1876*, Cambridge, Mass., Harvard University Press, 1948. doi.org/10.4159/harvard.9780674865716

Morris, Desmond, *The Human Zoo*, London, World Books, 1971.

Morrison, James, *The Journal of James Morrison*, Great Britain, The Golden Cockerel Press, 1935.

Mortimer, George, *Observations and Remarks Made During a Voyage … in the Brig Mercury Commanded by John Henry Cox, Esq.*, Dublin, P. Byrne et al., 1791.

Mulholland, M. & Tawhai, V. (eds), *Weeping Waters: The Treaty of Waitangi and Constitutional Change*, Wellington, Huia, 2010.

Mulrooney, M.A. & Ladefoged, T., 'Hawaiian *Heiau* and Agricultural Production in the Kohala Dryland Field System', *Journal of the Polynesian Society*, 2005, vol. 114, 45–67.

Munford, J.K. (ed.), *John Ledyard's Journal of Captain Cook's Last Voyage*, Corvallis, Ore., Oregon State University Press, 1963.

Munro, Doug, 'Who "Owns" Pacific History? Reflections on the Insider/Outsider Dichotomy', *The Journal of Pacific History*, vol. 29 (2), 1994, 230–36.

National Academy of Sciences, 'Recommended Dietary Allowances', in D.A. Wenck et al., *Nutrition* (2nd edn), Reston Publishing Co., 1983, pp. 630–34.

Nelson, Hank, 'Mobs and Masses: Defining the Dynamic Groups in Papua New Guinea', *State, Society and Governance in Melanesia Discussion Paper 2009/4*, State, Society and Governance in Melanesia Program, The Australian National University, 2009.

Nero, Karen, 'The Material World Remade', in Donald Denoon (ed.), *The Cambridge History of the Pacific Islanders*, Cambridge University Press, pp. 359–96.

Neves, Paki, 'Some Problems with Orthography Encountered by the Reader of Old Hawaiian Texts', *Oceanic Linguistics*, vol. 15 (1–2), Summer–Winter 1976, 51–74. doi.org/10.2307/3622776

Newbury, Colin, *Patrons, Clients, and Empire: Chieftaincy and Over-rule in Asia, Africa, and the Pacific*, Oxford University Press, 2003.

Newman, T. Stell, 'Man in the Prehistoric Hawaiian Ecosystem', in E. Alison Kay (ed.), *A Natural History of the Hawaiian Islands: Select Readings*, Honolulu, University of Hawai'i Press, 1972, pp. 599–603.

Niane, Djibril Tamsir (ed.), *Africa from the Twelfth to the Sixteenth Century CE* (volume 4 of *The UNESCO General History of Africa*), UNESCO, Paris, 1984.

——, *Sundiata: an epic of old Mali*, London, Longmans, 1965.

Nye, Joseph S. Jr., 'Old Wars and Future Wars: Causation and Prevention', *Journal of Interdisciplinary History*, vol. 18 (4), 1988, 581–90. doi.org/10.2307/204815

Obeyesekere, Gananath, 'Anthropology and the Cook Myth', in 'A Review Symposium on *The Apotheosis of Captain Cook: European Mythmaking in the Pacific*', *Social Analysis*, vol. 34, Dec. 1993, 70–85.

——, *The Apotheosis of Captain Cook: European Mythmaking in the Pacific*, Princeton University Press, 1992.

Odgers, S.J., 'Early Western Contact with Hawaii', BA Hons Thesis, The Australian National University, 1977.

Ohnuki-Tierney, E. (ed.), *Culture Through Time: Anthropological Approaches*, Stanford University Press, 1990.

Ortner, Sherry, 'Theory in Anthropology Since the Sixties', *Comparative Studies in History and Society*, vol. 26, 1984, 126–66. doi.org/10.1017/S0010417500010811

Osorio, Jonathan Kay Kamakawiwo'ole, *Dismembering Lāhui: A History of the Hawaiian Nation to 1887*, Honolulu, University of Hawai'i Press, 2002.

Otto, Ton, 'Conceptions of Warfare in Western Thought and Research: An Introduction', in Ton Otto, Henrik Thrane & Helle Vandkilde (eds), *Warfare and Society: Archaeological and Social Anthropological Perspectives*, Aarhus University Press, 2006, pp. 23–28.

Parsonson, G.S., 'The Life and Times of Hongi Hika', *Historical News*, vol. 44, May 1982, 1–8.

Peebles, Christopher, S. & Kus, Susan M., 'Some Archaeological Correlates of Ranked Societies', *American Antiquity*, vol. 42 (3), 1977, 421–48. doi.org/10.2307/279066

Peron, Pierre Francois, *A Frenchman in Hawaii, 1796*, Virginia Day (trans.), Honolulu, White Knight Press, 1975.

Perrin, Noel, *Giving up the Gun: Japan's Reversion to the Sword, 1543–1879*, Boulder, Colorado, Shambala Productions, 1979.

Pierce, Richard A., *Russia's Hawaiian Adventure, 1815–1817*, Berkeley, University of California Press, 1965.

Pogue, Rev. John F., *The Mooolelo of Ancient Hawaii*, Charles W. Kenn (trans.), Honolulu, Topgallant, 1978 (1858).

Polack, J., *New Zealand, Being a Narrative of Travels and Adventures*, vol. 2, Christchurch, Capper Press, 1974.

Portlock, Nathaniel, *A Voyage Round the World: But More Particularly to the North-West Coast of America, Performed in 1785, 1786, 1787 and 1788*, Bibliotheca Australiana no. 43, New York, Da Capo Press, 1968.

Pritchard, W.T., *Polynesian Reminiscences*, London, Chapman Hall, 1866.

Pukui, Mary Kawena, *'Ōlelo No'eau: Hawaiian Proverbs & Poetical Sayings*, Honolulu, Bernice P. Bishop Museum Press, 1983.

Pukui, Mary Kawena & Elbert, Samuel H., *Hawaiian Dictionary*, Honolulu, University of Hawai'i Press, 1986.

Purseglove, J.W., *Tropical Crops*, vol. 1: *Monocotyledons 1*, London, Longmans, 1972a.

——, *Tropical Crops*, vol. 2: *Monocotyledons 2*, London, Longmans, 1972b.

——, *Tropical Crops: Dicotyledons 2*, London, Longmans, Green & Co., 1968.

Ralston, Caroline, 'Sanctity and Power: Gender in Polynesian History – Introduction', *Journal of Pacific History*, vol. 22 (3), 1987, 115–22. doi.org/10.1080/00223348708572561

——, 'Hawaii 1778–1854: Some Aspects of Makaʻāinana Response to Rapid Cultural Change', *Journal of Pacific History*, vol. 19 (1), 1984, 21–40. doi.org/10.1080/00223348408572478

Reefe, Thomas Q., *The Rainbow and the Kings: A History of the Luba Empire to 1891*, Berkeley, University of California Press, 1981.

Reid, William, 'Carronades', *War Monthly*, vol. 8, 1974, 44–48.

Reilly, Ben, 'The Africanisation of the South Pacific', *Australian Journal of International Affairs*, vol. 54 (3), 2000, 261–68. doi.org/10.1080/00049910020012552

Renfrew, Colin, 'Space, Time and Man', *Transactions of the Institute of British Geographers*, New Series, vol. 6 (1981), 257–78.

Restarick, Henry B., 'John Young of Hawaii, an American', *21st Annual Report of the Hawaiian Historical Society for the Year 1912*, Honolulu, 1913, pp. 25–43.

Roe, Michael (ed.), *The Journals and Letters of Captain Charles Bishop on the North-West Coast of America in the Pacific and in New South Wales 1794–1799*, London, Cambridge University Press for the Hakluyt Society, 1967.

Rogers, H.C.B., *Weapons of the British Soldier*, London, Seeley Service and Co., 1960.

Rose, Debbie Bird, 'Worshipping Captain Cook', in 'A Review Symposium on *The Apotheosis of Captain Cook: European Mythmaking in the Pacific*', *Social Analysis*, vol. 34, Dec. 1993, pp. 43–49.

Ross, Alexander, *Adventures of the First Settlers on the Oregon and Columbia River*, London, Smith, Elder, 1849.

Ruggles, C., 'Cosmology, Calendar, and Temple Orientations in Ancient Hawaiʻi', in C. Ruggles & G. Urton (eds), *Skywatching in the Ancient World: New Perspectives in Cultural Astronomy*, Boulder, University Press of Colorado, 2007, pp. 287–329.

Ruru, Jacinta, 'The Right to Water as the Right to Identity: Legal Struggles of Indigenous Peoples of Aotearoa New Zealand', in F. Sultana & A. Loftus (eds), *The Right to Water: Politics, Governance and Social Struggles*, Abingdon, Earthscan, 2012, pp. 110–22.

Sahlins, Marshall, 'Structural Work: How Microhistories Become Macrohistories and Vice Versa', *Anthropological Theory*, vol. 5 (1), 2005, 5–30. doi.org/10.1177/1463499605050866

——, *Apologies to Thucydides: Understanding History as Culture and Vice Versa*, University of Chicago Press, 2004.

——, *How 'Natives' Think: About Captain Cook, For Example*, University of Chicago Press, 1995.

——, 'The Discovery of the True Savage', in Donna Marwick (ed.), *Dangerous Liaisons: Essays in Honour of Greg Dening*, History Department, University of Melbourne, 1994, pp. 41–96.

——, 'The Political Economy of Grandeur in Hawaii from 1810 to 1830', in Emikio Ohnuki-Tierney (ed.), *Culture Through Time: Anthropological Approaches*, Stanford University Press, 1990, pp. 26–56.

——, 'Captain Cook at Hawaii', *Journal of the Polynesian Society*, vol. 98 (4), 1989, 371–423.

——, *Islands of History*, Ann Arbor, University of Michigan Press, 1985.

——, 'Other Times, Other Customs: The Anthropology of History', *American Anthropologist*, vol. 85 (3), 1983, 517–43. doi.org/10.1525/aa.1983.85.3.02a00020

——, *Historical Metaphors and Mythical Realities: Structure in the Early History of the Sandwich Islands Kingdom*, Ann Arbor, University of Michigan Press, 1981.

——, *Stone Age Economics*, Chicago, Aldine, 1972.

——, *Social Stratification in Polynesia*, Seattle, University of Washington Press, 1958.

Sahlins, Marshall & Barrere, Dorothy, 'William Richards on Hawaiian Culture and Political Conditions of the Hawaiian Islands in 1841', *Hawaiian Journal of History*, vol. 7, 1973, 18–40.

Salmond, Anne, 'Whose God, or Not?', in 'A Review Symposium on *The Apotheosis of Captain Cook: European Mythmaking in the Pacific*', *Social Analysis*, vol. 34, Dec. 1993, 50–55.

Salmoran, Rolando Tamayo Y., 'The State as a Problem of Jurisprudence', in Henri J.M. Claessen & Peter Skalnik (eds), *The Study of the State*, The Hague, Mouton Publishers, 1981, pp. 387–407.

Samoan Reporter (9 Mar. 1849, 13 Jul. 1851), typescript copy in B.A. Tallentire, 'Samoa: The Eleven Years War', BA Hons Thesis, University of Otago, 1980, Appendices 106 ff.

Sand, C. & Bedford, S. (eds). *Lapita: Ancêtres océaniens/Oceanic Ancestors*, Paris, Musée du quai Branly/Somogy, 2010.

Schmitt, R.C., *The Missionary Censuses of Hawaii*, Pacific Anthropological Records no. 20, Honolulu, Bernice P. Bishop Museum, 1973.

——, 'New Estimates of the Pre-censal Population of Hawaii', *Journal of the Polynesian Society*, vol. 80 (2), 1971, 237–43.

——, 'Famine Mortality in Hawaii', *Journal of Pacific History*, vol. 5, 1970, 109–15. doi.org/10.1080/00223347008572167

Scrimshaw, Nevin S., 'The Phenomenon of Famine', *American Review of Nutrition*, vol. 7, 1987, 1–21. doi.org/10.1146/annurev.nu.07.070187.000245

Segraves, Barbara Abbott, 'Central Elements in the Construction of a General Theory of the Evolution of Societal Complexity', in Colin Renfrew, Michael J. Rowlands & Barbara Abbott Segraves (eds), *Theory and Explanation in Archaeology: The Southampton Conference*, New York, Academic Press, 1982, pp. 287–300.

Service, Elman R., *The Origins of the State and Civilization*, New York, W.W. Norton & Co., 1975.

Shaler, William, 'Journal of a Voyage Between China and the North-Western Coast of America Made in 1804', *American Register*, no. 3, 1808, 137–75.

Sharp, C.A. (ed.), *Duperrey's Visit to New Zealand in 1824*, Wellington, Alexander Turnbull Library, 1971.

Shineberg, Dorothy, 'Guns and Men in Melanesia', *Journal of Pacific History*, vol. 6, 1971, 61–82. doi.org/10.1080/00223347108572183

Sinoto, Yosihiko H., 'The Marquesas', in Jesse D. Jennings (ed.), *The Prehistory of Polynesia*, Canberra, Australian National University Press, 1979, pp. 110–34. doi.org/10.4159/harvard.9780674181267.c6

Sissons, Jeffrey, 'Rethinking Tribal Origins', *Journal of the Polynesian Society*, vol. 97 (2), 1988, 199–204.

Skocpol, Theda, *States and Social Revolutions: A Comparative Analysis of France, Russia and China*, London, Cambridge University Press, 1979. doi.org/10.1017/CBO9780511815805

Smith, Barbara M.D., 'The Galtons of Birmingham: Quaker Gun Merchants and Bankers', *Business History*, vol. 9 (2), 1967, 132–50. doi.org/10.1080/00076796700000014

Smith, Bernard, 'A Comment', in 'A Review Symposium on *The Apotheosis of Captain Cook: European Mythmaking in the Pacific*', *Social Analysis*, vol. 34, Dec. 1993, 61–65.

Smith, Robert S., *Warfare and Diplomacy in Pre-Colonial West Africa*, Norwich, Great Britain, Meuthen, 1976.

Smith, S. Percy, *Maori Wars of the Nineteenth Century* (2nd edn), Christchurch, Whitcombe and Tombs Ltd, 1910.

Spear, Thomas, 'Oral Traditions: Whose History?', *Journal of Pacific History*, vol. 16 (3), 1981, 133–48. doi.org/10.1080/00223348108572420

Stanish, C., 'The Origin of State Societies in South America', *Annual Review of Anthropology*, vol. 30, 2001, 41–64. doi.org/10.1146/annurev.anthro.30.1.41

Stannard, David, 'Disease and Infertility: A New Look at the Demographic Collapse of Native Populations in the Wake of Western Contact', *Journal of American Studies*, 24 (3), 1990, 325–50. doi.org/10.1017/S0021875800033661

——, *Before the Horror: The Population of Hawai'i on the Eve of Western Contact*, Honolulu, Social Science Research Institute, University of Hawai'i, 1989.

Steuer, Heiko, 'Warrior Bands, War Lords, and the Birth of Tribes and States in the First Millennium AD in Middle Europe', in Ton Otto, Henrik Thrane & Helle Vandkilde (eds), *Warfare and Society: Archaeological and Social Anthropological Perspectives*, Aarhus University Press, 2006, pp. 227–36.

Stiles, Daniel, 'Ethnoarchaeology: A Discussion of Methods and Applications', *Man*, vol. 12, 1977, 87–103. doi.org/10.2307/2800996

Stokes, John F.G., 'Nationality of John Young, A Chief of Hawaii', *47th Annual Report of the Hawaiian Historical Society for the Year 1938*, Honolulu, 1939, pp. 13–38.

——, 'Dune Sepulture, Battle Mortality and Kamehameha's Alleged Defeat on Kaua'i', *45th Annual Report of the Hawaiian Historical Society for the Year 1936*, Honolulu, 1937, pp. 30–46.

Sutton, Douglas G., 'Maori Demographic Change, 1769–1840: The Inner Workings of a Picturesque but Illogical Simile', *Journal of the Polynesian Society*, vol. 95 (3), 1986, 291–339.

Tainter, Joseph A., *The Collapse of Complex Societies*, Cambridge University Press, 1988.

Tcherkézoff, Serge, 'Is Anthropology about Individual Agency or Culture? Or Why "Old Derek" is Doubly Wrong', *Journal of the Polynesian Society*, vol. 110 (1), 2001, 59–78.

Thomas, Nicholas, *Out of Time: History and Evolution in Anthropological Discourse* (2nd edn), Ann Arbor, The University of Michigan, 1996. doi.org/10.3998/mpub.8667

——, 'Blood and Purity: A Comment on the Interpretation of Polynesian Culture', *Journal of the Polynesian Society*, vol. 98 (2), 1989, 207–11.

——, '"Le Roi de Tahuata" Iotete and the Transformation of South Marquesan Politics, 1826–1842', *Journal of Pacific History*, vol. 21 (1), 1986, 3–20. doi.org/10.1080/00223348608572525

Thompson, E.P., *The Making of the English Working Class*, London, V. Gollancz, 1980.

Thompson, William R., 'A Test of a Theory of Co-evolution in War: Lengthening the Western Eurasian Military Trajectory', *The International History Review*, vol. 28 (3), Sep. 2006, 473–503.

Thomson, Robert, *History of Tahiti*, L.M.S. Archives, G.S. Parsonson personal transcription – Hocken Library, Dunedin, n.d.

Thorton, John K., 'The Art of War in Angola, 1575–1680', *Comparative Studies in Society and History*, vol. 30 (2), Apr. 1988, 360–78. doi.org/10.1017/S0010417500015231

Thrane, Henrik, 'Warfare and the State: An Introduction', in Ton Otto, Henrik Thrane & Helle Vandkilde (eds), *Warfare and Society: Archaeological and Social Anthropological Perspectives*, Aarhus University Press, 2006, pp. 211–16.

Thrum, Thomas G. (ed.), *Fornander Collection of Hawaiian Antiquities and Folklore*, Honolulu, Bernice P. Bishop Museum, 1916–20.

——, 'Hana of Historic Tradition and Romance', in Thomas G. Thrum (comp.), *The Hawaiian Almanac for 1919*, Honolulu, Thos. G. Thrum, 1919, pp. 64–69.

——, 'The Battle of Nuuanu', in Thomas G. Thrum (comp.), *Hawaiian Almanac and Annual for 1899*, Honolulu, Press Publishing Co., 1899, pp. 111–12.

——, 'Some Noted Battles of Hawaiian History', in Thomas G. Thrum (comp.), *Hawaiian Almanac and Annual for 1889*, Honolulu, Press Publishing Co., 1889, pp. 55–60.

Thucydides, *History of the Peloponnesian War*, Rex Warner (trans.) (rev. edn), Middlesex, Penguin, 1972.

Tilly, Charles, 'States, State Transformation, and War', in Jerry H. Bentley (ed.), *The Oxford Handbook of World History*, Oxford University Press, 2011, pp. 176–93. doi.org/10.1093/oxfordhb/9780199235810.013.0011

——, *Regimes and Repertoires*, Chicago University Press, 2006.

——, *Trust and Rule*, Cambridge University Press, 2005.

——, *Coercion, Capital, and European States AD 990–1992* (rev. edn), Oxford, Blackwell, 1992.

—— (ed.), *The Formation of Nation States in Western Europe*, Princeton University Press, 1975.

Townsend, Ebenezer Jr., *Extracts from the Diary of Ebenezer Townsend Jr*, Honolulu, Hawaiian Historical Society, n.d.

Trask, Haunani-Kay, 'Natives and Anthropologists: The Colonial Struggle', *The Contemporary Pacific*, vol. 3 (1), 1991, 159–67.

——, 'Cultures in Collision: Hawai'i and England, 1778', *Pacific Studies* (Laie), vol. 7, 1983, 91–117.

Tregaskis, Richard, *The Warrior King: Hawaii's Kamehameha the Great*, London, Macmillan, 1973.

Trigger, B.G., *Understanding Early Civilizations: A Comparative Study*, Cambridge University Press, 2003. doi.org/10.1017/CBO 9780511840630

——, 'Generated Coercion and Inequality: The Basis of State Power in the Early Civilisations', in Henri J.M. Claessen, Pieter van der Velde & M. Estelle Smith (eds), *Development and Decline, The Evolution of Sociopolitical Organisation*, South Hadley, Mas., Bergin and Garvey, 1985, pp. 46–61.

——, *Times and Traditions: Essays in Archaeological Interpretation*, Edinburgh University Press, 1978.

Tuggle, H.D., 'Hawaii', in Jesse D. Jennings (ed.), *The Prehistory of Polynesia*, Canberra, Australian National University Press, 1979, pp. 167–99. doi.org/10.4159/harvard.9780674181267.c8

Tuggle, H.D. & Tuggle-Tomanari, M.J., 'Prehistoric Agriculture in Kohala, Hawaii', *Journal of Field Archaeology*, vol. 7 (3), 1980, 297–312. doi.org/10.1179/009346980791505347

Turnbull, John, *A Voyage Round the World in the Years 1800, 1801, 1802, 1803 and 1804*, Philadelphia, Benjamin and Thomas Kite, 1810.

Turner, G., 'The War on Upolu in 1969', typescript, 16 April 1869, Malua, Upolu, Hocken Library, Dunedin.

Urlich, D.U., 'The Introduction and Diffusion of Firearms in New Zealand, 1800–1840', *Journal of the Polynesian Society*, vol. 79 (4), 1970, 399–410.

US Department of the Interior, *Geological Survey*, Washington D.C., 1928, 1953–55.

Valeri, Valerio, 'Constitutive History: Genealogy and Narrative in the Legitimation of Hawaiian Kingship', in Emikio Ohnuki-Tierney (ed.), *Culture Through Time: Anthropological Approaches*, Stanford University Press, 1990a, pp. 154–92.

——, 'Blood and Impurity: A Counter-comment on Insufficient Scholarship and More Interesting Matters', *Journal of the Polynesian Society*, vol. 99 (3), 1990b, 319–24.

——, 'On Alan Howard's Review of *Kingship and Sacrifice*', *Journal of the Polynesian Society*, vol. 96 (3), 1987, 373–80.

——, *Kingship and Sacrifice: Ritual and Society in Ancient Hawaii*, Paula Wissing (trans.), University of Chicago Press, 1985a.

——, 'The Conqueror Becomes King: A Political Analysis of the Legend of 'Umi', in Antony Hooper & Judith Huntsman (eds), *The Transformation of Polynesian Culture*, Polynesian Society Memoir no. 45, Auckland, 1985b, pp. 79–103.

——, 'The Transformation of a Transformation: A Structural Essay on an Aspect of Hawaiian History (1809–1819)', *Social Analysis*, vol. 10, May 1982, 3–41.

Van Bakel, M., 'Ideological Perspectives on the Development of Kingship in the Early States of Hawaii', in H.J.M. Claessen & P. van de Velde (eds), *Ideology and the Formation of Early States*, Leiden, E.J. Bril, 1996a, pp. 321–38.

——, 'The Political Economy of an Early State: Hawaii and Samoa Compared', in H.J.M. Claessen & P. van de Velde (eds), *Ideology and the Formation of Early States*, Leiden, E.J. Bril, 1996b, pp. 265–90.

Vancouver, George, *A Voyage of Discovery to the North Pacific Ocean and Round the World*, London, John Stockdale, 1801.

Vansina, Jan, *Oral Tradition as History*, Madison, University of Wisconsin Press, 1985.

——, *Kingdoms of the Savanna*, Madison, University of Wisconsin Press, 1966.

Vason, George, *An Authentic Narrative of Four Years Residence at Tongataboo*, London, Longman, Hurst, Rees, Orme, 1810.

Vitousek, P., *Nutrient Cycling and Limitation: Hawai'i as a Model System*, Princeton University Press, 2004.

Vitousek, P.T., Ladefoged, A., Hartshorn, P.V., Kirch, M., Graves, S., Hotchkiss, S., Tuljapurkar, C. & Chadwick, O., 'Soils, Agriculture, and Society in Precontact Hawai'i', *Science*, vol. 304, 2004, 1665–69. doi.org/10.1126/science.1099619

von Kotzebue, Otto, *Voyage of Discovery in the South Sea Undertaken in the Years 1814, 16, 17 and 18*, London, Sir Richard Phillips and Co., 1821.

Vovelle, Michelle, *Ideologies and Mentalities*, Eamon O'Flaherty (trans.), Cambridge, Polity Press, 1990.

Waterhouse, Rev. J., *The King and People of Fiji*, London, Wesleyan Conference Office, 1864.

Watkins, J., *Journal 1830–1839*, Microfilm 298, Hocken Library, Dunedin, n.d.

Watson, R.M., *History of Samoa*, Dunedin, Whitcombe and Tombs Ltd, 1918.

Webb, M.C., 'The Abolition of the Taboo System in Hawaii', *Journal of the Polynesian Society*, vol. 74 (1), 1965, 21–39.

Weber, Max, *The Theory of Social and Economic Organisation*, A.M. Henderson & Talcott Parsons (trans.), New York, Oxford University Press, 1947.

Webster, D., 'Warfare and the Evolution of the State: A Reconsideration', *American Antiquity*, vol. 40, 1975, 464–70. doi.org/10.2307/279334

Weisler, M.I., 'Hard Evidence for Prehistoric Interaction in Polynesia', *Current Anthropology*, vol. 39 (4), 1998, 521–32. doi.org/10.1086/204768

Wenck, D.A., et al., *Nutrition* (2nd edn), Reston Publishing Co., 1983.

Wesley-Smith, Terence, 'Altered States: The Politics of State Failure and Regional Intervention', in Greg Fry & Tarcisius Tara Kabutaulaka (eds), *Intervention and State-building in the Pacific: The Legitimacy of 'Cooperative Intervention'*, Manchester and New York, Manchester University Press, 2008, pp. 37–53.

West, T., *Ten Years in South-Central Polynesia*, London, James Nisbet, 1865.

Westervelt, W.D., 'Kamehameha's Method of Government', *31st Annual Report of the Hawaiian Historical Society for the Year 1921*, Honolulu, 1922, pp. 24–38.

White, Gavin, 'Firearms in Africa: An Introduction', *Journal of African History*, vol. 12 (2), 1971, 175–82. doi.org/10.1017/S0021853700010628

Whiteley, Peter M., 'Archaeology and Oral Tradition: The Scientific Importance of Dialogue', *American Antiquity*, vol. 67 (3), Jul. 2002, 405–15. doi.org/10.2307/1593819

Wilks, I., 'Aspects of Bureaucratisation in Ashanti in the Eighteenth Century', *Journal of African History*, vol. 7 (2), 1966, 215–32.

——, *Asante in the Nineteenth Century: The Structure and Evolution of a Political Order*, London, Cambridge University Press, 1975. doi.org/10.1017/S0021853700006289

Williams, John, *A Narrative of Missionary Enterprises in The South Sea Islands*, London, J. Snow, 1838.

Wilson, J., *A Missionary Voyage to the Southern Pacific Ocean Performed in the Years 1796, 1797, 1798 in the Ship Duff*, London, T. Chapman, 1799.

Wilson, Peter J., *The Domestication of the Human Species*, New Haven, Yale University Press, 1988.

Withington, Antoinette, *The Golden Cloak: An Informal History of Hawaii*, Honolulu, Hawaiian Press, 1953.

Wittfogel, Karl, *Oriental Despotism*, New Haven, Yale University Press, 1957.

Wolforth, Thomas R., 'Searching for Archaeological Manifestations of Hawaiian Battles on the Island of Hawai'i', in Christopher M. Stevenson, José Miguel Ramirez Aliaga, Francis J. Morin & Norma Babacci (eds), *The Reñaca Papers: VI International Conference on Easter Island and the Pacific*, Los Osos, CA, Easter Island Foundation, 2004, pp. 161–79.

Wood, Michael, *In Search of the Trojan War*, London, Facts on File Publications, 1985.

Wright, Harrison, M., *New Zealand 1769–1840: Early Years of Western Contact*, Cambridge, Mass., Harvard University Press, 1959.

Wylie, Robert Crichton, *Supplement to the Report of the Minister of Foreign Relations*, Honolulu, Government Printer, 1856.

Yoffee, N., *Myths of the Archaic State: Evolution of the Earliest Cities, States, and Civilizations*, Cambridge University Press, 2005. doi.org/10.1017/CBO9780511489662

Young, John, *Manuscript Journal*, Hawai'i State Archives, n.d.

Young, Kanalu G. Terry, 'Kuleana: Toward a Historiography of Hawaiian National Consciousness, 1780–2001', *Hawaiian Journal of Law & Politics*, vol. 2, Summer 2006, 1–33.

——, *Rethinking the Native Hawaiian Past*, New York, Garland Publishing Inc., 1998.

Index

ahupua'a, 52, 62, 64, 74, 76, 100, 101, 105, 106, 121, 186, 268
'Aiea, battle of, 138, 141, 173–74, 227, 235, 253
akua, 66, 103
Alaloa, 72
Alapa'inui, 115, 139
ali'i, 24, 53, 55, 56, 59, 65, 78, 84, 88, 89–100, 103, 104, 110, 111, 113, 114, 117, 119, 121, 122, 123, 124, 125, 126, 127, 128, 129, 130, 133, 137, 138, 139, 140, 143, 145, 147, 150, 152, 153, 154, 155, 157, 166, 183, 188, 189, 192, 193, 194, 195, 198, 199, 200, 201, 202, 207, 208, 211, 212, 214, 217, 218, 239, 241, 242, 246, 247, 250, 251, 253
'aumakua, 90, 201n64

Beckwith, Martha, 268
breadfruit *see* 'ulu

cannon, 161–65, 167, 175–77, 190, 199, 205, 206, 217, 221, 231–34
chief, paramount *see* mo'ī
chiefs *see* ali'i
chiefs, lesser *see* kaukau ali'i
commoners *see* maka'āinana

demilitarisation, 181, 191–92, 194–99, 202–04, 237–38, 253–54

disease, 191–92, 194, 221–22, 225, 237, 243–46

enslaved underclass *see* kāuwa
European residents, role in Hawaiian society, 208–09, 226–27, 236–37

firearms, 26–27, 161–79, 190, 194, 195–96, 197, 198, 199, 202, 203, 204, 211, 212, 216, 217, 221, 225–31, 234–38
fishponds, 52, 76, 77, 79, 102, 134–35
Fornander, Abraham, 267

governor *see* kuhina

Hawai'i Island, 1, 26, 52, 53, 57, 59, 60, 61, 63, 64, 65, 66, 67–71, 105, 107, 112, 115, 125, 126, 133–34, 135, 136, 141, 143, 144, 145, 146, 148, 153–56, 159, 161, 164–69, 176, 179–80, 188, 190, 192, 194, 196, 199, 200, 207, 215–18, 236, 242, 245, 247–48, 251, 252
Hawai'inuiākea School of Hawaiian Knowledge, 3, 23
heiau, 58, 74, 98, 103, 104, 105, 128, 130, 143, 152, 164, 167, 186, 191, 193, 201, 241
see also luakini heiau
Honolulu, 44, 60, 134, 183, 194,

307

196, 197, 198, 199, 202, 205, 208, 209, 210, 216, 219, 237, 238, 239, 241, 244, 247
hoʻokupu, 101, 193
hoʻomana, 97

Iʻī, John Papa, 266
ʻĪao, battle of, 141, 163–64, 233–34, 253

Kaʻahumanu, 104, 124, 159, 181, 193, 194–95, 198, 201, 202, 206, 211, 212–13, 215–18
Kaʻeokulani, 110, 123, 146, 150, 153, 156, 170, 227, 237, 252, 253
Kahahana, 96, 128
Kahekili, 55, 93, 96, 101, 110, 118, 119, 123, 124, 125, 126, 128, 130, 136, 141, 143, 145, 147, 148–51, 156, 157–60, 167, 170–71, 249, 251, 252–53
Kahoʻolawe Island, 65, 66, 74, 148, 159
kahuna, 56, 90, 91, 94, 95–97, 98, 103, 128, 138, 151, 185, 187, 212
kalaimoku, 138
Kalaniʻōpuʻu, 93, 95–97, 99, 103, 115, 116, 118, 120, 122, 126, 128, 138, 139, 142, 148–52, 156, 189
Kalanikūpule, 93, 101, 119, 158, 159, 163, 166, 171–79, 227, 237, 253
kalo, 7, 62–63, 65, 68–69, 70, 71, 73, 74, 75, 77, 79, 102, 132, 133–35, 142, 209
Kamakau, Kēlou, 266–67
Kamakau, Samuel M., 266
Kameʻeleihiwa, Lilikalā, 23, 55, 224, 268
Kamehameha, 1, 25, 26, 34, 40, 46, 48, 49, 50, 55, 66, 93, 94, 116, 117, 122, 123, 124, 136, 140,
142, 145, 147, 148, 150, 152, 153–57, 159–72, 175–214, 223, 225, 226, 227, 231, 232, 236, 237, 240, 241, 242, 249, 250, 251, 252–54
kanaka, 113, 117
Kanaloa, 66, 86
Kāne, 66, 86
kapu, 62, 87, 88, 92–94, 97, 99, 103–04, 105, 186, 187, 191, 193, 200, 201, 212–18, 240, 241
Kauaʻi Island, 1, 26, 49, 59, 63, 65, 78–80, 97, 99, 105, 124, 134, 136, 140, 141, 145, 146, 148, 149, 150, 160, 167, 170–71, 179, 191, 199–200, 204–05, 245
Kauʻiki Head, 118, 136, 141, 144, 156, 157, 159
kaukau aliʻi, 24, 106, 110–13, 184
Kaumualiʻi, 1, 170, 179–80, 199–200
kāuwa, 103–04
Kealakekua Bay, 67, 71, 95, 106, 115, 139, 149, 231, 239, 242
Keʻeaumoku, 156
Kekūhaupiʻo, 114, 140, 150, 152, 153, 159
Keōpūolani, 164
Keōua Kuahuʻula, 116, 117, 161, 165–66, 167
Kepuwahaʻulaʻula, Battle of, 167, 234
Kīwalaʻō 1, 93–94, 120, 122, 124, 152–54, 164
Koapapa, battle of, 117, 165, 230
konohiki, 100–01
Kuamoʻo, battle of, 217–18
kuhina, 184, 192, 193, 194, 213
Kūkāʻili-moku, 58, 66, 86, 88, 95, 96, 97, 103, 112, 118, 120, 121, 145, 152, 167, 179, 186, 201, 215, 218, 242

Lānaʻi Island, 65, 74, 136, 148, 159, 171, 176
land manager *see* konohiki

INDEX

landless commoners *see* kanaka
Lono, 66, 86, 88, 95, 96, 97, 98, 103, 242–43
luakini heiau, 58, 66, 67, 103, 128, 130, 186, 191

maka'āinana, 8, 53, 54, 65, 66, 84, 88, 89, 90, 93, 98–107, 110, 111, 113, 114, 117, 118, 119, 120, 126, 127, 139, 143, 152, 207, 217, 241, 246, 250, 251
makahiki, 88, 94–95, 105, 127, 186, 200–01, 219, 242
Malo, David, 266
mana, 92, 128, 143, 146
Maui Island, 26, 52, 53, 55, 57, 58, 59, 61, 63, 65, 66, 71–74, 106, 107, 110, 117, 122, 125, 126, 128, 136, 140, 141, 142, 143, 144, 145, 148, 149, 151, 156, 157, 158, 159, 160, 162–64, 166, 167, 171, 172, 173, 236, 242, 251, 252
mo'ī, 1, 52, 54, 55, 59, 65, 67, 71, 72, 73, 74, 76, 78, 84, 89, 90, 91–92, 95, 96, 99, 101, 110, 114, 115, 116, 117, 118, 119, 120, 121, 122, 123, 124, 125, 126, 127, 128, 137, 139, 143, 145, 148, 149, 150, 156, 172, 175, 176, 183, 184, 185, 187, 191, 192, 193, 194, 207, 223, 225, 240, 250, 251, 253, 254
moku , 54, 59, 67, 127, 128, 152, 161, 251, 254
Moku'ohae, battle of, 93, 135, 137, 141, 143, 154–55
Moloka'i Island, 58, 63, 74–76, 102, 117, 128, 136, 139, 141, 144, 149, 150, 159, 164, 171, 175, 176, 210

Ni'ihau Island, 1, 49, 80, 105, 148
noa, 87

Nu'uanu, battle of (1795), 141, 176–77, 233–34, 250, 253

O'ahu Island, 26, 46, 52, 53, 57, 58, 59, 60, 65, 66, 76–78, 97, 110, 117, 119, 122, 124, 125, 128, 129, 136, 139, 143, 144, 145, 146, 149, 150, 151, 157, 158, 159, 160, 166, 171, 172, 173–78, 180, 181, 183, 188, 190, 191–92, 194, 196, 199, 200, 208, 210, 231, 235, 237, 252, 253
Osorio, Jonathon Kay Kamakawiwo'ole, 10, 23–25, 55, 224, 268

Pa'ahau, battle of, 165, 233–34
pahupū, 125
Pelei'ōhōlani, 117, 149, 150
political consolidation literature, 1, 2, 5–6, 7–25, 85
polities *see* moku
population estimates, 81–83
priests *see* kahuna
Pukui, Mary Kawena, 268
pu'uhonua, 144

refuge *see* pu'uhonua
religious festival *see* makahiki
religious offerings *see* ho'okupu

sacred status *see* kapu
sweet potato *see* 'uala

taro *see* kalo
temple *see* heiau

'uala, 62–63, 69, 70, 71, 73, 74, 77, 79, 80, 102, 133–35, 142
'ulu, 62, 63, 69, 73, 74, 79, 80, 133, 134, 142, 143
Umi-a-Līloa, 9, 52, 56, 57, 58, 71, 111

war counsellor *see* kalaimoku
warfare, Hawaiian, 2, 85, 109–46, 235–36
warfare literature, 2, 25–39, 85
Western influence on Hawaiian political consolidation, 39–45, 221–48

Young, John, 161, 183, 184, 186, 188, 191, 196, 210, 214, 225, 226, 233, 234, 236, 250, 264
Young, Kanalu, G. Terry, 10, 23–25, 55, 111–13, 223, 224, 268

www.ingramcontent.com/pod-product-compliance
Lightning Source LLC
Chambersburg PA
CBHW042042240426
43667CB00048B/2957